GRAMMAR EXPLORER 3

Amy Cooper and Samuela Eckstut-Didier

Series Editors: Rob Jenkins and Staci Johnson

NATIONAL GEOGRAPHIC LEARNING | CENGAGE Learning®

Australia • Brazil • Japan • Korea • Mexico • Singapore • Spain • United Kingdom • United States

Grammar Explorer 3
Amy Cooper and Samuela Eckstut-Didier

Publisher: Sherrise Roehr

Executive Editor: Laura Le Dréan

Managing Editor: Eve Einselen Yu

Senior Development Editor: Kimberly Steiner

Associate Development Editor: Alayna Cohen

Assistant Editor: Vanessa Richards

Senior Technology Product Manager: Scott Rule

Director of Global Marketing: Ian Martin

Marketing Manager: Lindsey Miller

Sr. Director, ELT & World Languages:
   Michael Burggren

Production Manager: Daisy Sosa

Content Project Manager: Andrea Bobotas

Print Buyer: Mary Beth Hennebury

Cover Designer: 3CD, Chicago

Cover Image: BRIAN J. SKERRY/National
   Geographic Creative

Compositor: Cenveo Publisher Services

For product information and technology assistance, contact us at
Cengage Learning Customer & Sales Support,
1-800-354-9706

For permission to use material from this text or product,
submit all requests online at **www.cengage.com/permissions.**
Further permissions questions can be e-mailed to
permissionrequest@cengage.com.

Student Book 3: 978-1-111-35111-3

National Geographic Learning
20 Channel Center Street
Boston, MA 02210
USA

Cengage Learning is a leading provider of customized learning solutions with office locations around the globe, including Singapore, the United Kingdom, Australia, Mexico, Brazil and Japan.

Cengage Learning products are represented in Canada by Nelson Education, Ltd.

Visit National Geographic Learning online at **ngl.cengage.com**

Visit our corporate website at **www.cengage.com**

Printed in the United States of America
Print Number: 02   Print Year: 2015

CONTENTS

UNIT 10   Beauty and Appearance   266

Causative Verb Patterns and Phrasal Verbs

UNIT 11   The Power of Images   294

Relative Clauses

National Geographic images introduce the unit theme—real world topics that students want to read, write, and talk about.

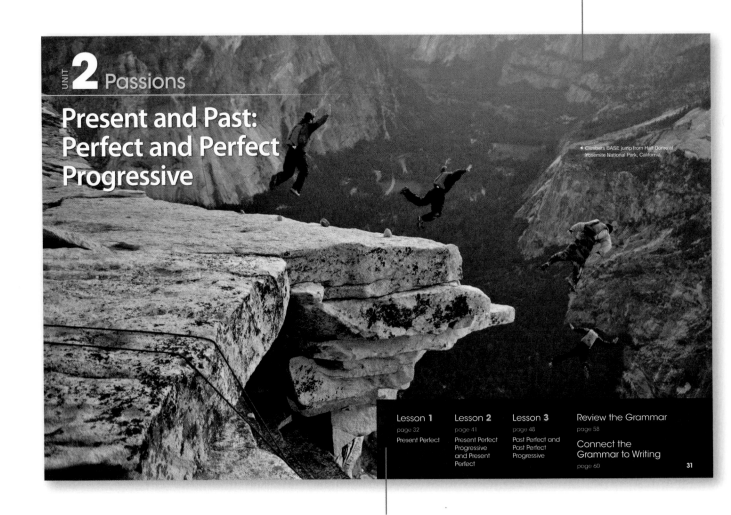

UNIT **2** Passions

Present and Past: Perfect and Perfect Progressive

◄ Climbers BASE jump from Half Dome at Yosemite National Park, California.

Lesson **1**	Lesson **2**	Lesson **3**	Review the Grammar
page 32	page 41	page 48	page 58
Present Perfect	Present Perfect Progressive and Present Perfect	Past Perfect and Past Perfect Progressive	Connect the Grammar to Writing
			page 60

31

Units are organized in **manageable lessons**, which ensures students **explore, learn, practice,** and **apply** the grammar.

Each lesson begins with the **Explore** section, featuring a captivating National Geographic article that introduces the target grammar and builds students' knowledge in a variety of academic disciplines.

LESSON 1 Present Perfect

EXPLORE

CD1-09 **1** **READ** the book review of *Polar Obsession*. What is Paul Nicklen's passion?

Paul Nicklen's *Polar Obsession*

For most people, the Arctic and Antarctica are strange places that we know very little about. Paul Nicklen's collection of photographs and stories, *Polar Obsession*, offers an excellent introduction.

Nicklen grew up on an island in Northern Canada, where he learned all about the outdoors from his Inuit[1] neighbors. Ever since that time, he **has loved** animals, cold weather, and adventure.

As a photojournalist, Nicklen **has spent** a lot of time in icy polar waters. He **has followed** sea lions, **dived** with whales, and **studied** polar bears. One of the most exciting parts of the book covers Nicklen's unforgettable encounter with a leopard seal in Antarctica.

As the photographs clearly show, leopard seals are very large—up to 12 feet (4 meters) long and weighing over 1000 pounds (450 kilograms). They have huge, sharp teeth, and they move quickly through the water searching for food such as fish and penguins.

Leopard seals can be dangerous, but this didn't stop Nicklen from trying to photograph one. When a huge seal approached his boat, Nicklen got into the water. He was shaking with fear, but much to his surprise the seal treated him gently. She even tried to feed him! The seal brought him penguins to eat, and he photographed her. Nicklen says it was the most incredible experience that he has

In *Polar Obsession*, He also helps us to un

[1] **Inuit:** indigenous people living

32 PRESENT AND PAST: PERFECT AND P

Present Perfect Progressive and Present Perfect **LESSON 2**

EXPLORE

CD1-13 **1** **READ** the magazine article about Helen Thayer. What advice does she have for other people?

Helen Thayer: A Lifelong Adventurer

Helen Thayer **has** never **let** age stop her. She and her husband, Bill, fulfilled a lifelong dream for their 40th wedding anniversary. They walked 1600 mile

In recent years, Thayer **has bee** to travel and bring back stories to sh people to follow goals, plan for s

[1] **nomads:** people who
[2] **inspire:** to make som
[3] **fulfill one's dream:**

The Gobi Desert covers parts of Mongolia and China

LESSON 3 Past Perfect and Past Perfect Progressive

EXPLORE

CD1-15 **1** **READ** the article about Alex Honnold. What big risk did he take to fulfill his dream?

Daring. Defiant. Free.
A new generation of superclimbers is pushing the limits in Yosemite

Every rock climber who has come to Yosemite has a dream. Alex Honnold's dream was to free solo Half Dome, a 2130-foot (649-meter) wall of granite. Free soloing means climbing with only rock shoes and some chalk to help keep the hands dry. Honnold couldn't use a rope or anything else to help him stick to the slippery stone. The few people who **had climbed** Half Dome before **had used** ropes, and it **had taken** them more than a day to do the climb.

On a bright September morning, Honnold was clinging[2] to the face of Half Dome, less than 100 feet (30 meters) from the top. He **had been climbing** for two hours and forty-five minutes, but all of a sudden he stopped. Something potentially disastrous had occurred—he had lost some of his confidence. He **hadn't felt** that way two days before when **he'd been racing** up the same rock *with* a rope. That climb **had gone** well. Today though, Honnold hesitated. He knew that even the slightest doubt could cause a deadly fall, thousands of feet to the valley floor below. He knew he had to get moving, so he chalked his hands, adjusted his feet, and started climbing again. Within minutes, he was at the top.

Bloggers spread the news of Honnold's two-hour-and-fifty-minute free solo, and climbers were amazed. On this warm fall day, 23-year-old Alex Honnold **had** just **set** a new record in one of climbing's biggest challenges.

[1] **granite:** a kind of very hard rock
[2] **cling:** to hold something tightly

◄ Alex Honnold free soloing in Yosemite National Park, California

48 PRESENT AND PAST: PERFECT AND PERFECT PROGRESSIVE

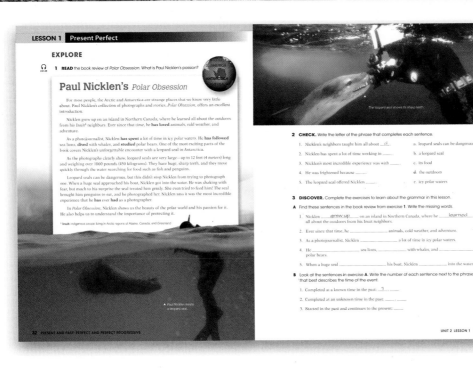

In the **Explore** section, students discover how the grammar structures are used in the readings and in real academic textbooks.

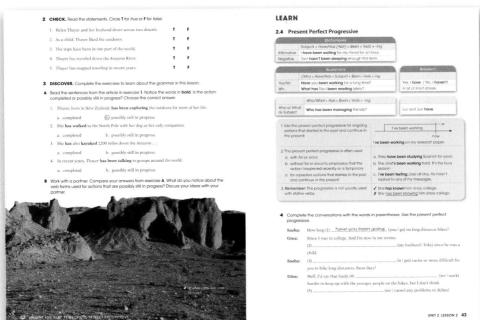

The **Learn** section features clear grammar charts and explanations followed by controlled practice of the grammar forms.

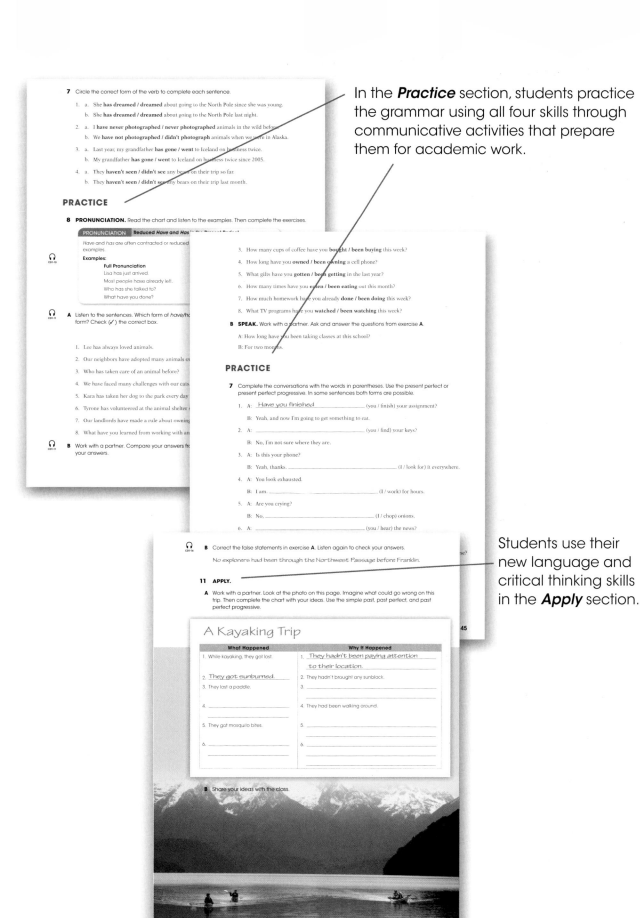

In the **Practice** section, students practice the grammar using all four skills through communicative activities that prepare them for academic work.

7 Circle the correct form of the verb to complete each sentence.

1. a. She **has dreamed / dreamed** about going to the North Pole since she was young.
   b. She **has dreamed / dreamed** about going to the North Pole last night.

2. a. I **have never photographed / never photographed** animals in the wild before.
   b. We **have not photographed / didn't photograph** animals when we were in Alaska.

3. a. Last year, my grandfather **has gone / went** to Iceland on business twice.
   b. My grandfather **has gone / went** to Iceland on business twice since 2005.

4. a. They **haven't seen / didn't see** any bears on their trip so far.
   b. They **haven't seen / didn't see** any bears on their trip last month.

PRACTICE

8 PRONUNCIATION. Read the chart and listen to the examples. Then complete the exercises.

PRONUNCIATION Reduced *Have* and *Has* in the Present Perfect

Have and *has* are often contracted or reduced examples.

Examples:
Full Pronunciation
Lisa has just arrived.
Most people have already left.
Who has she talked to?
What have you done?

A Listen to the sentences. Which form of *have/ha* form? Check (✓) the correct box.

1. Lee has always loved animals.
2. Our neighbors have adopted many animals o
3. Who has taken care of an animal before?
4. We have faced many challenges with our cats.
5. Kara has taken her dog to the park every day
6. Tyrone has volunteered at the animal shelter
7. Our landlords have made a rule about owning
8. What have you learned from working with an

B Work with a partner. Compare your answers fr your answers.

3. How many cups of coffee have you **bought / been buying** this week?
4. How long have you **owned / been owning** a cell phone?
5. What gifts have you **gotten / been getting** in the last year?
6. How many times have you **eaten / been eating** out this month?
7. How much homework have you already **done / been doing** this week?
8. What TV programs have you **watched / been watching** this week?

B SPEAK. Work with a partner. Ask and answer the questions from exercise **A**.
A: How long have you been taking classes at this school?
B: For two months.

PRACTICE

7 Complete the conversations with the words in parentheses. Use the present perfect or present perfect progressive. In some sentences both forms are possible.

1. A: _Have you finished_ _____ (you / finish) your assignment?
   B: Yeah, and now I'm going to get something to eat.

2. A: _____ (you / find) your keys?
   B: No, I'm not sure where they are.

3. A: Is this your phone?
   B: Yeah, thanks. _____ (I / look for) it everywhere.

4. A: You look exhausted.
   B: I am. _____ (I / work) for hours.

5. A: Are you crying?
   B: No, _____ (I / chop) onions.

6. A: _____ (you / hear) the news?

45

B Correct the false statements in exercise **A**. Listen again to check your answers.

No explorers had been through the Northwest Passage before Franklin.

11 APPLY.

A Work with a partner. Look at the photo on this page. Imagine what could go wrong on this trip. Then complete the chart with your ideas. Use the simple past, past perfect, and past perfect progressive.

Students use their new language and critical thinking skills in the **Apply** section.

A Kayaking Trip

What Happened	Why It Happened
1. While kayaking, they got lost.	1. They hadn't been paying attention to their location.
2. They got sunburned.	2. They hadn't brought any sunblock.
3. They lost a paddle.	3.
4.	4. They had been walking around.
5. They got mosquito bites.	5.
6.	6.

B Share your ideas with the class.

56 PRESENT AND PAST: PERFECT AND PERFECT PROGRESSIVE

Review the Grammar UNIT 2

Charts 2.1–2.7

1 Complete the paragraph. Use the correct form of each verb in parentheses.

I (1) _____ had _____ (have) a terrible car accident when I was sixteen. I (2) _____ (lose) a leg. As an athlete, this was especially devastating. I (3) _____ (be) a gymnast from the age of eight, and I (4) _____ (win) three national competitions. It (5) _____ (take) me a lot of time to recover, and I (6) _____ (not think) about competing again. Then, one of my coaches (7) _____ (tell) me about the Paralympics and (8) _____ (suggest) that I train for swimming. I could do that with only one leg. I (9) _____ (always / want) to be in the Olympics. In fact, I (10) _____ (train) for the Olympics at the time of my accident. So I (11) _____ (listen) to my coach and (12) _____ (start) swimming. I (13) _____ (swim) ever since that day and I love it. I (14) _____ (win) several competitions. Lately, I (15) _____ (train) for the next Paralympics. I hope to win a medal!

Charts 2.1, 2.3–2.7

2 EDIT. Read the text by a traveler on safari. Find and correct eight more errors with the simple past, present perfect, past perfect, or past perfect progressive.

Mason's Travels on Safari

It had always been our dream to travel to southern Africa, and we'd ~~make~~ ^{made} a lot of plans for our trip. I wanted to take a lot of wildlife photographs, so my friend has recommended that I bring two cameras. When I got to Namibia, I had panicked. One camera had been missing. Luckily, I was finding it later.

The next day, we had started out on our safari with a tour. By the end of our tour, we saw some amazing things. One time, when we stopped to take pictures, we were only a few feet away from a cheetah. Amazing!

We had never bothered the animals at night. How[...] and other noises outside our tent every night. At first, [...] but not by the end of the trip. It was really the most i[...]

Cheetah running, ▶ Namibia

58

Charts 2.1, 2.3–2.4, 2.6

3 LISTEN & SPEAK.

A Circle the correct form of the verb. Then listen to the conversation and check your answers.

CD1-17

1. Liu Yang is the first female astronaut that China **ever sent / has ever sent** into space.

2. She **trained / has trained** to be a pilot at China's Air Force College, and then she **joined / has joined** the Air Force.

3. She **flew / has flown** five different types of aircraft, and she **did / has done** 1680 hours of flight time.

4. She **also participated / has also participated** in military exercises and emergency rescues.

5. Liu started training to be an astronaut. She **has never experienced / had never experienced** anything so challenging.

CD1-18

B Listen to the next part of the conversation. Then work with a partner. Discuss the questions. Then listen again and check your answers.

1. What has Liu Yang done in her life?
2. Had she always wanted to be an astronaut?
3. How have her coworkers described her?
4. How long had she been in the Air Force before becoming an astronaut?

Review the Grammar gives students the opportunity to consolidate the grammar in their reading, writing, listening, and speaking.

Connect the Grammar to Writing

1 READ & NOTICE THE GRAMMAR.

A What is a goal that you have achieved? How did it affect you? Tell a partner your ideas. Then read the narrative.

Achieving a Goal

About a year ago, I was watching the Olympics, and I decided that I wanted to become a runner. I knew I should set an achievable goal, so I decided to train for a 5K race.

My parents were surprised when I told them about my goal, because I had never been interested in running before. In fact, I had never run more than a mile, and I had always been very slow. My friends thought I was joking. Everyone assumed that I would quit after a week.

Fortunately, I proved them all wrong. I did two things to achieve my goal. First, I went online and researched a good training plan. I found a website that helps you plan workouts. You start by walking, and then you gradually start running. After that, I joined a local running group. We ran in the park twice a week, and I made friends who had also decided to run a 5K.

Three months later, I achieved my goal: I ran in my first race. I didn't win, but I ran the whole way, so I was proud of myself. Since then, I have run in several races. I have also started training for a longer run. My next goal is to run in a 10K race. My friends have stopped laughing at me, and a few of them have even asked me to help them start running!

GRAMMAR FOCUS

In the narrative in exercise **A**, the writer uses these verb forms:

Simple past	• to tell about the main event of the story (*About a year ago . . . I **decided** that . . .*)
Past perfect	• to discuss events that happ... (*I **had** never **run** more than ...*)
Present perfect	• with *since* to tell about past... present (***Since** then, I **have** ...*)

B Read the narrative in exercise **A** again. Find and circle ... past. Underline two past perfect examples, and double ... examples.

Write a Personal Narrative

C Complete the time line with information from the narrative in exercise **A**. Write the letter of the events in the correct order. Then compare your answers with a partner.

a. Ran in several other races   e. Ran in 5K

b. Was never interested in running   f. Watched the Olympics

c. Joined a running club   g. Found a good website

d. Parents were surprised

  _b_   __   __   __   __   __

  Set a goal to run a 5K   Now

2 BEFORE YOU WRITE.

A Work with a partner. Make a list of goals that you have achieved. Discuss which goals would be the most interesting to write about.

B Create a time line for your personal narrative. Write the events of the story that you want to tell. Use the time line in exercise **1C** as a guide.

3 WRITE two or three paragraphs telling your story. Use your time line in exercise **2B** and the text in exercise **1A** as a guide. Remember to start your story with background information. At the end, tell how your life has changed.

WRITING FOCUS   Using *First* and *After that* to Show a Sequence

Notice *first* and *after that* in the narrative in exercise **1A**.

Use these words at the beginning of the sentence to explain the order of events in a text. Place a comma after *first* and *after that*.

***First**, I went online and . . .   **After that**, I joined a local running club.*

---

4 SELF ASSESS. Underline the verb forms in your narrative. Then use the checklist to assess your work.

☐ I used the present perfect and the present perfect progressive correctly. [2.1, 2.2, 2.4, 2.5]

☐ I used the simple past correctly. [2.3]

☐ I used the past perfect and the past perfect progressive correctly. [2.6, 2.7]

☐ I used commas correctly with *first* and *after that*. [WRITING FOCUS]

Connect the Grammar to Writing provides students with a clear model and a guided writing task where they first notice and then use the target grammar in one of a variety of writing genres.

ACKNOWLEDGMENTS

The authors and publisher would like to thank the following reviewers and contributors:

Gokhan Alkanat, Auburn University at Montgomery, Alabama; **Dorothy S. Avondstondt**, Miami Dade College, Florida; **Heather Barikmo**, The English Language Center at LaGuardia Community College, New York; **Kimberly Becker**, Nashville State Community College, Tennessee; **Lukas Bidelspack**, Corvallis, Oregon; **Grace Bishop**, Houston Community College, Texas; **Mariusz Jacek Bojarczuk**, Bunker Hill Community College, Massachusetts; **Nancy Boyer**, Golden West College, California; **Patricia Brenner**, University of Washington, Washington; **Jessica Buchsbaum**, City College of San Francisco, California; **Gabriella Cambiasso**, Harold Washington College, Illinois; **Tony Carnerie**, English Language Institute, University of California San Diego Extension, California; **Ana M. Cervantes Quequezana**, ICPNA - Instituto Cultural Peruano Norteamericano; **Whitney Clarq-Reis**, Framingham State University; **Julia A. Correia**, Henderson State University, Arkansas; **Katie Crowder**, UNT Department of Linguistics and Technical Communication, Texas; **Lin Cui**, William Rainey Harper College, Illinois; **Nora Dawkins**, Miami Dade College, Florida; **Rachel DeSanto**, English for Academic Purposes, Hillsborough Community College, Florida; **Aurea Diab**, Dillard University, Louisiana; **Marta Dmytrenko-Ahrabian**, English Language Institute, Wayne State University, Michigan; **Susan Dorrington**, Education and Language Acquisition Department, LaGuardia Community College, New York; **Ian Dreilinger**, Center for Multilingual Multicultural Studies, University of Central Florida, Florida; **Jennifer Dujat**, Education and Language Acquisition Department, LaGuardia Community College, New York; **Dr. Jane Duke**, Language & Literature Department, State College of Florida, Florida; **Anna Eddy**, University of Michigan-Flint, Michigan; **Jenifer Edens**, University of Houston, Texas; **Karen Einstein**, Santa Rosa Junior College, California; **Cynthia Etter**, International & English Language Programs, University of Washington, Washington; **Parvanak Fassihi**, SHOWA Boston Institute for Language and Culture, Massachusetts; **Katherine Fouche**, The University of Texas at Austin, Texas; **Richard Furlong**, Education and Language Acquisition Department, LaGuardia Community College, New York; **Glenn S. Gardner**, Glendale College, California; **Sally Gearhart**, Santa Rosa Junior College, California; **Alexis Giannopolulos**, SHOWA Boston Institute for Language and Culture, Massachusetts; **Nora Gold**, Baruch College, The City University of New York, New York; **Ekaterina V. Goussakova**, Seminole State College of Florida; **Lynn Grantz**, Valparaiso University, Indiana; **Tom Griffith**, SHOWA Boston Institute for Language and Culture, Massachusetts; **Christine Guro**, Hawaii English Language Program, University of Hawaii at Manoa, Hawaii; **Jessie Hayden**, Georgia Perimeter College, Georgia; **Barbara Inerfeld**, Program in American Language Studies, Rutgers University, New Jersey; **Gail Kellersberger**, University of Houston-Downtown, Texas; **David Kelley**, SHOWA Boston Institute for Language and Culture, Massachusetts; **Kathleen Kelly**, ESL Department, Passaic County Community College, New Jersey; **Dr. Hyun-Joo Kim**, Education and Language Acquisition Department, LaGuardia Community College, New York; **Linda Koffman**, College of Marin, California; **Lisa Kovacs-Morgan**, English Language Institute, University of California San Diego Extension, California; **Jerrad Langlois**, TESL Program and Office of International Programs, Northeastern Illinois University; **Janet Langon**, Glendale College, California; **Olivia Limbu**, The English Language Center at LaGuardia Community College, New York; **Devora Manier**, Nashville State Community College, Tennessee; **Susan McAlister**, Language and Culture Center, Department of English, University of Houston, Texas; **John McCarthy**, SHOWA Boston Institute for Language and Culture, Massachusetts; **Dr. Myra Medina**, Miami Dade College, Florida; **Dr. Suzanne Medina**, California State University, Dominguez Hills, California; **Nancy Megarity**, ESL & Developmental Writing, Collin College, Texas; **Joseph Montagna**, SHOWA Boston Institute for Language and Culture, Massachusetts; **Richard Moore**, University of Washington; **Monika Mulder**, Portland State University, Oregon; **Patricia Nation**, Miami Dade College, Florida; **Susan Niemeyer**, Los Angeles City College, California; **Charl Norloff**, International English Center, University of Colorado Boulder, Colorado; **Gabriella Nuttall**, Sacramento City College, California; **Dr. Karla Odenwald**, CELOP at Boston University, Massachusetts; **Ali Olson-Pacheco**, English Language Institute, University of California San Diego Extension, California; **Fernanda Ortiz**, Center for English as a Second Language, University of Arizona, Arizona; **Chuck Passentino**, Grossmont College, California; **Stephen Peridore**, College of Southern Nevada, Nevada; **Frank Quebbemann**, Miami Dade College, Florida; **Dr. Anouchka Rachelson**, Miami Dade College, Florida; **Dr. Agnieszka Rakowicz**, Education and Language Acquisition Department, LaGuardia Community College, New York; **Wendy Ramer**, Broward College, Florida; **Esther Robbins**, Prince George's Community College, Maryland; **Helen Roland**, Miami Dade College, Florida; **Debbie Sandstrom**, Tutorium in Intensive English, University of Illinois at Chicago, Illinois; **Maria Schirta**, Hudson County Community College, New Jersey; **Dr. Jennifer Scully**, Education and Language Acquisition Department, LaGuardia Community College, New York; **Jeremy Stubbs**, Tacoma, Washington; **Adrianne Thompson**, Miami Dade College, Florida; **Evelyn Trottier**, Basic and Transitional Studies Program, Seattle Central Community College, Washington; **Karen Vallejo**, University of California, Irvine, California; **Emily Young**, Auburn University at Montgomery, Alabama.

The publisher would also like to thank Heidi Fischer for her writing of Connect the Grammar to Writing in level 3 of this series.

From the Authors: We would like to thank Tom Jefferies for selecting us to work together on this project and Laura Le Dréan for steering it through to completion. We can't thank our editors, Eve Einselen Yu and Kim Steiner, enough for their expertise and perseverance through charts, drafts, and countless e-mails. We also wish to thank Heidi Fischer for her clear models and writing tasks in Connect the Grammar to Writing. In addition, we are grateful for the inspiration of our fellow authors Daphne Mackay and Paul Carne, as well as Daria Ruzicka in the early stages of the project. Their head start on Levels 1 and 2 set the high standards to which we knew we had to aspire.

Dedication: To Gary, for your patience, support, and invaluable native speaker intuitions.
À Robert, pour tous les bons repas et toutes les belles journées.

Text and Listening

4: Exercise 1. Source: National Geographic Magazine, January 2008. **64:** Exercise 1: National Geographic Magazine, August 2011. **12:** Exercise 1. Source: National Geographic Magazine, September 2011. **18:** Exercise 1. Source: National Geographic Magazine, January 2012. **32:** Exercise 1. Source: http://events.nationalgeographic.com/events/exhibits/polar-obsession. **41:** Exercise 1. Source: http://www.historylink.org/index.cfm?DisplayPage=output.cfm&file_id=9851. **46:** Exercise 1. Source: http://www.nationalgeographic.com/explorers/bios/barton-seaver. **48:** Exercise 1. Source: http://adventureblog.nationalgeographic.com/tag/alex-honnold. **59:** Exercise 3. Sources: http://scienceblogs.com/usasciencefestival/2012/11/08/women-who-changed-the-world-through-science-engineering-liu-yang-astronaut; http://www.huffingtonpost.com/2012/06/15/liu-yang-china-female-astronaut_n_1601063.html. **71:** Exercise 1. Source: http://natgeotv.com.au/videos/future-matters/clever-clothes 1707C4C2.aspx **78:** Exercise 1. Sources: http://environment.nationalgeographic.com/environment/sustainable-earth/11-of-the-fastest-growing-green-jobs/#/rio-20-green-jobs-roof-top-garden_55050_600x450.jpg; http://news.nationalgeographic.com/news/2012/07/pictures/120730-future-floating-cities-science-green-environment. **92:** Exercise 1. Sources: http://video.nationalgeographic.com/video/news/140402-mars-utah-vin; http://newswatch.nationalgeographic.com/2014/03/25/first-person-what-im-learning-on-a-simulated-mars-mission. **98:** Exercise 7C. Source: http://news.nationalgeographic.com/news/2007/09/070927-polynesians-sailors.html. **101:** Exercise 1. Source: http://www.nationalgeographic.com/adventure/0602/features/north-pole-expedition.html. **109:** Exercise 1. Sources: http://www.nationalgeographic.com/explorers/bios/albert-lin; http://www.nationalgeographic.com/explorers/projects/valley-khans-project. **120:** Exercise 1. Source: http://news.nationalgeographic.com/news/2005/03/0321_050321_babies.html. **124:** Exercise 1. Source: http://ngm.nationalgeographic.com/2011/10/teenage-brains/dobbs-text. **130:** Exercise 9. Source: http://www.mnn.com/lifestyle/eco-tourism/stories/5-teens-who-have-sailed-around-the-world-solo. **131:** Exercise 1. Source: http://news.nationalgeographic.com/news/2010/07/100701-boston-university-health-genes-live-100-longevity-genetic-science. **136:** Exercise 8. Source: assets.aarp.org/rgcenter/general/exercise-bulletin-survey.pdf. **139:** Exercise 3. Source: http://www.firstpeople.us/FP-Html-Legends/TheWonderfulTurtle-Lakota.html. **144:** Exercise 1. Sources: http://ngm.nationalgeographic.com/print/2010/05/sleep/max-text; http://www.npr.org/templates/story/story.php?storyId=4955790. **152:** Exercise 1. Sources: http://video.nationalgeographic.com/video/places/regions-places/south-america/paraguay_paraguayshaman; http://www.nature.org/ourinitiatives/urgentissues/rainforests/rainforests-facts.xml; http://www.sfgate.com/science/article/Amazon-deforestation-grows-outside-Brazil-3832770.php; http://www.wltus.org/shocking-deforestation-in-paraguay; http://rainforests.mongabay.com/1007.htm; http://www.rain-tree.com/article4.htm; http://news.nationalgeographic.com/news/2003/06/0626_030626_tvparaguaymedicine_2.html. **158:** Exercise 9. Source: National Geographic Magazine, February 2013. **161:** Exercise 1. Sources: http://www.looktothestars.org/news/7936-feliciano-dos-santos-says-lets-wash-our-hands; Milson, Andrew J. *Health.* National Geographic Global series. 2014; www.pbs.org/frontlineworld/stories/mozambique704/video/video index.html. **166:** Exercise 8. Sources: http://www.nationalgeographic.com/explorers/bios/hayat-sindi; http://education.nationalgeographic.com/education/news/real-world-geography-dr-hayat-sindi/?ar_a=1. **169:** Exercise 8. Source: http://www.nationmultimedia.com/opinion/Healthcare-in-Thailand-a-story-to-inspire-confiden-30180854.html. **170:** Exercise 2. Source: http://news.nationalgeographic.com/news/2013/06/130628-richard-louv-nature-deficit-disorder-health-environment. **184:** Exercise 1. Sources: http://www.youtube.com/watch?v=CRT4dU6r-KQ; http://www.jul.com; http://www.tripadvisor.com/Hotel_Review-g2237714-d1591061-Reviews-Khao_Sok_Nature_Resort-Phanom_Surat_Thani_Province.html; http://www.khaosoknatureresort.com. **208:** Exercise 1. Source: http://education.nationalgeographic.com/education/media/strange-rains/?ar_a=1. **212:** Exercise 5. Source: http://news.nationalgeographic.com/news/2007/02/070223-bees.html. **214:** Exercise 8. Source: http://news.nationalgeographic.com/news/2013/13/130507-talking-chili-plant-communication-science. **223:** Exercise 9. Source: http://news.nationalgeographic.com/news/2012/03/120312-leonardo-da-vinci-mural-lost-painting-florence-science-world. **216:** Exercise 1. Sources: http://ngm.nationalgeographic.com/2012/06/terra-cotta-warriors/larmer-text; http://science.nationalgeographic.com/science/archaeology/emperor-qin; http://www.livescience.com/25510-terracotta-warriors.html. **227:** Exercise 13. Source: http://news.nationalgeographic.com/news/2013/12/131208-roanoke-lost-colony-discovery-history-raleigh. **229:** Exercise 1. Source: http://www.globalpost.com/dispatch/news/regions/americas/united-states/130623/famed-tightrope-daredevil-nik-wallenda-cross-gra. **230:** Exercise 3. Source: http://news.nationalgeographic.com/news/2012/05/120510-maya-2012-doomsday-calendar-end-of-world-science. **236:** Exercise 1. Source: http://www.nationalgeographic.com/explorers/bios/sylvia-earle. **246:** Exercise 1. Source: National Geographic Magazine, March 2013, pp. 60–77. **254:** Exercise 1. Sources: http://environment.nationalgeographic.com/environment/natural-disasters/hurricane-profile; http://www.hurricanehunters.com/mission.html; Geiger, Beth. *Hurricane Hunters.* National Geographic Explorer Collection. **268:** Exercise 1. Source: National Geographic Magazine, August 2009. **274:** Exercise 9. Source: http://blogs.nybg.org/plant-talk/2013/04/science/alex-popovkin-botanist-extraordinaire. **275:** Exercise 1. Source: http://www.sciencedaily.com/releases/2010/01/100111112845.htm. **282:** Exercise 1. Sources: http://www.nationalgeographic.com/explorers/bios/lucy-cooke; http://animal.discovery.com/mammals/sloths-slow.htm; http://www.aviary.org/animals/two-toed-sloth; http://www.worldanimalfoundation.net/f/Sloth.pdf. **286:** Exercise 6. Source: http://www.ted.com/talks/denis_dutton_a_darwinian_theory_of_beauty. **288:** Exercise 9. Source: http://phenomena.nationalgeographic.com/2012/10/02/beauty-in-the-right-eye-of-the-beholder-finch-chooses-better-mates-with-its-right-eye. **290:** Exercise 1. Source: http://animals.nationalgeographic.com/animals/bugs/stick-insect. **296:** Exercise 1. Source: Dipanjan Mitra/National Geographic My Shot. **308:** Exercise 1. Source: www.michaelnicknichols.com. **310:** Exercise 4. Source: www.npr.org/blogs/pictureshow/2009/09/redwoods.html. **314:** Exercise 8. Source: rippleeffectimages.org. **316:** Exercise 10. Source: www.pbs.org/atcloserange/whoisjoel.html. **317:** Exercise 11. Sources: http://www.ted.com/speakers/913; http://www.ted.com/talks/jr_s_ted_prize_wish_use_art_to_turn_the_world_inside_out. **334:** Exercise 1. Source: http://www.nytimes.com/2011/02/13/books/review/Silver-t.html. **345:** Exercise 1. Source: http://www.bostonglobe.com/metro/2013/09/21/bicycling-dutch-way/kFRT0ABSPtUnXMIUj5zONM/story.html. **358:** Exercise 1. Source: www.adsvvy.org/the-power-of-framing-effects-and-other-cognitive-biases. **365:** Exercise 12. Source: http://blog.bufferapp.com/8-things-you-dont-know-are-affecting-your-decisions-every-day. **366:** Exercise 1. Sources: www.nationalgeographic.com/deextinction; news.nationalgeographic.com/news/2013/03/130311-deextinction-reviving-extinct-species-opinion-animals-science; National Geographic Magazine, April 2013. **377:** Exercise 1. Sources: National Geographic Magazine, December 2013; outofedenwalk.nationalgeographic.com **387:** Exercise 5. Source: http://www.decodedscience.com/doc-mallett-the-time-of-his-life/4431. **392:** Exercise 1. Sources: news.nationalgeographic.com/news/2012/10/121026-human-cooking-evolution-raw-food-health-science;

(continued on page C1)

Present and Past: Simple and Progressive

▶ A grizzly bear with four young cubs near Moraine Creek in Katmai National Park, Southwest Alaska, USA

EXPLORE

CD1-02

1 **READ** the article about lowland gorillas in northern Congo. What are researchers trying to learn about these animals?

AFRICA
Northern Congo

The Family Life of Lowland Gorillas

Scientists know very little about how lowland gorillas behave in the rainforests where they live. However, one thing is clear: their numbers **are** rapidly **declining**.[1] In order to help these animals survive, researchers **are trying** to learn as much as possible about their family relationships as well as their behavior and diet in the wild.

One family that scientists **are** currently **observing** belongs to Kingo. It includes Kingo, his four wives—each with her own baby—and one orphan.[2] The ten gorillas **live** comfortably in a rainforest in northern Congo. Together with a team of trackers,[3] the researchers **follow** the family everywhere. Today, they **are watching** Kingo at lunchtime.

Kingo always **eats** alone; his wives and babies never **go** near him. After he **eats**, he usually **takes** a nap. He **lies back** in the hot shade and instantly **falls** asleep. Then when he **wakes up**, he **leads** his family through the forest in search of more food. The young males **stay** close by his side, and they **copy** every move he **makes**. Kingo's wives **walk** behind him. When he **stops**, they **stop**, and when he **moves**, they **move**.

Kingo's stop today is a pond. Here he **is pulling up** plants, **washing** them in the water, and then **eating** them. This 300-pound (136-kilogram) king of the jungle couldn't be happier right now. The mothers **are resting**, and the young ones **are taking** naps or **playing**. As the researchers can clearly see, this is just one big, happy family.

[1] **decline:** become less
[2] **orphan:** a child whose parents have died
[3] **tracker:** someone who finds animals by following marks in the ground or other signs that show where the animals have been

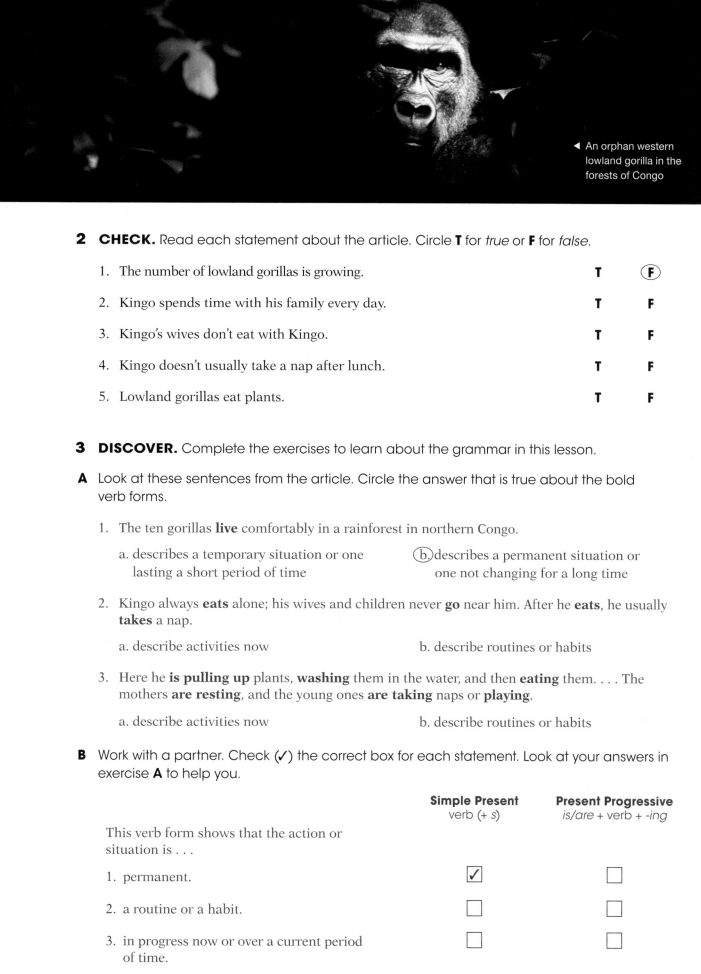

◄ An orphan western
lowland gorilla in the
forests of Congo

2 **CHECK.** Read each statement about the article. Circle **T** for *true* or **F** for *false*.

1. The number of lowland gorillas is growing.   **T**   (**F**)

2. Kingo spends time with his family every day.   **T**   **F**

3. Kingo's wives don't eat with Kingo.   **T**   **F**

4. Kingo doesn't usually take a nap after lunch.   **T**   **F**

5. Lowland gorillas eat plants.   **T**   **F**

3 **DISCOVER.** Complete the exercises to learn about the grammar in this lesson.

A Look at these sentences from the article. Circle the answer that is true about the bold
verb forms.

1. The ten gorillas **live** comfortably in a rainforest in northern Congo.

   a. describes a temporary situation or one   (b.)describes a permanent situation or
      lasting a short period of time   one not changing for a long time

2. Kingo always **eats** alone; his wives and children never **go** near him. After he **eats**, he usually
   takes a nap.

   a. describe activities now   b. describe routines or habits

3. Here he **is pulling up** plants, **washing** them in the water, and then **eating** them. . . . The
   mothers **are resting**, and the young ones **are taking** naps or **playing**.

   a. describe activities now   b. describe routines or habits

B Work with a partner. Check (✓) the correct box for each statement. Look at your answers in
exercise **A** to help you.

	Simple Present verb (+ *s*)	**Present Progressive** *is/are* + verb + *-ing*
This verb form shows that the action or situation is . . .		
1. permanent.	✓	☐
2. a routine or a habit.	☐	☐
3. in progress now or over a current period of time.	☐	☐

LEARN

1.1 Simple Present and Present Progressive Review

	Simple Present	Present Progressive
Affirmative Statements	I **eat** a healthy diet. Ana **eats** only vegetables.	I'm **eating** an apple now. She's **eating** a salad.
Negative Statements	We **don't work** on Saturdays. Ali **doesn't work** in a hospital.	We're **not working** today. Jim's **not working** now.
Yes/No Questions	**Do** you **eat** breakfast every day? **Does** Jana **study** at the library?	**Are** the children **eating** lunch now? **Is** Jana **studying** now?
Wh- Questions	Where **do** you **read** the news? How long **does** the train **take**?	What **are** you **studying** this semester? Why **is** he **staying** in a hotel this week?
Who or What as Subject	Who **lives** in this house? What **helps** a headache?	Who **is taking** math this semester? What **is cooking** in the oven?

1. Use the simple present for:
   a. routines and habits
   b. facts and general truths
   c. permanent actions or situations

   a. I **drink** coffee every day.
   b. The sky often **looks** blue.
   c. Tomo's parents **live** in a big house.

2. Use the present progressive for actions that are:
   a. happening now, at the moment of speaking
   b. happening over a current time period
      (today, this week, this month, this year)
   c. temporary

   a. I can't talk now. I'm **eating** dinner.
   b. She's **visiting** her grandmother this week.
   c. Jared **is living** in a dorm this semester.

3. Do not repeat the verb be when the same subject is doing two actions.

   Youssef is **singing** and **playing** the guitar in the video.

4. **Be careful!** Do not use do/does in questions when Who or What is the subject.

   ✓ Who **reads** the newspaper?
   ✗ Who does read the newspaper?

---

4 Complete the interview with the words in parentheses. Use the simple present or present progressive form of the verbs.

A: How (1) _____do you find_____ (you / find) the gorillas every day?

B: Every morning (2) _____ (I / go) with the trackers to look for them.

A: How long (3) _____ (it / take) to find the gorillas?

B: (4) _____ (it / usually / take) a few hours, but sometimes (5) _____ (we / not find) them for five or six hours.

A: (6) _____ (the trackers / follow) Kingo today?

B: No, they aren't. (7) _____

(the trackers / spend) time with their families for a few days and

(8) _____ (explore) the area.

A: Where (9) _____ (you / stay) this week?

B: (10) _____ (I / stay) at a campsite with my guides and trackers.

A: So, tell me, what (11) _____ (surprise) you about the gorillas?

B: Good question! I find it interesting that (12) _____ (gorillas / laugh).

A: (13) _____ (you / follow) other animal families?

B: Yes. This year (14) _____ (I / do) research on chimp families, too.

A: What (15) _____ (make) gorillas different from chimpanzees?

B: (16) _____ (young chimps and gorillas / stay)

with their mothers. (17) _____ (chimp fathers / usually / not stay)

with the family. Gorilla fathers (18) _____ (rarely / leave) their families.

1.2   More Present Progressive

1. Use the present progressive for changes that happen over time.	Her baby **is getting bigger** day by day. Children today **are eating** more sugar.
2. Use the present progressive with *always* to emphasize repeated actions. Sometimes, these actions are not typical or are unwanted.	I'm worried. Julie **is always sleeping**. My car **is always breaking down**.
3. Use the simple present with *always* if the action is normal or expected.	My son **always does** his homework.

5 Complete the paragraph with the words in parentheses. Use the simple present or the present progressive.

The Reed family (1) _____is growing_____ (grow) too big for their house. Rose and

Jeff Reed now have six children at home, and the kids (2) _____ (get)

bigger every day. The challenges for the family (3) _____ (grow), too.

For example, the cost of food (4) _____ (increase). It's hard to feed so

many people. Rose and Jeff (5) _____ (always / go) to the grocery store

together and (6) _____ (compare) prices, but it's still hard.

Different personalities are another challenge. Melissa Reed says, "I'm the oldest

child. I (7) _____ (always / take care of) my younger

brothers and sisters. I enjoy all of them most of the time, but my younger brother,

Charlie, can be difficult. He (8) _____ (always / get) into

trouble. In fact, he (9) _____ (become) impossible. Someone

(10) _____ (always / complain) about him."

6 ANALYZE THE GRAMMAR. Work with a partner. Identify the meaning of each verb form you wrote in exercise **5**. Write the number of the item next to the correct meaning.

1. A change over time: __1__, _____, _____, _____, _____

2. An unwanted repeated action: _____, _____

3. A regular or expected action: _____, _____, _____

PRACTICE

7 Complete the paragraphs with the words in parentheses. Use the simple present or the present progressive form of the verbs.

(1) I _'m enjoying_ (enjoy) my summer here in Japan. I (2) _____ (stay) with a very nice family, but they (3) _____ (do) things very differently than my family. Here, they (4) _____ (take) their shoes off at the entrance to the house and at school. Also, they (5) _____ (not eat) with forks and spoons; instead, they (6) _____ (use) chopsticks at every meal. I (7) _____ (get) better at eating with chopsticks, but I'm still not very good.

My host sister, Sachiko, is my age. She (8) _____ (speak) English pretty well. Her English is a lot better than my Japanese. My Japanese (9) _____ (improve) day by day, but Sachiko's younger brother (10) _____ (often / laugh) at my pronunciation. It (11) _____ (not bother) me because it is true that I (12) _____ (often / make) funny mistakes. They make me laugh, too.

8 WRITE & SPEAK.

A Use the words in parentheses to make questions. Use the simple present or the present progressive.

1. (you / eat / with chopsticks at every meal)
   Do you eat with chopsticks at every meal?

2. (your family / remove / their shoes inside the house)
   _____

3. (what / you / get better at)
   _____

4. (anyone in your family / speak / English well)
   _____

5. (what / language / you / speak / at home)
   _____

6. (who / you / live with)
   _____

A view of Mount Fuji from a field of sunflowers, Japan

7. (your English / improve / day by day)

   _____.

8. (you / ever / laugh / at your mistakes in English)

   _____.

B Work with a partner. Ask and answer the questions in exercise **A**.

A: *Do you eat with chopsticks at every meal?*   B: *No, I don't. How about you?*

9 Complete the exercises.

A Complete each sentence with the verbs in the box. Use *always* and the present progressive.

~~borrow~~	check	complain	lose
make	not return	talk	text

REAL ENGLISH

The present progressive with *always* is a common way to complain about other people's behavior.

*My neighbors **are always playing** loud music at night.*

1. My sister ___is always borrowing___ my things

   and _____ them.

2. My sons _____ their phone

   messages and _____ their friends.

3. My best friend _____ about her job. She needs to find a new one.

4. My neighbors _____ noise late at night. It's hard to fall asleep.

5. My cousin _____ about her clothes. It drives me crazy!

6. My husband _____ things. Yesterday it was his car keys!

B **SPEAK** Tell a partner which statements in exercise **A** are true about people you know. Replace the subjects with someone you know.

A: *My brother is always borrowing my things.*   B: *Oh, my friend is always doing that, too.*

10 Complete the exercises.

A Complete the sentences according to the information in the chart. Use the verbs in parentheses and the present progressive. Add *not* where necessary.

Current Trends in Family Life in the U.S.

Life Span	Marriage Rate	Divorce Rate	Age at Marriage	Number of Children	Number of Grown Children at Home	Children in Single-Parent Homes
⬆	⬇	⬇	⬆	⬇	⬆	⬆

1. People _____are living_____ (live) longer.

2. The number of marriages ___is decreasing___ (decrease). The number of marriages _____ (increase).

3. The divorce rate _____ (go) up. It _____ (come) down.

4. Fewer people _____ (get) married at a young age. More people _____ (wait) until their 30s to get married.

5. Most women _____ (have) a lot of children. They _____ (have) fewer children.

6. More grown children _____ (continue) to live with their parents when they become adults.

7. More children _____ (grow) up with only one parent than in the past.

B **SPEAK.** Work with a partner. Read the sentences in exercise **A**. Which trends are true about families in your country? Tell your partner.

A: *In my country, people are living longer. There are more doctors nowadays.*

B: *In mine, most people are not eating healthy food. I don't think they are living longer.*

11 **LISTEN & WRITE.**

CD1-03

A Listen to Julia tell a friend about her family. Match each family member with the correct activity.

1. grandmother __b__   a. play in an orchestra

2. father ____   b. ~~drive~~

3. brother Alex ____   c. stand next to Alex

4. twin sister ____   d. not get together often

5. brother Lucas ____   e. study in Scotland

6. whole family ____   f. live in New York City

B Write six sentences about Julia and her family. Use the simple present or the present progressive and the information in exercise **A**. Then share your answers as a class.

Julia's grandmother never drives at night.

_____

_____

_____

_____

_____

_____

12 EDIT. Read the paragraph. Find and correct five more errors with the simple present or present progressive.

          I am visiting
    This week, I ~~visit~~ my twin sister. We aren't getting together often because we live a couple of hours apart. We talk and text all the time, though, so we don't feel too far apart. We are telling each other our problems and try to help each other out. Another reason we don't see each other very often is because of my sister's job. She is very busy. We often make plans, but she is cancelling always our plans at the last minute. Sometimes this upsets me. It's almost summer, though, so her schedule becomes much less busy. This week, at least, we do a lot together. It's great!

13 APPLY.

A In your notebook, write a paragraph about a family member or a friend. Tell how often you see this person, what you do together, and what the person is doing now. Add other details.

    I don't see my older brother very often. He and his wife are very busy. They work full time, and they have a new baby. My sister-in-law is looking for a part-time job . . .

B Work with a partner. Read your partner's paragraph. Then ask him or her at least three follow-up questions.

A: *What kind of job is your sister-in-law looking for?*

B: *She is looking for a job as a nurse.*

EXPLORE

1 **READ** the article about the changing size of families in Brazil. How and why is the size of families changing?

The Shrinking **Families of Brazil**

Nowadays, families in Brazil are getting smaller. In the past, Brazilian women often had seven or eight children. Today, however, most women **think** that two children **are** enough. Ask any Brazilian woman, "Why **do you want** only two children? Why not four? Why not have eight like your grandmother did?" The answer **is** always the same: "It**'s** too expensive! It**'s** too much work!"

What **accounts for**¹ this change in Brazilian women's thinking? Why is this happening?

One reason **is** improved education for girls in Brazil. More education usually **means** that women wait longer to have children and have fewer of them. In Brazil, TV soap operas (*novelas*) **are** also a big influence. No one can deny² the popularity of these programs. People all over the country watch them every evening. In the average *novela*, 90 percent of the female characters **have** just one child or no children at all.

There **are** signs of this trend all over the country. As one business executive in Rio de Janeiro points out, "Look at the apartments. They**'re** designed for a maximum of four people. Two bedrooms. In the supermarkets, even the labels on frozen foods—always for four people." Clearly, many of today's Brazilian women **are not thinking** about having big families anymore.

¹ **account for:** cause or be the explanation for something
² **deny:** to say something is not true

▶ Smaller families like this one reflect the Brazilian birthrate. In 2013, women had an average of 1.8 children.

▼ In the past, Brazilian families were larger.

2 CHECK. Correct the error in each sentence to make it true according to the article in exercise **1**.

1. Brazilian women today ~~want~~ ˅don't want big families.

2. In Brazil today, women are having more children than their grandmothers did.

3. There is only one reason for smaller families in Brazil.

4. Most of the women in Brazilian soap operas have a lot of children.

3 DISCOVER. Complete the exercises to learn about the grammar in this lesson.

A Read the statements about the article in exercise **1**. Then underline the verb or verb phrase that agrees with each bold subject. Notice the different verb forms.

1. **The couple** <u>is thinking</u> about having more children.

2. **Most people** think that two children are enough.

3. **My mother** is looking at family photos.

4. **My sister** looks happy in the photo.

5. **Some large families** are having trouble finding big apartments.

6. **Most apartments** have only two bedrooms.

B Work with a partner. Read the statements below. Then decide which statement is true for each sentence in exercise **A**. Write the number of the sentence next to the correct statement.

1. The meaning of the verb is active; it expresses physical or mental action. __1__, _____

2. The meaning of the verb is not active; it expresses a state or condition. _____, _____, _____, _____

LEARN

1.3 Stative Verbs

1. Stative verbs* usually express states or conditions. Stative verbs are not usually used in the progressive.	✓ The baby **wants** the bottle now. ✗ The baby <u>is wanting</u> the bottle now.

2. Many stative verbs fall in the following categories:
  a. **Description:** *appear, be, look, look like, resemble, seem, sound*
  b. **Feelings:** *dislike, hate, like, love, miss*
  c. **Senses:** *feel, hear, see, smell, taste*
  d. **Possession:** *belong, have, own*
  e. **Desires:** *hope, prefer, want*
  f. **Mental states:** *agree, believe, know, think, understand*
  g. **Measurements:** *cost, weigh*
	a. Your niece **looks like** you.
	
	b. I **love** the picture of the whole family.
	c. I **hear** a phone ringing. Is it yours?
	d. That book **belongs** to Sofia.
	e. **Do** you **prefer** coffee or tea?
	f. He **understands** the assignment.
	
	g. How much **does** the red hat **cost**?

** Stative verbs are sometimes called non-action verbs. See page **A1** for a list of stative verbs.*

4 Look at the <u>underlined</u> verbs. Write **A** if it is an action verb and **S** if it is a stative verb.

1. _____ We <u>are</u> a very musical family.

2. _____ I <u>play</u> the piano.

3. _____ My older sister <u>owns</u> five guitars.

4. _____ My younger brother <u>sings</u> beautifully.

5. _____ He <u>has</u> a wonderful voice.

6. _____ My parents <u>love</u> to listen to us.

7. _____ Sometimes they <u>dance</u> to our music.

8. _____ My grandparents <u>know</u> a lot about classical music.

5 Complete the questions and answers with the subjects and stative verbs in parentheses.

1. A: ___Do most people have___ (most people / have) large or small families nowadays?

   B: Usually small ones. _____ (many families / have) only one child.

2. A: _____ (most people / own) their own homes these days?

   B: No, _____ (most people / not own) their own homes. They rent.

3. A: _____ (it / cost) a lot to own a home?

   B: Yes. _____ (it / cost) a lot of money.

4. A: What _____ (you / think) is the ideal number of children to have?

   B: Two. _____ (I / hope) to have one boy and one girl someday.

5. A: _____ (you / know) anyone with more than four brothers and sisters?

   B: No. _____ (it / seem) that everyone I know has only one brother or sister.

6. A: _____ (you / look like) anyone else in your family?

   B: Yes. _____ (I / resemble) my older brother a lot.

6 **SPEAK.** Work with a partner. Ask and answer the questions from exercise **5**. Use your own answers, not the answers in the book.

A: *Do most people in your country have large or small families nowadays?*

B: *Most families have two or three children.*

1.4 Stative Verbs: Stative and Active Meanings

Stative Meaning	Active Meaning
feel sick (state of body)	**feel** the soft material (touch)
have a car (own/possess)	**have** a good time (experience)
see something (perceive visually)	**see** a movie (watch); **see** a doctor (visit)
taste good (flavor)	**taste** the food (take a bite)
weigh 120 lbs (state of body)	**weigh** the apples (put on scale)

1. Some stative verbs have both stative and active meanings.*	Stative: The flowers **smell** wonderful! Active: **Smell** this perfume. Do you like it?
2. When the meaning is active, it is possible to use the progressive form of some stative verbs.	Stative: He doesn't **see** well. He wears glasses. Active: He's **seeing** a doctor monthly. He has a back problem. Stative: I **think** those people are nice. (*believe*) Active: I'm **thinking** of going to Mexico. (*considering*)
3. Use the simple present or the present progressive for verbs that describe physical conditions.	How **do** you **feel?** = How **are** you **feeling?** My foot **hurts.** = My foot **is hurting.** My back **aches.** = My back **is aching.**

*See page **A1** for examples of stative verbs that also have active meanings.

7 Circle the correct form of the verb in each sentence.

1. a. My sister's eyes are blue, and she **has** / **is having** brown hair.

   b. Linda's in the kitchen. She **has** / **is having** breakfast.

2. a. I **think** / **am thinking** Jon is her brother, but I'm not sure.

   b. I **think** / **am thinking** of going to the beach on Sunday.

3. a. Al should eat more. He only **weighs** / **is weighing** 120 pounds (55 kilograms).

   b. The store clerk **weighs** / **is weighing** the apples. Then, he'll tell us the price.

4. a. Henry **isn't / isn't being** very friendly today. I wonder if he's angry.

   b. The test **is / is being** difficult. You need to study very hard for it.

5. a. Jana **doesn't see / isn't seeing** well. She has to wear glasses when she drives.

   b. Farah **sees / is seeing** her accountant today. She needs help with her taxes.

6. a. Yoko **looks / is looking** at the beautiful sunset.

   b. Yoko **looks / is looking** wonderful. Her dress is beautiful.

7. a. I **smell / am smelling** the milk. I think it's sour.

   b. What are you cooking? It **smells / is smelling** delicious!

8. a. The storm **comes / is coming**. Look at the dark clouds.

   b. Jaime **comes / is coming** from Mexico. He was born in Puebla.

REAL ENGLISH

Sometimes, *being* + adjective is used to describe temporary changes in someone's personality or behavior.

*My son **is being bad**. He's usually good. The teacher **isn't being fair**.*

PRACTICE

8 Complete the conversations with the words in parentheses. Use the simple present or present progressive form of the verbs.

1. A: Why _____are you tasting_____ (you / taste) the soup, Mom?

   B: _____ (it / not smell) right. I want to make sure it's OK.

2. A: _____ (you / have) time to talk right now?

   B: Not really. _____ (I / be) busy at the moment.

3. A: Why _____ (you / look) so serious? What _____ (you / think) about?

   B: All the things _____ (we / need) to do for the family reunion.

4. A: What's wrong? _____ (you / seem) sad.

   B: _____ (I / miss) my family.

9 Complete the paragraphs with the stative verbs in parentheses. Use the simple present or present progressive form of the verbs.

I (1) _____like_____ (like) a TV show called *Modern Family*. My favorite character is Gloria. She (2) _____ (be) funny, and I (3) _____ (love) her accent. She (4) _____ (come) from Colombia and (5) _____ (have) a son, Manny, from a previous marriage. Gloria's husband on the show is a much older man named Jay.

Jay, Gloria, and Manny (6) _____ (not always / agree) with each other. In fact, I (7) _____ (watch) the program right now, and Gloria and Jay (8) _____ (have) an argument. Jay (9) _____ (be) stubborn, and Gloria is complaining about Jay's selfish behavior. She (10) _____ (sound) very angry. Manny (11) _____ (seem) like the only adult. It's very funny.

Gloria's son, Manny, (12) _____ (not resemble) her at all, and he (13) _____ (have) different ideas about everything, but Gloria (14) _____ (love) him very much. Jay makes a lot of money and they (15) _____ (own) a beautiful home, but you never actually (16) _____ (see) him at work in the show. This can only happen on television!

10 Complete the article about emperor penguins with the verbs in the box. Use the simple present or the present progressive. Use the present progressive when possible. Then listen and check your answers.

CD1-05

| be | have | know | not be | not have |
| not need | resemble | see | ~~seem~~ | weigh |

Some aspects of family life among Antarctica's emperor penguins (1) _____seem_____ strange to people. For example, the female lays one egg, and then she leaves. She (2) _____ a bad mother. She simply needs to find food, and she is depending on the male to keep the egg warm. In about two months, the female returns and the egg hatches.

The chick (3) _____ its parents, but it (4) _____ black and white feathers. It (5) _____ grey ones. Also, it (6) _____ much smaller, and it (7) _____ much less than the average 75-pound adult. The parents teach the chick how to take care of itself, but there's one thing the chick (8) _____ to learn: how to swim! When a penguin (9) _____ water, it (10) _____ exactly what to do. Emperor penguins are excellent swimmers!

▼ A penguin protects its chick by resting the chick on its feet.

11 APPLY.

A In your notebook, write a short paragraph about a family you know. Use at least five stative verbs that can have active meanings. Use chart 1.4 and the list on page **A1** to help you.

B Read your description to the class. Ask your classmates follow-up questions.

A: *How old is Manny?*   B: *I'm not sure. I think he's eleven or twelve.*

A: *Do Carla and James have any children?*   B: *Yes, they have a son and two daughters.*

EXPLORE

CD1-06

1 **READ** the newspaper article about twins and look at the photos. What do you think happens at a Twins Days Festival?

Notes from the Twins Days Festival

Jim Lodge, *The Sunset Times*

The opening day of the Twins Days Festival was an exciting one. Over 2000 sets of twins **arrived** for three full days of fun. Everyone **was looking** forward to all the scheduled events—picnics, talent shows, parades, and contests.

I found that there was a serious side to the festival, too. A lot of scientific research **was going on**. One afternoon, while I **was walking** around, I **stopped** by a research tent. Inside, technicians **were photographing** sets of twins, **collecting** their fingerprints, and **scanning** their irises.[1] They **were using** the latest face-recognition software to try to tell the twins apart. As one scientist explained, "Although identical twins may look the same to you and me, a digital imaging system can spot tiny differences in freckles,[2] skin pores,[3] or the curve of their eyebrows."

Some twins **were** a challenge for the researchers. For example, it **was** hard to tell Dave and Don Wolf apart because their beards **covered** half of their faces. I **looked** very carefully at the brothers, but I **didn't see** any difference at all. They **seemed** absolutely identical to me. But I **had** the very same reaction to almost every set of twins at the festival. It was like seeing double all the time!

[1] **iris:** round colored part of a person's eye
[2] **freckle:** a small light brown spot on someone's skin
[3] **pore:** a tiny hole in the skin

▼ A gathering of identical twins.

▲ Identical twins Dave and Don Wolf

2 CHECK. Answer the questions. Write complete sentences.

1. How many sets of twins were at the festival?

   Over 2000 sets of twins were at the festival.

2. What were some of the festival events?

3. Who was doing serious work at the festival?

4. Why were Dave and Don Wolf a challenge for the researchers?

3 DISCOVER. Complete the exercises to learn about the grammar in this lesson.

A Look at these sentences from the newspaper article in exercise **1**. Underline all of the verb forms.

1. One afternoon, while I <u>was walking</u> around, I <u>stopped</u> by a research tent.

2. Inside, technicians were photographing sets of twins, collecting their fingerprints, and scanning their irises.

3. I looked very carefully at the brothers, but I didn't see any difference at all.

B Work with a partner. Look at the sentences in exercise **A** and the verb forms you underlined. Then check (✓) the correct box for each statement below.

	Simple Past verb + -ed / didn't + base form	Past Progressive was/were (not) + verb + -ing
This verb form shows that an action or situation . . .		
1. continued for a period of time.	☐	☐
2. started and finished without interruption.	☐	☐
3. interrupted another action.	☐	☐

LEARN

1.5 Simple Past and Past Progressive Review

	Simple Past	Past Progressive
Affirmative Statements	Jim **left** the party at 8:00 last night. Jun and Kim **stayed** until 10:00.	Jim **was driving** home at 8:15. Jun and Kim **were talking** at 8:15.
Negative Statements	Javier **didn't go** to class yesterday. He **didn't feel** well.	Sue **wasn't taking** notes. We **weren't texting** during the class.
Yes/No Questions	**Did** Jan **read** the news this morning? **Did** you **eat** lunch yesterday?	**Was** Tim **reading** at age five? **Were** you **eating** lunch at 1:00?
Wh- Questions	**Where did** you **go** last night?	**What were** you **doing** at 8:00 last night?
Who or What as Subject	**Who went** to the movie after class?	**Who wasn't paying** attention in class?

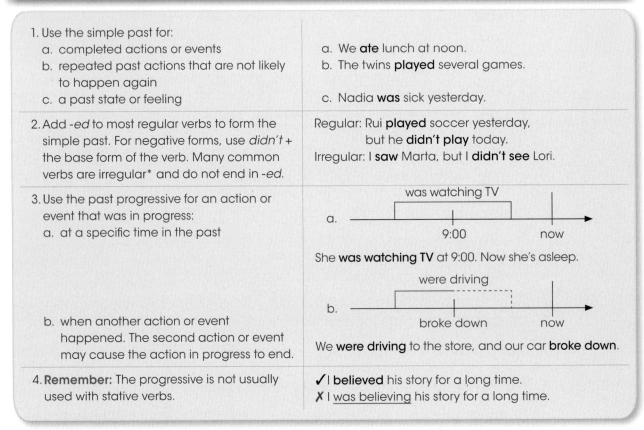

1. Use the simple past for:
   a. completed actions or events
   b. repeated past actions that are not likely to happen again
   c. a past state or feeling

   a. We **ate** lunch at noon.
   b. The twins **played** several games.
   c. Nadia **was** sick yesterday.

2. Add -*ed* to most regular verbs to form the simple past. For negative forms, use *didn't* + the base form of the verb. Many common verbs are irregular* and do not end in -*ed*.

   Regular: Rui **played** soccer yesterday, but he **didn't play** today.
   Irregular: I **saw** Marta, but I **didn't see** Lori.

3. Use the past progressive for an action or event that was in progress:
   a. at a specific time in the past

   She **was watching TV** at 9:00. Now she's asleep.

   b. when another action or event happened. The second action or event may cause the action in progress to end.

   We **were driving** to the store, and our car **broke down**.

4. **Remember:** The progressive is not usually used with stative verbs.

   ✓ I **believed** his story for a long time.
   ✗ I <u>was believing</u> his story for a long time.

* See pages **A1-A2** for a list of spelling rules for the -*ed* and -*ing* forms of verbs.
** See page **A3** for a list of irregular verb forms.

4 Complete the exercises.

A Complete the stories about twins. Use the simple past or the past progressive.

Story 1

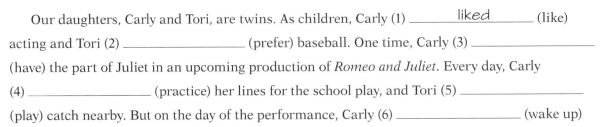

Our daughters, Carly and Tori, are twins. As children, Carly (1) ____liked____ (like) acting and Tori (2) _____ (prefer) baseball. One time, Carly (3) _____ (have) the part of Juliet in an upcoming production of *Romeo and Juliet*. Every day, Carly (4) _____ (practice) her lines for the school play, and Tori (5) _____ (play) catch nearby. But on the day of the performance, Carly (6) _____ (wake up)

sick. Luckily, Tori (7) _____ (know) all of Carly's lines. On the night of the play, Carly (8) _____ (stay) in bed at home, and Tori (9) _____ (perform) the part of Juliet instead of Carly. No one at school ever (10) _____ (find) out!

Story 2

My wife and I have twin daughters, and I'm a twin, too. As a child, I (11) _____ (not enjoy) sports like my twin, Ray, did. I (12) _____ (like) books. One summer day around noon, I (13) _____ (read) alone on the porch, and Ray (14) _____ (play) baseball in the yard with his friends. One of his friends (15) _____ (throw) the ball to him, but at that moment Ray (16) _____ (not look). So it (17) _____ (hit) him hard in the arm. Strangely, at the same time, I (18) _____ (feel) a sharp pain in my arm. It (19) _____ (be) a very unusual experience.

B Use the words and phrases to write simple past or past progressive questions about the stories in exercise **A**.

1. Why ____did Carly stay____ (Carly / stay) in bed on the night of the play?

2. Why _____ (Tori / perform) in the play?

3. Which twin _____ (read) alone on the porch?

4. What _____ (happen) to Ray?

5. Why _____ (Sam / feel) a pain in his arm?

6. Of the two stories, which one _____ (you / prefer)?

C **SPEAK.** Work with a partner. Take turns asking and answering the questions in exercise **B**.

A: *Why did Carly stay in bed on the night of the play?*   B: *Because she was sick.*

1.6   Past Time Clauses with *When* and *While*

Time Clause First
While Rob was eating lunch, the phone rang.

Time Clause	Main Clause

Time Clause Second
Dave was hiking when he hurt his foot.

Main Clause	Time Clause

1. Use a *when* or *while* clause + a main clause to show the relationship between two past actions or events. Use a comma after the time clause when it comes first in the sentence.	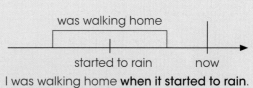 was walking home / started to rain / now I was walking home **when it started to rain.** **While I was walking home,** it started to rain.
2. Use *when* or *while* + the past progressive for an action or event that was in progress when another action happened. Use *when* + the simple past in the time clause to show an interrupted action.	**While the boy was running,** he dropped his book. **When the boy was running,** he dropped his book. ✓ The boy was running **when he dropped his book.** ✗ The boy was running <u>while</u> he dropped his book.

1.6 Past Time Clauses with *When* and *While* (cont.)

3. To show that one action or event happened before another, use a *when* time clause for the action that happened first. Use the simple past in both clauses.	**When** the phone **rang,** Lili **answered** it. First Event Second Event
4. To show that two actions were in progress at the same time in the past, use *while* in the time clause. Use the past progressive in both clauses.	 was studying were watching now **While** Li **was studying,** we **were watching** TV.

5 Circle the correct words to complete the tourist's notes about an elephant family.

We (1) **saw** / were seeing a family of elephants when we (2) **drove / were driving** down a road in Tanzania. We stopped to watch them. Some of the elephants (3) **drank / were drinking** water while others were eating grass. (4) **When / While** I raised my hand to say "hello," one of the elephants (5) **lifted / was lifting** its trunk as though to greet me. It made me laugh.

A little later, one big female elephant (6) **lead / was leading** her family across the river (7) **when / while** one of her babies slipped. It was OK, of course. Later, while another young elephant (8) **played / was playing** near us, it (9) **fell / was falling** in the water and (10) **got / was getting** us very wet. We (11) **decided / were deciding** to head back to the camp (12) **when / while** it started to rain. We were already wet enough!

▼ An elephant herd at a river bank in Sri Lanka

PRACTICE

6 WRITE & SPEAK.

A Work with a partner. Look at the time line and discuss the events
in Julio's family history.

Julio's Grandparents				Julio's Father, Jiro			Julio's Parents, Jiro & Susan	
saved money	emigrated to Peru	met & married	Jiro born	turned six	worked, went to high school	met Susan	got married in college	had Julio after college

Japan	Sugar Plantation in Peru	Lima, Peru

B Read each pair of sentences. Then combine the sentences into one sentence with a past
time clause. Use the simple past and the past progressive. Add a comma when necessary.
For some sentences, more than one answer may be possible.

1. Julio's grandparents lived in Japan. They didn't know each other.

    When _Julio's grandparents were living in Japan, they didn't know each other_ .

2. They saved enough money. They each emigrated to Peru.

    They each emigrated to Peru when _they saved enough money_ .

3. Julio's grandparents worked on a sugar plantation in Peru. They met.

    _____ when _____ .

4. Julio's father, Jiro, was born. They lived on the sugar plantation.

    _____ while _____ .

5. Jiro turned six. His family moved to Lima so he could go to school.

    When _____ .

6. Jiro worked in the family store. He went to high school.

    _____ while _____ .

7. Jiro saw Susan at school. He introduced himself.

    When _____ .

8. Jiro and Susan attended college in Lima. They got married.

    When _____ .

C In your notebook, write five questions about the information in exercise **B**. Use the simple past
and the past progressive with time clauses.

When Julio's grandparents were living in Japan, did they know each other?

D Work with a partner. Ask and answer your questions from exercise **C** on page 23.

A: *When Julio's grandparents were living in Japan, did they know each other?*

B: *No, they didn't. They met in Peru.*

7 LISTEN.

CD1-07

A Read the phrases about Bella's family history. Then listen to her talk about a secret in her family. Who does each phrase relate to? Check (✓) the correct box(es).

Story of Bella's Family Secret	Bella	Bella's Mother	Maria	Marina
1. found a copy of the family tree	✓	☐	☐	☐
2. told Bella about the secret	☐	☐	☐	☐
3. wanted to go to America	☐	☐	☐	☐
4. looked alike	☐	☐	☐	☐
5. did not move to America	☐	☐	☐	☐
6. was Bella's grandmother	☐	☐	☐	☐

CD1-07

B Work with a partner. Write the missing words to complete the story about Bella's family secret. Then listen again and check your answers.

One day, I (1) ___was cleaning___ out a desk drawer (2) _____when_____ I found a copy of my family tree. While I (3) _____ at it, my mother (4) _____ into the room. (5) _____ she saw it, she (6) _____ quiet. That's when she (7) _____ me the family secret.

It turns out that Grandma's name wasn't really (8) _____. Her real name was (9) _____. Many years ago back in Russia, my grandmother's sister planned to marry an American (10) _____ she turned 20. But while she (11) _____ to go to America, she started to cry. She (12) _____ to go anymore, but her sister, Marina, (13) _____. The two sisters (14) _____ alike, so when Maria's passport and boat ticket (15) _____, Marina took them and (16) _____ all the way from Russia to America.

(17) _____ my mother was growing up, no one, not even my grandfather,

(18) _____ the secret. Of course, they (19) _____ shocked when

they (20) _____ out. I certainly (21) _____!

8 EDIT.

A Read the phone conversation between Erica and her mother. Find and correct seven more errors with the simple past and the past progressive.

Erica: Hello?

Mother: Hello, Erica? Were you asleep? ~~Was I waking~~ *Did I wake* you up?

Erica: Yeah. I slept. I didn't sleep well last night, so I decided to take a nap.

Mother: Oh, I'm sorry. I just was wanting to say hello.

Erica: Well, I had the strangest dream when the phone rang. I talked to Aunt Jelena. We were sitting in her living room. While we were talking, a bear suddenly was appearing. It was terrifying! When the bear came toward us, we were running outside. That's when I heard the phone.

Mother: That sounds like a scary dream!

Erica: It was. It was a very strange dream. I'm glad I was waking up.

B Complete the chart with information about Erica's dream in exercise **A**.

Erica's Dream	Notes
1. Where was Erica in her dream?	In Aunt Jelena's living room.
2. What was she doing?	
3. What happened?	
4. What did they do when the bear came toward them?	
5. How did she feel when she woke up?	

9 APPLY.

A In your notebook, make a chart like the one in exercise **8B**. Write 5–6 questions for a partner about a strange dream or experience. Then ask your partner your questions. Write his or her answers in the chart.

A: *Where were you?*   B: *I was on a boat in the Mediterranean.*

A: *What were you doing?*   B: *I was on vacation with friends. We were taking pictures.*

B Write a paragraph about your partner's dream.

My partner had a dream about a vacation. She went away with two friends from college. They were celebrating their graduation. In her dream, they were taking pictures . . .

Charts
1.1–1.7

1 Complete the paragraphs with the correct forms of the words in parentheses. Use the simple present, present progressive, simple past, or past progressive. Add *not* where necessary.

I'm an only child. (1) I ___*don't have*___ (have) any brothers or sisters. A lot of people (2) _____ (feel) sorry for me when I tell them that, but I (3) _____ (know) why. They (4) _____ (believe) certain things to be true about all only children, but they're wrong. For example, many people (5) _____ (think) that all only children are lonely, but I (6) _____ (be) lonely as a child. I (7) _____ (go) to my friends' houses and (8) _____ (play) with the kids in my apartment building. Also, not all only children are spoiled. While I (9) _____ (grow up), my parents (10) _____ (give) me a lot of love and attention, but I (11) _____ (get) everything I asked for.

It's really not bad to grow up without siblings. Nowadays, more and more couples (12) _____ (decide) to have only one child. One reason is that it (13) _____ (cost) a lot of money to raise children. Also, many couples (14) _____ (wait) until their thirties to start a family. My husband and I (15) _____ (have) only one child, and we (16) _____ (plan) to have more. One child is just fine.

Charts
1.1, 1.2,
1.3, 1.5,
1.6

2 **EDIT.** Read the e-mail from Max's father to Anna, a family member. Find and correct eight more errors with present and past (simple and progressive) verb forms.

Hi Anna,

          are things going

How ~~do things go~~? Everything is great with Emily, Max, and me. Max grows day by day. He's four months old now. He is getting big! Emily is working part time now. She was going back to work last month, so she's always really tired. It's too bad babies aren't sleeping through the night. Max wakes up two or three times a night. I'm lucky. I'm never waking up. Emily does.

    I need my sleep. I'm working long hours these days. On top of that, my boss is always complaining about something. The other day, at 6:00 p.m., while I walked out the door to go home, he said, "Do you leave already?" These comments upset me, so now I think about changing jobs. Anyway, enough about me. What do you do nowadays? Write soon!

Love,
Carlos

3 LISTEN.

A Read the sentences about sibling relationships. Then listen to the interview and circle **T** for *true* or **F** for *false*.

1. Gender doesn't play a role in sibling differences.   **T**   **F**

2. Family relationships are different all over the world.   **T**   **F**

3. Parents often say that their children don't fight.   **T**   **F**

4. Children in the research study didn't fight very often.   **T**   **F**

5. When children are fighting about a toy, they are really fighting about something that is more important to them.   **T**   **F**

B Listen again and circle the word or phrase you hear in the interview.

1. Sometimes we **love / loved** them to death; other times we **don't / didn't**.

2. Our siblings **know / knew** us differently from the way our adult friends

   know / knew us because our siblings **know / knew** us when we were children.

3. The relationship **is / was** constantly changing.

4. **I'm not talking / I don't talk** about sibling relationships all over the world.

5. And my brother is ten years older than I am, so we **don't fight / didn't fight**.

6. . . . but in fact, the research studies **show / showed** that children between the ages of three

   and seven **fight / fought** about 3.5 times per hour.

4 SPEAK & WRITE.

A Work in a group of three or four students. Ask and answer questions using the phrases in the box. When a student in your group answers *yes* to one of the questions, get more details by asking follow-up questions.

comes from a large family	has a set of twins in the family
is an only child	enjoyed swimming as a child
is the youngest	played a sport while he/she was growing up
resembles a family member	won a competition while he/she was growing up

A: *Do you come from a large family?*

B: *Yes, I have a lot of relatives.*

A: *Oh really? Where do they live?*

B Write four or five sentences about your classmates based on your conversations from exercise **A**. Share your information with the class.

Andrea comes from a very large family. She has more than 20 cousins.

Misha won a pie-eating contest when he was 14 years old.

Connect the Grammar to Writing

1 READ & NOTICE THE GRAMMAR.

A Why do many adult children in their 20s and 30s live with their parents? Tell a partner your ideas. Then read the text.

Moving Back Home

The number of children who return home in adulthood to live with their parents is increasing. In the past, grown children left home as soon as they could afford it. For example, my father left his parents' house when he went to college. Then, he got a job and his own apartment. He never returned.

Today life is different. Many young adults cannot find jobs, so they return home. Plus, they want to save money. My sister and her husband, for example, are living at our parents' house to save money for a house.

This new trend is affecting both the parents and their children. Sometimes their children get too comfortable and think that their parents can support them forever. Often parents face economic challenges because of this and have to postpone retirement. It seems that young adults these days are taking longer to grow up.

GRAMMAR FOCUS

In this text, the writer uses simple and progressive verb forms in the following ways.

Present progressive	• to tell about current trends in society (*The number of children . . .* ***is increasing***.)
	• to tell about temporary situations (*My sister and her husband . . .* ***are living*** *. . .*)
Simple present	• to give facts (*. . . , so they* ***return*** *home.*)
	• with stative verbs (*It* ***seems*** *. . .*)
Simple past	• to give examples from the past (*Then, he* ***got*** *a job . . .*)

B Read the text in exercise **A** again. Find one more example of each verb form and identify its use. Complete the chart. Then work with a partner and compare your answers.

Verb Form	Example	Use
Present progressive		
Simple present		
Simple past		

C Complete the chart with information from the text in exercise **A**. Discuss your answers with a partner.

Short Essay Question	Why do many children in their 20s and 30s still live with their parents?
In the Past	
Today	
Final Thoughts	

2 BEFORE YOU WRITE.

A Work with a partner. Brainstorm more ways families are changing in the United States (or in your culture). Use exercise **10A** on page 10 for ideas. Write at least five questions that ask about these changes.

Why are people getting married at an older age?

B Choose one of your questions from exercise **A** to respond to. Make a chart like the one in exercise **1C** and write your question in the top row. Add notes to help you organize your ideas for your response.

3 WRITE a response to your question from exercise 2B. Write three paragraphs. Use your notes from exercise 1C and the text in exercise 1A to help you.

> **WRITING FOCUS**   Using *For Example* to Give Supporting Ideas
>
> Notice *for example* in the text in exercise **1A**.
>
> When *for example* starts a sentence, use a comma after it.
> > **For example,** *my father left his parents' house . . .*
>
> When *for example* is in the middle of a sentence, use a comma before and after it.
> > *My sister and her husband,* **for example,** *are living at our parents' house.*

4 SELF ASSESS. Read your response. Underline the verb forms in your response. Then use the checklist to assess your work.

- [ ] I used the simple present and simple past correctly. [1.1, 1.4]
- [ ] I used the present progressive and past progressive correctly. [1.1, 1.2, 1.4]
- [ ] I used the simple present with stative verbs. [1.3]
- [ ] I used commas correctly when using *for example*. [WRITING FOCUS]

Present and Past: Perfect and Perfect Progressive

◀ Climbers BASE jump from Half Dome at Yosemite National Park, California.

EXPLORE

1 READ the book review of *Polar Obsession*. What is Paul Nicklen's passion?

Paul Nicklen's *Polar Obsession*

For most people, the Arctic and Antarctica are strange places that we know very little about. Paul Nicklen's collection of photographs and stories, *Polar Obsession*, offers an excellent introduction.

Nicklen grew up on an island in Northern Canada, where he learned all about the outdoors from his Inuit[1] neighbors. Ever since that time, he **has loved** animals, cold weather, and adventure.

As a photojournalist, Nicklen **has spent** a lot of time in icy polar waters. He **has followed** sea lions, **dived** with whales, and **studied** polar bears. One of the most exciting parts of the book covers Nicklen's unforgettable encounter with a leopard seal in Antarctica.

As the photographs clearly show, leopard seals are very large—up to 12 feet (4 meters) long and weighing over 1000 pounds (450 kilograms). They have huge, sharp teeth, and they move quickly through the water searching for food such as fish and penguins.

Leopard seals can be dangerous, but this didn't stop Nicklen from trying to photograph one. When a huge seal approached his boat, Nicklen got into the water. He was shaking with fear, but much to his surprise the seal treated him gently. She even tried to feed him! The seal brought him penguins to eat, and he photographed her. Nicklen says it was the most incredible experience that he **has** ever **had** as a photographer.

In *Polar Obsession*, Nicklen shows us the beauty of the polar world and his passion for it. He also helps us to understand the importance of protecting it.

[1] **Inuit:** indigenous people living in Arctic regions of Alaska, Canada, and Greenland

▲ Paul Nicklen meets a leopard seal.

The leopard seal shows its sharp teeth.

2 CHECK. Write the letter of the phrase that completes each sentence.

1. Nicklen's neighbors taught him all about ___d___ .
2. Nicklen has spent a lot of time working in _____ .
3. Nicklen's most incredible experience was with _____ .
4. He was frightened because _____ .
5. The leopard seal offered Nicklen _____ .

a. leopard seals can be dangerous
b. a leopard seal
c. its food
~~d.~~ the outdoors
e. icy polar waters

3 DISCOVER. Complete the exercises to learn about the grammar in this lesson.

A Find these sentences in the book review from exercise **1**. Write the missing words.

1. Nicklen ___grew up___ on an island in Northern Canada, where he ___learned___ all about the outdoors from his Inuit neighbors.

2. Ever since that time, he _____ animals, cold weather, and adventure.

3. As a photojournalist, Nicklen _____ a lot of time in icy polar waters.

4. He _____ sea lions, _____ with whales, and _____ polar bears.

5. When a huge seal _____ his boat, Nicklen _____ into the water.

B Look at the sentences in exercise **A**. Write the number of each sentence next to the phrase that best describes the time of the event.

1. Completed at a known time in the past: ___1___ , _____

2. Completed at an unknown time in the past: _____ , _____

3. Started in the past and continues to the present: _____

LEARN

2.1 Present Perfect

Statements	
	Subject + *Have/Has (Not)* + Past Participle
Affirmative	I **have visited** many countries.
Negative	Tom **hasn't seen** the photos of my trip.

Questions		Answers
	(Wh-) + *Have/Has* + Subject + Past Participle	
Yes/No	**Have** you **visited** the Arctic? **Has** Paul **taken** many photos?	No, I **haven't**. Yes, he **has**.
Wh-	**What have** you **heard?** **Who has** he **met?**	Nothing. Why? An explorer.

	Who/What + *Has* + Past Participle	
Who or *What* as Subject	**Who has completed** the assignment? **What has happened?**	Only one student **(has)**. Nothing, yet.

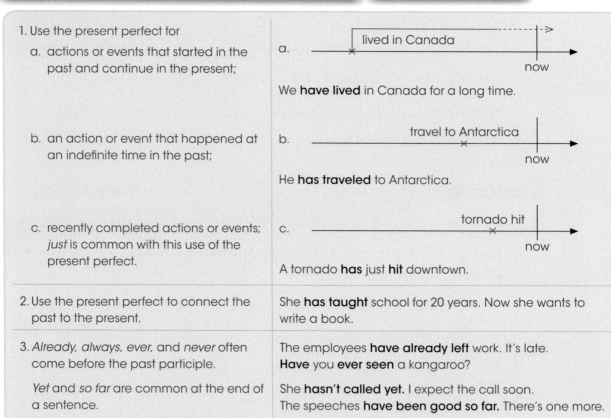

1. Use the present perfect for

   a. actions or events that started in the past and continue in the present;

   a. lived in Canada — now

   We **have lived** in Canada for a long time.

   b. an action or event that happened at an indefinite time in the past;

   b. travel to Antarctica — now

   He **has traveled** to Antarctica.

   c. recently completed actions or events; *just* is common with this use of the present perfect.

   c. tornado hit — now

   A tornado **has** just **hit** downtown.

2. Use the present perfect to connect the past to the present.

   She **has taught** school for 20 years. Now she wants to write a book.

3. *Already, always, ever,* and *never* often come before the past participle.

   The employees **have already left** work. It's late.
   Have you **ever seen** a kangaroo?

   Yet and *so far* are common at the end of a sentence.

   She **hasn't called yet.** I expect the call soon.
   The speeches **have been good so far.** There's one more.

4 Complete the conversations with the words in parentheses. Use the present perfect.

Conversation 1

Bev: How is your class going?

Ken: Great. (1) _____I've learned_____ (I / learn) a lot about the Arctic and polar explorers.

Bev: That sounds interesting. (2) _____ (you / see) that book by Paul Nicklen?

Ken: No, (3) _____. Who is he? (4) _____ (I / never / hear) of him.

Bev: He's a photographer. (5) _____ (he / live) and (6) _____ (work) in polar climates for many years. (7) _____ (he / take) amazing photos of all kinds of animals.

> **REAL ENGLISH**
>
> Do not repeat *have/has* between present perfect verbs connected by *and*.
>
> He **has followed** sea lions and **studied** polar bears.

Conversation 2

Lee: (8) _____ (Mr. Chin / just / cancel) today's class.

Jen: Really? (9) _____ (he / reschedule) it yet?

Lee: No, not yet. But I heard the class might be on Saturday.

Jen: Is that possible? (10) _____ (you / ever / have) a class on a Saturday?

5 **ANALYZE THE GRAMMAR.** Work with a partner. Look at each answer you wrote in exercise **4**. Then write the number of each answer next to the correct description below. Refer to chart 2.1.

1. Started in the past and continues to the present: _____, _____

2. Happened at an indefinite time in the past: __1__, _____, _____, _____, _____, _____

3. Happened recently: _____, _____

2.2 Present Perfect with *For* and *Since*

Use *for* or *since* with actions or events that started in the past and continue to the present.	graduated | worked at store - - - -> May now/December
a. Use *for* + an amount of time (number of days, months, . . .).	a. Jo has worked at this store **for six months**.
b. Use *since* + a specific past time (exact date, time, month, . . .).	b. He hasn't been a student **since May**.
c. Use a past time clause with *since*.	c. I've known him **since he graduated**.

6 Complete the sentences. Use the present perfect form of the verb in parentheses. Then write *since* or *for*.

1. People in many countries enjoy ice swimming. It became popular several decades ago.

   People ___have enjoyed___ (enjoy) ice swimming ___for___ several decades.

2. The first Canadian Polar Bear Swim was in 1920. It is still an annual event.

   The Canadian Polar Bear Swim _____ (be) an annual event
   _____ 1920.

3. Our town had its first New Year's Day swim in 2010. Our town still has this swim.

   Our town _____ (have) a New Year's Day swim _____ many years.

4. I wanted to swim with the Polar Bears when I was 13. I'm 23 and I still want to do it.

   I _____ (want) to swim with the Polar Bears _____ ten years.

5. The only sport my brother does is winter swimming. He _____ (not play)
   any other sport _____ he was a teenager.

6. My father doesn't participate anymore. His last winter swim was four years ago.

   My father _____ (not participate) _____ four years.

7. My cousin always jumps into the water first. He did this last year and the year before.

   My cousin _____ (always / jump) into the water first
   _____ he joined the Polar Bears.

8. We all love winter swimming. We loved our first experience, and we still love it.

   We _____ (love) winter swimming _____ we first tried it.

2.3 Present Perfect and Simple Past

1. The present perfect is used for
  a. actions or events that started in the past and continue to the present;
  b. completed actions or events with a connection to the present.
	a. Mary is our math teacher. She **has taught** here for five years.
	b. The children **have read** the rules. They're ready to play the game now.

2. The simple past is used for completed actions or events.	She **taught math** ten years ago. Now she works in finance.
3. With the present perfect, the exact time of the action or event is not given. With the simple past, the exact time of the past action or event is given or understood.	✓ They **have gone** to Morocco. ✗ They have gone to Morocco <u>last month</u>. ✓ They **went** to Morocco **last month**. ✓ **Did** you **sleep** well?
4. Use the present perfect with a time period that has not ended yet. Use the simple past with a completed past time period.	**I've called** her twice **this morning**. (It's still morning. I may call her again.) I **called** her twice **yesterday**.

7 Circle the correct form of the verb to complete each sentence.

1. a. She **has dreamed / dreamed** about going to the North Pole since she was young.

   b. She **has dreamed / dreamed** about going to the North Pole last night.

2. a. I **have never photographed / never photographed** animals in the wild before.

   b. We **have not photographed / didn't photograph** animals when we were in Alaska.

3. a. Last year, my grandfather **has gone / went** to Iceland on business twice.

   b. My grandfather **has gone / went** to Iceland on business twice since 2005.

4. a. They **haven't seen / didn't see** any bears on their trip so far.

   b. They **haven't seen / didn't see** any bears on their trip last month.

PRACTICE

8 **PRONUNCIATION.** Read the chart and listen to the examples. Then complete the exercises.

CD1-10

PRONUNCIATION	Reduced *Have* and *Has* in the Present Perfect

Have and *has* are often contracted or reduced in the present perfect. Repeat these examples.

Examples:

Full Pronunciation	**Reduced Pronunciation**
Lisa has just arrived.	*Lisəz just arrived.*
Most people have already left.	*Most peopləv already left.*
Who has she talked to?	*Whoz she talked to?*
What have you done?	*Whatəv you done?*

CD1-11

A Listen to the sentences. Which form of *have/has* do you hear, the full form or the reduced form? Check (✓) the correct box.

	Full	**Reduced**
1. Lee has always loved animals.	☐	✓
2. Our neighbors have adopted many animals over the years.	☐	☐
3. Who has taken care of an animal before?	☐	☐
4. We have faced many challenges with our cats.	☐	☐
5. Kara has taken her dog to the park every day for years.	☐	☐
6. Tyrone has volunteered at the animal shelter since 2012.	☐	☐
7. Our landlords have made a rule about owning pets.	☐	☐
8. What have you learned from working with animals?	☐	☐

CD1-11

B Work with a partner. Compare your answers from exercise **A**. Then listen again and check your answers.

▲ Eye of a green tree python snake, common to Australia

9 Complete the exercises.

A Complete the interview with the words in parentheses. Use the present perfect or simple past.

Sara: How long (1) _____ have you been _____ (you / be) a snake catcher, Tim?

Tim: (2) _____ (I / have) this job for over ten years.

Sara: When (3) _____ (you / become) interested in snakes?

Tim: When (4) _____ (I / be) a kid, and
(5) _____ (snakes / fascinate) me ever
since then. When (6) _____ (I / be) in middle school,
(7) _____ (I / not read) much about any other subject. During
my high school years, (8) _____ (I / often / volunteer)
at the local zoo, and then in college (9) _____ (I / major) in
herpetology—the study of reptiles.

Sara: And after college (10) _____ (you / spend) a few years in
Thailand. Isn't that right?

Tim: Yes, I was working with Thai snake experts. (11) _____
(I / really enjoy) my time with them.

Sara: (12) _____ (you / ever / experience) any
life-threatening situations since you started working with snakes?

Tim: (13) _____ (I / work) with many poisonous snakes over the
years, but (14) _____ (only one / bite) me. That was scary!
Since that time, (15) _____ (I / pay more attention)
to the snakes' behavior.

Sara: Why do you love your job?

Tim: (16) Because _____ (I / be) able to live my childhood dream.

B Listen and check your answers. Then practice the conversation with a partner. Notice your pronunciation.

10 **EDIT.** Read the e-mail. Find and correct eight more errors with the present perfect and simple past.

Dear Ms. Ramos,

I am writing to apply for the position of staff photographer that I ~~have seen~~ ᴠsaw on your website. I believe that my experience has prepared me well for this job.

Photography is my passion. I loved photography ever since I was a child. That is when I have gotten my first camera. The thrill of taking pictures never gone away, but my interests have changed over the years. While I was growing up, I liked to photograph people; however, as an adult, I have took more pictures of nature than people.

I lived in Hawaii since 2013, and I have traveled all over the islands to photograph rare birds and plants. I've learned a lot, and my technique has improved in the last few years. My photos has never appeared in a magazine or book, but several have been on display at a local gallery since several months. I would be happy to share my portfolio on request.

I have heared a lot about your magazine, and it would be a pleasure to work for you. I look forward to talking to you about this opportunity.

Sincerely,

Katy Mills

11 WRITE & SPEAK.

A Use the words to write questions. Use the present perfect or simple past.

1. what activities / you / always / love / to do

   What activities have you always loved to do?

2. what activities / you / enjoy / when you were younger

   _____

3. you / visit / any interesting places / when you were a child

   _____

4. you / visit any interesting places / recently

   _____

5. what dreams for the future / you / have / as a child

   _____

6. what / goals / you / achieved / in the last few years

   _____

B Work with a partner. Ask and answer the questions in exercise **A**.

   A: *What activities have you always loved to do?*

   B: *I've always loved listening to music.*

12 APPLY.

A What is your passion? What kind of job would allow you to follow your passion? Imagine that you are applying for your ideal job. Write an e-mail and apply for that job. Use ideas from the e-mail in exercise **10** on page 39 to help you. Use the simple past and present perfect.

B Read a partner's e-mail. Ask and answer questions about each other's passion.

   A: *So, you've been playing the flute ever since you were a child. I didn't know that.*

   B: *Yeah. I've always loved it.*

   A: *Have you always wanted to play in an orchestra?*

   B: *No. At first, I wanted to be a music teacher.*

EXPLORE

CD1-13

1 READ the magazine article about Helen Thayer. What advice does she have for other people?

Helen Thayer: A Lifelong Adventurer

Helen Thayer **has** never **let** age stop her. She and her husband, Bill, fulfilled a lifelong dream for their 40th wedding anniversary. They walked 1600 miles (2575 kilometers) in intense heat across the Gobi Desert. There they met Mongolian nomads[1] and learned about their culture. To celebrate 50 years of marriage, the Thayers walked almost 900 miles (1448 kilometers) across the Sahara Desert to study the customs of the people who live there. Now in her seventies, Thayer keeps on planning trips for the future.

Thayer, born in New Zealand, **has been exploring** the outdoors for most of her life. Since childhood, she **has traveled** widely in harsh climates and across rough lands. She **has walked** to the North Pole with her dog as her only companion. She **has** also **kayaked** 2200 miles (3541 kilometers) down the Amazon, and **done** several mountain climbs. These trips **haven't been** easy, but they**'ve been** very satisfying.

In recent years, Thayer **has been talking** to groups around the world. She **has continued** to travel and bring back stories to share with both children and adults. Thayer hopes to inspire[2] people to follow their passions and fulfill their dreams.[3] What is her advice? Set goals, plan for success, and never give up.

[1] **nomads:** people who move from place to place instead of living in one place

[2] **inspire:** to make someone want to do something

[3] **fulfill one's dream:** to manage to do what you hoped you would do

▶ The Gobi Desert covers parts of Mongolia and China

2 CHECK. Read the statements. Circle **T** for *true* or **F** for *false*.

1. Helen Thayer and her husband drove across two deserts.   T   F

2. As a child, Thayer liked the outdoors.   T   F

3. The trips have been in one part of the world.   T   F

4. Thayer has traveled down the Amazon River.   T   F

5. Thayer has stopped traveling in recent years.   T   F

3 DISCOVER. Complete the exercises to learn about the grammar in this lesson.

A Read the sentences from the article in exercise **1**. Notice the words in **bold**. Is the action completed or possibly still in progress? Choose the correct answer.

1. Thayer, born in New Zealand, **has been exploring** the outdoors for most of her life.

   a. completed   (b.) possibly still in progress

2. She **has walked** to the North Pole with her dog as her only companion.

   a. completed   b. possibly still in progress

3. She **has** also **kayaked** 2200 miles down the Amazon . . .

   a. completed   b. possibly still in progress

4. In recent years, Thayer **has been talking** to groups around the world.

   a. completed   b. possibly still in progress

B Work with a partner. Compare your answers from exercise **A**. What do you notice about the verb forms used for actions that are possibly still in progress? Discuss your ideas with your partner.

The Red Cliffs, Gobi Desert, Mongolia

LEARN

2.4 Present Perfect Progressive

Statements	
	Subject + *Have/Has (Not)* + *Been* + Verb + *-ing*
Affirmative	I **have been waiting** for my friend for an hour.
Negative	Tom **hasn't been sleeping** enough this term.

Questions		Answers	
	(Wh-) + *Have/Has* + Subject + *Been* + Verb + *-ing*		
Yes/No	**Have** you **been working** for a long time?	Yes, I **have.** / No, I **haven't.**	
Wh-	What **has** Raul **been reading** lately?	A lot of short stories.	

	Who/What + *Has* + *Been* + Verb + *-ing*		
Who or *What* as Subject	**Who has been managing** the lab?	Luz and Jun **have.**	

1. Use the present perfect progressive for ongoing actions that started in the past and continue in the present.

I've been working

now

I've been working on my research paper.

2. The present perfect progressive is often used
   a. with *for* or *since*
   b. without *for* or *since* to emphasize that the action happened recently or is temporary
   c. for repeated actions that started in the past and continue in the present

   a. They **have been studying** Spanish for years.
   b. The chef**'s been working** hard. It's the busy season.
   c. I**'ve been texting** Jose all day. He hasn't replied to any of my messages.

3. **Remember:** The progressive is not usually used with stative verbs.

   ✓ She **has known** him since college.
   ✗ She <u>has been knowing</u> him since college.

---

4 Complete the conversations with the words in parentheses. Use the present perfect progressive.

Sasha: How long (1) ___have you been going___ (you / go) on long-distance hikes?

Gina: Since I was in college. And I'm now in my sixties.

(2) _____ (my husband / hike) since he was a child.

Sasha: (3) _____ (it / get) easier or more difficult for you to hike long distances these days?

Gina: Well, I'd say that lately (4) _____ (we / work) harder to keep up with the younger people on the hikes, but I don't think

(5) _____ (we / cause) any problems or delays!

Jack: (6) _____ (you / enjoy) yourselves on the trip so far?

Katya: Oh, yes. (7) _____ (we / have) a wonderful time.

Jack: So what (8) _____ (you / do) during your stay

here in town?

Katya: Well, (9) _____ (we / visit) museums and

(10)_____ (take) tours of the major sights.

2.5 Present Perfect Progressive and Present Perfect

1. The present perfect is used for completed actions.	I've read the chapter. I'm ready to discuss it. Jill has made five phone calls.
The present perfect progressive is used for continuous actions that are not complete.	I've been reading the chapter. I'm almost finished. Jill has been making phone calls for two hours.
2. The present perfect and present perfect progressive have similar meanings with some verbs that express routines, such as *live, work,* and *teach*.	Tony has lived in New York for ten years. He has been living in New York for ten years.
3. The present perfect is often used to express the idea of *how many* or *how much*.	How many cookies has he eaten? He has eaten five cookies.
The present perfect progressive is often used to express the idea of *how long*.	How long have you been playing the piano? We have been playing for a long time.
4. **Remember:** The progressive is not usually used with stative verbs.	✓ I have loved that movie since I was a child. ✗ I have been loving that movie since I was a child.

5 Read the sentences. Circle **Y** for *yes* or **N** for *no* to answer the questions.

1. a. Tony has set high goals for himself.   Is he still setting goals?   **Y**   **(N)**

   b. Nick has been setting high goals for himself.   Is he still setting goals?   **Y**   **N**

2. a. We've been counting votes for hours.   Are they counting now?   **Y**   **N**

   b. We've counted the votes.   Are they counting now?   **Y**   **N**

3. a. Dana has lost 35 pounds.   Is she still losing the 35 pounds?   **Y**   **N**

   b. Dana has been losing weight.   Is she still losing weight?   **Y**   **N**

4. a. I've been working in a store this summer.   Is he still working?   **Y**   **N**

   b. I've worked in the store for 25 years.   Is he still working?   **Y**   **N**

6 Complete the exercises.

A Circle the best answer to complete each question.

1. How long have you **taken /** **been taking** classes at this school?

2. How many friends have you **made / been making** since you started studying here?

3. How many cups of coffee have you **bought / been buying** this week?

4. How long have you **owned / been owning** a cell phone?

5. What gifts have you **gotten / been getting** in the last year?

6. How many times have you **eaten / been eating** out this month?

7. How much homework have you already **done / been doing** this week?

8. What TV programs have you **watched / been watching** this week?

B SPEAK. Work with a partner. Ask and answer the questions from exercise **A**.

A: How long have you been taking classes at this school?

B: For two months.

PRACTICE

7 Complete the conversations with the words in parentheses. Use the present perfect or present perfect progressive. In some sentences both forms are possible.

1. A: Have you finished _____ (you / finish) your assignment?

   B: Yeah, and now I'm going to get something to eat.

2. A: _____ (you / find) your keys?

   B: No, I'm not sure where they are.

3. A: Is this your phone?

   B: Yeah, thanks. _____ (I / look for) it everywhere.

4. A: You look exhausted.

   B: I am. _____ (I / work) for hours.

5. A: Are you crying?

   B: No, _____ (I / chop) onions.

6. A: _____ (you / hear) the news?

   B: No, what happened?

7. A: How long _____ (Pat / study) Chinese?

   B: _____ (he / take) classes for about a year now,

   and _____ (he / learn) a lot.

8. A: _____ (Julio / take) his final exam?

   B: Not yet, but _____ (he / study) all week.

8 LISTEN, WRITE & SPEAK. Look at the photo and read the caption. What is chef Barton Seaver's passion?

CD1-14

A Read the sentences about Barton Seaver. Then listen to the interview with him. Circle **T** for *true* and **F** for *false*.

1. Barton Seaver hasn't been eating seafood for very long.　　**T**　　**F**

2. His family and childhood have influenced his career choices.　　**T**　　**F**

3. Seaver hasn't been focusing on his seafood restaurants recently.　　**T**　　**F**

4. Seaver has developed a list of popular fish to eat.　　**T**　　**F**

5. In his opinion, people have been eating too many vegetables.　　**T**　　**F**

6. Seaver hasn't written about oceans or seafood for a long time.　　**T**　　**F**

▲ Barton Seaver, chef and advocate for the oceans, believes that the choices we make directly affect the ocean and all the life it supports.

B Look at the false sentences from exercise **A**. Write a true sentence for each.

1. Barton Seaver has eaten seafood since he was a child.

2. _____

3. _____

4. _____

5. _____

6. _____

CD1-14

C Work in a group. Discuss the questions. Listen again if necessary.

1. Why did Barton Seaver create a list of substitute fish for people to eat?

2. What do you think he has been talking about in his lectures?

3. What is an aspect of eating/food production that you have heard about or feel is important?

9 Complete the exercises.

A Look at the checklist. Hank and Jake must complete these tasks by the end of next week to graduate from cooking school. Who is closer to graduating, Hank or Jake?

Tasks	Hank	Jake
1. Plan a daily menu	✓	✓
2. Take an online course on food science	✓	
3. Write a paper on food safety	✓	
4. Plan a food budget for one week	✓	✓
5. Serve a four-course holiday meal		

B Complete the paragraph with the words in parentheses. Use the present perfect or present perfect progressive. Add *not* where necessary.

(1) <u>Both Hank and Jake have planned</u> (plan) a daily menu.
(2) _____ (complete) the online food science course yet because he was sick for two weeks. The professor is letting him make up the final exam next week. (3) _____ (already / take) the course, so (4) _____ (help) Jake study for the exam.
(5) _____ (already / turn in) his food safety paper. (6) _____ (work) hard on his food safety paper, but (7) _____ (finish) it yet. (8) _____ (plan) the food budget and the menu for the holiday meal together for a few weeks.
(9) _____ (serve) the holiday meal yet, but they plan to serve it next Thursday. Both hope to graduate in December.

10 APPLY.

A Write a paragraph about a short or long-term goal you have for the future, such as passing a test or graduating from college. Write at least three things you have or have not done or been doing to achieve your goal.

> My goal is to get an A in my history class. I've been doing my homework every night and participating a lot in class. I've finished all my assignments on time. I haven't started my research paper yet, but I've been thinking about different topics.

B Share your goals with a group. Ask your classmates follow-up questions.

A: *Have you gotten As on your tests?*

B: *I've gotten one A and one B, but it was 89 percent, so that's a pretty high B.*

EXPLORE

CD1-15

1 **READ** the article about Alex Honnold. What big risk did he take to fulfill his dream?

Yosemite National Park, California

Daring. Defiant. Free.

A new generation of superclimbers is pushing the limits in Yosemite

Every rock climber who has come to Yosemite has a dream. Alex Honnold's dream was to free solo Half Dome, a 2130-foot (649-meter) wall of granite¹. Free soloing means climbing with only rock shoes and some chalk to help keep the hands dry. Honnold couldn't use a rope or anything else to help him stick to the slippery stone. The few people who **had climbed** Half Dome before **had used** ropes, and it **had taken** them more than a day to do the climb.

On a bright September morning, Honnold was clinging² to the face of Half Dome, less than 100 feet (30 meters) from the top. He **had been climbing** for two hours and forty-five minutes, but all of a sudden he stopped. Something potentially disastrous **had occurred**— he **had lost** some of his confidence. He **hadn't felt** that way two days before when **he'd been racing** up the same rock *with* a rope. That climb **had gone** well. Today though, Honnold hesitated. He knew that even the slightest doubt could cause a deadly fall, thousands of feet to the valley floor below. He knew he had to get moving, so he chalked his hands, adjusted his feet, and started climbing again. Within minutes, he was at the top.

Bloggers spread the news of Honnold's two-hour-and-fifty-minute free solo, and climbers were amazed. On this warm fall day, 23-year-old Alex Honnold **had** just **set** a new record in one of climbing's biggest challenges.

¹ **granite:** a kind of very hard rock
² **cling:** to hold something tightly

◀ Alex Honnold free soloing in Yosemite National Park, California

2 CHECK. Circle the correct answer to complete each statement.

1. When you free solo, you climb without **shoes / rope**.

2. Alex Honnold's free solo of Half Dome **was / wasn't** successful.

3. Honnold lost his **confidence / rope** for a moment on his way up Half Dome.

4. **No / Some** climbers before Honnold climbed Half Dome in under three hours.

3 DISCOVER. Complete the exercises to learn about the grammar in this lesson.

A Work with a partner. Read the sentences about the article. Write *1* above the underlined action or situation that happened first. Write *2* above the one that happened second.

1. Honnold <u>climbed</u>[2] Half Dome without a rope. Others <u>had climbed</u>[1] it with a rope.

2. He <u>had been</u> confident until he <u>got near the top</u>.

3. This time <u>was different</u> from the last time. The last time he <u>had used a rope</u>.

4. He <u>climbed the fastest</u>. Nobody <u>had ever climbed so quickly</u>.

B Look at the sentences in exercise **A** again. Did the sentences with *had* + past participle happen first or second? Discuss your answer with a partner and then your class.

LEARN

2.6 Past Perfect

Statements	
	Subject + *Had (Not)* + Past Participle
Affirmative	Lisa **had finished** her assignment by the due date.
Negative	Tim **hadn't revised** his essay before class.

Questions		Answers
	(Wh-) + *Had* + Subject + Past Participle	
Yes/No	**Had** you **been** to Tokyo before your trip?	Yes, I **had.** / No, I **hadn't.**
Wh-	**Where had** Raul **lived** before he came here?	Japan.

	Who/What + *Had (Not)* + Past Participle	
Who or *What* as Subject	**Who had left** the party when you arrived?	Most people **had.**

1. The past perfect is used to show that one action or event happened before another past action, event, or time.	finished dinner ordered dessert now We **had finished** dinner, so we **ordered** dessert.
2. Use the past perfect for the action or event that happened first. Use the simple past for the one that happened second.	When I **arrived,** the first band **had already played.** Second Event First Event
3. The past perfect is not necessary when the context is clear. Words like *before* and *after* make the order of events clear.	She **had left** home **before** he arrived. She **left** home **before** he arrived.
4. *Already, always, ever, just,* and *never* usually go before the past participle.	**Had** you **ever noticed** that sign before? She **had never eaten** a kiwi until her trip.
5. *By* + a time or *by the time* + subject + simple past are often used with the past perfect. *By* means *before* or *not later than.*	**By 5:00 p.m.,** it had rained two inches. **By the time we finished dinner,** the rain had stopped.

4 Complete the conversation with the words in parentheses. Use the simple past or past perfect. In some sentences both forms are correct. Use contractions where possible.

Deb: So tell me, why (1) _____ *did you take* _____ (you / take) the train from Moscow to Beijing?

Joe: Because it was my dream to ride the Trans-Siberian Railway. It was something

(2) _____ *I'd always wanted* _____ (I / always / want) to do.

Deb: How long (3) _____ (the trip / take)?

Joe: Seven days. By the time the train arrived at Beijing's main train station,

(4) _____ (I / travel) 4735 miles.

Deb: (5) _____ (you / ever / be) on such a long ride?

Joe: No, never. The longest train ride (6) _____

(I / ever / take) was only six hours long.

Deb: What (7) _____ (you / do) during those seven

days? Did you ever get bored?

Joe: No, not at all. It was fun on the train, and I had many conversations. By the time the

journey was over, (8) _____ (I / make) many new

friends. In fact, one of them (9) _____ (go) to

my high school. (10) _____ (I / never / meet) her

before!

2.7 Past Perfect Progressive

Statements	
	Subject + *Had (Not)* + *Been* + Verb + *-ing*
Affirmative	Nick **had been skiing** for years when he first skied the Alps.
Negative	We **hadn't been climbing** since 2008.

Questions		Answers
	(Wh-) + *Had* + Subject + *Been* + Verb + *-ing*	
Yes/No	**Had** Linda **been waiting** for a long time?	Yes, she **had**. / No, she **hadn't**.
Wh-	**How long had** you **been waiting** before he arrived?	Ten minutes.

	Who/What + *Had (Not)* + *Been* + Verb + *-ing*	
Who or *What* as Subject	**What had been causing** that noise?	A broken car alarm.

1. Use the past perfect progressive
   a. when an action or event was happening for a period of time until (or just before) another action, event, or time
   b. to talk about how long something happened

   a. She **had been climbing** for half an hour when she suddenly got a pain in her leg.

   b. We**'d been trying** to win the contest **for five years**.

2. **Be careful!** Use the past perfect to talk about how many times something happened.

   We**'d tried** to win the contest **five times**.

5 Complete the exercises.

A Complete the sentences with the words in parentheses. Use the past perfect progressive. Then compare your answers with a partner.

1. By the time Sylvia was 18, she _____*had been hiking*_____ (hike) for several years.

2. Two German hikers _____ (follow) a difficult trail when they lost their way.

3. The Danish hikers _____ (prepare) dinner when a bear approached their campsite.

4. Two young hikers were getting ready to go home. They _____ (not camp) for very long when they lost interest.

5. The rescue workers _____ (stay) at the park office before they moved into a house nearby the park.

6. Yesterday, George rescued a hiker who _____ (wait) for help for over 12 hours.

7. Some hikers were worried. They _____ (head) back to the camp when they heard thunder, and they had to look for shelter.

8. They _____ (not think) about the weather until the sky turned very dark.

B Complete the questions about the people in exercise **A**.

1. How long ____*had*____ Sylvia ____*been hiking*____ by the time she was 18?

2. What kind of trail _____ the German hikers _____ when they lost their way?

3. What _____ the Danish hikers _____ when the bear approached?

4. How long _____ the two young hikers _____ when they lost interest?

5. Where _____ the rescue workers _____ before they moved?

6. How long _____ the hiker _____ for help?

7. Where _____ the hikers _____ when they heard thunder?

8. _____ the hikers _____ about the weather before?

C **SPEAK.** Work with a partner. Ask and answer the questions in exercise **B**. Find the answers in exercise **A**.

A: *How long had Sylvia been hiking by the time she was 18?*   B: *For several years.*

PRACTICE

6 **WRITE & SPEAK.**

A Complete the questions with the words in parentheses. Use the simple past or past perfect.

1. What ____had you learned____ (you / learn) to do by the age of ten?

2. What ____did you learn____ (you / learn) to do in your teens?

3. How many languages _____ (you / study) by the time you were fifteen years old?

4. How many languages _____ (you / learn) as a child?

5. What things _____ (you / never / do) when you were a child?

6. What things _____ (you / never / do) until recently?

7. How many places _____ (your parents / live) by the time you were born?

8. Where _____ (you / live) when you were growing up?

B Work with a partner. Ask and answer the questions in exercise **A** with information about yourself. Answer with the simple past or past perfect.

A: *What had you learned to do by the age of ten?*

B: *I had learned to catch fish by then.*

7 **SPEAK & WRITE.**

A Work with a partner. Read the time line about an athlete who paid the ultimate price for his passion. What was his passion? Discuss your answer with your partner.

Dan Osman: A Passionate Life	
1963	Born in Reno, Nevada
1975	Starts rock climbing
1981	Moves to California and starts free solo climbing at Yosemite
1989	Gets bored with climbing and tries jumping from cliffs
1990s	Appears in the Masters of Stone videos
1995	Meets Andrew Todhunter, who starts to write a book about him
11/22/98	Makes a successful 925-foot jump off a cliff at Yosemite
11/23/98	Fails trying to make a 1000-foot jump at Yosemite; dies at age 35
1999	Todhunter's book about Osman is published

B Use information from the time line in exercise **A** on page 53 and the words in parentheses to complete the sentences. Use the past perfect. Add *not* where necessary.

1. Dan Osman _____ hadn't been _____ (be) a rock climber before the age of twelve.

2. Osman _____ (climb) free solo until he moved to California.

3. By 1989, he _____ (become) bored with climbing.

4. In 1989, Osman _____ (appear) in the Masters of Stone videos yet.

5. Andrew Todhunter didn't start his book about Osman until he _____ (meet) him.

6. When Osman died, Todhunter _____ (finish) the book yet.

7. Before his death, Osman _____ (already / jump) from many cliffs.

8. He _____ (complete) a jump of almost 1000 feet not long before his fatal jump.

C Write questions in your notebook about the sentences in exercise **B**. Then ask and answer the questions with a partner.

A: *Had Osman done any climbing before the age of twelve?*

B: *No, he hadn't. He did his first climb when he was twelve.*

8 Complete the story with the verbs in the box. Use the past perfect or the past perfect progressive. Add *not* where necessary.

~~go~~	eat	notice	plan	rest	ride	sleep	want

Ginny was about to start a mountain biking trip. She was excited because she (1) _____ hadn't gone _____ mountain biking alone before. She (2) _____ to go on a biking trip for a long time, and (3) _____ for this trip for five months.

> **REAL ENGLISH**
>
> The past perfect is often used to give a reason or explain an event that happened before another event in the past.
>
> *I didn't recognize her because she **had changed** her hairstyle.*

On the day of her trip, Ginny had a lot of energy because she (4) _____ well the night before. She started smoothly. She (5) _____ for several hours when she got a flat tire. Fortunately, she had a spare tire. A bit later, she was hungry because she (6) _____ anything since her mid-morning snack, so she stopped and ate a sandwich. Later, she decided to rest, so she rode back to a pond because she (7) _____ that it was shady there. She (8) _____ for long before she felt ready to get up and finish her ride.

▲ An image of the Canadian Arctic around 1834

9 READ & SPEAK.

A Read the paragraph about an expedition to the Canadian Arctic. Find and underline the simple past, past perfect, and past perfect progressive verb forms.

> By the mid-nineteenth century, Europeans <u>had been trying</u> to find a quick way to travel to Asia for hundreds of years. They had been looking for a waterway through the icy Canadian Arctic since the sixteenth century; however, no one had ever found it. Then in 1845, Sir John Franklin tried. He set out on the risky journey with an expedition of 128 men. Two years passed by, but Franklin did not return. What had happened to him and his men? Had their ship sunk? Had they gotten lost? A rescue team went to find out.

B Work with a partner. Read the questions about the text in exercise **A**. Discuss the answers with your partner and then your class.

1. What had the Europeans been trying to find since the sixteenth century?

2. Why do you think they wanted to find it?

3. What did Sir John Franklin do?

4. What do you think happened to Franklin and his men?

10 LISTEN.

CD1-16

A Listen to the interview with an author who wrote a book about the search for Franklin and his crew. Then read the sentences. Circle **T** for *true* or **F** for *false*.

1. The Northwest Passage was a popular route. Many explorers had been through before Franklin.   **T**   (**F**)

2. One rescue team found proof that Franklin had died.   **T**   **F**

3. A rescue team found a detailed message about the difficulties Franklin and his men had faced.   **T**   **F**

4. Franklin's men had abandoned their ships.   **T**   **F**

5. The men died from several different things, including starvation and disease.   **T**   **F**

CD1-16 **B** Correct the false statements in exercise **A**. Listen again to check your answers.

No explorers had been through the Northwest Passage before Franklin.

11 APPLY.

A Work with a partner. Look at the photo on this page. Imagine what could go wrong on this trip. Then complete the chart with your ideas. Use the simple past, past perfect, and past perfect progressive.

A Kayaking Trip

What Happened	Why It Happened
1. While kayaking, they got lost.	1. They hadn't been paying attention to their location.
2. They got sunburned.	2. They hadn't brought any sunblock.
3. They lost a paddle.	3. _____
4. _____	4. They had been walking around.
5. They got mosquito bites.	5. _____
6. _____	6. _____

B Share your ideas with the class.

56 PRESENT AND PAST: PERFECT AND PERFECT PROGRESSIVE

C Work in a group. Imagine what went wrong on the camping trip in the photo or any trip you know about. Follow the instructions below.

1. Discuss what happened and why.

2. Complete the chart below with the five most interesting ideas from your discussion. Use the chart from exercise **A** as a guide.

3. Share your answers with the class.

What Happened	Why It Happened
1.	1.
2.	2.
3.	3.
4.	4.
5.	5.

Charts
2.1–2.7

1 Complete the paragraph. Use the correct form of each verb in parentheses.

I (1) _____had_____ (have) a terrible car accident when I was
sixteen. I (2) _____ (lose) a leg. As an athlete, this was
especially devastating. I (3) _____ (be) a gymnast from
the age of eight, and I (4) _____ (win) three national
competitions. It (5) _____ (take) me a lot of time to recover,
and I (6) _____ (not think) about competing again. Then, one
of my coaches (7) _____ (tell) me about the Paralympics and
(8) _____ (suggest) that I train for swimming. I could do that with
only one leg. I (9) _____ (always / want) to be in the Olympics. In
fact, I (10) _____ (train) for the Olympics at the time of my accident. So
I (11) _____ (listen) to my coach and (12) _____
(start) swimming. I (13) _____ (swim) ever since that day
and I love it. I (14) _____ (win) several competitions. Lately, I
(15) _____ (train) for the next Paralympics. I hope to win a medal!

Charts
2.1, 2.3–2.7

2 EDIT. Read the text by a traveler on safari. Find and correct nine more errors with the simple past, present perfect, present perfect progressive, past perfect, or past perfect progressive.

Mason's Travels on Safari

    It had always been our dream to travel to southern Africa, and we'd ~~make~~ ᵛmade a lot
of plans for our trip. I wanted to take a lot of wildlife photographs, so my friend has
recommended that I bring two cameras. When I got to Namibia, I had panicked. One
camera had been missing. Luckily, I was finding it later.

    The next day, we had started out on our safari with a tour. By the end of our tour, we
saw some amazing things. One time, when we stopped to take pictures, we were only a
few feet away from a cheetah. Amazing!

    We had never bothered the animals at night. However, we heard their various calls
and other noises outside our tent every night. At first, I had been afraid of the sounds,
but not by the end of the trip. It was really the most incredible trip I've ever been taking.

Cheetah running, ▶
Namibia

CD1-17

3 LISTEN & SPEAK.

A Circle the correct form of the verb. Then listen to the conversation and check your answers.

1. Liu Yang is the first female astronaut that China **ever sent / has ever sent** into space.

2. She **trained / has trained** to be a pilot at China's Air Force College, and then
   she **joined / has joined** the Air Force.

3. She **flew / has flown** five different types of aircraft, and she **did / has done** 1680 hours
   of flight time.

4. She **also participated / has also participated** in military exercises and emergency rescues.

5. Liu started training to be an astronaut. She **has never experienced / had never experienced**
   anything so challenging.

B Listen to the next part of the conversation. Then work with a partner. Discuss the questions.
Then listen again and check your answers.

1. What has Liu Yang done in her life?
2. Had she always wanted to be an astronaut?
3. How have her coworkers described her?
4. How long had she been in the Air Force before becoming an astronaut?

Connect the Grammar to Writing

1 READ & NOTICE THE GRAMMAR.

A What is a goal that you have achieved? How did it affect you? Tell a partner your ideas. Then read the narrative.

Achieving a Goal

About a year ago, I was watching the Olympics, and I decided that I wanted to become a runner. I knew I should set an achievable goal, so I decided to train for a 5K race.

My parents were surprised when I told them about my goal, because I had never been interested in running before. In fact, I had never run more than a mile, and I had always been very slow. My friends thought I was joking. Everyone assumed that I would quit after a week.

Fortunately, I proved them all wrong. I did two things to achieve my goal. First, I went online and researched a good training plan. I found a website that helps you plan workouts. You start by walking, and then you gradually start running. After that, I joined a local running group. We ran in the park twice a week, and I made friends who had also decided to run a 5K.

Three months later, I achieved my goal: I ran in my first race. I didn't win, but I ran the whole way, so I was proud of myself. Since then, I have run in several races. I have also started training for a longer run. My next goal is to run in a 10K race. My friends have stopped laughing at me, and a few of them have even asked me to help them start running!

GRAMMAR FOCUS

In the narrative in exercise **A**, the writer uses these verb forms:

Simple past	• to tell about the main event of the story (*About a year ago . . . I **decided** that . . .*)
Past perfect	• to discuss events that happened before the main story (*I **had** never **run** more than a mile . . .*)
Present perfect	• with *since* to tell about past events that continue to the present (***Since** then, I **have run** in several races.*)

B Read the narrative in exercise **A** again. Find and circle two more examples of the simple past. Underline two past perfect examples, and double underline two present perfect examples.

C Complete the time line with information from the narrative in exercise **A**. Write the letter of the events in the correct order. Then compare your answers with a partner.

a. Ran in several other races

b. Was never interested in running

c. Joined a running club

d. Parents were surprised

e. Ran in 5K

f. Watched the Olympics

g. Found a good website

b __ __ ← __ __ __ __ __ →

Set a goal to run a 5K   Now

2 BEFORE YOU WRITE.

A Work with a partner. Make a list of goals that you have achieved. Discuss which goals would be the most interesting to write about.

B Create a time line for your personal narrative. Write the events of the story that you want to tell. Use the time line in exercise **1C** as a guide.

3 WRITE two or three paragraphs telling your story. Use your time line in exercise **2B** and the text in exercise **1A** as a guide. Remember to start your story with background information. At the end, tell how your life has changed.

> **WRITING FOCUS**   Using *First* and *After that* to Show a Sequence
>
> Notice *first* and *after that* in the narrative in exercise **1A**.
>
> Use these words at the beginning of the sentence to explain the order of events in a text. Place a comma after *first* and *after that*.
>
> ***First,*** *I went online and . . .*   ***After that,*** *I joined a local running club.*

4 SELF ASSESS. Underline the verb forms in your narrative. Then use the checklist to assess your work.

☐ I used the present perfect and the present perfect progressive correctly. [2.1, 2.2, 2.4, 2.5]

☐ I used the simple past correctly. [2.3]

☐ I used the past perfect and the past perfect progressive correctly. [2.6, 2.7]

☐ I used commas correctly with *first* and *after that*. [WRITING FOCUS]

The Future

▲ Supertrees act as vertical gardens, generating solar power and collecting rainwater, Supertree Glove, Singapore.

EXPLORE

1   **READ** the conversation about robots. What amazing things will robots do in the future?

Will robots be our friends one day?

HSM Open University

◀ **CLICK TO PLAY**

Unit 3 Robots: The New Generation
Course: Artificial Intelligence
Professor L. Lacy

Paulo: Wasn't Professor Lacy's online lecture last week amazing?

Kate: I haven't watched it yet. What did he say?

Paulo: He talked about a new generation of robots. Apparently they**'ll seem** almost human.

Kate: That's interesting, but why do scientists want to make them look real?

Paulo: Well, many of the new robots **will do** tasks for people at home. They **will** also **be** in schools and offices. Scientists are making robots look more human so people **will be** comfortable around them.

Kate: Hmm. What kind of tasks **are** the robots **going to do**?

Paulo: According to Professor Lacy, they**'ll cook, fold laundry, go shopping,** and even **babysit** children.

Kate: Don't you think the idea is a little creepy? I think a lot of people **won't want** robots in their homes.

Paulo: Maybe not. But scientists are working hard so robots **won't be** scary looking. These robots **are** even **going to be** responsive to our thoughts and feelings, and they**'re going to look** friendly.

Kate: I still think robots that look and act like humans **will make** people feel uncomfortable. And what about children? **Will** they **develop** normally if they have robots for babysitters?

Paulo: Good question. Nobody knows how robots **will affect** people and their relationships, but scientists are researching those issues.

Kate: Really? I want to hear more, but my class **starts** in five minutes. **Are** you **going** to the study session on Friday?

Paulo: No, but **I'll e-mail** you. Let's get together soon.

▲ "Actroid" is a human-looking robot made
by a Japanese robotics company.

2 CHECK. Read the statements. Circle **T** for *true* or **F** for *false*.

1. In the future, robots will look and act more like people.   **T   F**

2. The new robots won't prepare food.   **T   F**

3. Some robots are going to take care of people.   **T   F**

4. Everyone will want a robot helper at home.   **T   F**

5. Scientists are studying the effects of robots on humans.   **T   F**

3 DISCOVER. Complete the exercises to learn about the grammar in this lesson.

A Find these sentences in the conversation in exercise **1**. Write the missing words.

1. What kind of tasks _____*are*_____ the robots _____*going to do*_____?

2. Really? I want to hear more, but my class _____ in five minutes.

3. _____ you _____ to the study session on Friday?

4. No, but I _____ you later so we can get together.

B How many different verb forms are used in exercise **A** to talk about the future? _____

LEARN

3.1 Review of *Will* and *Be Going To*

	Will	Be Going To
Affirmative Statements	Patty **will be** a doctor someday.	Tim **is going to teach** high school.
Negative Statements	Ty **won't eat** that. He doesn't like fish.	Mari **isn't going to eat** with us.
Yes/No Questions	**Will** you **visit** us soon? We miss you.	**Are** you **going to visit** your sister this weekend?
Wh- Questions	Who **will** I **know** at the party?	**What are** you **going to do** on your birthday?
Who or *What* as Subject	Who **will bring** a cake?	Who **is going to watch** the game on Friday?

1. Use *will* and *be going to* for predictions. **Be careful!** Use *be going to* only when you are certain about something in the future because of evidence or information you have now.	I think the movie **will be** very popular. I think the movie **is going to be** popular. ✓ The score is five to zero. We**'re going to win** the game! ✗ The score is five to zero. We will win the game!
2. Use *be going to* for plans or intentions. (An intention is something you decide to do.)	We **are going to see** that new movie this weekend. Sue went to get her tools. She**'s going to fix** the door.

3. Use *will* for
  a. sudden decisions (made at the time of speaking)
  b. offers
  c. promises
  d. requests
	a. Amy's not home? I**'ll call** back later.
	
	b. Do you want some tea? I**'ll get** you some.
	c. I **won't be** late. I promise.
	d. **Will** you **give** the teacher the message?

4. Use *won't* for refusals.	My parents **won't lend** him any more money.

4 Complete the exercises.

A Complete the sentences with the words in parentheses. Use *will* or the correct form of *be going to* depending on the meaning (prediction, intention, etc.). Both *will* and *be going to* are possible in some sentences.

1. I think _____ robots will scare _____ (robots / scare) people if they look and

                            prediction
   act too human.

2. _____ (I / make) copies of my notes for a few other students.

               intention

3. _____ (I / make) you a copy of my notes if you like.

               offer

4. _____ (you / explain) the connection between robotics

               intention
   and students' everyday lives?

5. _____ (you / explain) the connection between robotics

               request
   and students' everyday lives?

6. I'm afraid there's no time to discuss your question now.

_____ (we / talk) about it next week.

               promise

7. I'm afraid there's no time to discuss your question now.

_____ (you / remind) me about it next class?

request

8. I have an appointment with my professor. _____

intention

(I / talk) to her about my test grade.

9. We want Mr. Lu to cancel the exam, but _____

refusal

(he / not do) it.

10. _____ (robots / be) common in everyday life in

prediction

the future?

11. _____ (you / help) me cook dinner tonight?

request

12. This room is a mess! _____ (I / help) you clean up.

offer

B **SPEAK.** Work with a partner. Compare your answers from exercise **A**.

3.2 Review of Present Progressive and Simple Present for the Future

1. Use the present progressive for definite plans. The plan is often in the near future, or the details of the plan (such as time or place) are known.	I'm **meeting** friends for dinner on Saturday. We're **eating** at Grimaldi's.
2. When the present progressive refers to the future, we often use a future time expression. The present progressive refers to *now* when it does not have a time expression and does not refer to the future.	Future: My parents **are leaving** Sunday. Now: My parents **are leaving**.
3. Use the simple present for future events that have a fixed or regular schedule.	The plane **leaves** at 8:30 Monday night. I'll be at the airport by 7:00.

5 Complete the conversations with the words in parentheses. Use the present progressive or simple present. More than one answer is sometimes correct. Then work with a partner and compare your answers.

REAL ENGLISH

The simple present is often used for scheduled future events with these verbs: *start, finish, begin, end, arrive, come, leave, open,* and *close.*

> Stores at the mall **open** at 11:00.
> The bus **leaves** at 10:30.

Conversation 1

A: What (1) ___are you doing___

(you / do) after class?

B: (2) _____

(I / go) to New York. In fact, I'm in a hurry. It's

3:30 and (3) _____

(my train / leave) at five o'clock.

A: (4) _____ (you / go) alone?

B: No. (5) _____ (I / go) with a few friends.

A: When (6) _____ (you / come) back?

B: (7) _____ (the train / get in) around 9:00 on Sunday night.

A: Do you want me to meet you at the train station?

B: No, that's OK. (8) _____

(my friends and I / share) a taxi.

Conversation 2

A: (9) _____ (you / work) tomorrow?

B: No, it's my day off.

A: (10) _____ (you / go) to the student government meeting tomorrow

afternoon? (11) _____ (it / begin) at 2:00.

B: I'd love to, but (12) _____ (I / play) tennis with a friend in the

morning. Then, (13) _____ (we / meet) another friend for lunch.

Conversation 3

A: (14) _____ (everyone / go) to the new *Star Wars* movie this weekend?

B: Yeah. Do you want to come?

A: Sure. What time (15) _____ (it / start)?

B: Around 7:00, I think. (16) _____ (we / meet) in front of the theater
at 6:30.

A: OK. Great. I'll see you then.

PRACTICE

CD1-20

6 Circle the correct answers to complete the
conversation. Then listen and check your answers.

> **REAL ENGLISH**
>
> With the verbs *go* and *come*, the
> present progressive is used more often
> than *be going to*.
>
> *We **are going** to the movies tonight.
> Cecilia **is coming** with us.*

Kesha: Steve, hi! Hey, (1) **are you going** / do you
go to the Robotics Club party at Chris
and Pat's place next Saturday?

Steve: I don't know yet. (2) **I'm playing / I'll play** basketball that afternoon.

Kesha: (3) **You're having / You'll have** plenty of time. The party (4) **is / will be** at 8:00.

Steve: Chris and Pat's house is really far away. The bus (5) **is taking / will take** a long time.

Kesha: (6) **I'm going to borrow / I'll borrow** my brother's car. I've already asked him, and he

said OK. So, (7) **I'm going to drive / I'll drive** you.

Steve: Great. Thanks. . . . Hey, watch out! That guy on the bike (8) **is going to / will** hit you!

Kesha: Wow! Thanks. I didn't see him!

7 ANALYZE THE GRAMMAR. Work with a partner. For each item in exercise **6**, decide how the
future form is used. Circle the correct letter.

1. a. plan   b. prediction   c. offer

2. a. plan   b. prediction   c. sudden decision

3. a. intention   b. prediction   c. schedule

4. a. prediction	b. offer	c. schedule
5. a. plan	b. prediction	c. offer
6. a. intention	b. offer	c. request
7. a. plan	b. prediction	c. offer
8. a. prediction	b. offer	c. sudden decision

8 **SPEAK.** Work with a partner. Ask and answer questions about your plans. Use the words in the box.

after class	tonight	tomorrow	this weekend

A: *Are you going home after class?*

B: *No, I'm going to the school play. Do you want to come?*

9 **LISTEN.**

CD1-21

A You will hear some people talking at a Robotics Club party. Choose the correct response to each statement or question you hear.

1. _____ it.

   a. I'll get   b. I get

2. Thanks. It's freezing out there. I think _____ snow tonight.

   a. it'll   b. it's going to

3. Do you want some? _____ pour you a cup.

   a. I'm going to   b. I'll

4. That's right. _____ help me set up the exhibits?

   a. Will you   b. Are you going to

5. That's great! _____ it at the tech fair next week?

   a. Are you showing   b. Will you show

6. OK, _____ quiet about it from now on. I promise.

   a. I'm going to keep   b. I'll keep

7. I'm really busy tomorrow, but I can try. What time _____?

   a. are you meeting   b. will you meet

8. Sorry, but the last bus _____. I don't want to miss it.

   a. will leave at 10:30   b. leaves at 10:30

CD1-22

B Work with a partner. Compare your answers from exercise **A**. Then listen to the complete conversations and check your answers.

10 LISTEN & WRITE.

CD1-23

A Listen and check (✓) the topics that Sasha talks about.

Sasha's immediate future

☐ Start high school next year

✓ Graduate from high school next year

☐ Do some research on engineering programs

☐ Begin an engineering program

☐ Plan to read about robot projects this year

☐ Work on robot projects this year

HERB and other robots

☐ Be a help in people's homes

☐ Drive cars

☐ Take care of children

☐ Take care of the elderly

Sasha's robot

☐ Respond to human questions

☐ Respond to human needs

☐ Understand what people say

☐ Not understand what people say

☐ Have an amazing name

☐ Be amazing

CD1-23

B Listen again. Then write at least six sentences about what Sasha said. Use *will/won't, be (not) going to,* and the present progressive. Use each subject in the box at least once.

Sasha	Sasha's robot	HERB and other robots

1. Sasha is graduating from high school next year.

2. _____

3. _____

4. _____

5. _____

6. _____

C Work with a partner. Share your sentences from exercise **B**.

11 APPLY.
Work in groups. Discuss your goals, plans, and predictions for the future. Discuss the topics below or your own ideas.

- The kind of work you want or hope to do in the future
- The things you are going to do in order to help you achieve your goals
- Some things you will probably do in your future job
- The feelings you will probably have about your work

I want to be a clothing designer someday. I'm going to take classes in design this summer.

EXPLORE

1 **READ** the article about the clothes of the future. Which item of clothing do you think is most useful?

Clever Clothes

These days we want clothes to make us look good and to protect us from the weather. However, scientists say that things are going to change. Thanks to technological advances, soon we will be wearing clever clothes such as the following.

▲ This jacket sleeve contains control buttons for a cell phone.

- **Cell Phone Jackets:** These jackets will power a cell phone **when we push a button on the sleeve.**[1]

- **Health-Monitoring Shirts:** These shirts will check our heart rate and blood pressure and will collect other important health information **while we go about our daily lives**. They will inform us of any possible problems.

- **GPS**[2] **Clothes for Kids:** These clothes have built-in GPS tracking systems. They will allow parents to watch their children on the computer and know where they are at all times.

- **Military "First-Aid"**[3] **Uniforms:** These uniforms will allow soldiers to turn the sleeve or leg of their clothing into casts[4] if they break a bone. This way, soldiers will be able to treat injuries **as soon as they happen**.

Scientists are developing all kinds of intelligent textiles in their labs. However, we won't see many clever clothes in stores **until researchers learn how to make them comfortable to wear. When that happens**, there will probably be a clothing revolution! Experts say that clever clothes will change not only the fashion industry but also the way we think. We will still want clothes to look good, but we will also want them to work for us.

[1] **sleeve:** the part of a piece of clothing that covers the arm or part of the arm
[2] **GPS (Global Positioning System):** a system that uses satellites to show exact locations on Earth
[3] **first aid:** medical treatment given as soon as possible after a person is injured
[4] **cast:** a hard covering used to prevent a broken bone from moving while it heals

2 CHECK. Work with a partner. Discuss the answers to these questions. Then share your answers with the class.

1. According to the article, what do we expect our clothes to do for us now?

2. What are two items of clever clothing that have a health purpose? Describe them.

3. What is one disadvantage of clever clothes?

4. What do we want our clothes to do for us in the future?

3 DISCOVER. Complete the exercises to learn about the grammar in this lesson.

A Read the sentences based on the article from exercise **1** on page 71. Circle the time word or phrase in each sentence.

1. Jackets will power a cell phone (when) we push a button on the sleeve.

2. Shirts will check our heart rate while we are wearing them.

3. This way, soldiers will be able to treat injuries as soon as they happen.

4. We won't see clever clothes in stores until they are more comfortable to wear.

5. When that happens, there will probably be a clothing revolution.

B Look at the time words you circled in exercise **A** and write them in the chart. Complete the chart with the subject and verb that follows each time word.

Time Word/Phrase	Subject	Verb
1. when	we	push
2.		
3.		
4.		
5.		

C What form are the verbs in the chart in exercise **B**: past, present, or future?

◀ Professor Takao Someya displays wearable electrical circuits. They can monitor blood temperature, blood pressure, and electrical impulses from the heart.

LEARN

3.3 Future Time Clauses

Time Clause First
Before I turn in my essay, I'm going to ask someone to read it.
Time Clause   Main Clause

Time Clause Second
I'll read your essay **before you turn it in**.
Main Clause   Time Clause

1. A future time clause tells when the future action in the main clause will happen. The time clause can come first or second. **Remember:** Use a comma after a time clause when it comes first in the sentence.	**After we do the dishes,** I'll serve dessert. I will wake up **before the alarm goes off.** **When we arrive,** we'll call your office.
2. A future time clause = a time word/phrase + subject + simple present form of a verb.	Will you call **as soon as you arrive?**
3. **Be careful!** Use a future form only in the main clause. Use a present form in the time clause.	✓ I'm going to take the trash out after the rain **stops**. ✗ I'm going to take the trash out after the rain <u>will stop</u>.
4. The present perfect can also be used in a future time clause. It emphasizes the completion of the action in the time clause.	I won't send the e-mail **until you have read it.** Present Perfect

4 Complete the exercises.

A Complete each prediction with the correct form of the verbs in parentheses. For future forms, both *will* or *be going to* are possible. Add a comma when necessary.

1. When scientists _____*develop*_____ (develop) clever clothes with cell phone controls, people _____ (not wear) ordinary clothes.

2. People _____ (purchase) clever clothes online before they _____ (see) them in stores.

3. In the future, clever car seats _____ (warn) a driver before he or she _____ (fall) asleep at the wheel.

4. Stores _____ (sell) **GPS** clothing before they _____ (offer) health-monitoring clothing.

5. Before people _____ (have) robots as friends they _____ (use) robots to help around the house.

6. When robots _____ (become) affordable everyone _____ (want) one.

B Read the predictions in exercise **A**. Tell a partner which you think will or will not come true.

A: *I don't believe number 6 is true. I won't want a robot when they become affordable.*

B: *Really? I think people are going to rush to the stores to get them.*

3.4 Future Time Clauses: *After, As Soon As, Before, Once, Until, When, and While*

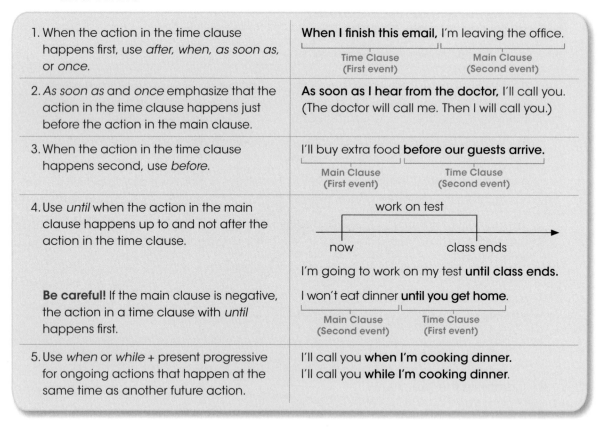

1. When the action in the time clause happens first, use *after, when, as soon as,* or *once.*	**When I finish this email,** I'm leaving the office. Time Clause (First event) — Main Clause (Second event)
2. *As soon as* and *once* emphasize that the action in the time clause happens just before the action in the main clause.	**As soon as I hear from the doctor,** I'll call you. (The doctor will call me. Then I will call you.)
3. When the action in the time clause happens second, use *before.*	I'll buy extra food **before our guests arrive.** Main Clause (First event) — Time Clause (Second event)
4. Use *until* when the action in the main clause happens up to and not after the action in the time clause. **Be careful!** If the main clause is negative, the action in a time clause with *until* happens first.	work on test now — class ends I'm going to work on my test **until class ends.** I won't eat dinner **until you get home.** Main Clause (Second event) — Time Clause (First event)
5. Use *when* or *while* + present progressive for ongoing actions that happen at the same time as another future action.	I'll call you **when I'm cooking dinner.** I'll call you **while I'm cooking dinner.**

5 Read each sentence. Circle the time clause and underline the main clause. Then write *1* above the action that will happen first and write *2* above the action that will happen second.

1. <u>Ron will receive a bionic arm,</u> (as soon as it is ready.)

2. Ron isn't going to be able to hold anything until he gets his bionic arm.

3. Before he has the new arm, he will learn as much as possible about bionics.

4. As soon as Ron gets the arm, he is going to try to use it.

5. When Ron thinks about moving his fingers, his brain will send messages to his hand.

6. The fingers in his bionic arm will move after they receive the messages from his brain.

7. Until he gets his bionic arm, Ron is going to need help with his everyday tasks.

8. He will be very happy once he is able to do everyday tasks again.

6 Complete the sentences about a home computer system that will change the way we live. Circle the letter of each correct answer.

1. The lights will come on _____ you get home.

   a. until   (b.) as soon as

2. While you _____, the home system is going to cook your dinner.

   a. are watching TV   b. are going to watch TV

3. Chairs will change their shape _____ different family members sit in them.

   a. until   b. when

4. Music will start playing _____ you enter the house.

   a. once   b. until

5. You will be able to turn on the oven _____ you are driving home.

   a. after   b. while

6. Your computer will create products for you _____ you give it instructions.

   a. when   b. before

7. While you _____ a bath, the home system will prepare your clothes.

   a. will take   b. are taking

8. The home system will stay on _____ you leave the house.

   a. until   b. as soon as

PRACTICE

7 Combine each pair of sentences into one sentence with a time clause. Use the time words in parentheses. Add a comma when necessary.

1. First: The car manufacturer is going to test its new self-driving car.
   Second: The manufacturer is going to sell the new car.

   (after) _The car manufacturer is going to sell its new_
   self-driving car after it tests it.

2. First: A car in front of you will stop.
   Second: Your self-driving car will stop automatically.

   (as soon as) _____

   _____

3. First: Your self-driving car will warn you.
   Second: You will make a wrong turn.

   (before) _____

   _____

4. First: People won't feel relaxed.
   Second: Engineers will make these cars safe.

   (until) _____
   _____

5. First: You will find a parking space.
   Second: Your car will park itself.

   (once) _____
   _____

6. First: People will name their destination.
   Second: Their cars will start up and drive there.

   (when) _____
   _____

7. First: Engineers are going to build more automated highways.
   Second: People will take more trips by car.

   (as soon as) _____
   _____

8. First: People are not going to buy self-driving cars.
   Second: Self-driving cars are going to become affordable.

   (until) _____
   _____

8 WRITE & SPEAK.

A Complete the sentences with your own ideas about the future. Add a comma when necessary.

1. I'll go out and buy something nice for myself after __I get my first paycheck__ .

2. Before I buy _____ .

3. I'm going to _____ when I have more time.

4. I won't _____ until _____ .

5. Once this course is over _____ .

6. I will look for a job as soon as _____ .

B Share your sentences with a partner. Ask follow-up questions for more information.

A: *I'll go out and buy something nice for myself after I pass all my exams.*

B: *When will you finish your exams?*

A: *December 15.*

9   **EDIT.** Read the paragraph. Find and correct five more errors with future time clauses.

> *is going to start*
>
> When Ari graduates from college next month, he ~~starts~~ working as a
> designer for a car company. It's a great job, but he's a little worried about it.
> When he will go to work on the first day, everything about the job will be new.
> Also, as soon as he begins, his long summer vacations are over. Ari will miss
> all that free time, but after he works for a couple of weeks, he loves his new job.
> He will learn a lot, and he definitely doesn't complain when he will get his first
> paycheck.

10   **LISTEN & WRITE.**

CD1-25

A   Listen to Ari talk about the first day at his new job. What are his worries? Take notes in your notebook. Then share what you heard with a partner.

won't remember everyone's name

A: *He's worried that he won't remember everyone's name.*

B: *Yes, I heard that, too.*

B   Work with a partner. Compare your notes from exercise **A**.

C   Ari needs encouragement. Write a main clause or a time clause to complete each sentence. Use your own ideas. Add a comma when necessary.

1.   Don't worry! ___*You'll learn everyone's name*___ after a few weeks.

2.   _____ you'll feel great.

3.   You'll learn all the information _____.

4.   While you are learning about the job _____.

5.   When you get your first paycheck _____.

11   **APPLY.**

CD1-26

A   Listen to Janet talk about her plans to study abroad. What are her fears? Take notes in your notebook. Then share your notes with a partner.

B   Imagine that you are Janet's friend. Write a paragraph to encourage her to go abroad. Use time clauses in at least five sentences. Use the ideas in exercise **10** to help you.

EXPLORE

 CD1-27

1 **READ** the web article about jobs in the future. Which job would you like to read more about?

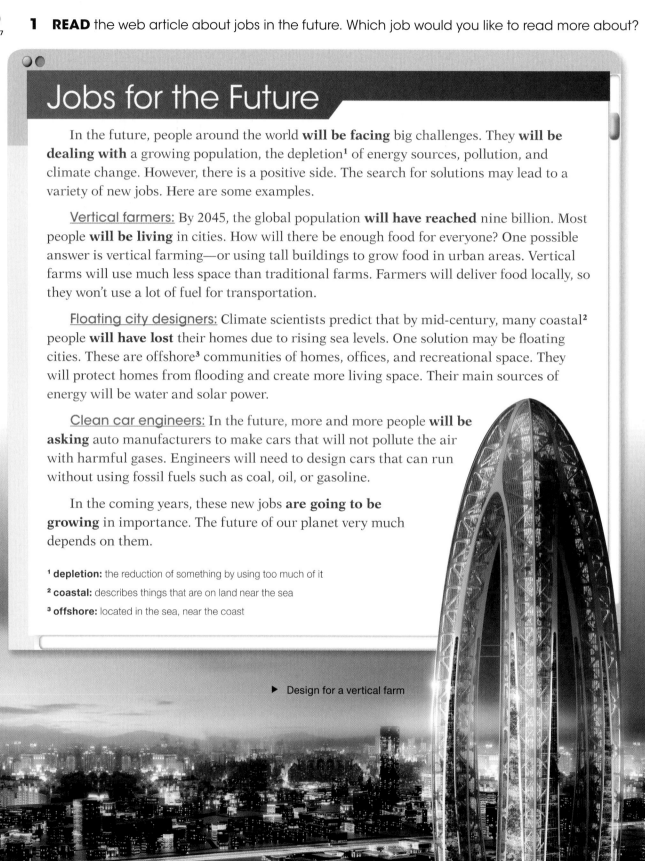

Jobs for the Future

In the future, people around the world **will be facing** big challenges. They **will be dealing with** a growing population, the depletion[1] of energy sources, pollution, and climate change. However, there is a positive side. The search for solutions may lead to a variety of new jobs. Here are some examples.

<u>Vertical farmers:</u> By 2045, the global population **will have reached** nine billion. Most people **will be living** in cities. How will there be enough food for everyone? One possible answer is vertical farming—or using tall buildings to grow food in urban areas. Vertical farms will use much less space than traditional farms. Farmers will deliver food locally, so they won't use a lot of fuel for transportation.

<u>Floating city designers:</u> Climate scientists predict that by mid-century, many coastal[2] people **will have lost** their homes due to rising sea levels. One solution may be floating cities. These are offshore[3] communities of homes, offices, and recreational space. They will protect homes from flooding and create more living space. Their main sources of energy will be water and solar power.

<u>Clean car engineers:</u> In the future, more and more people **will be asking** auto manufacturers to make cars that will not pollute the air with harmful gases. Engineers will need to design cars that can run without using fossil fuels such as coal, oil, or gasoline.

In the coming years, these new jobs **are going to be growing** in importance. The future of our planet very much depends on them.

[1] **depletion:** the reduction of something by using too much of it
[2] **coastal:** describes things that are on land near the sea
[3] **offshore:** located in the sea, near the coast

► Design for a vertical farm

◀ Design for a
floating city

2 CHECK. Match the problems on the left with the possible solutions on the right.

1. overpopulated cities __*a*__

2. the loss of some energy sources ____, ____

3. the loss of homes ____

4. polluted air ____

5. not enough food ____

a. vertical farms

b. floating cities

c. clean cars

3 DISCOVER. Complete the exercises to learn about the grammar in this lesson.

A Find these sentences in the article in exercise **1**. Write the missing words.

1. In the future, people around the world _____ will be facing _____ big challenges.

2. By 2045, the global population _____ nine billion.

3. Most people _____ in cities.

4. Many coastal people _____ their homes due to rising sea levels.

B Write the words from exercise **A** next to the correct pattern.

1. *will be* + verb + *-ing*: _____ will be facing _____, _____

2. *will have* + past participle: _____, _____

C Which pattern from exercise **B** expresses each idea below? Write the number on the line.

1. This verb form expresses something that will be in progress at a future time. ____

2. This verb form expresses something that happened before a time in the future. ____

LEARN

3.5 Future Progressive

Statements	
	Subject + *Will (Not)* + *Be* + Verb + *-ing*
Affirmative	I **will be sitting** on a beach this time next week.
Negative	We **won't be staying** at a hotel on our vacation.

Questions		Answers
	Will + Subject + *Be* + Verb + *-ing*	
Yes/No	**Will** you **be working** on your vacation?	Yes, I **will**. No, I **won't**.
Wh-	**What will** you **be doing** tomorrow at noon?	I'm not sure.

	Who/What + *Will* + *Be* + Verb + *-ing*	
Who or What as Subject	**Who will be studying** for exams Saturday?	Joe and Miriam.

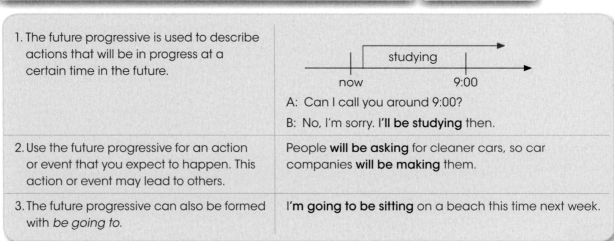

1. The future progressive is used to describe actions that will be in progress at a certain time in the future.	A: Can I call you around 9:00? B: No, I'm sorry. **I'll be studying** then.
2. Use the future progressive for an action or event that you expect to happen. This action or event may lead to others.	People **will be asking** for cleaner cars, so car companies **will be making** them.
3. The future progressive can also be formed with *be going to*.	**I'm going to be sitting** on a beach this time next week.

4 Complete the conversations with the words in parentheses. Use the future progressive.

1. A: Jim, do you and Pam want to get some lunch around 1:00?

   B: Sorry, we can't. (1) _____We're going to be meeting_____ (we / be going to / meet) with the engineers until 2:00.

   A: Then how about tomorrow at 1:00?

   B: That sounds good. (2) _____ (we / will / not do) anything then.

2. A: So, when do you think my car will be ready?

   B: Shortly. (3) _____ (I / be going to / test) it in a few minutes. If all goes well, (4) _____ (you / will / drive) home soon.

   A: Great. (5) _____ (I / will / shop) at the store across the street. Can you call my cell when it's ready?

3. A: What (6) _____
    (Julio and Ramon / will / do) tomorrow at 4:00?

   B: The same as today. (7) _____ (they / be going to /
      work) on their design project.

   A: (8) _____ (you / will / help) them?

   B: Yes, (9) _____ (I / be going to / write) a report
      about the project.

4. A: Excuse me. When (10) _____
    (the plane / will / take off)?

   B: In just a few minutes. Please sit down and fasten your seat belt.

   A: I'd like something to drink, please.

   B: (11) _____ (I / will / come) around with drinks once
      we are in the air.

3.6 Future Perfect and Future Perfect Progressive

Future Perfect	
	Subject + *Will (Not) Have* + Past Participle
Affirmative	By tomorrow, everyone **will have heard** about your job offer.
Negative	I **won't have finished** the work by the time you need it.

Future Perfect Progressive	
	Subject + *Will (Not) Have Been* + Verb + *-ing*
Affirmative	When I finally turn the essay in, I **will have been working** on it for a month.
Negative	They **won't have been working** on the project long when the new boss arrives.

1. The future perfect is used for
   a. an action or series of actions that will be complete before a specific time in the future
   b. a situation that continues for a period of time until and possibly after a particular time in the future

   a.

   build robots

   now   next month

   We **will have built** the robots by next month.

   b.

   25 years

   be married

   now   June 25th

   On June 25th, we **will have been married** for 25 years.

2. The future perfect progressive is used for actions or situations that will be in progress until a particular time in the future. They may continue after the future time.

   get home

   traveling

   now/2:00 p.m.   midnight

   I **will have been traveling** for ten hours when I get home.

3. *By* and *by the time* + clause are often used with the future perfect and the future perfect progressive.

   By 2018, my daughter **will have finished** college.
   By the time we get home, we **will have been driving** for two days.

5 Complete the sentences with the future perfect.

1. Rosa wrote one report yesterday. She is writing another report today and will write another one tomorrow. By the end of the week, she _____ will have written _____ three reports.

2. Tom built his first home in 2004 and then two more over the next ten years. He plans to build one more next year. By the end of next year, he _____ four homes.

3. Dr. Magano saw six patients in the morning and seven this afternoon. She is going to see two more patients in the evening. By the end of the day, she _____ 15 patients.

4. The photographer took over 500 pictures this morning. She is still at work. She _____ between 800 and 1000 photos by the end of the workday.

5. The building engineer has made seven designs and wants to make several more before next week's meeting. He _____ at least ten designs by the time of the meeting.

6. The guitarist is performing on Friday and Saturday evenings. He will perform again on Sunday afternoon. He _____ three times by Sunday night.

6 Complete the sentences with the future perfect progressive.

1. Yu-Ming started translating books at age 30. He is retiring next year at age 65. By the time he retires, he _____ will have been translating _____ books for over 30 years.

2. The flight attendants started serving food at 10:00 and will continue serving until shortly before landing at 12:30. Before the plane lands, the flight attendants _____ food for just over two hours.

3. Santana started playing baseball three years ago. At the end of the season, he _____ baseball for over three years.

4. Dale began to work at the restaurant six months ago. He plans to stay in the job for another six months. By the time he leaves, Dale _____ at the restaurant for a year.

5. Flora started to watch a movie at 6:00. It's a three-hour movie, and she wants to watch the whole thing. At 8:00, Flora _____ the movie for two hours.

6. The bike race began on May 15. Hari's team will ride for two weeks. By May 22, the team _____ for one week.

PRACTICE

7 WRITE & SPEAK.

A Kayden Lee is a worker on Floating City Island. Today is Wednesday. Look at his schedule for Thursday and Friday. Then complete the paragraph about his schedule for Thursday. Use the words from his schedule and the future progressive, the future perfect, or the future perfect progressive. Add *not* when necessary.

Early Thursday morning, Kayden (1) _____will be attending_____ a staff meeting. At 8:30, he (2) _____ the solar panels. By 10:30, (3) he _____ the trash, but he (4) _____ the repairs yet. When he finally finishes the repairs, he (5) _____ for eight and a half hours already. At 4:30, he (6) _____ the ferry boat to the mainland. By 6:00, he (7) _____ supplies for the next workday. At 7:00, he (8) _____ to Floating City Island.

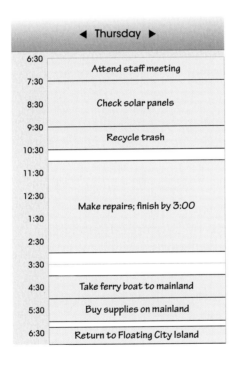

◄ Thursday ►	
6:30	
	Attend staff meeting
7:30	
8:30	Check solar panels
9:30	
	Recycle trash
10:30	
11:30	
12:30	
	Make repairs; finish by 3:00
1:30	
2:30	
3:30	
4:30	Take ferry boat to mainland
5:30	Buy supplies on mainland
6:30	Return to Floating City Island

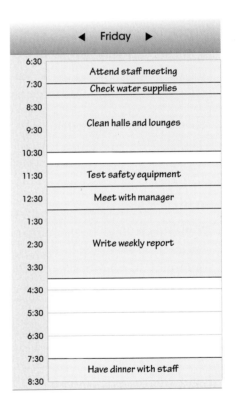

◄ Friday ►	
6:30	
	Attend staff meeting
7:30	Check water supplies
8:30	
	Clean halls and lounges
9:30	
10:30	
11:30	Test safety equipment
12:30	Meet with manager
1:30	
2:30	Write weekly report
3:30	
4:30	
5:30	
6:30	
7:30	
	Have dinner with staff
8:30	

B Write a paragraph about Kayden's schedule for Friday. Use the future progressive, future perfect, and future perfect progressive at least once each. Use the paragraph in exercise **A** as a model.

C Work with a partner. Compare your paragraphs from exercise **B**.

8 WRITE & SPEAK.

A Change the questions to polite requests. Use the future progressive.

REAL ENGLISH

The future progressive is often used to ask about someone's plans or make a request in a more polite way.

*Will you **be getting** the tickets for the concert?*

1. **Boss:** Who is going to take notes at the meeting?

   <u>Who will be taking notes at the meeting?</u>

2. **Auto Mechanic:** Are you picking up your car today?

   _____

3. **Student:** Are you going to return the homework next week?

   _____

4. **Teacher:** When are you going to hand in your project?

   _____

5. **Passenger:** Are you going to stop at the next bus stop?

   _____

B Work with a partner. Read each polite request in exercise **A**. With your partner, decide who the speaker is talking to. Then write another polite request for each situation. Role-play one short conversation for the class.

Boss ⟶ Employee

A: *How many days will you be taking off?*   B: *Just three.*

9 WRITE & LISTEN.

A By the year 2050, how will the workplace be different? Use the prompts to write affirmative or negative statements that express your own ideas. Use the future progressive, future perfect, or the future perfect progressive.

1. large numbers of people / work / in offices / in the years to come

   <u>Large numbers of people won't be working in offices in the years to come.</u>

2. fewer people / use / company office space

   _____

3. over the next few decades / more workers / have / video conferences

_____

4. desktop computers and phones / disappear / from offices / by the middle of the century

_____

5. almost everyone / communicate / with mobile phones and wireless computers / for years

_____

6. by 2050 / many companies / rethink / office space

_____

7. some offices / replace / office walls with electronic walls / by 2050

_____

8. people / not share / information in the same ways they do now

_____

CD1-28

B Listen to an office designer talk about the workplace of the future. Put a check (✓) before the statements you wrote in exercise **A** that the designer agrees with.

10 APPLY.

A In your notebook, write three responses to each question with the words and phrases in the boxes and your own ideas. Use each time phrase once. You can include ideas about your work, your studies, and your personal goals.

1. What do you think you are going to be doing . . . ?

| at 8 o'clock tomorrow night | this time next year | ten years from now |

This time next year, I'm going to be looking for a job.

2. What do you hope you will have done . . . ?

| by the end of this course | five years from now | by retirement |

By the end of this course, I hope I will have learned many useful new words.

3. What activity will you have been doing for a long time . . . ?

| when you graduate | by the time you're 40 | when you are 60 |

When I graduate, I will have been studying Chinese for almost six years.

B Work in a group. Discuss your answers to the questions in exercise **A**.

A: *What do you think you are going to be doing this time next year?*

B: *I'm going to be looking for a job, I think.*

Charts
3.1–3.4

1 Circle the correct words to complete the advertisement.

The future is now.

Get your degree in the comfort of your own home!

Your college application is ready, and you (1) **send / are going to send** it to the admissions office this afternoon. Then, you (2) **are waiting / are going to wait** for a reply. It (3) **will take / will be taking** time. (4) **After / While** you are waiting, you (5) **worry / will be worrying**. You'll think to yourself, "(6) **Will I be getting in / Will I get in**, or (7) **are they rejecting / are they going to reject** me?" You (8) **aren't receiving / won't receive** the answer for a few months.

That's not the only worry. When you (9) **go / will go** away to college, your friends and family (10) **will be / will have been** far away. You (11) **miss / are going to miss** them every day.

There's a way to avoid all this: Get your degree online! Yes, that's right. Online learning isn't something for the *future*. (12) **It happens / It's happening** right *now*. <u>Contact us</u> now. Classes (13) **begin / will begin** next Monday and every Monday after that. Don't wait. You (14) **aren't / won't be** sorry.

Charts
3.1–3.6

2 SPEAK, WRITE & LISTEN.

A Look at the information in the chart about three people's career paths. What are their plans and goals? Discuss them with a partner.

Hiro and Jamal are both going to do internships.

Time Period	Alex	Jamal	Hiro
By end of May	Send application	Send application	Start application
June to December	Take online classes in design and economics	Do internship	Do internship
January	Find a job	Start grad school	Start grad school
In 2 years	Work as urban designer	Get master's degree	Start job search
In 10 years	Start own company	Run urban planning company	Work as urban engineer
In 15 years	Sell company for a profit	Work on many helpful projects	Start own company

B In your notebook, write sentences about each person's career plans. Use the words below and the information from the chart in exercise **A**. Use the future progressive, the future perfect, and the future perfect progressive. Add *not* when necessary. More than one form is sometimes correct.

1. Hiro / send in his application / by the end of May

   Hiro won't have sent in his application by the end of May.

2. Jamal / do an internship / in August
3. Alex / finish his online classes / by January
4. Hiro / start a job search / later this year
5. Alex / work as an urban designer / in two years
6. Hiro / start his own company / in ten years

CD1-29

C Look at the chart in exercise **A** again. Then listen to the conversation. Circle the name of the person Sarah is talking to.

a. Alex   b. Jamal   c. Hiro

D In your notebook, write six sentences about the information from the conversation in exercise **C**. Use the phrases from the box and the future forms from this unit. Add *not* when necessary.

get a part-time job	make contacts	work on application
get some experience	take a year off	write full time

He will have made some good contacts by November.

Charts
3.1–3.6

3 EDIT. Read the blog. Find and correct eight more errors with future forms.

        ↙ It's going to work

    I finally have a plan for the future. ~~It is going to have worked~~ like this. Next week, I'm

starting my application for graduate school. I'm studying urban planning. At the end of

the month, I will sending in the application. While I'm going to wait for a response, I'm

going to do an internship. That will be between June and December. Hopefully, I'll start

classes in January. By the time I will graduate in two years, I'll take a variety of courses.

They will prepare me for the job market, and hopefully in ten years I'll be working as

an urban engineer for several years. In fifteen years, I will have been starting my own

company. At least, that's the plan right now.

Charts
3.1–3.6

4 SPEAK. Work with a partner. Discuss a plan you have for the future. It can be a plan about your studies, your job, or your family life.

Next year, my husband and I are going to buy a house.

Connect the Grammar to Writing

1 READ & NOTICE THE GRAMMAR.

A What do you want cars to do in the future? Tell a partner your ideas. Then read the text.

The Car of the *Future*

For many people in the world, having a car is a basic necessity, but it is a dangerous one. The World Health Organization estimates that 1.2 million people die each year in traffic accidents. Right now, the technology for self-driving cars exists, but not many people are taking it seriously. I hope that they will very soon. I strongly believe that self-driving cars are going to help us greatly in the future for two reasons: safety and productivity.

I believe that the cars of the future will be much safer because humans won't be driving them. Self-driving cars will take bad drivers, such as irresponsible teenagers and drunk drivers, off the road. They will also eliminate human error such as falling asleep at the wheel. In a generation or two, I think traffic fatalities[1] will have become a thing of the past.

Self-driving cars will also make the time we spend on the road more productive. For example, while we're sitting in traffic, we can read or study. This will help us to use our time more effectively. We will be more relaxed and happier, too.

Some people think that self-driving cars will never become popular, but I disagree. Once people realize how many lives can be saved by this technology, and how much more free time they will have, they will no longer want to drive themselves. When self-driving cars become available, everyone is going to want one.

[1] **fatality:** a death resulting from an accident, disease, natural disaster, or war

GRAMMAR FOCUS

In the text, the writer uses future forms and time clauses to make predictions and talk about future actions or events.

The writer uses *be going to* and *will* to make predictions.

> *I strongly believe that self-driving cars* **are going to help** *us . . . ; . . . cars of the future* **will be** *much safer . . .*

The writer uses future time clauses to talk about when future actions or events will happen.

> **When self-driving cars become available,** *everyone is going to want one.*

The writer uses the future perfect to talk about future actions or events that will be completed before a specific time in the future.

> *In a generation or two, . . . traffic fatalities* **will have become** *. . . .*

B Read the text in exercise **A** again. Find one more example of each of the following: *will, be going to,* and a future time clause. Then work with a partner and compare your answers.

C Complete the chart with the writer's ideas from the text in exercise **A**. Then work with a partner and compare your answers.

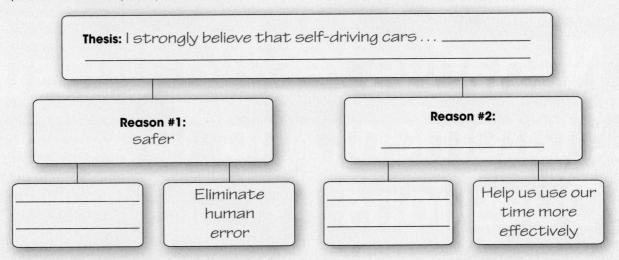

Thesis: I strongly believe that self-driving cars . . . _____
_____

Reason #1:
safer

Reason #2:
_____

_____ | Eliminate human error | _____ | Help us use our time more effectively

2 BEFORE YOU WRITE.

A Choose a current form of technology, such as cell phones. What are your predictions about this topic? Brainstorm a list of your ideas. Then share your ideas with a partner.

B In your notebook, make a chart like the one in exercise **1C**. Write a thesis statement and at least two reasons with examples to support it.

> **WRITING FOCUS** Using *Believe*, *Think*, and *Hope*
>
> Notice how *believe*, *think*, and *hope* are used in the text in exercise **1A**.
>
> Use *believe* and *think* to express opinions.
>
> > *I strongly believe* that self-driving cars are going to help us greatly . . .
> >
> > *Some people think* that self-driving cars will never become popular . . .
>
> Use *hope* to express a wish or desire.
>
> > *I hope* that they will (take them seriously) very soon.

3 WRITE your predictions and opinion about your topic. Write two or three paragraphs. Use your chart from exercise **2B** and the text in exercise **1A** to help you.

4 SELF ASSESS. Read your text again and underline the future forms. Then use the checklist to assess your work.

☐ I used the future with *will* and *be going to* correctly. [3.1]

☐ I used the simple present in future time clauses. [3.3]

☐ I used the future perfect correctly. [3.6]

☐ I used *believe*, *think*, and *hope* to express opinions or wishes. [WRITING FOCUS]

Negative *Yes/No* Questions; Statement and Tag Questions

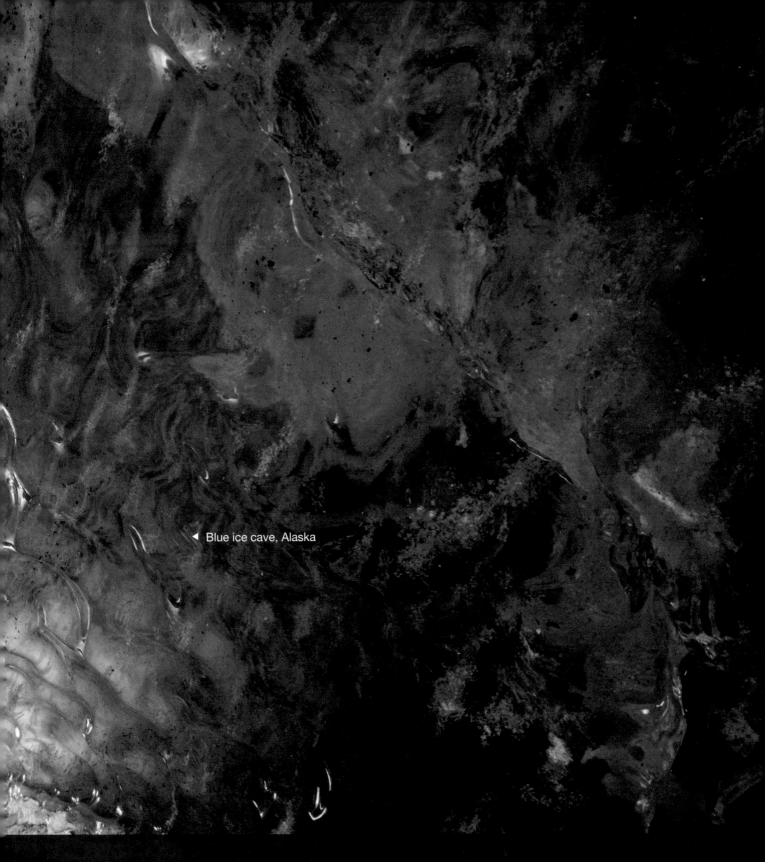

◀ Blue ice cave, Alaska

EXPLORE

CD1-30

1 **READ** the blog about how scientists are preparing for future travel to Mars. What are some of the challenges that the astronauts will face?

NORTH AMERICA
Utah, USA

MARS ON EARTH

Marta Mirsky 8 hours ago

It will be many years before humans can safely go to Mars, but space scientists have already begun to prepare. They've been trying to figure out what astronauts will need for extended stays on the red planet. One research project—the Mars Desert Research Station—is right here on Earth. The station is located in a remote[1] desert area in Utah in the United States, and the crew[2] members experience challenges similar to those they would face on Mars. The crew works closely with a space psychologist.[3] In fact, psychology, more than aerospace engineering, may be the key to sending human crews to Mars.

spacecrazy115   6 hours ago

So life on Mars can drive you crazy?

> **Reply**
>
> Sure. Think of the tight living space, the lack of privacy, and the stress of working together every day. The crew has to be able to handle all that.

martianhead   4 hours ago

Isn't another challenge the special suits they have to wear?

> **Reply**
>
> Yes, those suits have many parts and they take hours to put on! But they're essential.[4] They protect the astronauts from radiation when they go out to explore.

redplanetlover   1 hour ago

Don't the astronauts start to feel claustrophobic in the research station? I wouldn't want to work in such a small, crowded space.

> **Reply**
>
> Yes, after a while, it becomes very uncomfortable. In addition, the work is hard, and the crew is under a lot of pressure to get everything done.

martianhead   20 minutes ago

I guess that's why they need a psychologist?

> **Reply**
>
> That's part of the reason. The research project presents many challenges, and the astronauts need someone to help them to deal with everything.

[1] **remote:** far away from where most people live

[2] **crew:** the people who work on and operate a ship or spacecraft

[3] **psychologist:** someone who studies how the mind works

[4] **essential:** extremely important or absolutely necessary

2 CHECK. Answer the questions. Write complete sentences.

1. Where is the Mars Desert Research Station? _____

   _____

2. What kind of doctor helps the crew of astronauts? _____

   _____

3. What do the astronauts have to do before they go out to explore? _____

   _____

4. What are some of the challenges that astronauts have to deal with? _____

   _____

3 DISCOVER. Complete the exercises to learn about the grammar in this lesson.

A Find these sentences from the blog in exercise **1**. Write the missing punctuation—a question mark (?) or a period (.).

1. So life on Mars can drive you crazy

2. Isn't another challenge the special suits they have to wear

3. Don't the astronauts start to feel claustrophobic in the research station

4. I guess that's why they need a psychologist

B Look at the sentences in exercise **A** and answer the questions. Write the number of each sentence next to the correct statement.

1. These questions have the same word order as statements. ____, ____

2. These questions begin with negative contractions (-*n't*) ____, ____

▲ Surface of the planet Mars

LEARN

4.1 Negative *Yes/No* Questions

Negative *Yes/No* Questions	Answers
Aren't you going to class?	Yes, I'll be there. / No, I'm busy today.
Didn't she know the answer?	Yes, of course she did. / No. She had no idea.
Haven't you seen the news?	Yes, I have. / No, I haven't. What happened?
Isn't she a teacher?	Yes, she is. / No, she isn't.

1. Contract *not* to *n't* and add it to the end of the auxiliary verb* or the main verb *be* in a negative *Yes/No* question.	**Isn't** he a student? **Aren't** you **going** to class? **Didn't** she **know** the answer?
2. A negative *Yes/No* question is often used instead of an affirmative one when the speaker:	
a. expects or wants the answer to be *yes*	a. **Wasn't** that a terrible movie?
b. wants to check that information is correct	b. **Isn't** Lima the capital of Peru?
c. is annoyed	c. **Aren't** you going to say hello?
d. is surprised	d. **Haven't** you finished the book yet?
3. **Be careful!** The answers to negative and affirmative *Yes/No* questions are the same.	A: **Isn't** your house nearby? B: Yes, it is. / No, it isn't. A: **Is** your house nearby? B: Yes, it is. / No, it isn't.

* An auxiliary verb is used with a main verb. *Be, do, have, will*, and modals are auxiliary verbs. Auxiliary verbs are also called *helping verbs*.

4 Complete the exercises.

A Read the statements about space travel and underline the verbs. Then tell a partner which statements you believe are true and false.

Common Beliefs about Space Travel

1. The first person in space <u>was</u> American.

2. Space travel began in the 1960s.

3. The first astronaut stepped on the moon in 1969.

4. There have been trips to Mars already.

5. Space travel is expensive.

6. All objects are weightless in space.

7. Life in a space station seems exciting.

8. Everyone wants to travel to the moon.

▲ The NASA/ESA Hubble Space Telescope

B Write a negative question for each statement in exercise **A**.

1. <u>Wasn't the first person in space American?</u>

2. _____

3. _____

4. _____

5. _____

6. _____

7. _____

8. _____

CD1-31

C Choose the correct answer to the questions in exercise **B**. Then listen and check your answers.

1. a. Yes, it was not an American.   (b.) No, it was a Russian named Yuri Gagarin.

2. a. Yes, it began in the 1950s.   b. No, it actually began in the 1950s.

3. a. Yes, it was on July 21, 1969.   b. No, it was on July 21, 1969.

4. a. Yes, people haven't gone there yet.   b. No, nobody has gone there yet.

5. a. Yes, it's extremely expensive.   b. No, it's extremely expensive.

6. a. Yes, they float around in the air.   b. No, they float around in the air.

7. a. Yes, it seems amazing.   b. No, it seems really interesting.

8. a. Yes, I don't think so.   b. No, I don't think so.

4.2 Statement Questions

1. A statement question is a *yes/no* question with statement word order. Answers to statement questions are the same as to regular *yes/no* questions.	A: **That's the teacher?** B: **Yeah.** A: **Is that the teacher?** B: **Yeah.**

2. Statement questions are used:
  a. to check information
  b. to repeat and confirm information
  c. to show surprise or express annoyance
	a. **Your address is 22 Main Street?**
	b. **The lecture isn't on Friday?**
	c. **We're having fish again?**

3. Statement questions are more common in informal conversations. When using a statement question, the speaker expects the listener to agree with the statement.	A: **You went to the concert last night?** B: **Yes!** It was terrific! A: **You don't like the soup?** B: **No,** not really.
4. The speaker's voice usually rises at the end of a statement question.	The meeting is going to take five hours? ↗

5 LISTEN & SPEAK.

CD1-32

A Listen to the sentences. Add a question mark (?) if the sentence is a statement question and a period (.) if the sentence is a statement. There are six statement questions.

1. There's a Mars research station on Earth?

2. The training at the station isn't for everyone

3. There are people who specialize in space psychology

4. Astronauts haven't gone to Mars yet

5. It will take years for humans to travel to Mars

6. It takes longer to travel to Mars than to the moon

7. We aren't going to read about other planets

8. We have to learn all this information about Mars

CD1-33

B Match the six statement questions in exercise **A** with the correct responses below. Write the numbers on the lines. Then listen and check your answers.

_____ a. Yes, the moon is much closer to Earth.   _____ d. Yes, but I'm sure you'll find it interesting.

_____ b. Yes, but there aren't many.   _____ e. No, not this semester.

__1__ c. Yes. It's located in a desert.   _____ f. No. No humans have gone there.

▼ Artist's concept of NASA Mars Science Laboratory Curiosity rover, a mobile robot for investigating Mars

PRACTICE

6 Complete the exercises.

A Complete the conversation about a Pacific Ocean expedition. Write statement questions or negative questions with the words in parentheses.

Reporter: You traveled all that distance in a canoe. (1) _You weren't_____
(you / not be) afraid?
Statement Question

Explorer: Not really. I had done a lot of training before the journey.

Reporter: Yes, I think I read about that. (2) _____ (you / train) for
months to get ready? Negative Question

Explorer: Yes, I did. I had to be in excellent physical condition.

Reporter: Right. It would not be possible otherwise. But still . . .

(3) _____ (it / be) hard?
Negative Question

Explorer: Yes. It sure was. This kind of trip is not for everybody. Some people get lonely.

Reporter: What about for you? (4) _____ (it / not get) lonely?
Statement Question

Explorer: No, not for me. It was quiet, and I had a lot of time to think.

Reporter: How about the weather? Were there storms?

Explorer: Sometimes, but I was ready for them.

Reporter: (5) _____ (you / be) ever afraid?
Negative Question

Explorer: Not really. I had some good maps so I knew what I was doing. I can't wait to go
out again.

Reporter: (6) _____ (you / plan) another trip already?
Statement Question

Explorer: Yes, I am. In fact, I'm training for it now.

Reporter: You're kidding. (7) _____ (you / be) tired of the ocean by now?
Negative Question

Explorer: No, I'm not. I love it.

B Listen and check your answers.
CD1-34

7 Complete the exercises.

A Read the statements about early Polynesian explorers. Add a question mark to make a
statement question. Then write a negative question for each statement question.

1. The Polynesians were skilled explorers?

   Weren't the Polynesians skilled explorers?

2. It took only a short time to travel from Tahiti to Hawaii

   _____

   _____

3. The Polynesians discovered Hawaii and many other islands

_____

_____

4. The Polynesians traded with islanders thousands of miles away

_____

_____

5. Today's researchers are trying to find out how far the Polynesians traveled

_____

_____

B Work with a partner. Take turns reading each pair of questions.

C Look at the map and read the paragraph about Polynesian explorers. Which ocean did they sail on?

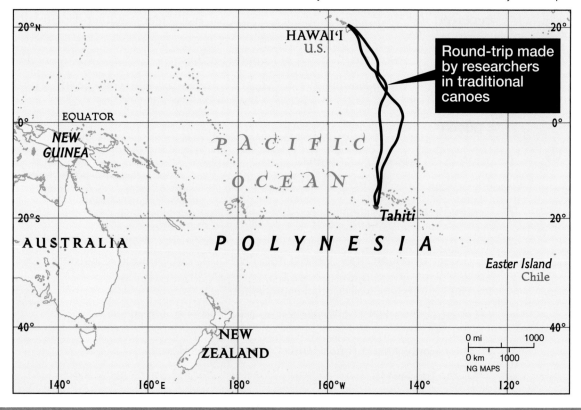

Polynesian Explorers

More than a thousand years ago, the Polynesians were skilled explorers of the Pacific Ocean. They sailed all over the South Pacific, including an extremely long journey from Tahiti to Hawaii. In addition to Hawaii, the Polynesians discovered many other islands, and they began trading goods[1] with the people on those islands, too. Why were the Polynesians so successful? Researchers today are trying to find out.

[1] **goods:** items that can be bought or sold

▼ Modern-day scientists follow an ancient route of Polynesian explorers.

A Polynesian canoe

D In your notebook, write the answer to each question in exercise **A** according to the information from the text in exercise **C**.

1. Yes, they were. They sailed all over the South Pacific.

8 LISTEN.

CD1-35

A Listen to the questions that a student asks his professor about the early Polynesians. Then read the responses. Which response do you think the professor will give? Choose the correct answer.

1. a. No, that's what the research shows.

   b. Yes, that's what the research shows.

2. a. No, they didn't. They had smaller boats called canoes.

   b. Yes, they did. They traveled in smaller boats called canoes.

3. a. No. They needed the wind.

   b. Yes. They waited for strong winds before they began their journeys.

4. a. Yes. They used the stars to find their way.

   b. No. They followed the direction of the stars.

5. a. No. They traveled in canoes.

   b. Yes. They didn't use sailboats.

6. a. No. They have proof.

   b. Yes. The proof is ancient Polynesian tools in Hawaii.

7. a. No. Hawaii is thousands of miles from Tahiti.

   b. Yes. Hawaii is thousands of miles from Tahiti.

8. a. No. They never had trouble.

   b. Yes. They never got lost.

CD1-36

B Listen to the full conversation and check your answers in exercise **A**.

▲ 1. Stonehenge

▲ 2. the Statue of Liberty

▲ 3. the Pyramid of the Sun

9 APPLY.

A Work with a partner. Look at the photos of famous places and match them with their locations. Ask and answer negative questions and statement questions about each place.

_____ 1. Stonehenge   a. New York City

_____ 2. The Statue of Liberty   b. Great Britain

_____ 3. The Pyramid of the Sun   c. Mexico

A: *Isn't that Stonehenge?*

B: *Yeah, it's that place in Great Britain with the mysterious stones.*

B Match the famous places in exercise **A** with the descriptions below. Then ask and answer negative and statement questions about each place.

a. It has around 250 steps. __3__

b. It's on an island. _____

c. It was built by the Aztecs. _____

d. It is over 500 years old. _____

e. It's over 5000 years old. _____

f. There are stones in a circle there. _____

A: *Isn't Stonehenge on an island?*

B: *Well, Stonehenge is in Great Britain, and that is an island. But what about the Statue of Liberty?*

C Work in a group. Tell your group the name of a famous place you have visited. The students in your group will then ask you negative and statement questions about the place. Can you answer all of the questions?

A: *I have been to St. Petersburg, Russia.*

B: *Interesting. Isn't there a famous museum there?*

A: *Yes. It's called the Hermitage.*

C: *You've been to St. Peterburg? I've always wanted to go there!*

EXPLORE

CD1-37

1 READ the information on the website about Børge Ousland. Then read the conversation between two friends below. Why do they enjoy videos about Ousland?

Børge Ousland, NORWEGIAN EXPLORER

Børge Ousland's solo crossing of the North Pole was a great challenge. Pulling a heavy sledge of food and fuel, he covered 1240 miles (1996 kilometers) by walking, skiing, and even swimming. Alone in the icy Arctic for 82 days, Ousland faced many problems—a broken sledge, thin ice, bad snowstorms, polar bears—but he never gave up.

Birthplace: Oslo, Norway

First Occupation: Deep-sea diver

First Expedition: Ski trip across Greenland

Favorite Expedition: First solo trip to the North Pole

Other Passions: Fishing, sailing, and everything that relates to nature

Favorite Use of Free Time: Being with friends and family

Concerns: Global warming and the loss of Arctic ice

Jeff:	Hey, what are you doing?
Flavio:	Just watching this guy Børge Ousland. There are some great videos of him online. You've seen some of them, **haven't you?**
Jeff:	Yeah. The guy is unbelievable! Did you see the one where he's swimming in the Arctic Ocean?
Flavio:	No, I missed that one. It didn't show this sledge, **did it?**
Jeff:	I think there was a quick shot of it. He was pulling 365 pounds of stuff everywhere . . . with all that snow blowing around. He's really incredible, **isn't he?**
Flavio:	Uh-huh. And the sledge broke at one point, too.
Jeff:	You're kidding! What did he do?
Flavio:	Well, he tried to repair it, but he couldn't, so he called for a new one. And he kept going.
Jeff:	He's not afraid of anything, **is he?**
Flavio:	No, definitely not. Do you remember that scene with the polar bears?
Jeff:	Yeah, that was great, **wasn't it?** That mother with her cubs looked so angry.

▶ Winter solstice during an Arctic expedition a few miles from the North Pole

2 CHECK. Read the statements. Circle **T** for *true* or **F** for *false*.

1. Børge Ousland is a Canadian explorer. **T** **F**

2. You can watch videos of Ousland's trip online. **T** **F**

3. Ousland fixed his sledge when it broke. **T** **F**

4. Ousland walked the whole way across the Arctic. **T** **F**

5. Ousland spends his free time with friends and family. **T** **F**

3 DISCOVER. Complete the exercises to learn about the grammar in this lesson.

A Underline the verbs in the sentences from the conversation in exercise **1** on page 101. Then complete each sentence with the missing words.

1. You've seen some of them, __haven't you__ ?

2. It didn't show this sledge, _____ ?

3. He's really incredible, _____ ?

4. Yeah, that was great, _____ ?

B Look at the sentences in exercise **A**. Notice the patterns with the main verb and auxiliary verb forms. Then check (✓) the two correct rules.

_____ 1. The main verb and auxiliary forms are either both affirmative or both negative.

_____ 2. If the main verb form is affirmative, the auxiliary form is negative.

_____ 3. If the main verb form is negative, the auxiliary form is affirmative.

◄ A man pulls a sled through a blizzard (North Polar Ice Cap, Arctic Ocean)

LEARN

4.3 Tag Questions

Negative Tag Question	
Affirmative Statement	Negative Tag
Vanessa **is** the teacher,	**isn't** she?
Class **starts** at 1:30,	**doesn't** it?
Carla and Luca **came** yesterday,	**didn't** they?
You'**ve** read that book,	**haven't** you?

Affirmative Tag Question	
Negative Statement	Affirmative Tag
Philip **isn't** the writer,	**is** he?
The test **doesn't start** at 1:30,	**does** it?
Matt and Fran **didn't come**,	**did** they?
They **haven't arrived** yet,	**have** they?

1. Tag questions are used to ask someone to agree with or confirm information. A tag question is a statement with a two-word tag (auxiliary verb + pronoun) at the end. A comma is always used before a tag.	A: That was a hard test, **wasn't it?** B: Yeah, it was really hard. (agreement) A: Carlos is from Mexico, **isn't he?** B: Yes, he is. (confirmation)
2. If the statement is affirmative, the auxiliary in the tag is negative. If the statement is negative, the auxiliary in the tag is affirmative.	The Smiths **are going** home, **aren't** they? The Smiths **haven't come** home, **have** they?
3. Use *doesn't, don't,* and *didn't* in the tag with simple present and simple past affirmative statements that have verbs other than *be.*	Pedro **likes** the school, **doesn't he?** Gina and Tim **play** a lot of sports, **don't they?** Mariko already **saw** the movie, **didn't she?**
4. The pronoun in the tag matches the subject. If *there is/there are* is used in the statement, use *there* in the tag.	<u>Carole</u> **is** a hard worker, isn't **she**? Subject Pronoun **There aren't** any eggs, are **there?**

4 Complete the tag questions about the Arctic. Use the tags from the box.

aren't there	doesn't it	do we	haven't they	isn't it
didn't they	don't they	hasn't he	isn't he	~~wasn't it~~

1. Børge Ousland's experience in the Arctic was different from his normal life, ___wasn't it___ ?

2. Ousland is worried about global warming, _____ ?

3. He has seen how warming temperatures are affecting Arctic ice, _____ ?

4. The Arctic is warming twice as fast as the rest of the planet, _____ ?

5. Scientists have collected a lot of information about sea ice, _____ ?

6. They used radar to show snow and ice thickness, _____ ?

7. There are many different types of ice, _____ ?

8. Arctic explorers have to wear many layers of warm clothing, _____ ?

9. The Arctic has one of the most extreme climates on Earth, _____ ?

10. We don't know exactly what will happen to Arctic ice in the future, _____ ?

4.4 Answering Tag Questions

1. When the statement in a tag question is affirmative, the speaker expects the answer to be affirmative.	A: You **are coming** to the party, aren't you? B: **Yes, I am.**
When the statement in a tag question is negative, the speaker expects the answer to be negative.	A: You **haven't eaten** lunch yet, have you? B: **No, I haven't.**
2. When the listener disagrees with the speaker or answers in an unexpected way, there is often an explanation.	A: Ahmed is from Egypt, isn't he? B: No, **he's from Canada.**
3. **Be careful!** The answers to tag questions and affirmative *Yes/No* questions are the same. It does not matter whether the tag is negative or affirmative.	A: Is Jim happy? B: Yes, he is. / No, he isn't. A: Jim is happy, isn't he? B: Yes, he is. / No, he isn't. A: Jim isn't happy, is he? B: Yes, he is. / No, he isn't.

5 Complete the interview with an explorer. Write *Yes* or *No*.

1. A: The life of an explorer is difficult, isn't it?

    B: _Yes_. It's hard, but it's very exciting.

2. A: Your journeys require a lot of planning, don't they?

    B: _____, I plan for months, and sometimes even years.

3. A: You take other people with you on these journeys, don't you?

    B: _____, most of the time I have two or three people with me.

4. A: There isn't a lot of free time, is there?

    B: _____, there's always something to do. We're busy all day long.

5. A: You're working on a new project now, aren't you?

    B: _____, I'm making plans for a trip next year.

6. A: You didn't get hurt on your last expedition, did you?

    B: _____. I didn't have any problems last time.

7. A: An expedition usually costs a lot of money, doesn't it?

    B: _____, supplies and equipment are very expensive.

8. A: You miss your family during these expeditions, don't you?

    B: _____, very much.

9. A: You don't go on more than one expedition a year, do you?

    B: _____, definitely not.

10. A: Your last journey was to the Gobi Desert, wasn't it?

    B: _____, I went to the Sahara Desert.

PRACTICE

6 Complete the exercises.

A Complete the conversation at a meeting of the Young Explorers Club. Write the missing tags.

Leon: You're new here, (1) _aren't you_ ?

Yuri: Yeah. I joined the club last month. It's a lot of fun, (2) _____ ?

Leon: I love it. Have you done any of the activities yet?

Yuri: Uh-huh. I did the cave trip two weeks ago.

Leon: Really? I did that one, too. That was great, (3) _____ ?

Yuri: Yeah. It was awesome. I didn't see you there. You weren't with the first group, (4) _____ ?

Leon: No, I was with the second. Hey, you probably don't know many people here, (5) _____ ?

Yuri: Not really.

Leon: OK. Let me tell you about some of them. That's Vera over there.

Yuri: Right. She collects spiders, (6) _____ ?

Leon: Really? How did you know that?

Yuri: She was in my group on the trip. I heard her talking about her spiders. They're a strange thing to collect, but she seemed really nice.

Leon: Look. She's coming over here. Let me introduce you. Hi, Vera. You haven't met Yuri, (7) _____ ?

Vera: I haven't met you, but I remember you. You were on the cave trip two weeks ago, (8) _____ ?

Yuri: Yeah. We were in the same group. So, how are your spiders?

Vera: They're great. I have one with me. You're not afraid of them, (9) _____ ?

▲ A Usofila cave spider

B Work with a partner. Compare your answers from exercise **A**.

7 **PRONUNCIATION.** Read the chart and listen to the examples. Then complete the exercises.

🎧
CD1-38

PRONUNCIATION	Intonation in Tag Questions

The intonation in a tag question helps the listener understand the meaning of the question.

1. When the voice falls at the end of a tag question, the speaker is certain about the answer and expects the listener to agree.	A: This is a terrific party, **isn't it?** B: Yeah. It's great!
2. When the voice rises at the end of a tag question, the speaker is not certain about the answer and wants to confirm that something is true.	A: You invited Paul to the party, **didn't you?** B: No, I forgot. Sorry.

◀ a Maya cave painting

A Listen to each interview question for an explorer. Does the speaker expect agreement or confirmation? Check (✓) the correct box.

CD1-39

	Agreement	Confirmation
1. It's very hot in the Maya caves, isn't it?	☐	✓
2. The Maya lived thousands of years ago, didn't they?	☐	☐
3. There were many interesting things in the caves, weren't there?	☐	☐
4. The cave paintings are unusual, aren't they?	☐	☐
5. We can learn a lot about the Maya from the paintings, can't we?	☐	☐
6. You don't know the meaning of the symbols on the walls, do you?	☐	☐
7. You needed the help of the local people to find the caves, didn't you?	☐	☐
8. There isn't a lot of information about Maya cave traditions, is there?	☐	☐

B Match each response with the correct question in exercise **A**. Write the number of the question on the line. Then listen and check your answers.

CD1-40

__7__ a. Yes, of course. They know the area very well.

_____ b. Yes, they're very unusual.

_____ c. No, not yet. We hope to figure out the meaning soon.

_____ d. No, actually the temperature is very comfortable.

_____ e. In fact, there is quite a lot. There are many books on the subject.

_____ f. Yes, and there are Maya people today who live in southern Mexico and parts of Central America.

_____ g. Yes, the artwork is full of information about how the Maya lived.

_____ h. Yes, many amazing things.

C Work with a partner. Ask and answer the questions in exercises **A** and **B**. Be sure to use the correct intonation.

8 LISTEN & SPEAK.

A Read the conversations. Does the speaker ask the question to confirm facts? Or does the speaker expect the listener to agree? Write *C* (confirm) or *A* (agree).

__A__ 1. A: Rock climbing seems dangerous, doesn't it?

   B: That's why I don't want to do it.

_____ 2. A: The view is beautiful, isn't it?

   B: It's gorgeous.

_____ 3. A: We start the hike tomorrow at eight o'clock, don't we?

   B: No, eight-thirty.

_____ 4. A: The climb was hard, wasn't it?

   B: Yeah, unbelievably hard.

_____ 5. A: There's plenty of water, isn't there?

   B: Let me check.

_____ 6. A: We're going to stop at four o'clock, aren't we?

   B: I'm not sure, but we stopped at four o'clock last time.

CD1-41

B Listen to the conversations in exercise **A** and check your answers.

9 Work with a partner. Read the conversations. Find eight more places where the speaker expects the listener to agree. Change those sentences to tag questions.

1. **Sandy:** The weather's great today ~~x~~ ,isn't it?

   Jessica: It's beautiful. And there are a lot of people here.

   Sandy: Yeah. I never knew so many people loved rock climbing.

   Jessica: We're going to see some great views today.

   Sandy: I hope so.

> People climbing the Eve Tooth rock formation in the Needles

REAL ENGLISH

Tag questions are often used to start conversations or to keep conversations going. Some topics that people talk about include the weather and their current surroundings.

It's a beautiful day, isn't it?
The band sounds great, doesn't it?

107

2. **Ray:**   Have we met before?

   Hamid: Right. We were in the same map and compass training course last month.

   Ray: Oh yeah. I remember now. That was hard.

   Hamid: It really was. But I don't think I'll ever get lost again.

   Ray: Me neither!

3. **Gisela:**   This climb can't get any harder.

   Luca: I hope not. We've walked through a lot of dangerous spots already.

   Gisela: I know. I'll be glad when it's over.

   Luca: The next mile is going to be the last hard part.

   Gisela: I think so. After that, the trail gets easier.

10 APPLY.

A Think of eight different ways to start a conversation with people at a party or other event. Use topics such as names, hometowns, weather, sports, the news, entertainment, school, or work. Write a statement to complete each tag question.

1. _____, aren't you?

2. _____, don't you?

3. _____, aren't there?

4. _____, isn't it?

5. _____, doesn't it?

6. _____, do you?

7. _____, are you?

8. _____, is there?

B Imagine that you are at a party. Stand up and walk around the room. Ask your classmates questions from exercise **A**.

A: *Hi, you're Yuri, aren't you?*

B: *Yeah, that's right. And your name is Jenny, isn't it?*

A: *That's right. You're from Russia, aren't you?*

Charts
4.1, 4.3–4.4

1 READ, WRITE & SPEAK.

A Read the fact sheet below and underline eight facts. Then write a negative question and a tag question for each fact.

Valley of the Khans Project Fact Sheet

Mongolia

ASIA

- Dr. Albert Lin is the creator of the *Valley of the Khans* project. He wants to help the Mongolian people locate Genghis Khan's tomb.

- Genghis Khan was the founder of the Mongol Empire, the largest land empire in history. He lived in the thirteenth century.

- Mongolians do not know the exact location of Genghis Khan's burial site.

- Genghis Khan conquered many different parts of Asia after years of war. He brought all these parts under one government.

- People from Mongolia honor the memory of Genghis Khan. He was the first ruler of their country.

◄ Dr. Albert Lin

Isn't Dr. Albert Lin the creator of the Valley of the Khans project?

Dr. Albert Lin is the creator of the Valley of the Khans project, isn't he?

B Work with a partner. Ask and answer the questions you wrote in exercise **A**.

Charts
4.1–4.4

CD1-42

2 LISTEN, SPEAK & WRITE.

A Listen to a radio interview with two volunteers who work on Dr. Lin's project. What kind of work is Dr. Lin doing? Take notes in your notebook.

B Work with a partner. Share your notes from exercise **A**. Discuss any other information you remember from the interview.

CD1-43

C Read each *Yes/No* question. Does the radio host ask this question as a statement question (S), a negative question (N), or a tag question (T)? Listen again and write *S*, *N*, or *T* for each question. Then edit the sentence to match.

            You're   aren't you?

1.   __T__ ~~Are you~~ working on Dr. Albert Lin's project?

2.   _____ Is the use of technology especially important in Mongolia?

3.   _____ Does Lin's team of explorers ever disturb the ground?

4.   _____ Do you do this right from your home computers?

5.   _____ Is Mongolia enormous?

CD1-43

D Listen again. Write the answer to each question from exercise **C**.

1. _____

2. _____

3. _____

4. _____

5. _____

◄ Some people believe that this rock shrine marks the burial place of Genghis Khan.

3 **EDIT.** Read the conversation. Find and correct seven more errors with questions and answers.

                                                                             aren't you

A: You're here for information about our University Explorers Club, ~~isn't it~~?

B: Yes. By the way, I'm only 18. I'm not too young for the program, do I?

A: No, you're not too young. The program is for anyone between the ages of 18 and 25.

B: I don't need a college degree?

A: Yes. A college degree is not necessary, but previous exploration experience is. You have some experience, do you?

B: Yes. Here is a list of the projects I've worked on.

A: You can keep that. First, you need to complete the application online.

B: Do not you want to see my list of projects?

A: No, I don't need to see anything. You're going to list your projects in your application.

B: There isn't a deadline, is it?

A: Yes. You can apply all year long.

B: And the application is online?

A: Yes, it is.

B: It isn't difficult to find, was it?

A: No. It's at the very top of the website. You can't miss it.

4 **WRITE & SPEAK.**

A Think of a nearby area to explore. In your notebook, write three negative questions and three tag questions about exploring the area.

You've been to Wildforest Park, haven't you?

B Work with a partner. Take turns asking and answering your questions from exercise **A**.

A: *You've been to Wildforest Park, haven't you?*

B: *Yes, I have. I went there once.*

A: *Doesn't it have some beautiful trails?*

B: *Yes, they're great. I'd like to go again sometime.*

Connect the Grammar to Writing

1 READ & NOTICE THE GRAMMAR.

A Read the short scene and visualize how it would look for a TV show or movie. Discuss your ideas with a partner.

The Great Maya Cave Quest

Characters: (1) Pierre L'Aventure, an archaeologist and adventurer

(2) Rosa Delacruz, Pierre's former coworker, an archaeologist

Situation: Pierre has not seen Rosa for ten years. He wants to find a hidden Maya cave. He thinks that there is a map in an old book that she owns. He goes to ask her if he can borrow it.

Scene: Rosa is at work putting books away. Suddenly, she hears a familiar voice behind her.

"Hello, Rosa," says Pierre. Rosa turns around in surprise.

"Pierre? You're here?" she cries out angrily.

"Yes, I am," he says. "What's wrong? Aren't you happy to see me again?"

Rosa does not answer. She only glares at him. Pierre continues, "I actually came to see you because I want to borrow something from you."

"You want to borrow something?" Rosa asks in disbelief.

"Yes—" Pierre starts to say, but then Rosa turns away and grumbles, "Don't you remember? You got that archaeology grant[1] instead of me. It wasn't fair!"

"You're not still upset about that, are you?" he asks.

"Yes, I am still upset about it. It was completely unfair," says Rosa, still angry.

"Look," says Pierre slowly, "I don't want to fight. I just want to borrow your old book about Maya caves. You know which book I'm talking about, don't you?"

Rosa looks surprised. She asks, "You want to borrow my Maya caves book? Why?"

"I can't explain," answers Pierre, "but it's important. You'll lend it to me, won't you?"

Rosa looks at him carefully for a minute. Then she continues putting books away as she says, "I'll think about it. Come back tomorrow."

[1]**grant:** money given for a specific purpose, such as research

GRAMMAR FOCUS

In this scene, the writer uses different questions to express emotions. For example:

Statement question: *"You're here?" she cries out.* (surprise)
Negative *yes/no* question: Rosa . . . grumbles, *"Don't you remember?"* (annoyance)
Tag question: *"You'll lend it to me, won't you?"* (expectancy)

B Read the scene in exercise **A** again. Underline one statement question, one negative *Yes/No* question, and a tag question. With a partner, decide which emotion the character is expressing with each question.

C Work with a partner. Look at the storyboard and tell your partner which part of the text in exercise **A** matches each picture. Draw a picture in the last square to match the scene. Then compare your drawings.

The Great Maya Cave Quest Storyboard

2 **BEFORE YOU WRITE.**

A Think of a scene in a movie or TV show in which two characters have an emotional conversation, or make up an imaginary scene. Draw four parts of the scene in your notebook. Use the storyboard in exercise **1C** as a model.

B Work with a partner. Share your storyboard from exercise **A** and describe the scene. Tell your partner what the characters are saying in each part.

WRITING FOCUS **Using Quotation Marks**

Notice how quotation marks ("...") and commas (,) are used in the story in exercise **1A**. Quotation marks are used around someone's exact words. Verbs such as *say* and *ask* often indicate quotes. Commas are used to separate the quote and the verb.

When the quote is first, put the comma inside the quotation marks and before the verb.
"Hello, Rosa," says Pierre.

When the quote is second, put the comma after the verb and outside of the quotation marks.
She asks, *"You want to borrow my old Mayan caves book? Why?"*

When the verb is in the middle of the quote, put the comma in both places.
"Look," says Pierre slowly, *"I don't want to fight. . . ."*

---

3 **WRITE** your scene as if it were part of a story. Make sure that the characters use the best question types to express their emotions. Use the scene from exercise **1A** and your storyboard from exercise **1C** to help you.

4 **SELF ASSESS.** Read your scene and underline the questions. Then use the checklist to assess your work.

- [ ] I used negative *Yes/No* questions and answers correctly. [4.1]
- [ ] I used statement questions correctly. [4.2]
- [ ] I used tag questions and answers correctly. [4.3, 4.4]
- [ ] I used commas and quotation marks correctly. [WRITING FOCUS]

Nouns, Articles, and Subject-Verb Agreement

◄ Navajo woman and girl stand in front of their hoja home in Nazlini, Arizona, USA.

EXPLORE

1 **READ** the web page about baby-naming traditions in different parts of the world. Are any of the customs similar to traditions in your culture or family?

Naming Customs

Naming a baby is an important **event** throughout the world, and different cultures have their own **traditions**. Just **a few examples** can demonstrate a wide variety of **customs**.

In Indonesia, Balinese children are named according to their birth order. Normally, **every** first-born **child** is named *Wayan* or *Putu*; the second child, *Made* or *Kadek*; the third child, *Nyoman* or *Komang*; and the fourth child, *Ketut*. The names can be given to either **boys** or **girls**, but there is a **way** to distinguish **gender**. Male **names** start with *I* and female **names** start with *Ni*. For example, *I Made* is the name of a second-born boy, and *Ni Ketut* is the name of a fourth-born girl.

The Luo people of East Africa typically give their newborns two names. The first is usually a Western name, and the second often refers to the **time**, the **weather**, or other **information** related to the day of the child's birth. For example, a baby boy born at night could be named Michael Otieno. *O* indicates "male," and *-tieno* means "night." A baby girl born on a rainy **day** might receive a name such as Vivianne Akoth. *A* indicates "female" and *-koth* is the word for "**rain**."

The Wikmungkan people of northeastern Australia conduct a naming **ceremony** during the **birth** of a baby. At the birth, the names of all the infant's living **relatives** are called out, one by one. The name that is called at the final stage of birth is the one that the baby receives. From that time on, there is a close **relationship** between the baby and the relative whose **name** the **newborn** shares.

◀ A father holds up his child, Bali, Indonesia.

2 CHECK. Read the statements. Circle **T** for *true* or **F** for *false*.

1. Balinese children's names are based on the order in which they are born.   **T**   **F**

2. The Balinese use *I* for the first-born child and *Ni* for the second-born.   **T**   **F**

3. A Luo baby's name often relates to the day the child was born.   **T**   **F**

4. In the Luo culture, *O* indicates male.   **T**   **F**

5. A Wikmungkan naming ceremony takes place after the birth of a baby.   **T**   **F**

3 DISCOVER. Complete the exercises to learn about the grammar in this lesson.

A Look at the underlined words in the sentences. Write **S** above the three singular count nouns, **P** above the three plural count nouns, and **NC** above the three non-count nouns.

1. The P
   names can be given to either boys or girls, but there is a way to distinguish gender.

2. . . . and the second often refers to the time, the weather, or other information related to the day of the child's of birth.

3. *A* indicates "female" and *-koth* is the word for "rain."

B Check (✓) the correct information about the nouns in exercise **A**.

	Singular Count Nouns (S)	Plural Count Nouns (P)	Non-Count Nouns (NC)
1. This type of noun cannot be plural.	☐	☐	☐
2. This type of noun follows *a/an*.	☐	☐	☐
3. This type of noun ends in *-s*.	☐	☐	☐

LEARN

5.1 Count and Non-Count Nouns

	Count Nouns	Non-Count Nouns
Singular	She wears that **necklace** every day. Is there a **copier** in the office? This English **assignment** looks hard.	She has beautiful **jewelry**. What **equipment** does the office need? The **homework** is pretty difficult.
Plural	She has two gold **necklaces**. Both **copiers** were broken. The **assignments** took a long time.	

1. Count nouns name things that can be counted. They have a singular and a plural form. To make most nouns plural, add *-s* or *-es*.*	We have a **son** at home and two **sons** in college. This **box** is small. Those **boxes** are large.
2. Non-count nouns name things that cannot be counted. They do not have plural forms. Use singular verbs and pronouns with non-count nouns.	Sugar **isn't** good for your teeth. ✓The information **is** interesting, isn't **it**? ✗ The informations <u>are</u> interesting, aren't <u>they</u>?
3. Do not use *a/an* before a non-count noun.	✓Do you have **homework** tonight? ✗ Do you have <u>a</u> homework tonight?
4. An abstract noun refers to an idea or quality rather than a physical object. Abstract nouns are usually non-count.	Feelings: **anger, happiness, hate, love** Ideas: **beauty, friendship, intelligence** School subjects: **art, history, math, science** Weather: **fog, rain, snow, sunshine, wind**
5. **Be careful!** Some nouns have both count and non-count meanings. Use the context to determine if the noun is countable or not.	He had a long **life**. / **Life** is wonderful. Here's a **glass** of water. / It's made of **glass**. Your horse is a **beauty**. / There's **beauty** in nature.

*See page **A2** for spelling rules for regular plural nouns.

4 Complete the paragraphs about naming traditions. Add a plural *-s/-es/-ies* when possible.

In China, (1) **girl** _____ often receive (2) **name** _____ that suggest (3) **beauty** _____.
(For example: *Mei Hua* means "beautiful flower.") (4) **Boy** _____ typically receive names that
represent (5) **health** _____ and (6) **strength** _____. (For example: *Gang* means "strong.") It is
customary to let some (7) **time** _____ pass before celebrating a (8) **birth** _____. Families have
parties called "Hundred Days" to celebrate the (9) **survival** _____ of (10) **baby** _____ during
the first three (11) **month** _____ of (12) **life** _____.

(13) **Buddhist** _____ in India name (14) **infant** _____ when they are certain that the baby
can hear. A (15) **mother** _____ writes the baby's name on a banana leaf and covers the leaf with
(16) **rice** _____. Then, she puts the baby on the leaf and whispers the name into the child's ear
three (17) **time** _____.

5 SPEAK. How do people in your country or culture choose names? Do you know where your name comes from? Discuss your answers with a partner.

A: *In my country, children are usually named after their parents or grandparents. I am named after my grandmother.*

B: *This is true in my country, too. I am named after my father.*

6 Complete the exercises.

A Read the non-count and count definitions of each noun in bold. Then complete each pair of sentences with *a*, *an*, or *Ø* for *no article*.

1. **light**   **Non-Count:** energy from the sun that lets you see things
                      Count: an electric lamp that produces light

   a. When I was a child, I always slept with __*a*__ light on.

   b. My house was filled with __*Ø*__ light every morning when the sun came up.

2. **appearance**   **Non-Count:** how someone looks and dresses
                      Count: an arrival of someone in a place

   a. My parents told me that intelligence is more important than _____ appearance.

   b. Once a famous person made _____ appearance at my school and talked to the students.

3. **paper**   **Non-Count:** thin, smooth material that you can write on or wrap things with
                      Count: a report or essay written by a student

   a. I always enjoyed making things out of _____ paper.

   b. I didn't know how to write _____ paper until high school.

4. **room**   **Non-Count:** enough empty space
                      Count: a separate area that has its own walls inside a building

   a. When I was young, I used to share _____ room with two siblings.

   b. At home, we didn't have _____ room for a lot of furniture.

5. **experience**   **Non-Count:** knowledge or skill in a particular job or activity
                      Count: something that happens to you

   a. I once had _____ very frightening experience.

   b. My babysitter had lots of _____ experience with children.

B SPEAK. Which sentences in exercise **A** are true for you? Tell a partner. Ask your partner follow-up questions for more information.

A: *Sentence 1a is true for me. When I was a child I always slept with a light on.*

B: *Really? Why?*

A: *I was afraid of the dark.*

5.2 Quantity Expressions with Count and Non-Count Nouns

Quantity Expressions	Singular Count Nouns	Plural Count Nouns	Non-Count Nouns
any, no	I'll read **any newspaper**. There is **no hotel** nearby.	Do you have **any ideas**? The store has **no eggs**.	I don't have **any advice**. He has **no patience**.
all, a lot of, lots of, more, most, some		I'll get **some candles**. Do **all babies** cry?	He has **more experience**. **Most fish** is good for you.
each, every, one	**Each photo** tells a story. **Every vote** counts.		
a couple of, a few, few, both, many		**Both parents** are here. Are there **many people**?	
a great deal of, a little, little, much			It's **a great deal of work**. There isn't **much time**.

1. A quantity expression is used before a noun to show the amount of the noun.

I got an e-mail from my friend. I get **a lot of e-mails** every day.

The blog posts are interesting. **Each blog post** is informative.

2. *Any* and *no* are negative in meaning. Use *any* with a negative verb. Use *no* with an affirmative verb.

Any can be used to mean *it doesn't matter which*.

They **haven't made any** progress.
They **have made no** progress.

Waiter: Would you like a table by the window?
Customer: **Any table** is fine. Thank you.

3. *A few* + a count noun and *a little* + a non-count noun mean *some*. They indicate a positive amount.

A few people have arrived. Let's begin.
We have **a little time**. Let's go for a walk.

4. *Few* + a count noun and *little* + a non-count noun mean *not many* or *not much*.

Few people went to the game. It was cold and windy.
We have **little time**. Let's take a taxi. It's faster.

5. **Be careful!** *Much* is not usually used in affirmative statements.

✓ His boss gave him **a lot of** praise for his work.
✗ His boss gave him <u>much</u> praise for his work.

7 Circle the correct words to complete the article.

Babies Recognize Faces Better Than Adults, Research Shows

Researchers believe that (1) **all** / **each** babies start out with an ability to recognize (2) **many** / **much** different faces. However, by nine months they lose the skill if they don't have practice. When babies have (3) **a couple of** / **some** training during their first few months, they are better at recognizing faces when they get older.

Researchers tested a group of six-month-old babies by showing them (4) **a little** / **some** photographs of monkeys' faces. Then, the infants were divided into two groups. One group of babies was shown the monkeys' faces again and again over the next three months, so those infants spent (5) **a lot of** / **much** time with the photos. The other group didn't see (6) **any** / **no** photos of the monkeys during the same three-month period.

After nine months, the researchers showed (7) **both / each** groups (8) **more / a great deal of** photos: some monkey faces that the babies had seen before and some new ones. The babies without training showed (9) **few / little** interest in the new faces, and they saw (10) **any / no** differences between the old and the new faces. However, the trained babies recognized the differences.

What did the study show? Babies that had had (11) **a few / some** training didn't lose their ability to recognize faces, but those with (12) **any / no** training lost this ability by the time they were nine months old.

8 Complete each statement with *few, a few, little,* or *a little.*

1. Our children need _____little_____ advice from us. They do everything right.

2. We have _____ problems with our children. They are very well behaved.

3. Our daughter is only sixteen months old, and she can already say _____ words.

4. Our daughter has _____ trouble learning anything new. She gets excellent grades.

5. Our son is seven and he already plays _____ musical instruments. He's gifted.

6. Our boys have _____ fights. They get along very well with each other.

7. Our girls have _____ free time. They are always busy studying.

8. Our children usually have _____ homework on the weekends, but not a lot.

PRACTICE

9 Complete the exercises.

A Circle the correct words to complete the paragraph.

Our daughter, Rosa, is already ten years old. Time (1) **has / have** gone so quickly! Before she was born, we had had (2) **few / little** experience with children. We didn't have (3) **any / some** knowledge about raising a child, but Rosa has taught us (4) **every / some** important things. She has (5) **a lot of / many** imagination, and so she always gives us (6) **a great deal of / many** pleasure. Fortunately, her health (7) **is / are** excellent, and that is the most important thing. We hope that Rosa meets (8) **many / much** kind people throughout her life and that she forms (9) **many / much** good relationships. We are happy that we're doing a good job as parents. There is (10) **little / a little** doubt in our minds that Rosa is going to be a successful adult with (11) **a lot of / much** self-confidence. (12) **Few / A few** of her teachers say that, too.

B **ANALYZE THE GRAMMAR.** Look at the chart. Then find at least four more examples of each kind of noun from the article in exercise **A** on page 121. Write them in the chart.

Singular Count Nouns	Plural Count Nouns	Non-Count Nouns
daughter	years	time

C Work with a partner. Compare your charts from exercise **B**.

10 **WRITE** eight sentences in your notebook. Use different quantity expressions, verbs, and nouns from the chart. Start each sentence with "When I was a child. . . ."

When I was a child, I didn't have many stuffed animals. I only had a few.

Verbs	Quantity Expressions	Nouns		
eat	a couple of	advice	fun	self-confidence
get	a great deal of	attention	game	stuffed animal
have	a lot of/lots of	candy	holiday	toy
like	a few/few	doll	junk food	truck
need	a little/little	fishing rod	money	video game
play	many/much	free time	praise	Use your own ideas
want	no	friend	problem	

◀ A child dressed up for *Shichi-Go-San*

122

11 EDIT. Read the paragraph about *Shichi-Go-San*. Find and correct six more errors with count and non-count nouns or quantity expressions.

Shichi-Go-San

Shichi-Go-San ("Seven-Five-Three")
           a
is ^ Japanese celebration. People have many fun at this time of year. *Shichi-Go-San* takes place on November 15 each year and celebrates different stages of childhood. Parents celebrate their children's growth and pray for their children's good healths. Every children receives a bag of candy. Boys receive bags of candy when they turn three and five years old. Girl receive them when they turn three and seven. In Japan, people think these are important ages in a child's life. The candy is shaped like a stick. All the candy bags have a picture of turtle and a crane on them. The candy, the crane, and the turtle are symbol of long life.

◄ A *Shichi-Go-San* candy bag

▲ *Shichi-Go-San* candy

12 APPLY.

A Write a paragraph in your notebook about a celebration from your childhood. It can be a national celebration or a personal one, such as a birthday. Answer the following questions.

What is the name of the celebration?
When does it take place?
What does the event celebrate?
Are there any symbols connected with the event?
Who celebrates this event?

Shichi-Go-San is a celebration in my country. It takes place on November 15th every year . . .

B Work with a partner. Read each other's paragraphs from exercise **A**. Then ask at least three questions about your partner's celebration.

A: *Do people wear any special clothing on that day?*

B: *Yes, the girls wear kimonos, and the boys wear traditional pants called hakama.*

EXPLORE

CD2-03

1 READ the article about why teenagers do the things they do. What are some typical teenage behaviors?

The Science of the Teenage Brain

Ask almost any parent of **a teenager** and you will hear **the** same **story**: adolescence[1] is a difficult time. Many parents will probably mention a few things that worry them such as high-speed driving, texting while driving, skateboarding, and other risky action sports.

Why do teens act the way they do? Nobody had **a** good **explanation** until **the** late **twentieth century** when **researchers** developed brain scanning. With this technology, scientists can see **the brain's** physical development and activity. **The brain scans** show that **the brain** develops slowly through childhood and adolescence. Therefore, **a** teenage **brain** is not yet fully developed. That's likely why most teens consider their desires more important than rules of behavior. For **the** same **reason**, they often don't consider **the consequences**, or results, of their actions.

In recent years, researchers have begun to view **the** teenage **brain** and teen behavior in **a** more positive **way**. Studies show that teens from all cultures have **some characteristics** in common such as **a desire** for thrills[2] and excitement. This desire may lead to **danger**, but it can also have **a** positive **effect**. Openness to new experiences can "get you out of **the house**," says brain researcher Jay Giedd. In other words, **the search** for excitement and risk prepares teens to leave **the safety** of their homes and move out into **the world**. According to this view, teens are very adaptable[3] human beings. When we look beyond their crazy behavior, we can see people who are getting ready to face **the challenges** of **the future**.

[1] **adolescence:** the stage of life between childhood and adulthood
[2] **thrill:** a strong feeling of excitement, fear, or pleasure
[3] **adaptable:** able to handle changes; flexible

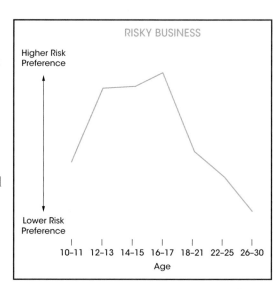

RISKY BUSINESS

Higher Risk Preference

Lower Risk Preference

10–11 12–13 14–15 16–17 18–21 22–25 26–30
Age

▼ For teens, pleasure is usually more important than its consequences.

2 CHECK. Answer the questions about the article in exercise **1**. Write complete sentences.

1. What did late twentieth-century researchers find out about the teenage brain?

   _____

2. What are two characteristics that teens from all cultures share?

   _____

3. According to the graph, at what ages do teenagers take the most risks?

   _____

4. What is the positive side of teenage risk taking?

   _____

3 DISCOVER. Complete the exercises to learn about the grammar in this lesson.

A Read the sentences from the the article in exercise **1**. If there is an article (*a/an* or *the*) before the underlined noun, circle it.

1. Ask almost any parent of ⓐ teenager . . .

2. Nobody had a good explanation until the late twentieth century.

3. The brain scans show that the brain develops slowly through childhood and adolescence.

4. . . . researchers have begun to view the teenage brain and teen behavior in a more positive way.

5. . . . the search for excitement and risk prepares teens to leave the safety of their homes and move out into the world.

B Check (✓) the statements that are true based on your answers in exercise **A**.

_____ 1. *A* or *an* is used before a plural count noun.

_____ 2. *The* is used before a singular count noun.

_____ 3. *The* is used before a plural count noun.

_____ 4. *The* is used before a non-count noun.

_____ 5. No article is used before a singular count noun.

_____ 6. No article is used before a non-count noun.

LEARN

5.3 Articles: Specific and Nonspecific

Articles	Singular Count Nouns	Plural Count Nouns	Non-Count Nouns
the	**The child** has brown eyes.	**The children** are tall.	Where is **the sugar**?
a/an	Do you have **a** blue **pen**?		
some		Do we need **some apples**?	I gave him **some advice**.

1. Use *the* to refer to a specific person, place, thing, or idea. A noun is specific when: 　a. it is clear which noun you mean 　b. there is only one of the noun 　c. a prepositional phrase or relative clause comes after the noun and defines the noun	a. Did you feed **the cat**? (our cat) b. Look at **the moon**. Isn't it beautiful? c. Do you know **the name** *of this lake*? 　I don't know **the people** *that arrived late*.
2. Use *a/an* before a singular count noun when: 　a. you are <u>not</u> referring to a specific person, place, thing, or idea; you are referring to one of many 　b. the listener or reader does not know which person, place, thing, or idea you mean	a. Do you have **a picture** of your family? 　(Any picture is fine.) b. I just read **an interesting article** about teenagers.
3. Use *some* before a plural count noun or non-count noun that is not specific. *Some* refers to an indefinite amount. Often the meaning with and without *some* is similar.	**Some people** are here already. **People** have already arrived. There's **some milk** in the fridge. There's **milk** in the fridge.
4. **Be careful!** Singular count nouns almost always need an article or other determiner (such as *this, many, . . .*).	✓ **The girl** has **a** new **bike**. ✗ <u>Girl has new bike</u>.
5. An article is not used in some common expressions (*to bed, in bed, in class, at work, after school/college, at home*).	I often read **in bed**. I went **to bed** late. **After college**, I plan to travel for a year.

4 Circle the correct articles to complete each sentence. Circle Ø for *no article*.

1. (**Some**) / **The** teens play soccer in Ø /(**the**) afternoon and others swim.

2. Nick had **an / the** injury, but he didn't let **an / the** injury stop him from playing soccer.

3. **A / The** coach of his soccer team told Raul to stay Ø / **the** home, but he didn't want to.

4. After Ø / **the** school, Mia babysits two young children in Ø / **the** neighborhood.

5. We have **a / Ø** test next Monday, so **a / the** teacher is going to review everything on Friday.

6. We have several schools in our town but only one hospital. **Ø / The** school that my children attend is near **a / the** hospital.

7. Gina sent me **a / the** text message when I got home, but I didn't understand **a / the** message.

8. Emily left **an / the** empty water bottle in **a / the** fridge.

9. **Ø / The** weather sometimes affects **the / Ø** people and makes them sad.

10. I'm so glad that I don't have to go to **a / Ø** work tomorrow. I can stay in **the / Ø** bed later.

5.4 Articles: Making Generalizations

Articles	Singular Count Nouns	Plural Count Nouns	Non-Count Nouns
No Article		**Cats** sleep during the day.	**Experience** is important in a job.
a/an	**A car** is a motorized vehicle.		

1. To make a generalization about something, use a plural count noun or a non-count noun without an article.	**Cows** are mammals. **Milk** comes from cows.
2. *A/an* can be used before a singular count noun to make a generalization, but it is less common.	**Less Common:** A computer is a useful tool. **More Common:** Computers are useful tools.
3. *The* can be used before certain adjectives to refer to a specific group of people.	**The poor** need our help. Sam works with **the elderly**.

5 Put the words in the correct order to make sentences. Add *a*, *an*, or *the* where necessary.

1. person's life / can be / difficult time in / adolescence
    <u>Adolescence can be a difficult time in a person's life.</u>

2. want / many teens / excitement
    _____

3. worries about / her / mother / children
    _____

4. risky things / young / sometimes do
    _____

5. like / their friends / to spend time with / teenagers
    _____

6. teenage behavior / elderly / often don't understand
    _____

7. enjoy / many teens / activities / dangerous
    _____

8. to have / teenagers / job / it is good for

    _____

9. responsibility / job / teaches

    _____

10. doesn't make / young people / happy / money

    _____

PRACTICE

6 Complete the exercises.

A Circle the correct articles to complete the statements. Circle Ø for *no article*.

1. "I love to play with (Ø) / **the** dolls."

2. "There's nothing that I like more than just looking up at **a** / **the** sky."

3. "I enjoy just hanging out with **Ø** / **the** friends."

4. "I can't wait until I'm big enough to go to **Ø** / **the** school."

5. "You never appreciate **a** / **Ø** time until you don't have a lot of it."

6. "It's fun to go to **Ø** / **the** parties and stay up all night."

7. "I don't see why students have to do **a** / **Ø** homework. We already do enough work
    at **Ø** / **the** school!"

8. "Swimming in **some** / **the** ocean is fun."

9. "I don't mind most household tasks, but I dislike cleaning **Ø** / **the** oven."

10. "I just learned to ride **a** / **the** bike."

B **SPEAK.** Work with a partner. Discuss who probably said each statement in exercise **A**:
a young child, a teenager, or an adult.

A: *I think a young girl said, "I love to play with dolls."*

B: *I agree, but I'm not sure about number two.*

7 **PRONUNCIATION.** Read the chart and listen to the examples. Then complete the exercises.

PRONUNCIATION	*The:* /ðə/ or /ði/

The is pronounced two ways: /ðə/ with /ə/ as in <u>o</u>f or /ði/ with /i/ as in h<u>e</u>.

1. Say /ðə/ before consonant sounds (b, c, d, . . .).
    the book   **the** question   **the** difficult exercise

2. Say /ði/ before vowel sounds (a, e, i, o, u).
    the exercise   **the** answer   **the** easy question

CD2-04

A Listen for the word *the* in each sentence. Then check (✓) the pronunciation you hear.

	/ðə/	/ði/
1.	✓	
2.		
3.		
4.		

	/ðə/	/ði/
5.		
6.		
7.		
8.		

B Listen again. Repeat each sentence. Then write the noun phrase with the word *the* from each sentence.

1. _____the flowers_____

2. _____

3. _____

4. _____

5. _____

6. _____

7. _____

8. _____

8 Complete the text. Write *a*, *an*, *the*, or Ø for *no article*.

Coming-of-Age Day in South Korea

What does it mean when (1) __a__ person comes of age? It means that (2) _____ person is moving from (3) _____ childhood to (4) _____ adulthood. This transition happens at different ages and is celebrated in a variety of ways in different cultures. It can be (5) _____ simple event or a celebration that involves special ceremonies.

In South Korea, the third Monday in May is Coming-of-Age Day. Everyone who is turning 20 years old that year celebrates (6) _____ day. When (7) _____ young reach this stage of (8) _____ life, they have more freedom than they did when they were (9) _____ children. For example, some start to drive, vote, or get married. In addition to (10) _____ independence, a 20-year-old needs to accept (11) _____ responsibility of becoming (12) _____ adult in his or her country.

It has become (13) _____ tradition for Korean "coming-of-agers" to receive three gifts: (14) _____ flowers, perfume, and (15) _____ kiss. In some places, there is (16) _____ ceremony, too, where the 20-year-olds wear traditional Korean clothing. The boys wear black hats made partially of (17) _____ horsehair, and the girls wear special (18) _____ dresses and hairstyles.

...ung women and ...n wear traditional ...thing at a ...oming-of-Age" ...y ceremony in ...uth Korea.

9 LISTEN.

CD2-06

A Listen to the news report about three young people—David Dicks, Zac Sunderland, and Laura Dekker. Check (✓) the sentence that best describes what they have in common.

_____ 1. They are all from the same part of the world.

_____ 2. Their parents encouraged them to do unusual things.

_____ 3. Each of them wanted to have an adventure.

CD2-06

B Listen again. Then complete the sentences based on what you heard in the news report. Use the words and phrases from the box and *a*, *an*, *some*, *the*, or *Ø* for *no article*.

after-school jobs	bad weather	difficult trip	government officials
problems with his boat	~~sailboat~~	West Coast	world young person

1. Each of the three teens had _____ *a sailboat* _____.

2. They all wanted to sail around _____ alone.

3. The two challenges David Dicks had to face were _____ and _____.

4. David Dicks completed _____ in nine months.

5. Zac Sunderland set out from _____ of the United States.

6. Zac Sunderland got money for his boat from _____.

7. _____ were worried about Laura Dekker's plans.

8. They thought the trip was too dangerous for _____.

10 APPLY.

A Work in a group. Discuss how being a child is different from being a teenager in your culture. Use the topics from the box in your comparison of children and teens.

interests	types of skills	rules to follow
responsibilities	types of worries	ways they get into trouble

Children in my culture are mostly interested in toys. Teens are interested in music and sports.

B Write five sentences about the ideas you and your group discussed.

_____

_____

_____

_____

_____

EXPLORE

CD2-07

1 READ the article about longevity, or how long people live. Why do some people live to be a hundred?

How long will you live?

Will you live to be a hundred? **There is** still no way to predict a person's life span, but **scientists are** getting closer. In a study of over 1000 centenarians (people who are 100 years old or older), researchers have discovered a set of "long-life" genes.[1] These genes allow scientists to guess, with 77 percent accuracy, whether a person can live into their late 90s or longer. **The authors** of the study **think** that long-life genes may prevent other genes from causing the usual illnesses of aging such as heart problems and dementia.[2] However, it is not true that **every person** with long-life genes **is going to live** to be a hundred. **A number of other important factors** greatly **influence** life span. For example, **lifestyle, the environment, and plain good luck** also **play** a big role. In fact, **23 percent of the people** in the study **were** not found to have long-life genes. Perhaps these people simply lived healthier lives.

The scientific community is excited by the study and its implications[3] for further research. For example, scientists are learning how to use genes to help predict and prevent certain illnesses. **Dan Buettner**, an expert in long-life studies, **believes** in the value of such studies. He says that scientists may even learn how to slow the aging process, although this won't happen for a long time. **Years** of research **have taught** him that, for now, we must accept the genes we have and live well. For Buettner that means eating a healthy diet, being physically active, and having a purpose in life.

[1] **gene:** the part of a cell that controls the physical characteristics, growth, and development of living things

[2] **dementia:** a serious illness of the mind

[3] **implication:** something that is likely to happen as a result of something else

▼ A 100-year-old man water-skis near his home in Washington State, USA.

► An Okinawan woman inspects a handful of edible seaweed.

2 CHECK. Correct the error in each sentence to make it true according to the article from exercise **1** on page 131.

                                   ∨centenarians

1. In a study of over 1000 ~~75-year-olds~~, researchers have discovered a set of "long-life" genes.

2. Long-life genes may cause the typical diseases of the elderly.

3. Lifestyle, the environment, and plain good luck have little effect on life span.

4. Scientists are learning how to destroy genes to help predict certain illnesses.

5. Dan Buettner believes that scientists may even learn how to stop the aging process.

3 DISCOVER. Complete the exercises to learn about the grammar in this lesson.

A Look at the underlined subjects in the sentences. Circle the verb or verb phrase that agrees with each subject.

1. <u>The authors of the study</u> (think) that long-life genes may affect aging.

2. <u>Every person with long-life genes</u> is not going to live to be a hundred.

3. <u>A number of other important factors</u> greatly influence life span.

4. In fact, <u>23 percent of the people in the study</u> were not individuals with long-life genes.

5. <u>Years of research</u> have taught him several things.

B Look the verb or verb phrase you circled in each sentence in exercise **A**. Then choose the noun or noun phrase that agrees with the verb or verb phrase.

1. (a.) the authors   b. the study   4. a. the people   b. study

2. a. every person   b. genes   5. a. years   b. research

3. a. a number   b. factors

LEARN

5.5 Subject-Verb Agreement

1. The main verb in a sentence must agree in number with the subject.	Singular: **The sofa looks** comfortable. Plural: **The chairs are** too hard.
2. When a subject includes a phrase or clause, the verb agrees with the head noun.	**The girl** with five brothers **is** very athletic. **A family** that has ten children **is** unusual.
3. Use a plural verb after subjects joined by *and*. Use a singular verb when *each* or *every* comes before subjects joined by *and*.	**Love and trust are** important to him. **Every day and night was** fun last summer.
4. Use a singular verb after an indefinite pronoun (*everybody, someone, anything, no one,* etc.).	**Everybody is going to come** to the party. **Someone has taken** the money. **Anything is** possible. **No one was sleeping** in the room.
5. **Remember:** Use a singular verb after *each* and *every*.	**Each class is** in a different room. **Every house costs** a different amount here.
6. In sentences beginning with *there is/there are* and *here is/here are*, the subject follows the verb. The verb still agrees with the subject.	There **is a dog** in the car. There **are two cats,** too. Here **is the lock,** and **here are the keys.**

4 Read the fact sheet about longevity, or long life. Circle the correct verb to complete each sentence.

Facts about Longevity

Here (1) **is / are** some information about longevity:

- There (2) **is / are** several factors other than genes that affect longevity.

- Lifestyle and the environment (3) **contributes / contribute** to the length of a person's life.

- Not every centenarian (4) **chooses / choose** the same lifestyle.

- Every man and woman (5) **needs / need** to exercise regularly.

- People who eat a balanced diet usually (6) **lives / live** longer.

- A good set of genes (7) **helps / help** some people stay active into their 90s.

- The people of Monaco (8) **has / have** the highest life expectancy in the world.

5.6 More Subject-Verb Agreement

1. Use a singular verb after a plural amount of money, time, or distance when it refers to one thing or idea (a price, a time period, a distance, . . .).	**Two hundred dollars is** a lot of money. **Three weeks seems** like a long time to wait. **Five miles isn't** too far to walk.

2. Some nouns look plural, but are used with singular verbs. For example:
    a. subjects ending in *-ics (physics, economics, . . .)*
    b. the noun *news*
	
	a. **Physics is** hard.
	
	b. **The news wasn't** good.

3. Use a singular verb with the names of:
    a. books, movies, and plays
    b. countries
    c. businesses ending in *-s*
	
	a. **"Romeo and Juliet" is** a famous play.
	b. **The United States is** a large country.
	c. **GREX Works is** a company near Boston.

4. When using *the* + adjective to refer to a group of people (*the young, the elderly, . . .*), use a plural verb.	**The wealthy live** in houses along the river. **The young are** comfortable with technology.
5. Use a singular verb with *the number of*. Use a plural verb with *a number of*.	**The number of** gardens in the city **is** small. **A number of** questions **are** impossible to answer.
6. The verb after a percentage (%), fraction (¼, ½), or quantity expression (*all, most*) agrees with the noun after *of*.	**Fifty percent of** the students **know** the answer. **Half of** the class **knows** the answer. **Most of** the survey **is** about aging.

5 Complete the sentences with *is* or *are*.

1. The average human life span __is__ 82 years in some countries.

2. Eighty-two years _____ not quite a century. There are 100 years in a century.

3. In Japan, more than one-fifth of the population _____ over the age of 65.

4. In India, more than 10 percent of the people _____ 60 or older.

5. Geriatrics _____ the name of medical care for older adults.

6. The number of centarians _____ increasing worldwide.

7. The elderly today _____ healthier than 50 years ago.

8. *Blue Zones* _____ the name of a book about longevity.

9. A number of interviews in the book _____ with centenarians.

10. The young _____ not likely to learn from the experience of the elderly.

PRACTICE

6 Complete the exercises.

A Circle the correct verb to complete each quotation.

> ## ⁓ Quotations about Aging ⁓
>
> 1. An old man (1) **continues / continue** to be young in two things – love of money and love of life. (Proverb)
> 2. There (2) **is / are** no medicine against old age. (Nigerian proverb)
> 3. To me, old age (3) **is / are** always 15 years older than I am. (Bernard Baruch, businessman)
> 4. Everyone (4) **is / are** the age of their heart. (Guatemalan proverb)
> 5. The elderly (5) **has / have** so much to offer. They're our link with history. (From the movie *Being John Malkovich*)
> 6. Anyone who stops learning (6) **is / are** old, whether at twenty or eighty. (Henry Ford, car manufacturer)
> 7. As we get older, things (7) **seems / seem** less important. (From the movie *Red*)
> 8. No man (8) **knows / know** he is young while he is young. (G. K. Chesterton, writer)

B **SPEAK.** Work with a partner. Choose one or two quotations in exercise **A** that you believe are true. Then tell your partner why you believe the quotations you chose are true.

7 LISTEN.

A You are going to hear an interview with Elvira Caceres Montero, a participant in a research study on the elderly. Before you listen, predict which three things she will say are the most important as she looks back at her life.

- ☐ communication
- ☐ health
- ☐ money
- ☐ education
- ☐ honesty
- ☐ volunteer work
- ☐ family
- ☐ marriage
- ☐ technology

CD2-08

B Listen to the interview. Were your predictions correct?

CD2-08

C Listen again. Circle the correct word(s) to complete each sentence about Ms. Montero.

1. **All / Some** of her family **was / were** together for her 80th birthday.
2. **Some / All** of her family **live / lives** in Puerto Rico.
3. **One experience / Her experiences** in life **has taught / have taught** her to be a better listener.
4. **One / All** of her grandchildren **has been / have been** successful.
5. She believes that **education / experience is / are** important for success.

8 **EDIT.** Read the company newsletter. Find and correct six more errors with subject-verb agreement.

Meet Gene Guerro, 92, Briteroom Electronics's 60-Year Employee

Gene Guerro has been working at Briteroom for 60 years and nothing ~~have~~ has ever prevented him from going to work. Briteroom Electronics are going to be honoring him next month for being the company's longest-working employee. When he first started college, Gene majored in economics. But economics just weren't very interesting to him, so he changed to physics. "There was many exciting things to learn in every physics class. In fact, physics still excites me today," says Gene. "Everybody tell me I should retire." And I say, "Why should I do that? Watching TV all day isn't for me. Half of my friends does that, but they aren't happy. Every day are exactly the same for them." As Lucy Guerro says about her father, "Work is my dad's hobby."

9 **READ, SPEAK & WRITE.**

A Work with a partner. Read the chart about the results of a survey. Then discuss these questions with your partner.

What is the survey about?

Who responded to the survey questions?

Are your answers to the questions similar?

Survey Results: Physical Activity of Adults 45+

1. Are you physically active now?
   - 71%
   - 29%

2. Do you plan to start an exercise program in the next month?
   - 9%
   - 91%

3. Do you prefer walking to other forms of exercise?
   - 50%
   - 50%

4. Do you do four or more hours of physical activity every week?
   - 53%
   - 47%

5. Are you more active now than you were five years ago?
   - 39%
   - 61%

0%   50%   100%

■ Yes ■ No

Source: Based on data from the American Association of Retired Persons (AARP)

B Complete each statement about the survey results in exercise **A**. Use a phrase from the box and the correct form of the verb. Add *not* where necessary. More than one answer is sometimes correct.

~~be over 45 years old~~
be physically active now
have the same level of activity as five years ago
be more active now than five years ago
plan to start an exercise program next month
do a few hours of physical activity per week
prefer walking to other forms of exercise

1. All of the respondents _were over 45 years old_ .

2. A little less than 40 percent of the group _____ .

3. Almost three-quarters of the respondents _____ .

4. Nearly a third of the group _____ .

5. Almost nobody _____ .

6. Fifty percent of the people _____ .

7. A little over half of the group _____ .

8. Almost two-thirds _____ .

10 APPLY.

A Work in a group. Brainstorm *Yes/No* questions to ask your classmates about their physical activity. Write as many questions as you can.

Do you exercise regularly?

Do you prefer going to the gym to exercising outdoors?

B Choose the four best questions from exercise **A** and write them in the chart. Then walk around the classroom and ask five students to take your survey. Ask each student all four of your questions. Record each student's answers in your chart. Write **Y** for *Yes* or **N** for *No*.

Class Survey on Physical Activity	Classmates (Y or N?)				
Questions	1	2	3	4	5
1.					
2.					
3.					
4.					

C Return to your group and discuss the results of your survey. Then write five sentences about the results.

Every person in the class exercises on a regular basis now.

Two-thirds of the students do not prefer exercising in the gym to exercising outdoors.

Charts
5.1,
5.3–5.5

1 Complete the exercises.

A Read about storytelling in Native American culture. Circle the correct answers.

Storytelling: A Native American Tradition

There (1) **is / are** a long tradition of (2) **the / Ø** storytelling among many Native American (3) **person / people**. Stories are often told by elders to teach younger generations important lessons about (4) **a / Ø** history and culture. Virginia Driving Hawk Sneve, (5) **a / the** Native American writer, remembers how it felt to sit with a group of other children and listen to the fascinating stories that her grandmother told. Sneve and her family (6) **is / are** Lakota Indians; however, (7) **a / the** tradition is not unique to them.

(8) **The / A** Lakota culture is just one example of a society in which grandmothers became the storytellers. Hunting for food was (9) **the / Ø** responsibility of the adult men, and household tasks such as food preparation (10) **was / were** the job of the strong, younger mothers. Therefore, it was up to the grandmothers to educate the children, and they told stories to do it.

◄ A Lakota language class at Red Cloud Indian School in South Dakota

B ANALYZE THE GRAMMAR. Find four singular count nouns, four plural count nouns, and four non-count nouns from the text in exercise **A**. Write them in your notebook. Then work with a partner and compare your lists of nouns.

Charts
5.1–5.6

2 EDIT. Read the information about stories. Find and correct eight more errors with nouns, articles, and subject-verb agreement.

                                                   has

Every culture and country ~~have~~ stories to pass down to the younger generation, and the young learns a lot of things from the stories. The stories also bring joy to a great deal of children.

There are many different kinds of stories, but a number of themes is common across cultures. For example, the importance of family relationships appear again and again. Hard work and honesty is also important theme in children's stories. What else do the children learn? Perhaps most importantly, they learn that all human beings are the same. There is a little difference between people. Everybody have the same dreams, hopes, and fears.

Charts
5.1–5.5

3 LISTEN, WRITE & SPEAK.

A You are going to listen to an excerpt from a traditional Native American story told by the Chippewa people of North America. The title of the story is "The Wonderful Turtle." Read the first part of the story. Write the articles and verbs that you think are missing.

Near a Chippewa village was (1) _____ large lake, and in (2) _____ lake there lived (3) _____ enormous turtle. This (4) _____ no ordinary turtle because he would often come out of his home in that lake and visit with his Indian neighbors. He made most of his visits to (5) _____ head chief of the tribe, and on these occasions he stayed for hours talking with him.

The chief, seeing that (6) _____ turtle was very smart and showed great wisdom, took a great fancy to him,[1] and whenever (7) _____ difficult question came up before the chief, he generally asked Mr. Turtle to help him decide.

One day there (8) _____ a great misunderstanding between two different groups in (9) _____ tribe. Each side became so angry that the argument threatened to become (10) _____ bloody fight. The chief was unable to decide which side was right, so he said, "I will call Mr. Turtle. He will judge for you."

[1] **took a great fancy to him:** liked him a lot

B Work with a partner. Compare your answers from exercise **A**. Then listen and check your answers.

CD2-09

C Listen to the next part of the story. Take notes to help you answer the questions that follow. Then ask and answer the questions with a partner.

CD2-10

1. Who did Mr. Turtle listen to carefully?
2. Who did the turtle say was right?
3. Why did he make this decision?
4. How did the people react to the turtle's decision? What did they do?

D Work in a group. Make up an ending to the story. Then tell your ending to the class. Decide as a class which group had the best ending.

Connect the Grammar to Writing

1 READ & NOTICE THE GRAMMAR.

A What are some kinds of risks have you taken in your life? Discuss them with a partner. Then read the narrative.

Teen Daredevil: A SURVIVOR'S STORY

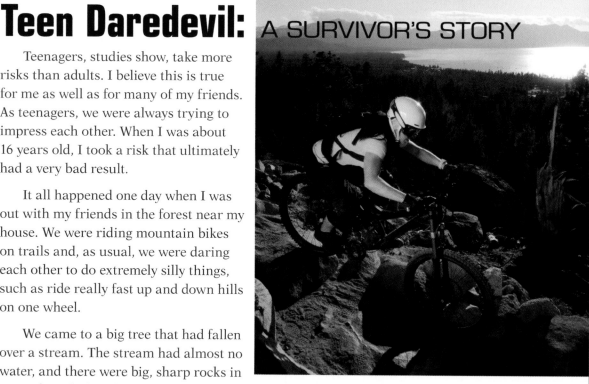

Teenagers, studies show, take more risks than adults. I believe this is true for me as well as for many of my friends. As teenagers, we were always trying to impress each other. When I was about 16 years old, I took a risk that ultimately had a very bad result.

It all happened one day when I was out with my friends in the forest near my house. We were riding mountain bikes on trails and, as usual, we were daring each other to do extremely silly things, such as ride really fast up and down hills on one wheel.

We came to a big tree that had fallen over a stream. The stream had almost no water, and there were big, sharp rocks in it. My friends dared me to ride my bike over the fallen tree. "No problem," I said coolly. There was no way I was going to chicken out[1] now. Everybody was cheering as I rode my bike at top speed. My fear was not as strong as my desire to impress my friends.

Suddenly, I lost control and slipped off the tree, crashing onto the rocks below. I landed on my right arm and felt a sharp pain unlike any I'd ever experienced before. Hours later at the hospital, where my parents had driven me after the accident, I learned that my arm was broken in several places.

After that experience, I became much more cautious. To this day, whenever someone dares me to do something, I think twice before doing it.

[1] **chicken out:** to agree to do something and then not do it because of fear

---

GRAMMAR FOCUS

In this story, the writer follows these rules of subject-verb agreement.

Subjects follow *be* in sentences with *there*.
    . . . and ***there were big, sharp rocks*** in it.

Subjects with *every-, some-, any-,* or *no-* take a singular verb.
    Everybody was cheering . . .

Non-count nouns as subjects take singular verbs.
    My fear was not as strong as . . .

B Read the narrative in exercise **A** again. Underline more examples of *subject + verb* combinations such as those in the box. Then work with a partner and compare your answers.

2 BEFORE YOU WRITE. Work in a group of three or four students. Use the information about the writer of the narrative in exercise **1** as an example. Then tell your group about a risk that you have taken. What were the results of your actions? Complete the chart with notes about people in your group.

Name	Risky Action	Result
Lucy	rode her bike over a tree	broke her arm

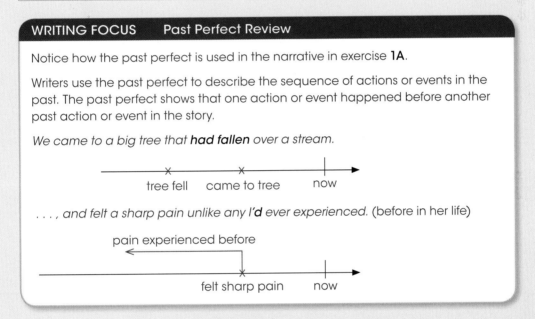

WRITING FOCUS   Past Perfect Review

Notice how the past perfect is used in the narrative in exercise **1A**.

Writers use the past perfect to describe the sequence of actions or events in the past. The past perfect shows that one action or event happened before another past action or event in the story.

*We came to a big tree that **had fallen** over a stream.*

tree fell   came to tree   now

. . . , and felt a sharp pain unlike any I'd ever experienced. (before in her life)

pain experienced before

felt sharp pain   now

3 WRITE about a risk that either you or a classmate once took. Write three or four paragraphs. Use your notes from exercise **2** and the narrative in exercise **1A** to help you.

4 SELF ASSESS. Read your narrative again. Underline the subjects and verbs in your sentences. Then use the checklist to assess your work.

☐ I used count and non-count nouns with the correct quantity expressions. [5.1, 5.2]

☐ I used articles correctly. [5.3, 5.4]

☐ I used proper subject-verb agreement with count and non-count subjects. [5.5, 5.6]

☐ I used the past perfect to describe actions or events that happened before other actions or events in the past. [WRITING FOCUS]

Gerunds and Infinitives

▲ Young Afghan girls play on swings in Kabul, Afghanistan.

143

EXPLORE

1 READ the article about sleeping. What are sleep researchers trying to find out?

The Mysteries of Sleep

Sleeping takes up about one-third of our lives, and most people need seven to nine hours of sleep a night. Why do we need so much sleep? After decades of research, scientists still don't have an answer, but they do have some theories.

Sleep seems to benefit both the mind and the body. According to some researchers, **sleeping** may improve our memory. It might be that the sleeping brain helps us remember important things **by letting** us forget unimportant things. Other research suggests that the body repairs damaged cells during sleep. Therefore, **not sleeping** may slow the healing process when we get injured. There is also a theory that sleep helps protect us from infection.

Although theories on sleep differ, researchers agree on its importance. Sleep is a necessary part **of living** a healthy life. Unfortunately, conditions such as insomnia are common. In the United States, for example, one-fifth of the population **has difficulty sleeping**. **Working** long hours and **managing** the stresses of modern life are common causes of sleeping problems.

Not getting enough sleep can have serious consequences, including traffic accidents and low productivity at work. Some people are trying to find solutions. In Spain, for example, businessman Ignacio Buqueras y Bach thinks that **watching** late-night television is a problem. In his opinion, TV networks should **consider changing** their schedules so that people can **spend** more **time sleeping**. Now, prime-time[1] programs don't end until midnight or later. Buqueras y Bach's words are relevant[2] for people throughout the world: "Every once in a while we have to close our eyes. We're not machines."

[1] **prime time:** the hours, usually in the evening, when the largest number of people are available to watch television or listen to the radio
[2] **relevant:** important or appropriate

▲ A hiker rests in the grass on the Mount Fox trail. Mount Fox, Westland National Park, Southern Alps, South Island, New Zealand.

2 **CHECK.** Write answers to the questions with information from the article.

1. What is one theory that researchers have for the reason we sleep?

   _____

2. What is one reason that some people don't get enough sleep?

   _____

3. What can happen if you don't get enough sleep?

   _____

4. What does Ignacio Buqueras y Bach think TV networks should do?

   _____

3 **DISCOVER.** Complete the exercises to learn about the grammar in this lesson.

A Write the missing words in the sentences from the article in exercise **1**.

1. _____Sleeping_____ takes up about one-third of our lives.

2. It might be that the sleeping brain helps us remember important things by _____By letting_____ us forget unimportant things.

3. Sleep is a necessary part of _____living_____ a healthy life.

4. _____Not getting_____ enough sleep can have serious consequences.

5. In his opinion, TV networks should consider _____changing_____ their schedules so that people can spend more time _____sleeping_____ .

B The words you wrote in exercise **A** are gerunds. Look back at exercise **A**. Then read the statements below. Circle **T** for *true* or **F** for *false*.

1. A gerund can be the subject of a sentence.   (T)   F

2. A gerund can be the object of a preposition.   (T)   F

3. A gerund can be the main verb in a sentence.   T   (F)

LEARN

6.1   Gerunds as Subjects and Objects

	Gerund as Subject	Gerund as Object
Gerund	**Reading** is my favorite hobby.	I love **cooking**.
Negative Gerund	**Not eating** at restaurants saves money.	We considered **not going**.
Gerund Phrase	**Running in the park** is good exercise.	They enjoy **baking cookies**.

1. A gerund is an *-ing* form of a verb.* It functions as a noun (subject or object) in a sentence.	**Hiking** is fun for all ages. We enjoy **traveling**.
2. A gerund can be part of a gerund phrase. A gerund phrase can be the subject or object of a sentence.	**Seeing a movie** is a great idea. They enjoyed **hearing that song**.
3. Add *not* to make a gerund negative.	**Not sleeping** enough is a problem.
4. These common verbs can be followed by gerunds: *avoid, consider, dislike, enjoy, finish, keep, involve, mind, quit, practice, require, suggest.***	Have you **finished eating**? **Keep practicing**. Your skills will improve.
5. Use the third-person singular form of the verb when a gerund or gerund phrase is the subject.	<u>Winning the race</u> **was** an accomplishment. Gerund Phrase Verb
6. **Remember:** The *-ing* form of a verb can be a progressive verb or a gerund.	Progressive: She **was jogging** on the beach. Gerund: **Jogging** is her hobby.

*See page **A2** for spelling rules for the *-ing* form of verbs.
See page **A4 for a longer list of verbs followed by a gerund.

4   Complete the exercises.

A   Check (✓) the sentences with gerunds or gerund phrases. Then underline each gerund or gerund phrase.

_____   1.   The baby is taking a nap. Try to be quiet.

✓   2.   <u>Taking a nap in the afternoon</u> is good for you.

_____   3.   Not getting eight hours of sleep a night is often a problem for adults.

_____   4.   I haven't seen a sleep expert yet, but I'm considering the idea.

_____   5.   Meditating helps some people sleep better.

_____   6.   Most people dislike waking up early in the morning.

_____   7.   Do you mind sleeping with a light on?

_____   8.   Staying up late is a common habit of teenagers.

_____   9.   I like exercising. It helps me sleep.

_____   10.   Too many teens aren't getting enough sleep.

B ANALYZE THE GRAMMAR. Work with a partner. Label each gerund or gerund phrase in exercise **A** with **S** for *subject* or **O** for *object of a verb*.

S
<u>Taking a nap in the afternoon</u> is good for you.

6.2 Gerunds as Objects of Prepositions

1. A gerund is the only verb form that can follow a preposition (*about, at, by, for, in, of . . .*).	✓ You can achieve your goals **by working** hard. ✗ You can achieve your goals by <u>work</u> hard.
2. These common verb + preposition combinations can be followed by a gerund: *believe in, dream about, succeed in, think about.*	She has finally **succeeded in getting** a license. He is **thinking about getting** his own apartment.
3. These common noun + preposition combinations can be followed by a gerund: *advantage of, benefit of, purpose for/of, reason for.*	What's the **advantage of taking** vitamins? I don't know his **reason for writing** the letter.
4. These common adjective + preposition combinations can be followed by a gerund: *afraid of, interested in, tired of, worried about.*	I'm **interested in learning** more about baseball. I'm **tired of waiting** for the bus.

*See page **A4** for a list of verbs, nouns, and adjectives often followed by a preposition + gerund.

5 Complete the sentences with the correct preposition and the gerund form of the verb in parentheses.

1. Not everyone is interested ____in thinking____ (think) about their dreams.

2. What is the purpose _____ (dream)?

3. What is a possible reason _____ (have) bad dreams?

4. Have you ever succeeded _____ (understand) your dreams?

5. Sometimes I dream _____ (meet) a famous person.

6. In other dreams, I'm afraid _____ (stay) home alone.

7. Some people don't believe _____ (analyze) their dreams.

8. I never get tired _____ (try) to figure out my dreams.

6.3 Gerunds with Nouns and Special Expressions

1. Some common nouns are often followed by gerunds. For example: *fun, difficulty, experience, problem, trouble.*	I had **fun playing** the video game. Did you have **difficulty finding** the house?
2. Some common expressions with *time* and *money* are often followed by gerunds. They occur with these verbs: *spend, waste,* and *have.*	She didn't **spend time exercising** yesterday. Don't **waste money buying** a new exercise bike. I've always **had a hard time losing** weight.

6 Complete the exercises.

A Complete the conversations with the correct form of the words in parentheses.

1. **A:** Lately, I've had _____trouble staying_____ (trouble / stay) awake at my job.

   B: Why? Are you having _____d... falling_____ (difficulty / fall) asleep?

2. **A:** Yes. I'm wasting _____t... lying_____ (time / lie) in bed for hours.

   B: I'm sorry to hear that. Do you have _____p... d...ing_____ (problems / deal) with stress?

3. **A:** Sometimes I worry about work. Then I have _____t... c...ing d..._____ (trouble / calm down).

   B: You know, I have _____e... teaching_____ (experience / teach) people effective sleep techniques.

4. **A:** Really? It would be _____fun... learning_____ (fun / learn) from you.

   B: Come to my class tonight. We have a great _____time p...ing_____ (time / practice) relaxation techniques.

B **SPEAK.** Work with a partner. Discuss any techniques you know for falling asleep.

I like doing yoga or meditating.

PRACTICE

7 Complete the paragraph with the words in parentheses. Use a gerund and add a preposition when necessary.

(1) _____Dreaming about_____ (dream) insects can be scary. However, not all insects are bad. In fact, many people in the world have positive feelings about insects. People in Eastern Europe, for example, believe that if a person sees a red butterfly, it means that he or she will have good health. In addition, some people (2) _____b... e...ing_____ (believe / eat) insects as part of a healthy diet.

People (3) _____e... dining_____ (enjoy / dine) on insects in many parts of the world. (4) _____C...ing & e...ing_____ (cook and eat) these creatures is common, for example, in Asia and Latin America.

▶ Grasshopper, cricket, and giant scorpion lollipops. France and the Netherlands are two countries making insect sweets.

▼ Peacock butterfly in the Netherlands.
Butterflies have symbolism in many countries,
including China, Russia, and Japan.

There are actually many (5) _____ b.. to . e i aq _____ (benefits / eat)

bugs. If you (6) _____ (have difficulty / believe) this,

I (7) _____ (suggest / look) at the facts. Insects have a high amount of

protein. Just take grasshoppers. They have 60 percent protein and they are rich in calcium.

Do people ever have any (8) _____ (problems / eat) insects? Yes. Some

contain toxins. It's best to (9) _____ (avoid / eat) yellow, red, or orange

bugs and any bugs that smell strong. Black, brown, or green bugs are generally fine.

Are you interested (10) _____ (try) something new and healthy? Then

(11) _____ (think / include) more bugs in your diet.

8 LISTEN, WRITE & SPEAK.

CD2-12

A Work with a partner. Read the choices to complete each tip for losing weight. Which do you
think are good? Tell your partner. Then listen and choose the answers you hear.

TIP 1: Eat _____ .

     a. food with bread   b. food cut in pieces   c. one piece of food

TIP 2: Schedule your biggest meal _____ .

     a. in the morning   b. in the afternoon   c. at night

TIP 3: Eat _____ and stop when you are full.

     a. slowly   b. quickly   c. slowly or quickly

B Listen again. Then complete the sentences with the words you hear. You can use a verb more than once.

1. a. _____Cutting your food_____ into small pieces may help you eat less.

   b. _____ of food may satisfy people more than having one large piece.

2. a. Some researchers believe that _____ the largest meal of the day in the early afternoon helps people control their weight better than _____ late in the day.

   b. One theory is that when we eat late in the day, it causes our body to have problems _____ .

3. a. _____ gives your body a chance to process food properly.

   b. _____ the total amount of food you eat helps you avoid _____ and other health problems.

C Work in groups. Discuss your ideas for eating well. Use gerunds

A: *Eating several small meals a day is better than eating one large one.*

B: *I have problems finding time to eat during the day. That's why I eat at the end of the day.*

9 WRITE & SPEAK.

A Read the sentences about healthy habits that help you live longer. Then rewrite the sentences with gerunds. Use *by* where necessary.

1. If you floss your teeth every day, it could add three to five years to your life.

   Flossing your teeth every day could add three to five years to your life.

2. You may add six years to your life if you don't smoke.

   _____

3. You should lift weights. It could add five to six years to your life.

   _____

4. You could add five years to your life if you eat fruits and vegetables.

   _____

5. You should get enough sleep. It may add three years to your life.

   _____

6. You could add two years to your life if you walk every day.

   _____

B Work with a partner. Suggest five more pieces of advice to help people live longer. Use gerund form of the verbs *avoid, consider, think about, spend time,* and *practice.*

People should spend more time relaxing.

10 **EDIT.** Read the paragraph about fitness and technology. Find and correct seven more errors with gerunds.

Tech Tools for Healthy Living

<u>Using</u>
~~Use~~ technology is a big part of daily life. Today there are many products that can help us succeed in reach our dietary and fitness goals. Is planning meals a problem for you? Are you tired of spend time search for healthy recipes? Downloading diet-related apps to your cell phone may be the answer. Apps can put the fun back into eat well.

Apps are also great for helping you get a good workout. If you are a runner, perhaps improve your speed is your goal. If so, a GPS watch is perfect for you. Do you need to be especially careful during your run? Take advantage of the heart monitor. It will prevent you from overdo your workout. If you swim, you may find that doing laps can get boring, especially when you are swimming long distances. But swimming is much more fun with a pair of waterproof headphones that play your favorite music.

Try these different products—you will have no excuse for being not able to stay fit!

11 **APPLY.**

A Complete the sentences about your habits. Use gerunds.

1. I don't have fun _____.

2. I have thought about _____ in order to stay fit.

3. When I exercise, I avoid _____.

4. _____ doesn't bother me.

5. I am always worried about _____.

6. A while ago I quit _____ because
   _____.

7. _____ gives me a headache.

8. When I was younger, I had a hard time _____.

B Work in groups. Tell each other four of your sentences from exercise **A**. Ask questions to get more information. Use gerunds when possible.

A: *I don't have fun exercising.*

B: *Why not?*

A: *I think being in the gym is boring.*

EXPLORE

CD2-13

1 **READ** the article about a place where ancient healing is helping to advance modern medicine. Why are scientists in a hurry to learn as much as they can?

Medical Riches in the Rainforests

The world's rainforests are of great interest to medical scientists. In those forests, scientists have found treatments for a wide range of conditions, from headaches to malaria. Researchers also **hope to find** cures for cancer there. According to the National Cancer Institute, 70 percent of plants that may be useful in cancer treatment grow only in rainforests. Only some of them have been studied so far.

Scientists often depend on the knowledge of traditional healers. The scientists **want the healers to show** them where plants are growing in the rainforest. Gervasio Noceda, for example, is a well-known healer in Paraguay. He is a shaman[1], and his knowledge of medicinal plants equals that of a medical library. When Noceda **prepares to lead** a group of researchers on a search for plants, he chants and prays. Perhaps he **is hoping to establish** a spiritual connection with the forest. When he is ready, the search begins.

The researchers often **ask him to find** a plant root[2] called *suruvi*. When *suruvi* is made into a tea, it is used to treat a variety of illnesses. With Noceda's help, some researchers have published a book on medicinal plants. It is a rich source of information that **helps people to identify** and **study** plants more easily.

Scientists feel **fortunate to have** the benefit of the healers' knowledge. They **need to work** quickly, though. Deforestation[3] is a serious problem, so it is urgent[4] **to identify**, **record**, and **analyze** the plants of the rainforests before it is too late.

[1] **shaman:** a wise person who is thought to have magic or spiritual powers
[2] **root:** the part of a plant that grows underground
[3] **deforestation:** the cutting down or destruction of trees for farming, wood, or fuel
[4] **urgent:** needing attention as soon as possible

▲ A shaman in the Cofan region, Ecuador

► The cinchona tree grows in the rainforests of South America. Its bark is used in a medicine for malaria.

2 CHECK. Check (✓) the statements that are true according to the article.

_____ 1. There is a large number of medicinal plants that you can find only in rainforests.

_____ 2. Researchers have studied most of the medicinal plants of the rainforest.

_____ 3. Scientists and healers work together to find and identify useful plants.

_____ 4. Gervasio Noceda learned about plants in a medical library.

_____ 5. The loss of rainforests in the future is a possibility.

3 DISCOVER. Complete the exercises to learn about the grammar in this lesson.

A Write the missing words in the sentences from the article in exercise **1**.

1. Researchers also hope _____to find_____ cures for cancer there.

2. The scientists want the healers _____ them where plants are growing in the rainforest.

3. The researchers often ask him _____ a plant root called *suruvi*.

4. Scientists feel fortunate _____ the benefit of the healers' knowledge.

5. They need _____ quickly, though.

B The verbs you wrote in exercise **A** are infinitives. Look back at the word that comes before each infinitive. Write it in the chart. Then check (✓) the correct column.

	Adjective	Noun	Pronoun	Verb
1. hope				✓
2.				
3.				
4.				
5.				

LEARN

6.4 Infinitives: Verbs (+ Object) + Infinitive

Verb + Infinitive	Verb + Object + Infinitive	Verb (+ Object) + Infinitive
We **have decided to go** to Chile. She **promised to be** on time.	He **reminded his son to study**. He **convinced me to study** medicine.	I **want to see** the doctor. I **want you to see** the doctor.

1. Certain verbs can be followed by an infinitive (*to* + the base form of a verb) or an infinitive phrase.	I like **to eat**. *Infinitive* I like **to eat chocolate cake**. *Infinitive Phrase*
2. These verbs can be followed by an infinitive: *afford, decide, hope, know how, plan, promise, seem.*	I **hope to get** better at diving. Do you **know how to swim**?
3. These verbs can be followed by an object + an infinitive: *advise, allow, convince, encourage, remind, teach, tell, urge, warn.**	The teacher **encourages us to ask** questions in class. I **urge you to consider** your plans carefully.
4. Some verbs can be followed by either an infinitive or an object + an infinitive, but the meaning is different: *ask, expect, need, pay, want, would like.**	He **expected to pay** for dinner. He **expected me to pay** for dinner.
5. Add *not* before the infinitive to make the infinitive negative.	They promised **not to be** late.
6. **Be careful!** Use an infinitive after *want* and *would like*, not *that*.	✓ I want you to exercise more. ✗ I want <u>that you</u> exercise more.

*See page **A5** for a list of verbs followed by an infinitive and verbs followed by an object + an infinitive.

4 Circle the correct answers.

Dear Professor Bartoli,

I'm writing to tell you that I've decided (1) **not to continue** / to not continue my medical research here. My family in Paraguay (2) **needs / needs me** to come home. While I still plan (3) **to finish / me to finish** my degree, I will do so in Paraguay. Thank you so much for everything you have taught me. I now know how (4) **to present / me to present** my research findings in a professional way. You have also taught (5) **to use / me to use** lots of new techniques to study plants. I promise (6) **not to forget / to not forget** anything I have learned. Please tell me if you would like (7) **to return / me to return** any of your papers before I leave. Finally, I want to encourage (8) **to come / you to come** to Paraguay in the future. It will give me great pleasure to show you some of our wonderful rainforest plants.

Sincerely,

Mariana Vera

5 Complete a health care worker's statements. Use the words given. Put the words in the correct order. Use the infinitive form once in each sentence.

1. ask / people / we / be patient

   We ask people to be patient _____ in the waiting room.

2. follow / my patients / would like / I

   _____ their doctors' orders.

3. everyone / I / stop smoking / advise

   _____

4. our patients / we / exercise / encourage

   _____ every day.

5. avoid / advise / we / them

   _____ certain foods.

6. be careful / older people / need

   _____ about their diet.

7. not worry / I / urge / our patients

   _____

8. people / I / not lose / remind

   _____ their sense of humor.

6.5 Verbs Followed by a Gerund or Infinitive without a Change in Meaning

1. Some verbs can be followed by a gerund or an infinitive with no or almost no difference in meaning. These verbs include: *begin, (not) bother, can't stand, continue, hate, like, love, prefer, start.*	I **began exercising** regularly last year. I **began to exercise** regularly last year. Don't **bother making dinner**. We'll go out tonight. Don't **bother to make dinner**. We'll go out tonight.

2. You can use *prefer* to compare two activities in the following ways:
  a. *prefer* + gerund + *to* + gerund/noun
  b. *prefer* + infinitive + *rather than* + verb
	
	a. I **prefer swimming** to **running**.
	b. I **prefer to swim** rather than **run**.

6 Complete the exercises.

A Rewrite the sentences. Change the gerunds to infinitives (sentences 1–4) and the infinitives to gerunds (sentences 5–8).

1. I can't stand staying in bed all day long when I'm sick.

   I can't stand to stay in bed all day long when I'm sick.

2. I prefer using medicinal plants to taking medicine.

_____

3. I like getting phone calls from my friends when I'm sick.

_____

4. When I feel ill, I start looking up my symptoms on the Internet.

_____

5. I begin to worry right away when I have symptoms.

_____

6. I prefer to wait rather than go to the doctor immediately.

_____

7. I don't bother to tell anyone when I don't feel well.

_____

8. I hate to sit in the waiting room at the doctor's office.

_____

B SPEAK. Work with a partner. Say which sentences in exercise **A** are true for you.

A: *When I don't feel well, I can't stand to stay in bed all day long.*

B: *Me neither. I get bored and my back starts to bother me.*

6.6 Verbs Followed by a Gerund or Infinitive with a Change in Meaning

1. Some verbs can be followed by a gerund or infinitive, but with a change in meaning. These verbs are *stop*, *remember*, and *forget*.	I'll never **forget meeting** you for the very first time. Sorry, I **forgot to meet** you at the gym yesterday.
2. Use *stop* + a gerund to say that a person or thing ended an activity.	He **stopped drinking** coffee a year ago. My car **stopped working**.
Use *stop* + an infinitive to tell the reason why a person or animal stopped. The infinitive gives the reason.	It was a long drive. We only **stopped to eat** lunch. The cat **stopped to watch** the bird.
3. Use *remember* + a gerund to talk about a memory or something in the past.	I **remember calling** last week, but I don't remember what day it was.
Remember + an infinitive means you remember to do a necessary task or action.	He never **remembers to call** when he arrives safely.
4. Use *forget* + a gerund to talk about a memory. It is often used with a negative.	I'll never **forget hiking** to the top of the mountain. I **didn't forget meeting** him. I just forgot his name.
Forget + an infinitive means someone did not remember to do a necessary task or action.	He often **forgets to do** his homework. Did you **forget to pay** the rent?

7 Complete the stories with the gerund or infinitive form of each verb in parentheses.

Nina Garfield, Avalanche Survivor

Nina Garfield almost didn't survive her recent ski trip. She remembers
(1) _____enjoying_____ (enjoy) a beautiful day on the mountain with her friends,
all expert skiers. All of a sudden, the snow started moving underneath her. Nina
remembers (2) _____ (fall) and rolling around in the snow. Luckily, the
snow didn't bury her. What saved Nina's life? When she was packing, she remembered
(3) _____ (put) airbags into her backpack. When the avalanche began, the
airbags opened and helped Nina keep her head above the snow. She says that she'll never
forget (4) _____ (bring) airbags with her on ski trips in the future.

Juan Ramos, K2 Climb Survivor

When Juan Ramos was close to the top of K2, the second highest mountain in the
world, it was evening and already getting dark. He stopped (5) _____
(admire) the view. Then, he began his return trip down to the camp. However, it began
to snow hard, so he had to stop (6) _____ (move) because he couldn't see.
He stayed on the mountain for two freezing, stormy nights before the weather cleared.
Fortunately, he had not forgotten (7) _____ (bring) a lot of water with him.
Not drinking enough can be life-threatening in high altitudes. Ramos says he'll never forget
(8) _____ (feel) such fear.

PRACTICE

8 Complete the exercises.

A Read each statement. Complete the sentence so that it is similar in meaning to the statement. Use infinitives in your answers.

1. "Last time I had a cold, I forgot about taking vitamin C. This time, I took it." (Aaron)

   Aaron remembered _to take vitamin C_____.

2. "My grandfather thinks I should take a walk by the sea." (James)

   James's grandfather wants James _____.

3. "I don't like to take medicine. I think drinking hot milk is much better." (Suzana)

   Suzana prefers _____.

4. "Make sure you rub plant oil on your back." (Li's mom)

   Li's mom reminded him _____.

5. "My parents say that I can't drink coffee or soda." (Lisa)

   Lisa's parents don't allow Lisa _____.

6. "My mother can make noodle soup that cures colds." (Sang)

Sang's mother knows how _____.

7. "I still have a cold, so I need to keep resting as much as possible." (Felipe)

Felipe should continue _____.

8. "My mother said adding garlic to my soup will cure anything." (Oscar)

Oscar's mother reminded him _____.

B SPEAK. Work in groups. Discuss ways you deal with a cold. Use gerunds and infinitives.

My mother always told me to drink a lot of orange juice.

9 Complete the exercises.

A Complete the article. Use the correct form of the verbs in parentheses. Add an object pronoun where necessary. Sometimes either the gerund or the infinitive form of the verb is correct.

Can venom be good for you?

While Michael was on vacation in Mexico, he (1) _____*decided to go*_____ (decide / go) for a swim. It was very hot, and he (2) _____ (want / get) some cool relief. He jumped into the pool, but instead of relief, all of a sudden he (3) _____ (start / feel) a burning pain in his leg. He looked down and saw his attacker—a poisonous scorpion. Michael got to a local hospital quickly, and about 30 hours later, the pain (4) _____ (seem / disappear). He was very relieved.

But that isn't the end of the story. Before the scorpion bite, Michael had been suffering from back pain. Doctors had often (5) _____ (encourage / him / do) regular exercise such as swimming. Surprisingly, days after the scorpion bite, his back pain went away, and it never came back. The scorpion's venom had cured him. Whenever he (6) _____ (remember / suffer) from his horrible back pain, he is grateful for that scorpion.

Experts (7) _____ (advise / people / not go) anywhere near scorpions or snakes. But if scorpion researchers (8) _____ (stop / work) with these creatures, we might not find out more about the medical benefits their venom can provide.

◄ A venomous
bark scorpion,
Arizona, United
States

B Listen and check your answers.

10 **EDIT.** Read the poster. Find and correct seven more errors with gerunds and infinitives.

First-Aid Tips for Treating Cuts

Do you remember ~~to cut~~ ^cutting yourself when you were a child? Did you know how take care of the cut, or did you ask to someone to help you? Of course, it's not only children who cut themselves. That is why we urge everyone having a first-aid kit at home. We also want you follow this advice.

- For minor cuts: After the cut stops to bleed, start rinsing the wound with clear water. Clean the area around the wound with soap and a washcloth. Avoid getting soap directly in the wound.

- For deep cuts: Put pressure on the cut to stop the bleeding. Continue to putting pressure on the wound for 20 or 30 minutes.

- If the wound can get dirty, put a bandage on it and remember changing it every day.

- Remember! Teach your children about first aid, and remind them to not play with sharp objects.

11 Read the situations about sports injuries. Then complete the sentences. Use infinitives and gerunds where necessary.

> Lucy used to run every weekend, but she doesn't now because her feet have been hurting her a lot. She hates to miss her runs, and she's tired of being in pain, so she goes to see a foot specialist. The specialist's advice: "Wear proper shoes. Ice your feet often. Your feet will always give you trouble unless you follow my advice."

1. Lucy has stopped _running every weekend_ .

2. Lucy can't stand _____ .

3. Lucy decides _____ because of the problem with her feet.

4. The foot specialist warns Lucy _____ or she will continue to have pain.

5. The specialist also tells Lucy _____ often.

6. The specialist tells her she needs to follow his advice or her feet will continue _____ .

Jake's favorite sport is mountain biking, but recently he's been biking less because of pain in his knees. It costs him a lot of money, but Jake goes to see a sports injury specialist. Some advice from the specialist: "Raise the seat of the bike. Do leg muscle exercises in the gym." Jake will remember to do the exercises every day because he wants to go mountain biking again soon.

7. Jake loves _____ .

8. Jake pays _____ .

9. The specialist has advised Jake _____ .

10. The specialist wants Jake _____ in the gym.

11. Jake won't forget _____ .

12. Jake hopes _____ .

12 APPLY.

A Check (✓) the medical problems you have had. Then make notes about how you have dealt with the problems.

Medical Problems	(✓)	Ways That I Have Dealt with the Problem
Burn		
Earache		
Headache		
Muscle pain		
Sprained ankle		
Toothache		
Other:		

B Write six sentences about the problems you checked in exercise **A**. Use some of the verbs in the box. Remember to use gerunds and infinitives appropriately.

advise	begin	encourage	forget	remember	start	want
ask	continue	expect	prefer	remind	stop	warn

The last time I had a burn, my friend advised me to put ice on the burn. I felt better right away, and I think my burn healed faster.

C Work in groups. Share your sentences. Ask questions to get more information.

EXPLORE

1 READ the article about the work of one man, Feliciano dos Santos, in his home country. What are some serious problems in the part of Mozambique where he is from?

The Guitar Man

For Feliciano dos Santos, a guitar is an excellent weapon in the fight against disease. Along with his band, Massukos, Santos plays music to educate people about how personal hygiene[1] helps to prevent illness. In fact, one of the band's greatest hits is *Tissambe Manja*, which means "Wash Our Hands."

Santos performs in some of the poorest, most remote[2] villages of his home country, Mozambique. His songs provide information and motivation for villagers. He uses traditional music, rhythms, and local languages to get his message across.

Santos has focused his efforts on Niassa, the part of Mozambique where he is from. He has not forgotten the challenges of growing up there. In Niassa, there is **not enough clean water to meet** people's needs. Unclean water is the cause of many diseases, including polio. As a child, Santos had polio, and he knows how it feels to be ill. He also knows that many of the people are **too poor to travel** for medical care.

> Music has the power to change people.
> —Feliciano dos Santos

▼ Feliciano dos Santos

In addition to performing, Santos works on projects to improve sanitation.[3] Thanks to Santos, there are now water pumps and low-cost, environmentally friendly toilets in many villages. **It wasn't easy to make** these changes, but the project was **effective enough to provide** Niassa with a basic sanitation system. Santos's projects have been so successful that they now serve as models for other development programs around the world.

[1] **hygiene:** the practice of keeping yourself and your surroundings clean
[2] **remote:** far away from places where most people live
[3] **sanitation:** the process of keeping a place clean and healthy

2 CHECK. Correct the error in each sentence so that it is true according to the article.

guitar

1. Feliciano dos Santos uses a ~~piano~~ to teach people about keeping clean.

2. Santos's band plays songs in English to communicate their message.

3. Santos does most of his work in small cities in Mozambique.

4. Santos thinks that Niassa needs more traditional music.

5. Other countries have little to learn from Santos's sanitation projects.

3 DISCOVER. Complete the exercises to learn about the grammar in this lesson.

A Underline the infinitives in the sentences from the article on page 161.

1. In Niassa, there is not enough clean water to meet people's needs.

2. He also knows that many of the people are too poor to travel for medical care.

3. It wasn't easy to make these changes.

4. The project was effective enough to provide Niassa with a basic sanitation system.

B Look back at the sentences in exercise **A**. Pay attention to the words before the infinitive and after the main verb. Write the number of the sentence that has each pattern.

_____ a. adjective + *enough* + infinitive   _____ c. *enough* + (adjective) + noun + infinitive

_____ b. adjective + infinitive   _____ d. *too* + adjective + infinitive

Feliciano dos
Santos

162

LEARN

6.7   Infinitives after the Subject *It*; Infinitives after Adjectives

1. An infinitive phrase is often used in a sentence that has *it* as the subject. *It* has the same meaning as the infinitive phrase at the end of the sentence.	**It** is fun **to go to the beach**. Subject Infinitive Phrase
2. The following verbs are common between *it* and the infinitive phrase: *appear, be, cost, seem, take*.	**It costs** a lot **to take** the course. **It takes** time **to lose** weight.
3. The following adjectives are common between *it* and the infinitive phrase: *challenging, difficult, easy, exciting, important, necessary, rewarding*.	**It** is **easy to learn** English. **It** is **important to pay** attention in class.
4. The following adjectives do not follow *it*, but they are also common before an infinitive: *afraid, determined, disappointed, easy, glad, lucky, relieved, reluctant, willing.**	I'm **determined to get** a good score on the exam. I'm **reluctant to pay** for private lessons. We're **not willing to share** one book.
5. When an infinitive follows an adjective, use *for* + an object (*for someone*) before the infinitive to indicate who or what the adjective refers to.	The exercises are hard **for young children** to do.

*See page **A5** for a list of adjectives followed by infinitives.

4   Rewrite the first part of each sentence with *it* as the subject. Use infinitives.

1. Helping people from Niassa is rewarding for Feliciano dos Santos.

   _____It is rewarding for Feliciano dos Santos to help_____ people from Niassa.

2. Communication is possible through music.

   _____ through music.

3. Learning about sanitation is important for children.

   _____ about sanitation.

4. Educating people about good hygiene takes a lot of thought.

   _____ about good hygiene.

5. Washing your hands frequently is necessary to prevent disease.

   _____ to prevent disease.

6. Getting clean water to a remote village takes time.

   _____ to a remote village.

5 Complete the sentences. Use the verb *be*, the adjectives in parentheses, and infinitives.

1. Some people are uncomfortable with trying new health practices.

   Some people _are reluctant to try new health practices_ (reluctant).

2. Governments must be open to solving problems.

   Governments _____ (willing).

3. Some countries are afraid of making changes.

   Some countries _____ (unwilling).

4. Many people feel strongly about getting good health care.

   Many people _____ (determined).

5. Some people do not like talking about illness.

   Some people _____ (hesitant).

6. We really want to make the world a healthier place.

   We _____ (ready).

6.8 *Too* and *Enough* with Infinitives

Too + Infinitive	*Enough* + Infinitive
The hospital is **too small to treat** everyone.	The hospital is **big enough to treat** everyone.
We have **too much homework to do**.	Is there **enough food to feed** everybody?
The doctor has **too many patients to see**.	Are there **enough eggs to make** an omelet?

1. *Too* + an adjective means "more than what is wanted or possible." You can use the infinitive after *too* + an adjective to explain why something is not possible.	He is **too weak to walk**. The medicine is **too strong to take daily**.

2. You can also use the infinitive after *too* + a noun to explain why something is not possible. Use these patterns:
  a. *too much* + non-count noun + infinitive
  b. *too many* + plural count noun + infinitive
	
	a. I have **too much work to do**.
	b. There are **too many children to take** care of.

3. *Enough* means "an amount that is wanted or possible." *Not enough* means "less than is wanted or possible." Use the infinitive after an adjective + *enough* or after *enough* + a noun.	They are **(not) tall enough to reach** the shelf. We have **enough data to write** the report.
4. A noun object or pronoun may come before the infinitive in sentences with *too* and *enough*. Use *for* before the noun or pronoun.	The music isn't loud enough **for <u>me</u> to hear**. The chair is too small **for <u>my father</u> to sit** in. There is not enough time **for <u>her</u> to visit**.

6 Circle the correct words to complete the paragraph about an African health clinic that is mobile (on wheels).

Sometimes people don't have (1) **(enough information)** / information enough to make the right health choices. At our mobile clinic, it's hard for the staff to explain (2) **too many / too much** things at one time. That's why we hold educational workshops several times a week. Our meeting room is (3) **enough big / big enough** to hold 30 people. The doctors and nurses have learned to speak the local language, so their language skills are good enough (4) **for them / for they** to communicate with the villagers. At the meetings, we explain all the medical services we offer. At the end of the meetings, we always have (5) **enough / too many** time to answer questions.

If people find that it costs (6) **too many / too much** money to use our services, we treat them for free. When they live (7) **far enough / too far** away to travel to a hospital, we can help them instead. There aren't (8) **enough health clinics / health clinics enough** in many areas of Mozambique, so it's really important to have mobile health clinics that can come to the areas that need them.

6.9 Infinitives of Purpose

	Purpose
She went to the store	**in order to** get bread.
	to get bread.

1. Use an infinitive of purpose to say why someone does something or what something is for.	He teaches **in order to help** others. We use this scale **to weigh** ourselves.
2. Use *in order not to* for negative purposes.	I drink a lot of water **in order not to get** dehydrated.
3. **Be careful!** Do not use *for* to say why someone does something.	✓ I'm taking this class **to learn** English. ✗ I'm taking this class <u>for</u> learning English.

7 Complete the sentences. Use *to* or *in order not to* and the verbs in parentheses.

1. Paulo practices medicine <u>to help</u> (help) people around the world.

2. He follows several steps _____ (make) mistakes or waste supplies at work.

3. He volunteers _____ (bring) health care to poor places.

4. Paulo is working in a lab _____ (develop) a new medicine for diabetes.

5. He writes papers _____ (inform) other doctors about his research.

6. He also pays attention to other doctors' work _____ (learn) as much as he can.

7. He avoids complex language _____ (confuse) patients.

8. He listens to people _____ (try) to understand their health concerns.

9. Paulo's organization always needs money _____ (pay) for projects.

10. It organizes concerts with famous performers _____ (raise) money.

PRACTICE

8 Read the paragraph about Dr. Hayat Sindi and her research to improve health care. Insert *to* where it is missing in each sentence in **bold**.

Dr. Hayat Sindi is a medical researcher from Saudi Arabia. (1) **She has co-invented and developed a way ~~to~~ detect disease with a tiny piece of paper.** (2) **It appears be an ordinary piece of paper, but it is not.** (3) **It took a lot of time for her develop the device**; (4) **however, she was determined find a simple, inexpensive way monitor health.** Sindi's organization, Diagnostics for All (DFA), brings affordable health diagnoses to the world's poorest people.

(5) **There has never been a problem too great for Sindi solve.** (6) **When she moved to England continue her studies,** (7) **her English was not good enough attend university.** But that did not stop her. She improved her English by watching news broadcasts, and (8) **she studied up to 20 hours a day prepare for college entrance exams.** (9) **She was the first Saudi woman study at Cambridge University in the field of biotechnology.**

Sindi's accomplishments have made her a role model for women and girls around the world. (10) **She feels it is important for women know that they can transform society.**

▶ Hayat Sindi, emerging explorer and science entrepreneur

9 Read the information in the chart about medical innovations. Then use the words to write sentences with infinitives. Use the simple present. Add *not* and *for* when necessary.

Medical Innovations		
Device	How It Works	Purpose
Diagnostics for All (DFA) patterned paper	The paper "reads" a sample from a patient. If there is an illness, the paper changes color.	Detects illness cheaply and without a lot of equipment
CellScope Oto™ cell phone attachment by CellScope, Inc.	People use their smartphone as a microscope.	Lets parents diagnose their children's ear infections easily, without going to a doctor
Headache-curing implant by Autonomic Technologies, Inc.	The device sends a message to the brain before a headache starts.	Improves the lives of headache sufferers

Patterned Paper by Diagnostics for All

1. the paper / cost / too much / produce

   The paper doesn't cost too much to produce.

2. DFA / produce / the paper / provide inexpensive medical care

   _____

3. it / be / difficult / detect / an illness / with DFA

   _____

The CellScope Oto™ by CellScope, Inc.

4. parents / use / a cell phone / diagnose their children's ear infections

   _____

5. the CellScope Oto / is / hard / parents / use

   _____

6. parents / have / enough time / go to the doctor for every earache

   _____

Headache-Curing Implant by Autonomic Technologies, Inc.

7. people / are / glad / have / relief from headaches

   _____

8. the device / act / early enough / prevent a headache

   _____

10 WRITE & SPEAK. Work with a partner. Answer the questions about health using infinitives and your own ideas. Then share your answers with your partner.

REAL ENGLISH

Infinitives of purpose are often used to answer questions with *Why*.

A: **Why** are you going to the store?
B: **To buy** some fruit.

1. Why shouldn't people eat too many sweets?
   <u>To avoid problems with their teeth.</u>

2. Why do researchers invent new things?
   _____

3. Why should we support health research?
   _____

4. Why should every home have a first-aid kit?
   _____

5. Why do people choose to be medical workers?
   _____

11 LISTEN & WRITE.

CD2-16

A Listen to an interview with a public health researcher in Thailand. Check (✓) the statements that are true according to what you hear.

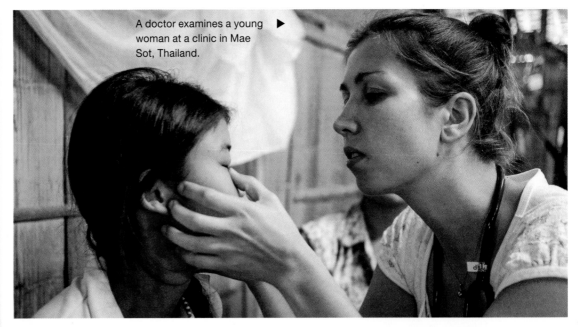

Thailand: A Health Care Success Story

_____ 1. The government of Thailand has universal health care for Thai people.

_____ 2. Thailand was a wealthy country 20 years ago but is not as wealthy today.

_____ 3. Other countries are studying the health model in Thailand to improve their own health care.

A doctor examines a young woman at a clinic in Mae Sot, Thailand. ▶

CD2-16

B Listen again. Then complete the chart about public health in Thailand with information from the interview. Use infinitives of purpose, *too,* and *enough.*

1. **Problem**: People in rural areas _____ lived too far away _____ to get medical treatment in hospitals.

   Solution: The government of Thailand _decided to spend money on the countryside_ in order to bring health care to the rural areas.

2. **Problem**: There wasn't _____ to meet people's needs.

   Solution: The government gave more people safe _____ drink.

3. **Problem**: People lived _____ to access health services.

   Solution: The government built highways _____ remote areas to the cities.

4. **Problem**: There _____ medical workers to give people medical care in remote areas.

   Solution: New medical graduates must serve in rural areas, so there will always be

   _____ people who live outside cities.

12 APPLY.

A Work in groups. Discuss areas in the world where changes could help solve people's health problems. Then complete the chart with two more problems and possible solutions.

Country	Problem	Possible Solutions
	not enough food to feed all people	give farmers seeds to plant more vegetables

B Write five sentences for the problems and solutions you listed in the chart. Use infinitives.

In ____, there isn't enough food to feed all the people. The government should give farmers seeds to plant more vegetables.

Charts
6.1–6.4,
6.6, 6.7,
6.9

1 Circle the correct words to complete the sentences.

1. When Sam doesn't remember **taking** / **to take** his allergy medicine in the morning, he sometimes has difficulty **breathing** / **to breathe** later in the day.

2. Marina stopped at the pharmacy **buying** / **to buy** some tissues because she couldn't stop **sneezing** / **to sneeze**.

3. Jamal would like **tasting** / **to taste** the bread, but he had to stop **eating** / **to eat** bread of any kind because he's allergic to it.

4. Henry has to be careful **not eating** / **not to eat** eggs or anything made with eggs. That's why he often has a hard time **ordering** / **to order** food in a restaurant.

5. Ana's allergy to cats prevents her from **visiting** / **to visit** any of her friends with cats. It's hard for her **being** / **to be** around cats for more than an hour or so.

6. Ali tried allergy pills for his hay fever. They didn't work, so he stopped **taking** / **to take** them.

7. Gina was surprised **learning** / **to learn** that she had a peanut allergy. She remembers **eating** / **to eat** bowls of peanuts when she was younger.

8. Ed is pretty good at **cleaning** / **to clean** his apartment every week. If he doesn't clean it, he is likely **to having** / **to have** an allergic reaction to the dust.

2 **LISTEN.**

Charts
6.1–6.4,
6.8

CD2-17

A Listen to the radio broadcast. Then complete the answers to the questions with the word in parentheses. Use gerunds, infinitives, prepositions, *too*, and *not enough* where necessary.

1. How do many people spend a lot of their time?

   They spend a lot of time ___sitting at a computer___ (sit).

2. Why are many people unable to enjoy nature?

   They are _____ (busy) outside.

3. What does Richard Louv write about?

   He writes about the _____ (benefits) outside.

4. What did Louv's first book do?

   It encouraged _____ (start) nature programs.

5. When the high school principal gave him a choice, what did Martinez do?

   Martinez decided _____ (join).

6. According to Louv, what changed Juan Martinez's life?

_____ (connect) changed his life.

7. What does Martinez think many children don't have enough of?

They _____ (connect) with nature.

8. What does Martinez emphasize in his lectures?

He emphasizes the importance _____ (get) outdoors.

CD2-17
B Listen again and check your answers.

Charts
6.1–6.7
3 **EDIT.** Read the article about student stress. Find and correct eight more errors with gerunds and infinitives.

A Furry Solution to Student Stress

Dealing
~~Deal~~ with stress is becoming more and more of a problem for young people. Many

students say that they are having trouble falling asleep at night because of the pressures

of school. They also say that they are constantly worried about get good grades.

Some schools are trying to do something about the problem. In one high school,

five-year-old Maddy greets the students as they enter the building every morning. Maddy

seems happy being there, and the students like to see her. They have fun greeting her, and

they walk away with smiles on their faces. It doesn't cost much for the school have Maddy

there every day because Maddy is a dog.

The school considered to set up a special room where students could go to relax, but

it was too expensive do. In addition, some parents didn't want their children to take time

out from classes in order relax. They thought that it was important for their children to be

in class as much as possible.

Experts disagree and warn parents not putting too much pressure on their children.

Encouraging children to relax are the best way for parents to help them.

Charts
6.1–6.7
4 **SPEAK.** Work in groups. Have a discussion about stress in people your age. Then draw a chart like the one below. Write five things in every column.

Causes of Stress	Physical and/or Emotional Effects	Things You Can Do to Relieve Stress

Connect the Grammar to Writing

1 READ & NOTICE THE GRAMMAR.

A Have you ever bought a product after you read a review of it? What kind of product was it? Tell a partner. Then read the product review.

Keeping Fit with the Zip by Fitbit

Starting a new exercise routine is not a problem for me, but I always have difficulty sticking to one. However, things have changed ever since I got my Zip by Fitbit. The Zip is a small device that measures the number of steps you take every day. It also measures your distance and the number of calories that you burn. It really encourages you to be active. Exercising becomes more fun!

One great thing about the Zip is its small size. Also, it's very easy to clip on. Knowing that it is measuring your steps encourages you to get out of your chair more often. With your Zip on, you will probably decide to walk or take the stairs instead of driving or taking the elevator.

Another great aspect of Zip is that it is easy to connect to your smartphone or computer, so you can share your goals and progress with others. It challenges you to try to take the most steps and burn the most calories. I convinced my brother to get a Zip a few months ago, and now we are competing with each other. I am determined to beat him; sometimes, I go for long walks at night in order to get a higher score. The competition is fun, but more important is my achievement: I've started to exercise regularly, and I feel great.

GRAMMAR FOCUS

In this product review, the writer uses gerunds and infinitives with the following patterns:

Gerunds
- as the subject of the clause (**Starting** *a new exercise routine is not a problem . . .*)
- after certain nouns (*. . . I always have **difficulty sticking** to one.*)
- after prepositions (*. . . instead **of driving** or **taking** the elevator.*)

Infinitives
- after a verb + an object (*It really **encourages you to be** active.*)
- after a verb + an adjective (*I **am determined to beat** him . . .*)
- after *it* + a verb + an adjective (***It's** very **easy to clip on** . . .*)

B Read the product review in exercise **A** again. Find one more gerund and one more infinitive. Write the pattern for each. Use the box above and the grammar charts in the unit to help you.

Gerund/Infinitive	Pattern

C Look at the graphic organizer that the writer used to generate ideas for the product review in exercise **A**. Cross out the features that the writer did NOT choose to write about.

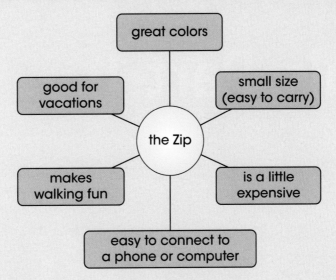

2 BEFORE YOU WRITE.

A Work with a partner. Discuss a product that you like or dislike. Brainstorm its positive or negative features. Then write your ideas in a graphic organizer like the one in exercise **1C**.

B Look at your graphic organizer and choose two or three features to include in your product review. Cross out the features that you do not want to write about.

3 WRITE two or three paragraphs about the product. Your review can be either positive or negative. Use your ideas from exercise **2B** to organize your writing.

WRITING FOCUS   Avoiding Comma Splices

A comma splice is an error that occurs when two independent clauses are separated by a comma. A comma splice can be fixed by:
- adding a conjunction (*and, but, so*) after the comma
- changing the comma to a period and beginning a new sentence with the second clause
- changing the comma to a semicolon (**;**) between the two clauses

Comma splice:
✗ I went for a walk in the forest, at 9 o'clock I came home.

Corrected:
✓ I went for a walk in the forest, **and** at 9 o'clock I came home.
✓ I went for a walk in the forest. **At** 9 o'clock I came home.
✓ I went for a walk in the forest; **at** 9 o'clock I came home.

---

4 SELF ASSESS. Read your product review. Underline the infinitives and circle the gerunds. Use the checklist to assess your work.

- [ ] I used gerunds as subjects and objects. [6.1]
- [ ] I used gerunds and infinitives after the correct verbs. [6.3, 6.4, 6.5]
- [ ] I used infinitives with *it* as the subject or with *too* and *enough*. [6.6, 6.7]
- [ ] I avoided comma splices. [WRITING FOCUS]

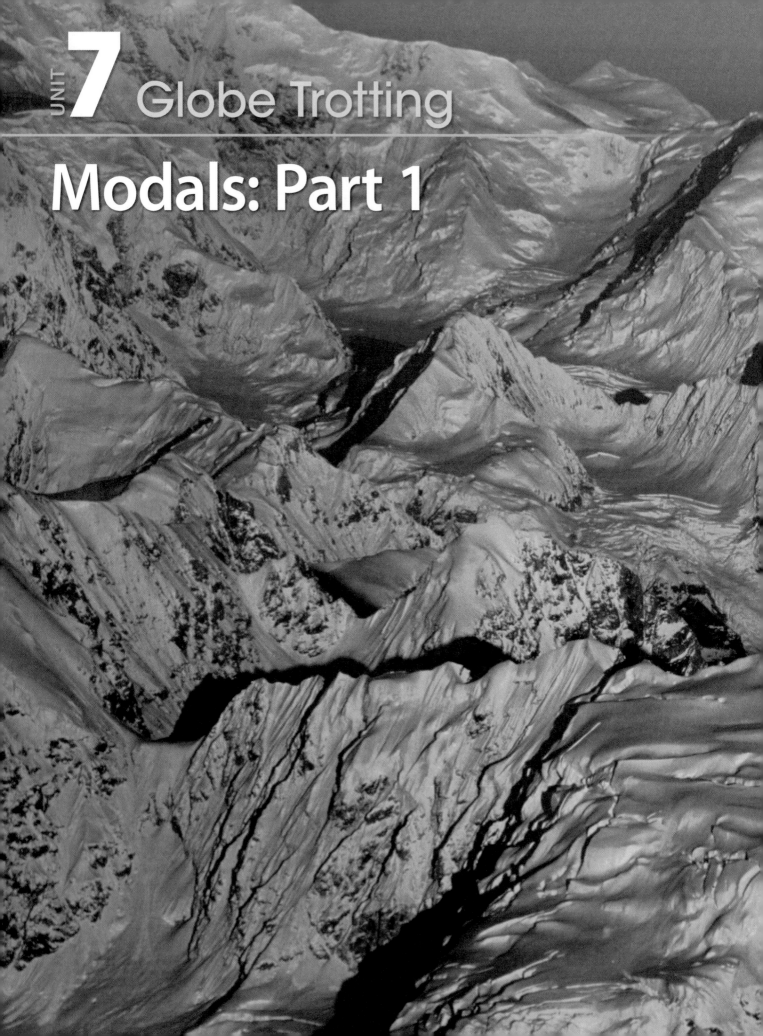

Modals: Part 1

▼ Plane flying over mountains, Wrangell St. Elias National Park, Alaska

175

EXPLORE

1 READ the web page. What should people think about when they scuba dive?

Best Dive Vacations International

HOME ABOUT US CLASSES FAQS TRIPS

What is scuba diving? SCUBA refers to the equipment that divers **must wear** so that they can stay underwater for long periods of time. When you scuba dive, you can explore exotic places, take terrific pictures, and exercise your body and mind. It's also a great way to make friends because you **have to** dive with other people. In the past, divers could not stay underwater very long. They often **had to hold** their breath.[1] Now, divers have air tanks that give them fresh oxygen so they can stay down for a long time.

Here are answers to some common questions.

Q: Do I **have to be** a great athlete to scuba dive?

A: No, but you **have to be** healthy. Before taking a diving class, you **must fill out** a medical questionnaire. You **will have to take** a water-skills assessment[2] test, too.

Q: Is scuba diving dangerous?

A: It can be. At the end of the dive, for example, you **must not come** to the surface too quickly. If you do, you can get sick.

Q: Where is a good place to scuba dive? I've heard that Bali **is supposed to be** great. Is that true?

A: Yes, Bali is a popular destination for diving. Go in June, and you **won't have to worry** about heavy rain at that time of year.

[1] **hold your breath:** take air in and not let the air out
[2] **assessment:** evaluation

2 CHECK. Write the missing words to make true sentences according to the web page.

1. Scuba equipment allows divers to stay underwater for _____ periods of time.

2. Not all scuba divers are great _____.

3. It's very important for a scuba diver to be _____.

4. A diver should avoid coming to the surface of the water very _____.

5. Springtime in Bali is good for scuba diving because there won't be a lot of _____.

3 DISCOVER. Complete the exercises to learn about the grammar in this lesson.

A Use information from the web page in exercise **1** to complete these sentences about SCUBA.

1. SCUBA refers to the equipment that divers _____ wear.

2. They often _____ hold their breath.

3. You _____ be healthy.

4. You _____ come to the surface too quickly.

5. Bali _____ great.

B The words you wrote in exercise **A** change the meaning of the main verbs. Match the words with their meanings.

_____ 1. *have to*   a. prohibition

_____ 2. *be supposed to*   b. expectation

_____ 3. *must not*   c. necessity

LEARN

7.1 Expressing Necessity and Prohibition

Must	Have To
You **must check** your luggage. She **must fill in** another form.	We **have to get up** early for the tour. He **has to be** careful when he flies.

Must Not	Not Have To
You **must not text** while driving. She **must not miss** any more classes.	We **don't have to get up** early tomorrow. **Doesn't** he **have to go** to class tonight?

1. *Must* and *have to* are used before a verb to show that something is necessary.	Sue **must pass** the course in order to graduate. Sue **has to pass** the course in order to graduate.
2. *Have to* is a modal-like expression. It has different forms for the present, past, future, and present perfect.	He always **has to arrive** at work by 9:00. She **had to work** late yesterday. I **will have to read** the notes tomorrow. I **have had to work** on this problem all night.
3. *Must* is often used with rules, laws, and commands. It is not usually used in questions. *Have to* is used to express necessity in most other situations. *Have to* is more common in conversation than *must*.	Drivers **must obey** the rules of the road. To get a license, you **must take** a test and **complete** a written exam. I **have to finish** the report today. You **have to think about** your future. **Do** we **have to hand in** our homework?
4. *Must not* means that something is prohibited or not allowed. *Not have to* means that it is not necessary to do something.	Workers **must not enter** the building until the doors open at 9:00. I **don't have to go** to school tomorrow. It's a holiday.
5. *Have got to* is also used to talk about necessity, but it is less formal than *have to* or *must*. It is usually used only in affirmative statements, not in questions or negative statements.	✓ I **have got to study** more next time. ✓ I**'ve got to study** more next time. ✗ <u>Have you got to study</u> more next time? ✗ I <u>haven't got to go</u>.

*Modals are words such as *can*, *could*, *should*, and *will*. They add meaning to the main verb that follows them. Modals do not have different forms and are always followed by the base form of a verb.

4 Circle the correct words to complete the conversation. In some sentences, more than one answer is possible.

A: How was the scuba diving trip?

B: It was terrific. But I (1) **must /(had to)** get my diving certification first.

A: Really? (2) **Did you have to / Must you** get it, or did you want to get it?

B: Well, I (3) **didn't have to / must not** have the certification to do basic diving, but that got boring after a while. I (4) **must / had to** do the certification training in order to dive more freely.

A: So what (5) **do people have to / have people got to** do for the certification? Are there a lot of tests?

B: Well, everyone (6) **has got to / must** float or tread water for 10 minutes, and you (7) **have got to / must** be able to swim 200 yards.

A: Oh, about 180 meters. That's not very much. I guess you (8) **don't have to / haven't got to** be an excellent swimmer to get the certification.

B: No, you don't. There are also written tests, pool work, and diving practice; but you can do it all over a period of several weeks. It (9) **doesn't have to / must not** be an intensive course. I actually think it's better to do the training over a period of time.

A: I (10) **have got to / have to** try it soon. I've always wanted to go scuba diving.

5 Complete the paragraph with *must, must not,* or a form of *have to/not have to*. More than one answer is sometimes possible.

Diving Safely

You can have a great time scuba diving, but you (1) ____have to____ remember that it can be dangerous. In order to dive safely, you (2) _____ forget the possible dangers underwater. For example, watch out for sea creatures. Divers don't get attacked very often, but you (3) _____ know which animals to stay away from. You also (4) _____ consider the effect of the force of the water on the body. A diver (5) _____ go down slowly to avoid ear pain or injury. Coming up slowly is important, too. You (6) _____ rise to the surface too quickly, or you could get very sick. Most importantly, a diver (7) _____ stay alert. If you follow these rules, you (8) _____ worry, and you will enjoy your dive.

▼ A green turtle swims near a scuba diver.

7.2 Expressing Obligation and Expectation: *Be Supposed To*

Be Supposed To

I'm **supposed to buy** textbooks before the first class.
You're late. You **were supposed to be** here an hour ago.

1. *Be supposed to* is a modal-like expression. It expresses an obligation because of expectations, rules, laws, or other people's requests.	You **are supposed to call** the hotel to cancel the reservation. Aren't you going to do that?
2. *Be supposed to* can also express an expectation based on a schedule, plan, or a person's opinion.	We **are supposed to be** at the boarding gate a half hour before departure.
3. *Was/were supposed to* means that the action or event was expected, but it did not happen.	I **was supposed to drive** my friend to the station, but my car broke down.

6 Complete the paragraphs. Use the correct form of *be supposed to*.

According to some travel websites, volunteering on a boat (1) _is supposed to_ be a great way to see the world without spending a lot of money. You help out on a boat and you get a place to sleep in exchange. Everyone on the trip (2) _____ share the cost of food.

This kind of volunteering seemed like a great idea, so I read the blogs of a couple of people who had done it. One person, Manny, went on a trip to the South Pacific with an older couple. Their daughter (3) _____ travel with them, but she changed her mind at the last minute. The couple heard about the volunteer program and asked Manny to come with them instead for six months. While he was on the trip, he (4) _____ help with the cooking, cleaning, and boat chores.

Unfortunately, the trip turned out to be much shorter than expected. Manny and the couple (5) _____ go around the world, but they had to end the trip in the South Pacific because of a problem with the boat. Manny enjoyed himself anyway and said he can't wait to do it again. He (6) _____ meet some new boat owners soon to arrange a couple months at sea.

PRACTICE

7 Complete the statements about the Galápagos Islands. Use the words in the box. You can use some words more than once.

didn't have to	had to	was supposed to	have got to
~~don't have to~~	are supposed to	were supposed to	will have to

1. There are a lot of optional day trips. You ___don't have to___ go on any of them, but some are really great. You _____ sign up for the trips the night before, but I think you can also just show up in the morning and go.

2. Our plane _____ arrive at 4:30 in Quito, but it didn't land until 11:00 at night. Our tour guide _____ wait at the airport for over six hours. Then, when our luggage was not on the plane, the guide located it for us. We _____ do anything.

3. We _____ bring our own wetsuits. We didn't know that, so we _____ rent some.

4. You _____ check out my photos of the iguanas! I took this shot from just a few feet away. Next time, I _____ try to get a shot of the sea lions, too.

8 **PRONUNCIATION.** Read the chart and listen to the examples. Then complete the exercises.

CD2-19

> **PRONUNCIATION** **Reduced Forms of *Have To* and *Have Got To***
>
> *Have to, has to, have got to,* and *has got to* are often reduced.
>
> **Examples:** | **Full Pronunciation** | **Reduced Pronunciation**
> We have to help Mom. | We /hæftə/ help Mom.
> Nobody has to know. | Nobody /hæstə/ know.
> You don't have to pay right away. | You don't /hæftə/ pay right away.
> I have got to go now. | I've /gatə/ go now.
> Jack has got to get up. | Jack's /gatə/ get up.

CD2-20

A Listen to the statements. Write the full form of the words you hear.

1. We ___have to___ be there in 20 minutes, or we'll miss the plane.

2. Everybody _____ be back on time. We leave at 6 o'clock sharp.

3. You _____ call us every day.

4. Max _____ learn some basic Chinese before he goes.

5. I'm sorry that I'm late. I _____ take an earlier train next time.

6. We _____ buy gifts before we go back home.

CD2-20

B Listen again and repeat the sentences from exercise **A**.

9 READ, WRITE & SPEAK.

A Look at the airport arrival and departure information. Complete the sentences with the correct form of *have to*, *have got to*, or *be supposed to*. Add *not* where necessary. More than one answer is sometimes possible.

✈ **DEPARTURES**			
Destination	**Scheduled Departure Time**	**Status**	**Gate**
Beijing	8:00	Now boarding	E4
London	7:30	1 hour delay	B3
Seoul	9:45	On time	C1
Istanbul	11:30	Canceled	
Addis Ababa	3:10	Departed 3:40	

🛬 **ARRIVALS**			
Departure City	**Scheduled Arrival Time**	**Actual Arrival Time**	**Status**
Tokyo	6:30		Expected 8:30
Jakarta	2:40	2:15	Arrived
Cairo	4:30		5-hour delay
Quito	5:45	5:45	Arrived
Mexico City	6:30		2-hour delay

1. It's 7:35 A.M. Lynn is flying to Beijing. She's just finished going through security. She ___*has to OR has got to*___ get to the gate quickly.

2. It's 8:00 A.M. The passengers for the flight to London are still at the gate, and they're not happy. The plane _____ depart at 7:30.

3. It's 9:40 A.M. The flight to Seoul _____ take off in five minutes, but the doors of the plane are still open.

4. Hank _____ fly to Istanbul at 11:30 A.M. Now he _____ find another way to get there.

5. It's 2:20 P.M. Mr. Halim is on the flight from Jakarta. He was worried about getting to his meeting at 4:00 P.M. Now, he _____ worry about being late.

6. It's 7:00 P.M. Celia is returning from Mexico City. Her brother thought he _____ leave for the airport at 5:45 P.M., but now he _____ rush to get there.

B Imagine that it's 12:00 P.M. Write two sentences about the arrival and departure information in exercise **A**. Leave a blank for the names of the cities. Use the correct forms of *have got to*, *have to*, or *be supposed to*. Add *not* where necessary.

Passengers from _____ *are supposed to arrive at the airport very early in the morning.*

C Read your sentences to the class. Ask your classmates to say the correct city for each of your sentences.

182 MODALS: PART 1

10 EDIT. Read the e-mail. Find and correct eight more errors with modal verbs and modal-like expressions.

Hi Tom,

    I'm writing to tell you some exciting news. I'm suppose~~d~~ to go to Ethiopia in May. I know you had a great time there last year, so I want to ask you a few questions. First of all, when you were there, must you stay in Addis Ababa, or were you able to find good accommodations outside the capital? I also want to go to Bale Mountain National Park. Have I got to camp there, or is there a hotel? Either way, I got to make a reservation very soon, so let me know. How about food? According to my travel guide, visitors are suppose to try *injera*, an interesting kind of bread. I also read that in Ethiopia you have to use a fork. It's not the custom. You're supposed to use *injera* as both the fork and the plate. Is that true?

    I don't have a visa yet, but I know that I got to have one. What am I supposed to doing to get one? Do I have to go to the Ethiopian embassy, or can I do the application online? I'm sorry about all these questions. I promise that you must not answer anymore . . . until my next e-mail!

Best,

Linda

Addis Ababa, Ethiopia

11 LISTEN to the podcast about coffee ceremonies in Ethiopia. Then complete the sentences with an appropriate modal or modal-like expression. More than one answer is sometimes possible.

1. You _____ must _____ plan to spend a lot of time at a coffee ceremony.

2. You _____ leave the ceremony early.

3. You _____ say that the coffee and its preparation are excellent.

4. According to tradition, the oldest person _____ get the first cup of coffee.

5. You _____ say "no" to any of the cups of coffee.

6. You _____ speak the language of your host in order to enjoy yourself.

12 APPLY.

A Write six sentences about a ceremony or ritual in your country or in a country you know. Use *have to, have got to, must,* and *be supposed to.* Add *not* where necessary.

The host of a Japanese tea ceremony must serve Matcha tea, a kind of green tea.

B Read your sentences to the class. Answer any questions your classmates may have.

CD2-21

EXPLORE

1   READ the web page from a travel website. Which of the hotels would you like to stay in?

Traveling Feet

When you travel, your accommodations should be as interesting as the rest of your trip. Today's post is about some of the world's most unusual places to stay.

Nine Hours capsule hotel, Kyoto, Japan

Capsule hotels became popular years ago in Japan, especially among businessmen who worked late and **couldn't catch** the last train home. Nine Hours is a modern capsule hotel with a simple, clean design. Each tiny boxlike room for sleeping has a special alarm clock that wakes guests up with light, not noise. The hotel is right in the center of Kyoto, so it's a quick walk to shops, buses, and subways. Capsule hotels are also good for people who **can't afford** expensive hotel rates.

Jules' Undersea Lodge, Florida, USA

This hotel is completely underwater. In fact, you **have to be able to scuba dive** down 21 feet (6 meters) to reach it. The lodge **is able to accommodate** four people and has showers, a microwave, and a refrigerator. For entertainment, see if you **can identify** the different fish that swim past your window.

▲ Khao Sok Rainforest Resort

Khao Sok Rainforest Resort, Phanom, Thailand

Here you **will be able to observe** the plants and animals of the rainforest from your room in the treetops. Visitors like taking boat trips on the river or elephant rides through the jungle.[1] One guest reports that she **was** even **able to enjoy** visits from monkeys.

---

[1] **jungle:** a hot, humid area with many trees and plants growing close together

2 CHECK. Match the accommodations with the features.

_____ 1. Nine Hours   a. a view of fish

_____ 2. Jules' Undersea Lodge   b. special alarm clocks

_____ 3. Khao Sok Rainforest Resort   c. monkeys

3 DISCOVER. Complete the exercises to learn about the grammar in this lesson.

A Read the sentences from the web page in exercise **1**. Underline the words that show ability or lack of ability.

1. Capsule hotels became popular years ago in Japan, especially among businessmen who worked late and <u>couldn't</u> catch the last train home.

2. Capsule hotels are also good for people who can't afford expensive hotel rates.

3. In fact, you have to be able to scuba dive down 21 feet (6 meters) in order to reach it.

4. For entertainment, see if you can identify the different fish that swim past your window.

5. Here you will be able to observe the plants and animals of the rainforest from your room in the treetops.

▲ A monkey, Thailand

6. One guest reports that she was even able to enjoy visits from monkeys.

B Look at the words you underlined in exercise **A**. Circle **T** for *true* or **F** for *false*.

1. There is more than one way in English to express ability.   **T**   **F**

2. We use *can* with infinitives   **T**   **F**

3. We use *can* after *will*.   **T**   **F**

4. There are two ways to talk about ability in the past.   **T**   **F**

LEARN

7.3 Expressing Ability: Present and Future

Can	*Be Able To*
I **can speak** Chinese, but I **can't speak** Japanese.	Ana and Ella **are able to swim**, but they **aren't able to dive**.

1. *Can* and *be able to* both express ability. *Can't* and *be not able to* express a lack of ability.	We **can speak** English fairly well now. We **are able to speak** English fairly well now. She **can't speak** English very well. She **isn't able to speak** English well.
2. *Can* is used more frequently than *be able to*. *Be able to* is used in more formal situations than *can*.	Sam, I **can come** over now. Mr. Lugo, I'**m able to come** to your office now.
3. *Be able to* has different verb forms.	We **are able to buy** tickets online. He **hasn't been able to go** on vacation all summer.
4. Use *will be able to* (or *be going to*), not *can*, for a future ability that will be learned or new. Use *will be able to* or *can* when the future ability is possible or true now. **Remember:** Do not use *can* with *will*.	I **will be able to read** French after my course. I **am going to be able to write**, too. I'**ll be able to finish** the paper tonight. I **can finish** the paper tonight. ✗ I <u>can will</u> speak English well a year from now.

4 Circle the correct words to complete the travelers' comments. Sometimes both answers are correct.

Flora and Federico

If you visit Nanuku Island in the South Pacific, you won't regret it. We
(1) **can /** (have been able to) do a lot of wonderful things since we got here. With coconut
trees all around, you (2) (can) / (are able to) eat coconuts all day long. The food is delicious,
too. We have been lucky on this trip because we (3) **can / have been able to** go fishing
almost every day so far. It's too bad that we have to leave tomorrow. We (4) **can't / won't be
able to** forget this paradise in the South Pacific.

Lucia

Here we are on beautiful Nanuku Island. We wake up every morning to the sound of
the ocean. The accommodations aren't great, though. We (5) **can't / haven't been able to**
take a shower since yesterday because of a problem with the hot water. The air-conditioning
isn't perfect either. Hopefully, they (6) **are going to be able to / can** fix both problems soon.
On the bright side, we (7) **can / have been able to** kayak around the island three times
since we got here. Yesterday, I learned how to surf and stood up on the surfboard for over
five seconds. Maybe next time I (8) **can / will be able to** stand up longer.

7.4 Expressing Ability: Past

Could	Was Able To
I **could ski** when I was 12, but I **couldn't ski** when I was 8.	I **was able to go** on the tour last week, but my friends **weren't able to join** me.

1. *Could* and *was able to* refer to general ability in the past.	My dad **could** always **fix** broken toys. My dad **was** always **able to fix** broken toys.
2. *Could* is used more frequently than *was/were able to*. *Was/Were able to* is more formal.	Informal: The kids **could ski** when they were four. Formal: The child **was able to read** by age four.
3. Use *was/were able to* (not *could*) to talk about ability at one time in the past. In the negative, use either *couldn't* or *wasn't/weren't able to*.	✓ I **was able to fix** the clock when it stopped. ✗ I <u>could fix</u> the clock when it stopped. ✓ I **couldn't fix** the clock when it stopped. ✓ I **wasn't able to fix** the clock when it stopped.
4. With verbs of perception (*see, hear, understand, remember*), you can use *could* or *was/were able to* to talk about ability at a time in the past.	We were at the back of the theater, but we **could hear** everything. He **was able to see** clearly from the front row.

5 Complete the paragraphs. Write the affirmative or negative forms of *could, was able to,* or *were able to* as appropriate. If two forms are correct, write both.

We drove up and down the narrow streets of Cerbère, but we

(1) _couldn't/weren't able to_ find a parking space. After driving around for 20 minutes,

I finally (2) _____ find a space, but it was tiny. I'm not good

at parking, so I (3) _____ get into the space. My friend had to get out of

the car to direct me. Then, I (4) _____ park the car.

We had to walk a long way to the hotel and carry our bags. On my last hiking trip,

I (5) _____ carry my backpack without difficulty. But this time, I had

packed too much stuff, and the bags were heavy. It was very hot, too. When we saw that we were

lost, we stopped and asked a woman for directions. My friend (6) _____

speak a little French, so he (7) _____ understand her directions. I (8)

_____ understand anything. Believe me, we were very glad when we

finally got to the hotel.

▼ Cerbère, France

7.5 *Be Able To:* Gerunds, Infinitives, and with Modals

Be Able To	
Gerund	**Being able to speak** Russian was helpful during her visit to Moscow.
Infinitive	I want **to be able to travel** by myself.
Modal	People near the emergency exit **must be able to open** the door.

1. *Be able to* describes the ability to do something. Use *being able to* when you need a gerund.*	We were upset about not **being able to** sit together on the plane.
2. Use *to be able to* when you need an infinitive.	She hopes **to be able to** work in Rome after she learns Italian.
3. Use *be able to* after another modal or modal-like expression.	You **should be able to** open the door quickly.

*To review gerunds and infinitives, see Unit 6, starting on page 142.

6 Complete the sentences about alternative travel ideas. Use the correct form of *be able to.*

1. On this yoga retreat, the instructors want you _____ to be able to _____ relax. You will
   enjoy _____ spend a whole month focusing on your mind and spirit.

2. Do you want _____ speak Italian or maybe Chinese? Studying a
   language abroad is a great way to travel. _____ communicate with
   people in a foreign country can be very satisfying.

3. Why not take a cooking class in another country? You don't have to
   _____ speak the local language, because many of the classes are
   in English. However, _____ speak the local language is helpful
   when you visit the local markets to buy ingredients. It's fun _____
   eat at popular restaurants and meet their chefs. And when you return home, you are going
   _____ cook some delicious food.

4. Archaeological digs make great vacations for people who love history and museums.
   When I went on a dig in Tanzania, I was worried about not _____
   do such hard work in the hot sun. But after a few days, I was happy about
   _____ work for hours without any difficulty.

PRACTICE

7 Complete the conversation. Use the correct form of *be able to.* Add *not* when necessary.

Irene: Welcome back, Terry. How was your trip to Turkey? You stayed in a cave, right?

Terry: It wasn't really a cave. It was a cave house in Cappadocia, and it was wonderful. We
(1) _____ were able to _____ experience how our ancestors lived, but we had all the modern
conveniences. Our host was great. He (2) _____ answer all of our
questions.

▲ Cave houses in Cappadocia, Turkey

Irene: Was there a lot to do?

Terry: Tons. And we (3) _____ walk everywhere. I really enjoyed
(4) _____ do that. We didn't need to take buses at all! The only
thing we (5) _____ do was go up in a hot-air balloon because
the weather wasn't good enough. That was a disappointment.

Irene: I was wondering . . . Do you have to (6) _____ speak Turkish in
order to get around?

Terry: No, you don't have to, but it's great if you do. Hopefully, I (7) _____
speak some Turkish next time. I'm taking a class now. I really want
(8) _____ communicate with the local people.

8 ANALYZE THE GRAMMAR. Read the sentences. Underline the form of ability in each
sentence. If possible, write *can, can't, could,* or *couldn't* above the underlined words.
Write **NC** if no change is possible.

1. <u>NC</u>
   <u>Being able to</u> ride in a hot-air balloon was the best part of my trip to Turkey.

2. <u>can</u>
   You <u>are able to</u> see so many things when you go up in a hot-air balloon.

3. I was able to see dozens of caves from the air, and they were beautiful.

4. We were able to take a lot of great pictures from the balloon.

5. My sister wasn't able to come with us on the balloon ride because she was sick.

6. If my sister visits Turkey again, she will be able to go up in a balloon.

9 Complete the sentences. Use an affirmative or negative form of *can, could,* or *be able to.* If two forms are correct, write both.

1. In Catalonia, Spain, people _____have been able to_____ keep the tradition of human tower building alive since the eighteenth century.

2. Participants in the competition _____ build enormous towers using only their bodies.

3. It requires a lot of practice _____ build a tower.

4. Men are usually on the lowest level of the tower because they _____ support the weight of the others.

5. Children need courage. They have to _____ stand on the top of the tower.

6. When children get older and heavier, they _____ be on the top.

7. One year, a team _____ build ten levels.

8. Perhaps sometime in the future, people _____ form even taller towers.

9. _____ trust the other people in the tower is important.

10. There is a competition every two years, so if you _____ see it last year, you will have to wait another year to attend.

10 APPLY.

A Complete the sentences so that they are true about you.

1. When I travel, I can _____, but I can't _____.

2. The first time I went on a trip, I couldn't _____.

3. I have never been able to _____ on a trip.

4. One day, I would like to be able to _____.

5. When people travel, they have to be able to _____.

6. Being able to _____ is important in a foreign country.

B Work in groups. Take turns reading your sentences from exercise **A**. Then ask each other follow-up questions. Use the affirmative or negative of *can, could,* or a form of *be able to.*

A: *When I travel, I can communicate with people in French or Greek, but I can't speak Chinese or Arabic.*

B: *Can you answer when people ask you questions in Greek and French?*

EXPLORE

CD2-23

1 READ the web page. Who would find this information useful?

WWOOFing It!

HOME   FEATURE ARTICLES   PHOTOS   CONTACT US

*Farm work isn't for everybody, but if you want an adventure that will give you hands-on experience on an organic farm, you **should check out** World Wide Opportunities on Organic Farms (WWOOF). This organization connects volunteers with farmers who offer accommodations, food, and learning opportunities in exchange for work. Read some comments from WWOOFers on their experiences:*

WWOOFer in Greece

"Last summer, I helped a Greek family start an olive orchard. We spent hours every day digging stones out of a field to prepare it for planting. It was extremely hard work, and my muscles were sore by the end of the day. I really **should have gotten into** better shape before my trip. But I learned a lot about farming, and I picked up a little Greek, too."—*Angie, Scotland*

WWOOFer in Argentina

"I'm a city kid from Tokyo, so I didn't know what to do on a small Argentinian farm. On my first day I pulled up a whole row of carrot seedlings[1] because I thought they were weeds.[2] My hosts were nice about it, but I know they weren't happy. I **should have asked** more questions before I got started."—*Michio, Japan*

WWOOFer in Ireland

"I **should have found out** more about the accommodations before arriving. I had a tiny room and no electricity. I got used to it after a while, but it wasn't easy. WWOOF hosts will rarely be able to offer you the comforts of home; if you're not willing to rough it,[3] then you **ought to look into** other travel options."—*Marie, Canada*

[1] **seedling:** a young plant that has been grown from a seed
[2] **weed:** a wild plant that is not wanted in a yard or garden
[3] **rough it:** live without modern comforts

▶ Sarah MacClellan, WWOOF volunteer on an organic farm in Richmond, Virginia

▼ WWOOF volunteers have many possibilities, including working with herbs and flower gardens.

2 CHECK. Correct the mistake in each sentence to make it correct according to the information from the web page in exercise **1** on page 191.

volunteer
1. Through WWOOF, you can ~~work for money~~ at an organic farm.

2. Angie was in great shape when she went to Greece.

3. Michio came from a village in Japan to work on a farm in Argentina.

4. Marie didn't get used to her accommodations in Ireland.

3 DISCOVER. Complete the exercises to learn about the grammar in this lesson.

A Look back at the web page in exercise **1** to find these sentences. Then circle the correct meanings.

1. You **should check out** World Wide Opportunities on Organic Farms (WWOOF).

   a. It is a bad idea for you to check out WWOOF.

   b. It is a good idea for you to check out WWOOF.

2. I really **should have gotten** into better shape before my trip.

   a. I didn't get into better shape before the trip, and I'm sorry I didn't.

   b. I got into better shape before the trip, and I'm glad I did.

3. I guess I **should have asked** more questions before I got started.

   a. I didn't ask enough questions before I got started.

   b. I asked enough questions before I got started.

4. You **ought to look** into other travel options.

   a. It is a bad idea for you to look into other travel options.

   b. It is a good idea for you to look into other travel options.

B Match the meanings with the grammar from exercise **A**.

1. advice about the present or future _____, _____

2. a regret about something in the past _____

   a. *should* + verb

   b. *should have* + past participle

   c. *ought to* + verb

LEARN

7.6 Asking for or Giving Advice

Should, Ought To, and *Had Better*	
	Subject + Modal/Modal-like Expression + Base Form
Should	You **should get** your passport soon. You **shouldn't forget** to buckle your seat belt.
Ought To	You **ought to buy** your tickets online.
Had Better	We **had better take** a taxi, or we will be late. We **had better not be** late, or we will miss the plane.

1. *Should* or *ought to* + the base form of a verb can be used to give advice. *Should* is more common than *ought to*.	You **should pack** some warm clothes. Everyone **ought to watch** the video about the plane's safety procedures.
2. *Had better* + the base form of a verb is used to express strong advice or a warning. *Had better* suggests that there will be serious consequences if the advice is not followed.	You **had better stop shouting,** or the other passengers will get angry. We**'d better take** a taxi, or we'll miss the bus.
3. In negative statements, use *should not* or *had better not*. To ask for advice or an opinion, use *should*.	You **shouldn't put** your laptop in your bag. You**'d better not be** late. **Should** we **take** umbrellas, too?
4. To give advice in the progressive, use *should (not) be, ought to be,* or *had better (not) be* + verb + *-ing*.	You **shouldn't be texting** your friends. You **ought to be sleeping**. You**'d better be taking** notes.
5. **Be careful!** *Had* in *had better* does not refer to the past. It refers to the present or future.	You **had better** hurry, or we'll be late. We**'d better check out** ticket prices today.

4 Complete the exercises.

A Complete the sentences. Use *should* or *ought to* and the words in parentheses. Add *not* when necessary. If both *should* and *ought to* are correct, write both.

1. Marc is good at planting seeds. He __should do / ought to do__ (do) that job all the time.

2. Lucy is a good worker. _____ (we / offer) her a full-time job?

3. Tarek is scared of dogs. I _____ (keep) them away from him.

4. Sarah has a fever. She _____ (work) tomorrow.

5. Ru is always late, and it's causing problems. She _____ (get) to work on time.

6. All the volunteers did a really good job today. We _____ (tell) them.

7. We _____ (pick) the apples yet. They aren't ready.

8. _____ (we / ask) WWOOF to send us more volunteers?

B **ANALYZE THE GRAMMAR.** Which four sentences in exercise **A** can also use *had better* or *had better not*? Write the number of the sentences.

___3___, ___, ___, ___

5 Complete the conversation between people on a trip to Peru. Use modals and the progressive form of the verbs in parentheses. Add *not* when necessary.

Joe: It's hot today. We (1) ___shouldn't be wearing___ (should / wear) jeans.

Ani: I know. We (2) _____ (should / wear) shorts.

Joe: You know, maybe it was a mistake to go to the market today. I feel like we
(3) _____ (ought / work) at the farm today. And I'm
worried about the animals. Dan (4) _____ (had better / feed)
them right now, or I'll be very upset.

Ani: Don't worry. I talked to Señor Ortega, and he said that we've been working too hard lately.
He thinks we (5) _____ (should / have) some fun during our stay,
too. And I'm sure Dan is taking good care of the animals.

Joe: I guess you're right . . . So where is this market anyway? We
(6) _____ (should / get) close to it by now. I think we
(7) _____ (ought / walk) the other way.

Ani: I'm pretty sure it's this way . . . Wow! Look at the cool hat that woman is wearing! Let me
take her picture.

Joe: Ani, you (8) _____ (should / take) pictures of people without
asking them first!

Ani: Oops! I forgot. I'll put my camera away.

▼ A view of mountains in Chinchero, Peru

7.7 Expressing Regret or Criticism: *Should Have* + Past Participle

Statements
Subject + *Should (Not) Have* + Past Participle
I **should have bought** my ticket online. The online tickets were cheaper.
I **shouldn't have bought** my ticket from a travel agent. It was more expensive.

Questions
(*Wh-* Word) + Subject + *Should Have* + Past Participle
Should I **have arrived** here earlier?
What **should** we **have done** to prepare for the test?

Answers
Yes, you **should have**. / No, you **shouldn't have**.
You **should have started** studying earlier.

1. *Should (not) have* + past participle is often used to express regret about something that happened or did not happen in the past.	We **should have researched** hotels before we left. I **shouldn't have stayed up** so late last night. Now I'm tired.
2. *Should (not) have* + past participle is also used to talk about mistakes or to criticize someone for something they did or did not do in the past.	You **should have told** me about the cost. I can't afford to go. He **shouldn't have made** a reservation without asking me.

6 Complete the exercises.

A Read the situations. Then complete the sentences about the travelers' mistakes. Use *should have* and *shouldn't have* and the verbs in parentheses.

1. Carlos got thirsty during his train trip. He left his bag on his seat and went to get something to drink. When he came back, the bag was gone. He ___should have taken___ (take) his bag with him. He ___shouldn't have left___ (leave) it on the seat.

2. Anna made a photocopy of her passport, but she kept the copy with her passport. Then, she lost her passport. She _____ (keep) the copy with the passport. She _____ (put) the copy in a different bag.

3. Sylvia drank tap water and got sick. She _____ (drink) water from the sink. She _____ (buy) bottled water.

4. Jake went on a backpacking trip, and he packed too many things in his backpack. He couldn't carry it, and he had to throw away some of his belongings. He _____ (pack) so much in his backpack. He _____ (take) only a few important things with him on the trip.

5. Ira and Gina saw a crowd of people marching and carrying signs. They also saw police, but they went closer anyway. When they started to take photos, the police began to question them. They _____ (take) photos. They _____ (go) back to their hotel.

B Write questions about the people in exercise **A**. Use *should have*.

1. Carlos / leave / his bag on the seat

   Should Carlos have left his bag on the seat?

2. what / Carlos / do / with his bag

   _____

3. Anna / keep / the copy and the passport together

   _____

4. who / Anna / notify / about the lost passport

   _____

5. Jake / throw away / some of his belongings

   _____

6. what / Jake / bring / with him on his trip

   _____

7. Ira and Gina / take / photos of the crowd

   _____

8. where / they / go / when they saw the crowd

   _____

C **SPEAK.** Work with a partner. Ask and answer the questions in exercise **B**.

A: *Should Carlos have left his bag on the seat?*

B: *No, he shouldn't have.*

PRACTICE

7 Read the conversation about a homestay in India. Use the modals and the correct form of the verbs in parentheses. Add *not* where necessary.

Lee: So how was your homestay in that village? Was it everything you expected?

Ben: It was even better. You (1)_____ought to try_____ (ought to / try) it some time.

Lee: Did you stay with a family in their home?

Ben: No, we had meals with the family, but my brother and I stayed in a mud hut. It had two beds, a fan, lighting, and a bathroom. It wasn't like home, but when you travel, you (2) _____ (should / expect) everything to be just like home.

Lee: So you had no complaints?

Ben: None. You (3) _____ (should / miss) the chance to do a homestay some day. I'm sure you'll love it. For us, the whole experience was great. In fact, we think we (4) _____ (should / stay) longer. We were in the village for only two days. We (5) _____ (should / spend) at least four days there, maybe even six or seven.

Lee: Did you do a lot of sightseeing, too?

Ben: Yes, but we were in big cities most of the time. We (6) _____ (should / spend) so much time there. I wish we had spent more time in the villages. Being with a family and learning about local customs was much more interesting than visiting temples and palaces.

Lee: It sounds interesting. Maybe I'll do it this summer.

Ben: Homestays in Rajasthan are becoming pretty popular. You (7) _____ (had better / make) arrangements soon, or the homestays will all be booked.

Lee: That's good to know.

Ben: Before you go, you (8) _____ (ought to / practice) eating with your hand, because you often eat meals that way. I (9) _____ (should / practice) before my visit because I wasn't very good at it. I held the bread the wrong way to eat my vegetables. I (10) _____ (should/fold) the bread the way I did. Finally, my host got me a fork and knife. He called them "gardening tools"!

8 PRONUNCIATION. Read the chart and listen to the examples. Then complete the exercises.

PRONUNCIATION	Reduced *Should Have, Shouldn't Have*

Should have and *shouldn't have* are often reduced. *Have* sounds like the word *of*.

Examples:

Full Pronunciation	**Reduced Pronunciation**
We should have helped them.	We *should of* helped them.
Chris should have asked for a ride.	Chris *should of* asked for a ride.
I shouldn't have left so early.	I *shouldn't of* left so early.
The children shouldn't have gone.	The children *shouldn't of* gone.

In informal conversation, *should have* is often pronounced *shoulda*.

We should have helped them.	We *shoulda* helped them.

A Listen to the sentences. Do you hear *should have* or *shouldn't have*? Write the correct words.

1. I __shouldn't have__ bought a ticket for her.

2. I _____ taken the bus.

3. We _____ come early.

4. She _____ invited her friend.

5. We _____ worn jeans today.

6. He _____ made a reservation online.

7. They _____ stayed at a hotel on the beach.

8. You _____ eaten the soup.

B Tell a partner two things you should have done and two things you shouldn't have done in the past. Use reduced pronunciation.

I should've studied harder for the last test. I shouldn't have made so many mistakes.

9 WRITE & SPEAK.

A Read a family's comments about their trip to Marrakesh, Morocco. Complete the next sentence in each comment. Use *should have* or *shouldn't have*.

1. We left the *suq* (marketplace) after two hours. The kids loved it and didn't want to leave.
   <u>We shouldn't have left the suq</u> so soon.

2. When the snake charmer gave our son some snakes to hold, my wife and I got scared.
   _____ our son the snakes to hold.

3. We got into trouble when we took pictures of some people in the *suq*.
   _____ of people in the *suq*.

4. I told a vendor that I really liked one of his lamps. He didn't lower the price.
   _____ that I liked the lamp.

5. We were never able to find the Bahia Palace because we didn't know how to get there.
   _____ for directions.

6. We took a day trip to the Atlas Mountains, but without a guide we missed a lot.
   _____ a guide.

7. We walked around the walls of the old city in the heat of the day. That wasn't a good idea.
   _____ in the heat of the day.

8. We hurried past the storytellers and didn't stop to listen. We were sorry later.
   _____ to the storytellers.

B Work with a partner. Compare the sentences you wrote in exercise **A**.

▼ The suq, Rif Mountains, Chefchaouen, Morocco

🎧 CD2-26

10 **LISTEN** to the conversation between a business consultant and the owner of a hotel with organized tours. Then check (✓) the things that the owner is doing already. Write **X** next to the things that the owner should have done.

_____ 1. Provide comfortable accommodations

_____ 2. Employ local people

_____ 3. Serve food from the local area

_____ 4. Start a recycling program at the hotel

_____ 5. Use local tour guides

_____ 6. Offer walking tours and camel tours

11 **EDIT.** Read the comment on the blog. Find and correct seven more errors with *should, ought to,* and *had better.*

Tina Grant:

    The message of your recent blogs has been that we ~~have~~ ^had better limit our traveling because it is bad for the planet. Yes, travel has some negative effects on the environment, but people should be know the positive effects as well. You should have spend some time discussing the benefits of travel. People should to realize that the income from tourism helps local economies.

    We had not better forget that without foreign money it is hard for some countries to build airports, roads, bridges, schools, and hospitals. All these things are very important, so tourists had better to keep visiting these countries and bringing their money with them! I believe we should thinking about the cultural benefits of tourism, too. When tourists are interested in another culture, it can encourage a sense of pride and identity in that culture. That's very important, so I think you ought to mentioned that as well.

12 **APPLY.**

A Work with a partner. List four ways that travel can have a negative effect on the environment.

B Write four sentences, two affirmative and two negative, with *should(n't) have* + past participle about a recent travel experience. Explain the effect your trip had on the environment.

My friends and I shouldn't have driven to Jakarta in separate cars. We should have gone in one car in order to save energy.

C Work in groups. Read your sentences to each other. Ask questions to find out more about your classmates' trips.

Charts
7.1, 7.2,
7.4, 7.6,
7.7

1 Circle the correct words to complete the story about David's first day in Moscow.

1. The train **had to / was supposed to** arrive at 10:00 P.M., but it didn't arrive until 2:00 A.M.

2. It was so late that I **can't / wasn't able to** call my friends to tell them about the delay.

3. I hadn't booked a hotel room because my friends **could / were supposed to** meet me and take me to a hotel near their apartment.

4. That was a big mistake. I **had to book / should have booked** a room before I arrived.

5. I **had to walk / should have walked** around for hours before I found accommodations.

6. I **could / was able to** find a hotel that had rooms, but it was expensive.

7. It was a good thing I **didn't have to pay / shouldn't have paid** cash because I didn't have any.

8. I **could / was supposed to** be at a language school at 10:30 A.M. for a job interview the next morning, but unfortunately, I didn't fall asleep until 6:00 A.M.

9. I **didn't have to go / shouldn't have gone** to sleep because I didn't wake up until 1:00 P.M.

10. I went to the school and apologized. I **had to / was supposed to** set up another interview time. I knew that I **don't have to / shouldn't** be late again.

Charts
7.1–7.3,
7.5–7.7

2 **LISTEN & SPEAK.**

A Complete the conversation with the modals or modal-like phrases in the box. Use the correct forms of the the verbs in parentheses. Add *not* where necessary. More than one answer is sometimes possible.

be able to	be supposed to	can	have to	should

The night before

Mara: OK. So we're going to start at the Lincoln Memorial, right? Everyone says we

(1) _____shouldn't miss_____ (miss) that.

Paul: Yeah. It's good to start at the Lincoln Memorial because we

(2) _____ (visit) it early in the morning. It's open 24 hours a day.

Mara: Do we (3) _____ (buy) tickets?

Paul: No, it's free.

At the Lincoln Memorial

Mara: Look how clearly you (4) _____ (see) the Washington Monument from here. Isn't it a spectacular view?

Paul: It is. Are you ready to walk over there?

◄ Washington Monument,
Washington DC, USA

Mara: Almost. Let's take pictures of the monument first. Oh, no. The flash isn't working again! I (5) _____ (get) the flash to work at all on this trip.

Approaching the Washington Monument

Mara: Look at that line of people. Isn't it only a quarter to nine? The Monument (6) _____ (open) until 9 o'clock. Why are they standing there?

Paul: For tickets. You (7) _____ (have) a ticket to take the elevator. And you (8) _____ (go) to the top to see the view. It's great. You (9) _____ (see) the whole city from up there. And the Washington Monument is free. We (10) _____ (spend) any money on tickets. It's the same at the Jefferson Memorial.

A few hours later, leaving the Jefferson Memorial

Mara: That was great. I'm so glad we (11) _____ (wait) in a long line here. One long line a day is enough for me.

CD2-27

B Listen to the conversation. Compare your answers from exercise **A** to what the people actually say. Then work with a partner. Discuss the sentences in exercise **A** that have more than one correct answer.

C Use the map to complete Paul and Mara's conversation below with modals, modal-like expressions, and the verbs in parentheses. Then share your answers with the class.

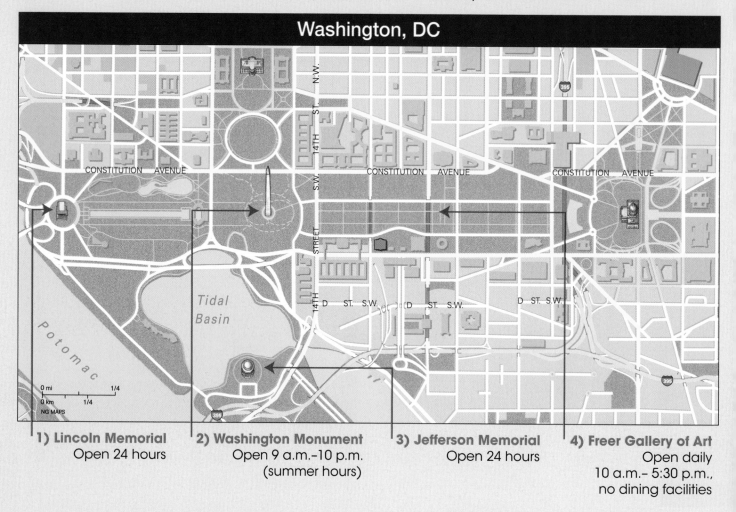

Washington, DC

1) Lincoln Memorial
Open 24 hours

2) Washington Monument
Open 9 a.m.–10 p.m.
(summer hours)

3) Jefferson Memorial
Open 24 hours

4) Freer Gallery of Art
Open daily
10 a.m.– 5:30 p.m.,
no dining facilities

Looking for the Freer Gallery

Paul: OK. So how do we get to the Freer Gallery from here?

Mara: First, we go up 14th Street. Then, we (1) _____ (make) a right.

A half hour later

Mara: I think we turned too soon. The map says we (2) _____ (turn) on Constitution Avenue. This is D Street.

Paul: I think we (3) _____ (ask) that police officer for directions.
I don't want to walk all the way back to 14th Street.

At the Freer Gallery

Paul: I'm starving. (4) We _____ (bring) sandwiches with us.

Mara: It's a good thing we didn't. Do you see that sign? People (5) _____ (eat) here.

Paul: OK, then we (6) _____ (find) a café nearby.

CD2-28

D Listen to the rest of Paul and Mara's conversation. Check your answers from exercise **C**.

Charts 7.1–7.7

3 EDIT. Read the paragraph about staying home for vacation. Find and correct nine more errors with modals and modal-like expressions.

Save Money: Take a Staycation!

      Friends are always telling me that I should ~~taking~~ ^take^ a trip abroad. "You can learn so much. You will able to have new experiences," they say. "You had better to travel before you get married and have a family. When you have a family, you can't afford to travel so easily." I'm sure it's wonderful to go abroad, but I think people are able to learn a lot and have new experiences right at home. When I'm on vacation, I enjoy be able to see all the exciting things right in my hometown. I should not go abroad to visit a great museum. There's a great museum ten miles from my home. I went there yesterday. I could go for free. I had a wonderful time. I also don't have to go far to hear good music. I can enjoy the performances at our great concert hall. In fact, I ought go there more often. No, traveling isn't for me. At the end of the day I want to be able sleep in my own bed. I think all of my friends should had stayed in town for their last vacation like I did. I had a terrific time, and I must not to spend as much money as my friends did.

Charts 7.1–7.3 7.6

4 SPEAK. Work in groups. Describe a good place for visitors to see in your town or country. Take turns answering the questions.

What place do you think visitors should see?

What are visitors able to see and do there?

How much do they have to pay to visit?

What do they have to bring with them?

Are they supposed to wear anything special?

What must people avoid doing to stay out of trouble there?

I think visitors should see the Forbidden City. Tourists are able to walk around the palace and its gardens . . .

1 READ & NOTICE THE GRAMMAR.

A Do people tip in your country? Have you ever made a mistake when tipping someone in your country or abroad? Tell a partner about it. Then read the text.

When should I tip?

A tip is a small amount of money that you pay to certain service workers. In most countries, you don't have to tip much, if anything. However, in the United States, you are supposed to tip in a number of different situations.

- **Restaurants:** When you eat in a restaurant, you are supposed to leave your server a 15–20 percent tip. You don't have to tip when you order food and pick it up yourself, but you are supposed to offer a delivery person about 10 percent if he brings it to your home. Of course, if it's terrible weather, you probably ought to include a few extra dollars.

- **Hotels:** Hotels can be complicated. A lot depends on how much help you need. You are supposed to tip the concierge about $10–$20 when you check out. You should also leave some money for the cleaning staff, especially if you left your room a mess! Also, you really ought to hand anyone who carries your suitcases a small tip of about one or two dollars.

- **Taxis:** People generally tip taxi drivers about 15–20 percent. If the driver helps you with your bags, then you should probably offer him or her a few dollars more.

If you follow these basic rules, you won't have any problems traveling in the United States. If you get confused, don't be afraid to ask what to do.

GRAMMAR FOCUS

In this text, the writer uses the following modals and modal-like expressions.

be supposed to	• is used to express an obligation (*When you eat in a restaurant, you **are supposed to leave** your server . . .*)
not have to	• is used to show that something is not necessary (*In most countries, you **don't have to tip** much . . .*)
ought to/should	• are used to offer advice (*. . . you probably **ought to include** . . .*) (*You **should** also **leave** some money for the cleaning staff . . .*)

B Read the text in exercise **A** again. Underline one more example of each of the following:

  1. something that the writer considers a rule (with *supposed to*)

  2. something that is not necessary (with *not have to*)

  3. advice (with *should* or *ought to*)

C Complete the chart with information from the text in exercise **A**. Discuss your answers with a partner.

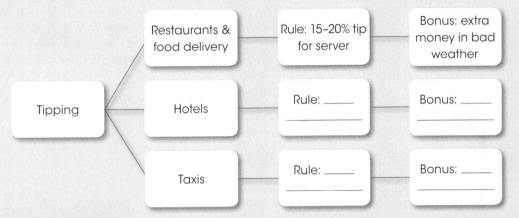

2 BEFORE YOU WRITE.

A Work with a partner. Brainstorm customs that visitors often find confusing when they visit your country, such as tipping, giving gifts, greeting people, arriving on time, and so on.

B Choose one custom from your list in exercise **A**. Then in your notebook, make a chart like the one in exercise **1C**. Write the basic "rules" for the custom.

3 WRITE two to three paragraphs explaining the custom to a visitor to your country. Use your chart from exercise **2B** and the text in help **1A** to guide you.

> ### WRITING FOCUS   Using Bullets to Organize Points
>
> Notice how bullets are used in the text in exercise **1A**. In this text, after each bullet, the author uses a word in **bold** followed by a colon (:) to introduce a topic.
>
> • **Restaurants:** When you eat in a restaurant . . .

4 SELF ASSESS. Underline the modals and modal-like expressions in your paragraphs. Then use the checklist to assess your work.

☐ I used *not have to* correctly. [7.1]

☐ I used *be supposed to* correctly. [7.2]

☐ I used *should* and *ought to* correctly. [7.6]

☐ I used the same pattern and punctuation after each bullet in my text. [WRITING FOCUS]

Modals: Part 2

▶ Giant statues on Mount Nemrut in Turkey show King Antiochus I, Theos of Commagene, lions, eagles, and gods.

EXPLORE

CD2-29

1 READ the conversation about a mysterious weather event. What is unusual about this kind of weather?

The Weather That Nobody Forecast

Krista: Hey, Gino. You're not going to believe the article I just read on the Internet. It's called *The Weather That Nobody Forecast.* Listen to this:

"Brignoles, France . . . London, England . . . Naphlion, Greece . . . Odzaci, Serbia . . . Kansas City, United States. What do these towns and cities have in common? They have all been the scene of a mysterious weather event. In all these locations, people have reported at one time or another that they saw frogs coming down like rain from the sky."

Gino: That **can't be** true!

Krista: Well, the article says that a lot of climate scientists have tried to come up with an explanation. That **must mean** they take the reports seriously, right?

Gino: I guess so. Have they figured out[1] why? What **could** possibly **be causing** frogs to fall from the sky?

Krista: Well, according to some scientists, it **could be** waterspouts.

Gino: What's a waterspout?

Krista: It's a tornado[2] that forms over water and travels over land. Sometimes a waterspout picks up animals and objects and carries them over long distances. So this is what **might be happening** to the frogs. According to the theory, the strong winds pick up the frogs and carry them along until they finally drop to the ground.

Gino: Incredible!

Krista: I know, but not everyone agrees with the waterspout theory. That **may not be** the right explanation. The cause **might be** a powerful flow of air called an updraft, which can lift small things such as frogs into the sky. However, no one has been able to prove either theory, so frog rainfall is still a bit of a mystery.

[1] **figure out:** to solve, understand
[2] **tornado:** a violent wind storm with a tall column of air that spins very fast

2 **CHECK.** Correct the error in each sentence according to the information in the conversation.

frogs

1.   Many people said that they saw ~~lizards~~ fall from the sky.

2.   Some biologists have tried to explain frog rain.

3.   A snowstorm is a possible reason for frog rain.

4.   Strong winds can transport frogs short distances.

5.   Scientists agree about the causes of frog rainfall.

3 **DISCOVER.** Complete the exercises to learn about the grammar in this lesson.

A Find these sentences in the conversation from exercise **1**. Write the missing words. Then circle the modals.

1.   That _____ (can't) be _____ true!

2.   That _____ they take the reports seriously, right?

3.   Well, according to some scientists, it _____ waterspouts.

4.   That _____ the right explanation.

5.   The cause _____ a powerful flow of air. . .

B Look at the modals in exercise **A** again. What do they mean in this context? Write each modal in the correct column.

Very Certain	Not Certain
can't	

LEARN

8.1 Possibility: Present and Future

	Not Certain about Present or Future Events
Could/May (Not)/Might (Not)	The exam **could last** two hours. I'm not sure. It **may rain**. The sky looks a bit gray. Let's take an umbrella just in case. You **might have to** wait until the fall to take Chinese. Ask the professor. He **might not be** well today, so he **may not** come.
	Very Certain about Present or Future Events
Couldn't/Can't	That **couldn't be** Bill over there. Bill is much shorter. That **can't be** Mary. Mary isn't that tall.

1. Modals can be used to express possibility about something happening now or at some future time.
  a. *Could, may,* and *might* express the possibility that something will happen or that something is true.
  b. *May not* and *might not* express the possibility that something will not happen or is not true.
  c. *Couldn't* and *can't* express certainty that something is not possible or true.
	a. The hurricane **may change** its path. It **might go** south, not east.
	
	b. He **may not come** to work today. I hear he's having car trouble.
	
	c. It **couldn't be** a bird. It doesn't have feathers.
	He won the lottery? You **can't be** serious!

2. Do not use contractions for *may not* or *might not*.	✓ I may not finish my paper on time. ✗ I <u>mayn't</u> finish my paper on time.
3. Use *could* to ask questions about possibility. Do not use *may* or *might*.	Where **could** my wallet **be**? It's not in my bag.

4 Rewrite the statements. Use *may (not), might (not), could(n't),* or *can't* and the words in parentheses. More than one answer is sometimes possible.

1. It's possible that next summer will be hotter than usual.

   Next summer ___*might be/may be/could be*___ (be) hotter than usual.

2. The paper says it's 120 degrees outside, but I don't believe it.

   It _____ (be) that hot outside.

3. There's a 50 percent chance that it will snow tomorrow.

   It _____ (snow) tomorrow.

4. There's a chance that you will see red rain someday, but it's not likely.

   You _____ (see) red rain someday.

5. It's snowing very hard, so it's possible that we won't have class this afternoon.

   We _____ (have) class this afternoon

6. Marc isn't here.

   Where _____ he _____ (be)?

7. I really don't think that animal is a frog. It has a tail.

   That animal _____ (be) a frog.

8.2 Logical Conclusions: Present and Future

	Almost Certain about Present or Future Events
Must (Not)/Has (Got To)	She just got a promotion at work. She **must be** happy. He **must not know** the address. That's why he's checking online. That **has (got) to be** a letter from Claire. I recognize her handwriting.

1. A logical conclusion is a judgment that we come to based on knowledge or evidence. We are almost 100 percent certain that the statement is true.	Robin lost her wallet. She **must be** upset.
2. Use *must, have to,* and *have got to* in affirmative statements that are logical conclusions.	My keys **must be** in my backpack. I saw them there last night. My wallet **has to be** somewhere in the house. I'm sure I left it there. The bill **has got to be** wrong. There **is** no way we used this much electricity.
3. Use *must not* for negative statements that are logical conclusions. Do not use *have to* or *have got to* with *not*.	She **must not be** his sister. They don't look anything alike.
4. Do not use a modal of logical conclusion when you state a fact. Instead, use a simple present or future form of the verb (*will, be going to*).	The store is closed. The sign says so. . He**'ll be** here later. He called to let me know.

5 Complete the exercises.

A Read each statement about honeybees. Then complete each logical conclusion. Use *must* or *must not*.

1. These honeybees aren't moving.

   They _____must_____ be dead.

2. Many honeybees are flying away from their hives and dying.

   There _____ be a reason for this behavior.

3. It's a mystery why so many bee colonies are dying.

   Scientists _____ know the reason.

4. The research on bees is taking a long time.

   It _____ require a lot of work.

5. Fruit farmers depend on bees to pollinate their crops.

   The fact that there are fewer bees _____ worry farmers.

6. Scientists still have a lot of questions about the situation.

   The scientists _____ be able to give fruit farmers much information.

7. Some beekeepers have lost up to 90 percent of their bees.

   The beekeepers _____ be happy.

8. There will be less honey available for sale.

   That _____ mean that the price of honey will increase.

B **SPEAK.** Work with a partner. Find the sentences in exercise **A** in which *must* can be replaced by *have to* and *have got to*.

They must be dead.
They have to be dead.
They have got to be dead.

6 **ANALYZE THE GRAMMAR.** Read the sentences about bee research. Decide how *must* and *must not* are used in each sentence. Write **LC** for *logical conclusion*, **O** for *obligation*, or **P** for *prohibition*.

> **REAL ENGLISH**
>
> *Must* has three different uses. Its meaning depends on the context of the sentence.
>
> > *You look pale. You **must** be sick.* (conclusion)
> > *You **must** take your medication.* (obligation)
> > *You **must not** smoke here.* (prohibition)

_O_ 1. The researchers must observe the bees carefully. If they don't, they might make mistakes in their research.

_____ 2. Other people must not go near the bees. Bees are dangerous.

_____ 3. The researchers always look calm. They must not be afraid of bees.

_____ 4. They must write down all their observations. That's an important part of the work.

_____ 5. They must not talk to anybody about their findings until their study is complete.

_____ 6. Some of their observation notes are missing. The researchers must not be happy.

_____ 7. The bees are leaving. There must be a problem.

_____ 8. The researchers must think that something in the environment is harming the bees.

8.3 Possibility and Logical Conclusions: Progressive

	Modal (*Not*) + *Be* + Verb + *-ing*	
May (Not)/Might (Not)/Could	**Not Certain about Present or Future Events**	
	Professor Wang **may be giving** a lecture now. He's in the lecture hall. Sam **might be meeting** with his study group. It sometimes meets on Mondays. Lisa **could be coming** by taxi. She often takes one when she's late for class.	
Can't/Couldn't/Must (Not)	**Very Certain about Present or Future Events**	
	The teacher **can't be holding** office hours. His door is locked. They **couldn't be taking** an exam now. The class ended 15 minutes ago. Jen **must be studying**. She picked up her laptop and went to the library.	

1. To express a possible continuing action in the present or future, use modal + *be* + verb + *-ing*.	Jay **might be talking** to Professor Angad in the lab. I saw them in there a minute ago. Suki's team **may be playing** basketball tonight. She was wearing her uniform when she left.
2. *May/Might/Could* + *be* + verb + *-ing* can be used to talk about possible future plans.	I **may be moving** in six months. I'm waiting to hear about the job I applied for. I **might not be taking** math next semester.
3. *Must* + *be* + verb + *-ing* can be used to talk about something that is very likely in the present or in the future.	The team **must be feeling** great. They just won the championship. Alan **must be graduating** next month. He has finished his coursework and passed his exams.
4. *Can't/Couldn't* + *be* + verb + *-ing* are used to express certainty that an action is not taking place.	Ben **can't be driving** to work. His car is in the driveway.

7 Complete each conversation. Use the modal and the progressive form of the verb in parentheses.

1. **A:** What do you think those researchers are doing here?

   B: They ___must be studying___ (must / study) the 17-year cicadas.
   These insects come out of the ground every 17 years, and this is the year.

2. **A:** Why are those people talking to the scientist?

   B: They _____ (may / describe) the cicadas they saw.

3. **A:** One woman looks angry. She's pointing at all the cicadas in her garden.

   B: She _____ (might / complain) about them.

4. **A:** What is that researcher doing with the audio equipment?

   B: He _____ (could / record) the sound of the cicadas.

5. **A:** Wow! Listen to that noise.

   B: I know. It _____ (must / keep) people up at night.

◀ A 17-year cicada

6. **A:** Look at the cicadas on that man's arm. He's just standing there calmly.

   B: I see. The cicadas _____ (must not / bother) him.

7. **A:** The researchers look like they're counting the cicadas. Are they?

   B: No, they _____ them (could not / count). There are too many to count—probably billions this year.

8. **A:** Why are there so few cars on the road tonight?

   B: I'm not sure, but people _____ (might not / drive) because it's dangerous. When cicadas fly into car windshields, it's difficult to see.

PRACTICE

8 Circle the correct modals to complete the paragraph.

Can Plants Hear?

According to a recent study, plants (1) **have got to /** ⟨**might**⟩ be able to "listen to" other nearby plants. You might think this theory is impossible and (2) **can't / might not** be true. However, the study suggests that some plants—such as basil—are good neighbors. Researchers think that they (3) **may / must** be helping other plants grow better. This (4) **could / must** be because the plants are communicating through sound vibrations (movements), but there will need to be more research before we know for sure. It (5) **must / can't** be difficult to get money for research, though, because the researchers say they have very little money left to continue their plant study. If they do not get more funding, they (6) **may not / must not** be able to continue their work. This would be a shame because the research is important. The results of these studies (7) **could / must** help humans in the future. For example, farmers (8) **could / have to** use sound to encourage or discourage the growth of certain plants. Just imagine, one day a farmer might even use music to help crops grow. It (9) **must not / may not** happen anytime soon, but it's possible.

9 Read the headlines. Then complete the statements about them. Use *might, may not, must,* or *can't* and the correct form of the verbs in parentheses. Add *not* where necessary. More than one answer is sometimes possible.

Residents Want to Stop New Building Near Bat Cave

1. "The residents _____ must like _____ (like) bats and, and they _____ must not think _____ (think) the new building is a good idea."

Plants Unhappy Without Other Plants Nearby

2. "Plants don't have feelings. The writer _____ (joke)."

Shark Seen on Subway Car in New York City

3. "That _____ (be) true. There are no sharks in the city."

Goats Replace Gardeners in Washington, DC, Cemetery

4. "Hmm. That _____ (be) a good idea for a lot of parks. Goats could control the number of weeds and keep down costs."

Study Suggests That Dogs Respond to Owners' Emotions

5. "So that _____ (explain) why my dog usually yawns when I yawn."

Bear Walks into Hotel in Juneau, Alaska; Eats Candy in Lobby

6. "Bears _____ (love) candy."

10 LISTEN & SPEAK.

A Listen to each group of sounds. Take notes in your notebook about what you think you hear.

B Work with a partner. Compare and discuss your notes. Use *may, might, could,* or *must.* Then share your ideas with the class.

A: *The first one must be a scary place. It could be an old house in a horror movie.*
B: *Yeah, it sounds really creepy. Did you hear the footsteps? It could be a ghost!*

11 APPLY.

A The photo shows an unusual relationship. In your notebook, answer the questions below. Use *may (not), might (not), could (not), can't,* or *must (not).*

What kind of animals are in the picture?

Is the small animal afraid of the big animal?

Is the large animal asleep or awake?

Do you think the big animal will hurt the small animal?

What do you think the relationship between these two animals is?

B Work in groups. Discuss your answers. Give reasons for what you wrote.

The large animal can't be a tiger because tigers have stripes . . .

EXPLORE

CD2-31

1 READ the article about an archaeological discovery of a strange army. What questions did the discovery raise?

The Emperor's Terra Cotta Army

Near the city of Xian, China, in 1974, two farmers found a piece of terra cotta[1] that looked like a human head. Archaeologists began digging at the site, and they soon realized that the head belonged to a clay soldier. Over time, the archaeologists uncovered an entire army of such soldiers . . . over 6000 of them. These soldiers and their weapons[2] were found near the tomb of China's first emperor, Qin Shi Huang Di. Qin **must have wanted** the clay army to protect him in the afterlife.

Creating the soldiers **must have been** extremely challenging. The craftsmen[3] first had to find clay that was strong enough to shape into huge figures. Each soldier is about six feet tall (1.8 meters) and weighs over 600 pounds (272.2 kilograms). The most surprising finding was that each figure is unique—no two are exactly alike. How **could** the craftsmen **have produced** this collection? It's a mystery.

According to some sources, the workers **may have used** molds.[4] Molds allow for mass production because they produce objects that are the same. However, with molds it isn't possible to make individual features. That's why some scholars now believe that the craftsmen **must have added** details to the molded pieces by hand. They **might have wanted** the figures to look like people in the emperor's service, but no one knows for sure.

Archaeologists have explored only a fraction of the emperor's burial ground so far. In the coming years, they hope to learn even more about his unusual army, created over 2000 years ago.

[1] **terra cotta:** brownish-red clay that has been baked and is used for making things
[2] **weapon:** a tool used to harm or kill
[3] **craftsman:** a man who is skilled at making things with his hands
[4] **mold:** a form with an empty space inside into which materials are put to shape objects

2 **CHECK.** Read the statements. Circle **T** for *true* or **F** for *false*.

1. Archaeologists found a village made out of clay.   **T**   **F**

2. Experts believe that the emperor was worried about his safety after he died.   **T**   **F**

3. Each figure weighs about the same as an average human.   **T**   **F**

4. The figures were completely made by molds.   **T**   **F**

5. Archaeologists have completed their work at the site of Qin's tomb.   **T**   **F**

3 **DISCOVER.** Complete the exercises to learn about the grammar in this lesson.

A Find these sentences in the article from exercise **1**. Write the missing words.

1. Qin __must have wanted__ the clay army to protect him in the afterlife.

2. Creating the soldiers _____ extremely challenging.

3. How _____ the craftsmen _____ this collection?

4. According to some sources, the workers _____ molds.

5. . . . the craftsmen _____ details to the molded pieces by hand.

6. They _____ the figures to look like people in the emperor's service, but no one knows for sure.

B Look at the sentences in exercise **A**. Write the number of each sentence next to the correct statement.

1. The writer is very certain that this is true. _____

2. The writer thinks this is possible, but is not certain. _____

LEARN

8.4 Possibility: Past

	Modal + (*Not*) + *Have* + Past Participle
May (Not)	Charlie **may have done** the painting, but I'm not sure. Pat **may not have gone** to bed yet. It's only 9:30 p.m.
Might (Not)	Pam **might have been** sick. I know she went home early. They **might not have wanted** to go to the party.
Could/ Couldn't	We **could have crashed**. We were lucky you saw the other car coming. Alex **couldn't have stolen** the money. He was at work at the time of the robbery.

1. To express possibility in the past, use a modal + *have* + the past participle of a verb.
  a. Use *may (not) have*, *might (not) have*, or *could have* when it's possible that something happened.
  b. *Could have* is also used to express something that was possible but did not happen.
	a. He **may have gotten** lost. Give him a call. The mail **might not have come** yet. I'll check.
	
	b. He **could have dropped** the class, but he decided not to.

2. **Be careful!** *Couldn't have* is used when the speaker or writer believes the past action was not possible.	Her computer crashed while she was working, so she **couldn't have finished** the research. (It was impossible for her to have finished the research.)
3. Use *could have* to ask questions about possibility. *May have* is not used to ask about possibility. *Might have* is rarely used.	✓ **Could I have signed up** for the wrong class? ✗ <u>May</u> I have signed up for the wrong class?

4 Complete the exercises.

A Complete the conversation about the terra cotta warriors. Use the words in parentheses and the correct form of the verbs.

Guide: Notice how realistic the faces of the warriors are.

Rita: How (1) _could the ancient artists have created_ (the ancient artists / could / create) such realistic faces?

Guide: I don't know, but (2) _____ (they / could / ask) people to pose for them while they carved the statues, just like artists do today.

Felix: And why is there one soldier with a green face?

Guide: Some experts think (3) _____ (the artist / could / not do) that on purpose. They think the artist made a mistake.

Felix: (4) _____ (the artist / could / be) color blind?

Guide: Yes, maybe, but there's another possible explanation. The color green was a symbol of youth and energy in ancient China. (5) _____ (the artist / could / paint) the soldier's face green to show his bravery.

▲ A terra cotta warrior

Ryan: It's amazing that the tombs weren't discovered until the 1970s. How

(6) _____ (people / could / not know)

about the tombs for such a long time?

Guide: Before the discovery, the figures were under a beach.

(7) _____ (no one / could / notice) that the

figures were there. Remember, the villagers had to dig down over 16 feet before they

found the tomb with the soldiers.

Cara: I understand that archaeologists also found models of horses and carriages in the tombs.

Guide: Yes, that's true. It's not entirely clear why they were built . . . but

(8) _____ (the emperor / could / want)

them for his travels during the afterlife.

B **ANALYZE THE GRAMMAR.** Work with a partner. Role-play the conversation in exercise **A**.
Replace *could* with *may* or *might* in each sentence where possible. When it is not possible to
replace it, discuss the reason.

5 Complete each conversation with *might not have* or *couldn't have* and the past participle of
the verb(s) in parentheses.

1. **A:** The craftsmen probably needed a month or so to create each statue.

   B: No, they ___*couldn't have made*___ (make) the statues that quickly. It was a
   lot of work.

2. **A:** The guide didn't answer my question about the weapons.

   B: She _____ (hear) the question.

3. **A:** Why did Frank leave the tour early?

   B: I don't know. He _____ (like) it.

4. **A:** Uh oh. I think I left my camera at the hotel this morning.

   B: You _____ (leave) it there. You had it this afternoon.

   A: Then maybe I left it on the tour bus.

   B: Let's hurry. You can check with the driver. He _____ (leave) the parking area yet. Let's hope he hasn't.

5. **A:** You know, it's too bad we didn't get to the museum earlier this morning.

   B: But we _____ (see) the exhibit any earlier. The place doesn't open until 8:00 a.m.

8.5 Logical Conclusions: Past

Subject + *Must (+ Not)* + *Have* + Past Participle
She **must have loved** art. She collected paintings and sculptures. He **must not have heard** the question. He didn't answer it.

1. Use *must* or *must not* + *have* + the past participle of a verb to express a logical conclusion about something in the past. The conclusion is based on knowledge or evidence.	I **must have left** my laptop at home. It's not in my backpack.
2. *Had to have* + past participle can also be used to express a logical conclusion about the past.	Those statues **had to have been** very difficult to make.

6 Complete the exercises.

A Complete each logical conclusion with *must have* or *must not have* and the verb in parentheses.

1. Hannah works on archaeological digs in Rome. She _____must have studied_____ (study) archaeology in school.

2. She can't find her hand shovel. That's strange. She _____ (leave) it at the work site yesterday.

3. Glen didn't find any stone cooking tools at the site. The ancient Romans _____ (prepare) food there.

4. He spent a lot of time in the lab last year. He _____ (spend) much time digging outside at the work site.

5. Sam's team won an award for their work. They _____ (make) an unusual discovery.

6. The team leader has Cathy's report. She _____ (complete) it last night.

7. Ruth's team worked in the hot sun for ten or more hours every day.

   They _____ (be) exhausted when they got home.

8. They gave up after a year of disappointing archaeological research.

   They _____ (discover) anything interesting at the site.

9. Megan almost fainted from the heat the other day, and she had to lie down.

   She _____ (drink) enough water.

10. Victor's team finally left the site. They _____ (decide) there was

    nothing interesting to find there.

7 Complete the conversation with the words in parentheses. Use *must have* for logical conclusions. Use *had to* for obligations.

Andy: So, Cara, you used to be an archaeologist, right?

(1) ___ *Your job must have been* ___

(your job / be) very interesting.

Cara: Yes, it was.

Ben: (2) _____ (you / go) to college to become an archaeologist?

Cara: Yes, and I went to graduate school, too. (3) _____
(I / not have) a master's degree, but I wanted to get one, anyway.

Dan: (4) _____ (you / work) on a lot of digs?

Cara: I did early in my career. It was fun, but it was tough at times, because I didn't get to see my husband very often.

Ben: (5) _____ (it / be) hard to spend all that time away from him.

Cara: Yes, it was. That's why I switched to working in the lab after a few years. During my career (6) _____ (I / spend) thousands of hours analyzing material in the lab, though of course, I never kept track of the time. Sometimes, (7) _____ (I / analyze) things that the police found underground. They always needed the information quickly.

Ben: That (8) _____ (work / be) fascinating.

8.6 Possibility and Logical Conclusions: Progressive

	Modal (+ *Not*) + *Have Been* + Verb + *-ing*	
	Not Certain about Past Events	
Could/May (Not)/ Might (Not)	We **could have been experiencing** a small earthquake. I felt the ground move. Stress at work **might have been contributing** to his health problems.	
	Certain about Past Events	
Couldn't/Must (Not)	She **couldn't have been lying**. She always tells the truth. He **must not have been taking** calls. I kept getting his voicemail.	

To draw conclusions about a continuing action in the past, use a modal (+ *not*) + *have been* + verb + *-ing*.	Rena **might have been studying** in the library last night. I know she likes the peace and quiet there. Katie's hair is wet. She **must have been swimming**.

8 Use the words in parentheses to write an answer for each question.

1. How could the archaeological site have been robbed? It was closed to visitors at 5:00 p.m. yesterday, right?

   Yes, no one could have been touring the site after 5:00.

   (no one / could / tour / the site after 5:00)

2. The looters were familiar with the tour schedule. How is that possible?

   _____

   (they / must / watch / the site / for several days)

3. It's strange that the guard didn't hear anything when the looters arrived.

   _____

   (he / might not / pay / attention)

4. The looters knew exactly what they were doing. Why were they so successful?

   _____

   (they / could / plan / the theft / for months)

5. It's strange that the looters took only coins. Why didn't they take anything else?

   _____

   (they / might / plan / to return / for more things later)

6. It took a long time for the police to arrive at the site.

   _____

   (they / must / have / trouble finding the site)

7. The police searched the site, but they didn't find anyone. Why not?

_____

(the looters / may / hide in a secret cave)

8. The police finally caught the looters this morning. The police looked really tired. Why?

_____

(they / must / wait / all night for the looters to come out)

PRACTICE

9 READ & WRITE.

A Look at the photograph and read the paragraph. Who painted the mural?

> This photo shows the Palazzo Vecchio in Florence, Italy. Leonardo da Vinci made a famous painting in this room in 1505. Later, another painter, Vasari, painted the mural that we now see in the photograph. Some people believe that Leonardo da Vinci's missing painting is under Vasari's mural. They think it is possible that Vasari protected Da Vinci's painting by building a wall over it and then painting his own mural on the new wall.

▼ Palazzo Vecchio, Florence, Italy

B Complete the sentences about the painting in exercise **A**. Use *may, might, could,* or *must.* Add *not* where necessary. More than one answer is sometimes possible.

1. It's possible that someone destroyed *The Battle of Anghiari* years ago.

   Someone ___may OR might OR could have destroyed___ the painting.

2. It wasn't possible for Vasari to remove Leonardo's painting from the hall.

   Vasari _____ Leonardo's painting from the hall.

3. It's possible that Vasari painted over Leonardo's painting.

   Vasari _____ over Leonardo's painting.

4. It's almost certain that Vasari wanted to save Leonardo's painting.

   Vasari _____ to save Leonardo's painting.

5. It's possible that Vasari built a second wall to protect Leonardo's painting.

   Vasari _____ a second wall to protect the painting.

6. It was impossible for Leonardo's assistants to steal Leonardo's painting.

   Vasari's assistants _____ Leonardo's painting.

7. At first, the Italian government tried to look beneath Vasari's mural. I'm sure they wanted to search for Leonardo's painting there.

   They _____ to search for Leonardo's painting beneath Vasari's.

8. The Italian government decided to leave the paintings alone. I think that they left the paintings alone because they didn't want to damage them.

   They _____ to damage either of the paintings.

10 PRONUNCIATION. Read the chart and listen to the examples. Then complete the exercises.

PRONUNCIATION	Reduced Past Modals

The *have* in modals of past possibility and logical conclusion is often pronounced like the word *of.*

CD2-32

Examples:	**Full Pronunciation**	**Reduced Pronunciation**
	They may have left the house.	They *may of* left the house.
	It might have happened fast.	It *might of* happened fast.
	I could have screamed.	I *could of* screamed.
	She must have known the truth.	She *must of* known the truth.
	You might not have known that.	You *might not of* known that.
	He could not have called my number.	He *couldn't of* called my number.

In informal conversation, some people say *mighta, coulda,* and *musta* instead of *might of, could of,* and *must of.*

	It might have happened fast.	It *mighta* happened fast.

A Listen to the sentences. Write the full form of the missing words.

1. We ___may have___ forgotten to lock the door.

2. Everybody _____ been at the game that night.

3. You _____ dropped your keys on the way home.

4. Max _____ noticed the footprints in the yard.

5. You _____ left the window open.

6. We _____ checked the security system last night.

7. You _____ heard the footsteps outside.

8. It _____ happened yesterday.

B Complete each sentence with your own ideas. Then read the sentences aloud to a partner. Practice the reduced pronunciation of the modals.

1. I could have _____ yesterday, but I didn't.

2. My grandparents might have _____, but I don't know for sure.

3. My parents must have _____ when I _____
_____ .

4. Our English teacher must not have _____ when _____
_____ .

5. In the past, people might not have _____ .

11 **EDIT.** Read the text about a strange robbery. Find and correct six more errors with modals.

It was a strange crime. One night, a man climbed into a 5000-gallon fish tank. He

~~been~~
must have ~~be~~ crazy! The fish were halibut, and he wanted to steal them. He must not have

know how to catch fish properly because he attacked them with a heavy piece of metal.

The tank became a mess. The man must not cleaned up the area because he left a trail of

evidence that led the police to his house. The police were looking for the most important

fish that was stolen—a 50-pound halibut. She may been a well-loved fish because everyone

called her "Big Mamma." Unfortunately, the police never found Big Mamma because

she had been eaten at a dinner party at the man's house. The people at the party were

shocked. They could not have know that they were eating Big Mamma at the time. Those

guests must been very angry because they spoke against the man at his court trial. The

court gave the man a sentence of four years in prison. He offered to catch a new halibut

to replace Big Mamma. He was a diver and surfer, so it's possible he could had caught

another big fish. The court said thanks, but no thanks.

12 SPEAK & WRITE.

A Look at the time line about Roanoke, an English colony that mysteriously disappeared from North America in 1590. Work with a partner. Answer the questions.

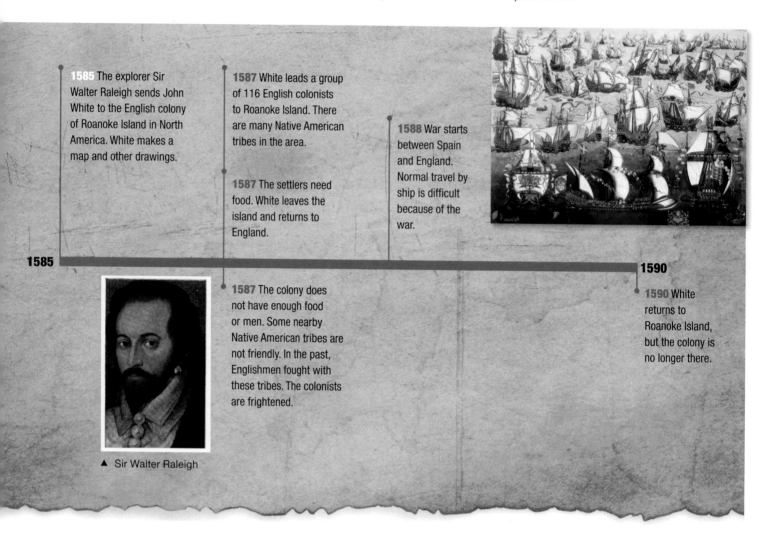

1585 The explorer Sir Walter Raleigh sends John White to the English colony of Roanoke Island in North America. White makes a map and other drawings.

1587 White leads a group of 116 English colonists to Roanoke Island. There are many Native American tribes in the area.

1587 The settlers need food. White leaves the island and returns to England.

1588 War starts between Spain and England. Normal travel by ship is difficult because of the war.

1585 ———— **1590**

1587 The colony does not have enough food or men. Some nearby Native American tribes are not friendly. In the past, Englishmen fought with these tribes. The colonists are frightened.

1590 White returns to Roanoke Island, but the colony is no longer there.

▲ Sir Walter Raleigh

1. Who do you think John White was?

   A: *John White might have been a leader in a town in England.*

   B: *Or he could have been an explorer.*

2. Why do you think John White decided to travel to Roanoke Island?

3. What did he make drawings of?

4. Why did he return to England shortly after he brought the colonists to Roanoke?

5. Why didn't White return to Roanoke Island for three years?

6. When White returned to Roanoke Island, why didn't he find the colony?

B Write your answers to the questions in your notebook. Use *may, might, could,* and *must.* Add *not* where necessary.

John White might have been a leader in a town in England.

🎧 **13** Listen to some popular theories about what happened to the settlers on Roanoke Island.
CD2-34   Then choose the correct way to complete each theory.

1. According to Theory 1, Native Americans _____ killed the colonists.

   a. must not have   b. may have

2. According to Theory 2, the colonists _____ died from a disease.

   a. may have   b. couldn't have

3. According to Theory 3, the fence shows that a storm _____ destroyed the Roanoke colony.

   a. might have   b. couldn't have

4. According to Theory 4, the colonists and the Croatoan Native American tribe _____.

   a. could have lived together

   b. could have had a big fight

5. According to Theory 5, the colonists _____.

   a. could have built a fort 70 miles away

   b. must not have moved to a different place

▼ Hand-colored woodcut showing John White's return
   to Roanoke Island in 1590

14 APPLY.

A Work with a partner. Complete the sentence based on the information in exercises **12** and **13**.

Roanoke Island must have gotten its nickname "The Lost Colony" because . . .

B Work in a group. Look at the list of unusual place names listed. Suggest reasons for the names. Write a sentence for each place name. Use *may have, might have, could have,* or *must have* + past participle.

Seven Sisters (Alberta, Canada)   Disappointment Islands (South Pacific)

Burnt Hill (Berkshire, England)   Moneygold (County Sligo, Ireland)

Cape Farewell (South Island, New Zealand)   Nowhere Else (Tasmania, Australia)

Crazy Corner (County Westmeath, Ireland)   Bearskin Neck (Massachusetts, USA)

Seven sisters may have discovered the town of Seven Sisters.

_____

_____

_____

_____

_____

_____

_____

_____

C Share your group's sentences with the class.

Charts
8.1–8.5

1 Complete the sentences about Nik Wallenda's tightrope walk. Use *may/might/could/must (not) or can't* and the verbs in parentheses. More than one answer is sometimes possible.

1. When people learned of Wallenda's plan to walk above the Grand Canyon on a wire, they thought, "He _____must be_____ (be) crazy."

2. One tourist watching Wallenda said, "It's so dangerous.
   He _____ (fall). I hope he doesn't."

3. The wind started blowing and Wallenda stopped twice.
   The wind _____ (bother) him.

4. His family looked nervous. They _____ (be) worried.

5. Of course, Wallenda had practiced.
   He _____ (do) it without a lot of training.

6. Wallenda successfully crossed the Grand Canyon. He _____
   (succeed) without luck, skill, and self-confidence.

▲ Nik Wallenda crossing
the Grand Canyon

229

2 Read the sentences. Then rewrite the second sentence. Replace the underlined words with appropriate modals. Do not change the meaning of the sentence.

1. I can't find my ring. <u>It's probably</u> on my bedside table.

   It _____*must be*_____ on my bedside table.

2. Matilda was late for work yesterday. <u>Maybe she got</u> stuck in traffic.

   She _____ stuck in traffic.

3. Paul lost his job. <u>I'm sure</u> he's upset.

   He _____ upset.

4. Kendra studied for weeks, but she failed the exam. How <u>was it possible for her to fail</u>?

   How _____ ?

5. I called Ana's name, but she didn't look up. She <u>probably didn't hear</u> me.

   She _____ me.

6. Henry didn't steal the car. It <u>was impossible for him to have stolen</u> it because he was at work.

   He _____ it because he was at work.

Charts
8.1, 8.2,
8.4, 8.5
CD2-35

3 LISTEN.

A Listen to the report about a surprising archaeological discovery. Before the discovery, what did many people believe about the Maya?

CD2-35

B Listen again. Mark the statements **T** for *true* or **F** for *false* according to the information in the report.

__F__ 1. The Maya must have predicted 2012 as the end of the world.

_____ 2. The room that was discovered must have been the workroom of a Maya king.

_____ 3. Kings may have wanted scribes to tell them what was going to happen in the future.

_____ 4. Scribes may have used past events and complex arithmetic to predict the future.

_____ 5. Archaeologists think they might understand everything about the murals soon.

_____ 6. The Maya must have been afraid that their world was going to end.

4 EDIT. Read the text. Find and correct six more errors with modals.

People sometimes believe in strange things. Some people believed that the Maya predicted the

end of the world in 2012. They must *have been* be surprised when the world did not end. In fact, the Maya

never made such a prediction. Other people used to believe in the existence of the Loch Ness

Monster. They may have saw a photo once of an odd creature in the water. The picture, taken many

years ago, looked real, so they thought the monster must existed. But there must not be another

explanation. In fact, the Scottish doctor who took the famous photo of the creature said that it

wasn't a monster. It was just an animal he didn't recognize. Now some people have a new theory:

the Loch Ness Monster may have die because of global warming!

Some people also believe in crop circles. They think the circles may contain messages from aliens.

The circles first appeared in England in the 1970s. In 1991, two Englishmen announced that they had

made some of the circles. However, that announcement didn't stop people from believing that aliens

had made them. The believers say that the men maybe have made the crop circles in England, but they

could not made all the other circles in Europe, Australia, North America, and Japan.

So, the mystery is not why strange events happen. The mystery is really why people believe that

such events happen, even when there is evidence that they didn't.

▲ Crop circles

5 SPEAK. Work in groups. Discuss your opinions about the headlines. Use modals of possibility and logical conclusion.

Spaceship Flies Over London

Mother Finds Son on Social Media Site After 22 Years

Man Has Heart Attack While Driving, Gets 3 Tickets

Bear with Head in Jar Rescued

Ghost Saves Man's Life

Bank Employee Drops 90,000 Euros in River

It couldn't have been a spaceship. It must have been an airplane or a star.

1 READ & NOTICE THE GRAMMAR.

A Who is the most interesting or mysterious person in your family? Think about what you know and don't know about this person. Tell a partner. Then read the article.

Family Exploration

You never know what you might find out about your family. I must have been about ten years old when I first discovered that I had a distant relative who had been an explorer. I loved to go exploring myself. One day I went on an "expedition," and I must have forgotten to tell my grandmother. I couldn't have been away for more than three hours, but she was worried. "Pedro!" she said angrily when I came back, "Something could have happened to you. Next time, tell me where you're going. You must have some of my great-uncle's blood in you!"

This is how I discovered that I am distantly related to a man called Bruno, who knew the famous Brazilian explorer, Cândido Rondon. In fact, Bruno was one of the members of the famous expedition in Mato Grosso in 1909. They ran out of supplies on the long journey, and they almost didn't survive.

Bruno never married, and he died young. I don't know much about him. He must have been very brave. He couldn't have been much older than I am now when he went on his first expedition in the Amazon. I'm not sure, but he may have gone on ten different expeditions in that area. He might have seen tribes that had never met outsiders before.

Bruno had to have been one of the most adventurous people in Brazil at that time. I'm proud that he was part of my family.

▲ Cândido Rondon

GRAMMAR FOCUS

In the article in exercise **A**, the writer uses the following modals:

must have + past participle	• to express a logical conclusion about the past (He **must have been** very brave.)
might/may have + past participle	• to express possibility in the past (. . . he **may have gone** on ten different . . .)
could not have + past participle	• to express that the past action was not possible (I **couldn't have been** away for more than . . .)

B Read the article in exercise **A** again. Find and underline other examples of logical conclusions, possibilities, and impossibilities about the past.

C Complete the chart with information from the article in exercise **A**. Discuss your answers with a partner.

What the author knows for sure	What the author guesses
He has a distant relative who was an explorer.	Bruno must have been very brave.

2 BEFORE YOU WRITE.

A Draw a family tree going as far back as you possibly can. What do you know about your relatives who lived a long time ago? Share your family tree with a partner.

B Choose one family member to write about. Make a chart like the one in exercise **1C**. Write logical conclusions or possibilities about the past in the right-hand column.

3 WRITE two or three paragraphs about a distant relative or ancestor. Give information you know about him or her. Then discuss what may or must have happened in his or her life. Use your chart from exercise **2B** and the article in exercise **1A** to help you.

> **WRITING FOCUS** Using *In Fact* to Emphasize an Interesting Idea
>
> *In fact* is used to introduce and add emphasis to an interesting idea that builds on information in the previous sentence.
>
> *This is how I discovered that I am distantly related to a man called Bruno, who knew the famous Brazilian explorer, Cândido Rondon.* **In fact**, *Bruno was one of the members of the famous expedition in Mato Grasso in 1909.*

4 SELF ASSESS. Underline the verb forms in your paragraphs. Then use the checklist to assess your work.

☐ I used modals of possibility and logical conclusion about the present correctly. [8.1, 8.2]

☐ I used modals of possibility about the past correctly. [8.4]

☐ I used modals of logical conclusion about the past correctly. [8.5]

☐ I used *In fact* to emphasize an interesting idea. [WRITING FOCUS]

UNIT 9 The Natural World

The Passive

▲ Borneo red flying frog in mushroom, Sabah, Borneo

EXPLORE

1 READ the article about oceanographer Sylvia Earle. What message is she trying to communicate to the world?

Sylvia Earle and the Deep Blue Sea

Ever since Dr. Sylvia Earle **was knocked over** by a wave as a young child, she **has been fascinated** by the ocean. She has led more than a hundred ocean expeditions and spent more than 7000 hours underwater. Her research **is guided** by her commitment to preserving ecosystems[1] and developing new technologies for exploring the sea.

People sometimes ask Earle, "Why is the ocean so important?" She explains how the natural cycles that balance Earth's water, air, and climate **are** all **regulated** by the ocean. She also notes our dependence on the ocean's food chain,[2] from the biggest fish to the tiniest organisms.[3] If just one link in the chain **is removed**, it will affect the whole system. For example, if the plants that feed the small fish **are destroyed** by pollution, the small fish will die. Then, the larger fish that depend on the small fish will disappear as well.

In the past, people behaved as though the ocean **could not be harmed**. However, today, the ocean **is being damaged** at a rapid rate, and it is clear that humans are responsible. More trash and chemicals **are being dumped** into the water. This damages delicate ecosystems, such as coral reefs, and all the life that they support. People are also overfishing. In fact, over 90 percent of big fish such as tuna **have been killed** for food.

Earle firmly believes that the ocean **must be protected** from further harm. She urges people around the world to help support what she calls "the blue heart" of the planet.

[1] **ecosystem:** the plants and animals living in an area together, and the relationship that exists between them and the environment
[2] **food chain:** a series of living things that are linked to each other because each feeds on the one next to it
[3] **organism:** an animal or plant, especially one that is so small that you can't see it without a microscope

◀ Dr. Sylvia Earle shows a plant to a researcher while exploring Great Lameshur Bay, the Virgin Islands.

▶ Dr. Sylvia Earle

2 **CHECK.** Read the statements. Circle **T** for *true* or **F** for *false*.

1. Sylvia Earle became interested in the ocean when she was a teenager.　　**T**　**F**

2. Earle studies the connections between living things in the ocean.　　**T**　**F**

3. Smaller numbers of big fish will result in smaller numbers of little fish.　　**T**　**F**

4. In the past, people thought that nothing could harm the ocean.　　**T**　**F**

5. The condition of the ocean is changing slowly.　　**T**　**F**

3 **DISCOVER.** Complete the exercises to learn about the grammar in this lesson.

A Look at the underlined verbs in the sentences based on the article in exercise **1**. Circle the forms of *be*.

1. Dr. Sylvia Earle (was) knocked over by a wave as a young child.

2. Earth's water, air, and climate are regulated by the ocean.

3. Ocean plants are destroyed by pollution.

4. The world's oceans could be harmed.

5. More trash and chemicals are being dumped into the water.

6. The ocean must be protected from further harm.

B Write the number of each sentence in exercise **A** in the correct column.

Simple Present Passive	Simple Past Passive	Present Progressive Passive	Passive with Modal
	1		

LEARN

9.1 Active and Passive

Active	Passive
Big fish **eat** small fish. Object	Small fish **are eaten** by big fish. Subject

	Active	Passive
	Subject + Verb (+ Object)	Subject + *Be* + Past Participle*
Simple Present	People **take** lots of pictures here.	Lots of pictures **are taken** here.
Simple Past	They **saw** a shark near the beach.	A shark **was seen** near the beach.
Present Progressive	People **aren't protecting** the whales.	The whales **are not being protected**.
Past Progressive	They **were washing** the elephants.	The elephants **were being washed**.
Present Perfect	I **haven't walked** the dog.	The dog **hasn't been walked**.

* See page **A3** for a list of irregular verb forms.

1. In an active sentence, the subject performs the action of the verb. The subject is the *agent* or *doer*. In a passive sentence, the subject receives the action of the verb. Sometimes *by* + the agent comes at the end of the sentence to show who or what is performing the action.	Active: The fishermen **caught** ten bluefish. Subject/Agent Passive: Ten bluefish **were caught** by the fishermen. SubjectAgent
2. The passive occurs in different verb tenses. It always includes a form of *be* + the past participle form of the verb. The form of *be* shows the verb tense.	The animals **are being fed**. The research **has not been completed**. Seven new species of mushrooms **were identified**.
3. Only transitive verbs (verbs that take a direct object) can be used with the passive. Intransitive verbs cannot be made passive.	Transitive Verb: discover A new type of sea animal **was discovered**. Intransitive Verb: disappear ✗ Those birds <u>are disappeared</u>.
4. To make questions in the passive, put a form of the auxiliary *be* or *have* before the subject.	The applications **were completed**. **Were** the applications **completed**? The animals **have been trained**. **Have** the animals **been trained**?

4 Underline the verb in each sentence. Then write **A** if the sentence is *active* and **P** if the sentence is *passive*.

___P___ 1. During the expedition, Sylvia Earle's instructions <u>were followed</u> by the team.

___P___ 2. Most of our oxygen on Earth is <u>generated</u> by the ocean.

___A___ 3. The changes in the ocean ecosystem affect all of us.

___A___ 4. Nearly half of the world's coral reefs have disappeared.

_____ 5. The sea around the Galápagos Islands is being polluted by boats.

_____ 6. In the last 50 years, more than 90 percent of the big fish in the sea have been eaten.

_____ 7. Many sea creatures have been dying from water pollution.

_____ 8. Action is being taken to protect the California and Oregon coasts.

_____ 9. An area of Antarctica is protected by scientists and international governments.

_____ 10. The efforts of researchers have increased public awareness of our ecosystem.

5 Read each sentence and underline the object of the verb. Then rewrite the sentences in the passive. Do not include the agent of the action. Use the correct form of the verb.

1. We protect <u>about 12 percent of the land on Earth</u> in some way.

   About 12 percent of the land on Earth is protected in some way.

2. Local officials are considering new guidelines for beach preservation.

   New guidelines are considered by local officials for beach preservation.

3. The mayor has created a nature preserve near the river.

   A nature preserve creates the major near the river.

4. Were guides giving tours yesterday at the nature preserve?

   Were tours were given by guides yesterday at the nature preserve?

5. Villagers have cut down all the trees in that forest.

   All the trees are cut down by Villagers in that forest.

6. Did swimmers see dolphins near the beach?

   Did dolphins were seen by swimmers near the beach?

7. Is the parks department protecting the birds on the island?

   Are the birds were protected by the parks department on the island?
   being

8. Volunteers cleaned up the trash on the riverbank.

   The trash was cleaned up by volunteers on the riverbank.

9. Fishermen catch tens of thousands of fish every day.

   Tens of thousands of fish were catched by fisherman every day.

10. Has anyone reported the environmental problems to government officials?

   Have the environmental problems reported by anyone to government officials?
   been

9.2 Passive with Modals

Active	Passive
They **should solve** the problem.	The problem **should be solved**.
Object	Subject

Present and Future Passive	
	Modal *(Not)* + *Be* + Past Participle
Present	The plans **must be approved**.
Future	The research **might be done** next month. The report **won't be seen** by the public.

Past Passive	
	Modal *(Not)* + *Have Been* + Past Participle
Past	The money **may have been taken**. She **should not have been told** the news.

1. The passive form with a modal is the modal + *be (not)* + the past participle of the verb.	The monkey **can be trained**. The elephant **couldn't be moved**.
2. For passive sentences with the modal expressions *be going to* or *have to*, use: a. *be going to* + *be* + past participle b. *have to* + *be* + past participle	a. The work **is going to be completed** soon. b. The project **has to be done** now.

6 Complete the sentences. Use the modal and the passive form of the verbs in parentheses.

1. Sea turtles <u>must not be disturbed</u> (must / not disturb) during the nesting season.

2. Rules about proper behavior around sea turtles <u>should be followed</u> (should / follow).

3. Information about the turtles <u>can be found</u> (can / find) at nature preserves.

4. New beach rules <u>are going to be posted</u> (be going to / post).

5. In many coastal towns, no street lights <u>will be turned on</u> (will / turn on) when the turtles are nesting.

6. Photographs <u>should only be taken</u> (should only / take) from far away.

7. The effects of human behavior on sea turtles <u>might be understood</u> (might / understand) more clearly now.

8. Perhaps more sea turtles <u>will be saved</u> (will / save) in the future.

PRACTICE

7 Read the sentences. Circle the correct verb form to complete each sentence.

1. The Grand Canyon **has shaped** / **has been shaped** by the once powerful Colorado River.

2. Now the great Colorado River **is drying up** / **is being dried up**.

3. About seventy percent of the water **uses** / **is used** to grow crops.

4. People in far-off cities, for example, Los Angeles, **are using** / **are being used** the water.

5. Miles of dried up river beds **can see** / **can be seen** now.

6. A lot of animals **have not survived** / **have not been survived** the dry conditions.

7. Climate change **is also harming** / **is also being harmed** the Colorado River.

8. In the next few decades, the amount of available water **may reduce** / **may be reduced** significantly because of climate change.

9. What **could do** / **could be done** to save the river?

10. More water **should conserve** / **should be conserved**.

8 Complete the exercises.

A Complete the questions with the words in parentheses. Use the correct passive forms of the verbs.

1. How many sharks _____are killed_____ (kill) every year?

2. How many people _____are attacked_____ (attack) by sharks every year?

3. When _____was the mega_____ (the megamouth shark / discover)?

4. How many shark species _____were threaten_____ (threaten) by human activity?

5. Which part of a shark _____is sette sold_____ (sell) for food?

▶ A pregnant sand tiger shark swims over coral. Bonin Islands, Japan.

6. Where _____ (shark-fin soup / eat) the most?

7. When _____ (shark-fin soup / serve)?

8. How _____ (can / sharks / protect)?

B SPEAK. Work with a partner. Take turns answering the questions in exercise **A** with the choices in the box. See page A12 to check your answers.

Asia	at weddings	fewer than 100	More than 100
the fins	~~60 million~~	1976	stop hunting them

A: *How many sharks are killed every year?*

B: *Sixty million.*

9 SPEAK & WRITE.

A Work with a partner. Look at the map of Madagascar and some of the endangered species that live there on page 243. Do you know other endangered animals? Tell your partner at least one other endangered animal and where it lives.

B Write sentences about Madagascar using the words in parentheses. Use a correct active or passive form of each verb. Use negative forms when correct according to the map and information on page 243.

1. (Madagascar / locate / off the coast of Africa)

   Madagascar is located off the coast of Africa.

2. (Baobab trees and lemurs / find / in Madagascar)

   _____

3. (A few areas of Madagascar / protect / by the government)

   _____

4. (Most of the island / protect)

   _____

5. (Many of Madagascar's plants and animals / live / in small, unprotected areas)

   _____

6. (Many of these plants and animals / endanger)

   _____

7. (A lot of the rain forest areas in Madagascar / destroy)

   _____

8. (Some rain forest areas / preserve)

   _____

9. (Every year, they / cut down / more and more trees)

_____

10. (The rain forest in Madagascar / should / protect / to save endangered species)

_____

▲ Grandidier baobab

AFRICA

MADAGASCAR

MADAGASCAR

INDIAN OCEAN

▲ Silky sifaka (lemur)

▲ Lesser chameleon

▲ Long-tailed ground roller

▲ Harlequin mantella frog

■ Rain forest
■ Rain forest in bad condition because trees are being cut down
■ Other forest
⫽ Area where endangered animals live
▫ Protected area

10 LISTEN.

CD3-03-06

A You will hear a tour guide talk about a cruise in Antarctica. Listen to each part of his story. Then choose the correct sentence for each item.

Part 1   1.   a. The cruise ship rescued passengers from two other ships.

b. The passengers on M/S Explorer were rescued by two other ships.

Part 2   2.   a. Fewer ships are coming to Antarctica than in the past.

b. Antarctica is visited by thousands of tourists every year.

Part 3   3.   a. Some plants have been harmed.

b. Some animals have been bothering people.

4.   a. Tours to Antarctica will be stopped.

b. Tours to Antarctica should be limited and controlled.

Part 4   5.   a. Guidelines have been created to protect Antarctica.

b. The IAATO has promised to create guidelines to protect Antarctica.

6.   a. Only twenty people can join each tour group.

b. One hundred people can be included in each tour group.

7.   a. The situation is considered to be better now.

b. The situation is not any better now.

8.   a. Tour companies are required to obey the new rules.

b. Tour companies don't have to obey the new rules.

CD3-03-06

B Listen again and check your answers.

▼ Cruise ship and iceberg at Deception Island, Antarctica

11 **EDIT.** Read the paragraph. Find and correct seven more errors with passives.

Three Gorges Dam: Success or Failure?

Construction on the Three Gorges Dam[1] on the Yangtze River began in 1994. It $\overset{\text{was}}{\vee}$ completed in 2012. The dam is considered a great success because it has had some positive effects on the environment. In the past, a lot of coal is used for energy. Now, the dam generates water power, and the need for coal has been reduced. This means that there is less carbon dioxide in the air. Unfortunately, there have also been some negative effects. Many places were flood because of the dam. Over a million people had to being moved. Also, the dam located in a region with many plants and animals. Many plant species in this region have being harmed by the dam. More could be harm in the future. The dam has also caused changes to the temperature and increased the amount of pollution in the water. This has been threatened the freshwater fish in the area. Changes should been made to improve the situation soon. Authorities have promised to make these changes.

[1] **dam:** special walls built across rivers to stop the water from flowing; used to create electricity

12 **APPLY.**

A Work in a group. Discuss some environmental problems that you know about. Make a chart in your notebook like the one below and write notes for each category.

Problem	Cause	Changes in Environment	What Should Be Done?
river in my town has been polluted	chemicals from nearby factory	fish and plants are dying	make rules that control how factories get rid of chemical waste

B In your notebook, write five sentences about one of the problems your group discussed. Use the passive and the verbs in the box or your own ideas.

damage	endanger	improve	poison	preserve
destroy	harm	limit	pollute	rescue

C Exchange sentences with someone from a different group. Ask each other questions to learn more.

A: *Are any steps being taken to clean up the river?*

B: *Yes, the harmful chemicals are being removed with special equipment.*

A: *Have all the fish been killed?*

B: *No, some species have survived.*

EXPLORE

CD3-07

1 **READ** the article about night gardens. How are night gardens different from the gardens that we see during the day?

Night Gardens

Take a walk through a garden at night. You will probably notice that flowers look different from how they look during the day. At nighttime, colors **are transformed**[1] when they **are lit by** moonlight. White and yellow flowers shine, and reds and oranges glow.[2]

Glowing colors are especially important for plants that bloom[3] only at night, such as the cereus cactus plant and some tropical water lilies. Night-bloomers **are pollinated by** bats and moths. Most of these creatures are active only at night. They don't have good vision, but they can easily locate flowers that glow in the dark. In addition, night-bloomers have a sweet smell, so their pollinators **are attracted by** their scent as well as their color.

That's the scientific explanation for the colors and fragrance of night gardens, but it does not explain their peacefulness or the magical effect they have on us.

[1] **transform:** to change from one appearance to another
[2] **glow:** to give off light
[3] **bloom:** to flower

▶ A night-blooming cereus flower unfolds in Honolulu, Hawaii.

2 CHECK. Correct the error in each sentence according to the article.

    different

1. Flowers look ~~the same~~ at night and during the day.

2. The colors of flowers change in sunlight.

3. Bees pollinate night bloomers.

4. Pollinators locate flowers that are hard to see in the dark.

5. Science can explain the effect that night gardens have on us.

▲ Hummingbird hawk moth

3 DISCOVER. Complete the exercises to learn about the grammar in this lesson.

A Look at the sentences based on the article in exercise **1**. Underline the passive in each sentence.

1. At nighttime, the colors of flowers <u>are transformed</u>.

2. They are lit by moonlight.

3. Night-bloomers are pollinated by bats and moths.

4. Their pollinators are attracted by scent as well as color.

B Look at the sentences in exercise **A** again. Write **A** if the agent is mentioned. Write ✗ if the agent is not mentioned.

1. _____   2. _____   3. _____   4. _____

C Look at the sentences in exercise **A** again. What word is used before the agent?

LEARN

9.3 Using the Passive

1. The passive can be used when you want to emphasize *what* happened more than *who* or *what* performed the action (the agent).	Coffee **is produced** in Colombia.
2. The passive can also be used when you do not know the agent.	Look! The car **has been stolen**!
3. The passive is sometimes used when it is not necessary to state or repeat the agent.	✓ My car was stolen. ✗ My car was stolen <u>by a car thief</u>.
4. The passive can also be used to avoid criticizing or blaming someone.	My manager told me in a nice way, "This report **was not done** correctly."

4 Rewrite the sentences in the passive. Do not include the agent.

1. People love flowers for their beauty and scent.

   Flowers are loved for their beauty and scent.

2. In Australia, people chose the golden wattle as the national flower.

   _____

3. You can see wax flowers in Western Australia.

   _____

4. The media reported an unusual story from Sydney, Australia.

   _____

5. Australian police discovered a destroyed flowerbed outside a museum.

   _____

◄ Gary the Goat with his owner, comedian Jimbo Bazoobi, outside an Australian courthouse

6. A goat named Gary had eaten the museum's flowerbed.

_____

7. The police ordered Gary's owner to pay a fine.

_____

8. The owner brought Gary to the courthouse for his trial.

_____

9.4   Using *By* with the Passive

1. In a passive sentence, use *by* + the agent when it is important to say who or what performed the action.	Her roses were destroyed **by insects**. Agent
2. Sometimes the agent is clear from the context, so you do not need *by* + agent.	Charles Dickens wrote many books. *Oliver Twist* **was written** in the 1830s.

3. It is common to mention the agent when it is:
   a. a number
   b. a person's name
   c. someone or something specific
	a. This magazine is read **by millions of people**.
	b. The portrait was painted **by Picasso**.
	c. Many animal habitats are threatened **by pollution**.
	✗ Many animal habitats are threatened <u>by something</u>.

5   Look at each verb and agent. Then complete the sentence with the correct form of the verbs. Use the passive. If the agent is important, include *by* + the agent. If the agent is not important, cross it out.

1. write / Jack London

   The Call of the Wild __was written by Jack London_____.

2. pick / ~~farm workers~~

   The peaches on this farm _____*are picked*_____ in late summer.

3. release / people

   The wolf _____ into the wild last week.

4. visit / millions of tourists

   The Taj Mahal in India _____ every year.

5. steal / someone

   My cell phone _____ last night.

6. give / the president of South Africa

   Tomorrow, an important speech _____.

7. eat / birds

   Many baby sea turtles _____ before they reach the
   ocean.

8. destroy / a forest fire

   Our house _____ last year.

PRACTICE

6 Complete the article with the words in parentheses. Use the passive and the correct form of
each verb. Add *by* + agent when necessary.

Nearly one-third of parrot species (1) __are threatened__ (threaten) in the
wild. The World Parrot Trust (2) _____ (start) in 1989 to help
parrots survive and also to help protect parrots in captivity. Educational materials
(3) _____ (post) on the World Parrot Trust's website. They teach
the public about the dangers parrots face around the world.

The Cape Parrot of South Africa (4) _____ (endanger).
This parrot (5) _____ (have to / protect) because of three
problems. First, their population (6) _____
(reduce / disease). Now only 1000 to 1500 of these parrots still live in the wild.
Second, the parrots' natural habitat (7) _____ (damage
/ deforestation). The third problem relates to business. Although it is against the
law, large numbers of these birds (8) _____ (catch / wild-parrot
traders). Then they (9) _____ (sell) to people who want
them as pets.

7 Complete the article about one of the natural wonders of the world with the words in parentheses. Use the active or passive and the correct form of the verbs. Add *by* when necessary.

Table Mountain (1) __is considered__ (consider) to be one of the most amazing places in South Africa. It (2) _____ (be) in the beautiful city of Cape Town. The flat top of the mountain measures 2 miles (3 km) across. A tall pile of stones (3) _____ (place) on the highest point of the mountain. The pile of stones (4) _____ (call) *Maclear's Beacon*. Table Mountain (5) _____ (visit) many tourists who like to hike and bike there.

In 1926, Trygve Stromsoe, a Norwegian engineer, (6) _____ (propose) a plan for a cable car system on the mountain. The cableway (7) _____ (complete) in 1929. Since the opening of the cableway, over 16 million people (8) _____ (take) the trip to the top of the mountain. Table Mountain offers visitors an incredible view of Cape Town. The mountain (9) _____ (also / know) for something else: Mensa, a group of stars. These stars (10) _____ (name) after Table Mountain. (*Mensa* means "table" in Latin.)

▲ Table Mountain in Cape Town, South Africa

8 Read the article. Then complete the sentences below. Use the active or passive and the correct form of the verb. Include *by* + the agent when necessary.

Tourists who visit Cape Town, South Africa, shouldn't miss the Cape of Good Hope. It's a rocky piece of land that sticks out into the Atlantic Ocean. The Cape of Good Hope is a very important place because when ships reach the cape, they have to turn east to sail around Africa.

Bartolomeu Dias was the first European explorer to discover the cape in the 15th century. He called it the Cape of Storms because it was very stormy there. Its discovery had opened up a trading route between Europe and Asia, so it got a new name: Cape Hope. Over the years, many European traders stopped at the cape to buy food and supplies from the local people. Eventually these traders built the city of Cape Town. Many ships also sank near the cape. People told stories about *The Flying Dutchman*. This was a ghost ship that tried to sail around the cape over and over again, but never succeeded.

Nowadays, the Cape of Good Hope is part of Table Mountain National Park. You can find many unusual plants and animals at the cape, including African penguins. You can also see different kinds of whales in the waters around the cape.

1. The Cape of Good Hope _shouldn't be missed by tourists_ who visit Cape Town, South Africa.

2. Ships _____ east when they reach the Cape of Good Hope.

3. The Cape of Good Hope _____ in the 15th century.

4. At first, the cape _____ the Cape of Storms because it was very stormy there.

5. The cape _____ the Cape of Good Hope because it had opened up an important trading route.

6. European traders _____ food and supplies from the local people at the cape.

7. The city of Cape Town _____ these traders.

8. Stories _____ about *The Flying Dutchman*, a ghost ship.

9. Unusual plants and animals _____ at the Cape of Good Hope.

10. Whales _____ in the waters around the cape.

9 Read the headlines. Then complete the sentences using the passive. Use the correct form of the verb. Add *by* when necessary.

1. **LION-MEAT BAN PROPOSED**

   A ban on lion meat _____ .

2. **SWORDFISH EYEBALL FOUND ON FLORIDA BEACH**

   A swordfish eyeball _____ on a Florida beach.

3. **SINGING MICE OBSERVED IN 2005 STUDY**

   Singing mice _____ in a 2005 study.

4. **BRAZILIAN FAMILY RAISING TIGER**

   A tiger _____ .

5. **THREE BILLION BIRDS KILLED EVERY YEAR; CATS TO BLAME**

   Three billion birds _____ every year.

6. **68 BURMESE PYTHONS CAUGHT IN FLORIDA**

   Sixty-eight Burmese python snakes _____ in Florida.

7. **REPAIRMAN DISCOVERS BEAR IN BASEMENT**

   A bear _____ last Tuesday.

10 APPLY.

A Listen to the conversation. Which headline in exercise **9** is the conversation about? [CD3-08]

B Complete the sentences. Use the passive form of six of the verbs from the box. Add *not* and *by* when necessary.

bite	catch	chase	contact
~~find~~	give	release	repair

   Last Tuesday a 500-pound black bear (1) ___was found___ in the basement of a home near the state park. A repairman discovered the bear while he was working in the basement. The repairman ran out, and fortunately he (2) _____ the bear or hurt in any other way. The animal control department (3) _____ and some officers came right away. They shot the bear with tranquilizers. The tranquilizers were not effective at first, and the bear managed to escape. The bear (4) _____ for nearly 45 minutes before it (5) _____ . The bear (6) _____ into the wild after it (7) _____ a medical exam.

C Work with a partner. Use your imagination to write a news report for another headline from exercise **9**. Use the report in exercise **B** as a model.

EXPLORE

1 **READ** the article about hurricane hunters. What important work do they do?

Hurricane Hunters

One September morning, Captain Chad Gibson boarded an airplane in Mississippi. A violent hurricane had been reported in Cuba. It was raining hard, and winds were over 110 miles per hour (177 kph). Gibson was planning to fly right through the storm.

Being caught in the middle of a storm was no problem for Gibson, because he is a hurricane hunter. His job is to collect information about powerful storms. Most of this information **gets collected** when the plane flies through the calm eye of the storm.[1] The pilots use a device called a dropsonde to record humidity,[2] temperature, and wind speed. With this information, they determine the strength of a hurricane and where it is heading. Then they send the information to weather forecasters.

After considering the data, the weather forecasters issue warnings about areas that they expect **to be affected**. Sometimes, people in these areas have to prepare **to be evacuated**.[3] Sometimes people do not want **to be evacuated**, but it is safer if they leave the area. That way, they can avoid **getting caught** in dangerous situations.

The damage caused by past hurricanes has been considerable, but without the work of the hurricane hunters, it would have been even worse. Pilots like Chad Gibson know that their work can save lives. They don't mind **being asked** to track dangerous storms. As Gibson says, "It's just a job. You know, a lawyer goes to his office. We get on our plane."

[1] **eye of the storm:** calm area in the center of a storm or hurricane
[2] **humidity:** the amount of water in the air
[3] **evacuate:** to move out of a place of danger for a period of time

▲ A satellite image of Hurricane Katrina, which devastated New Orleans and the Gulf Coast of the US in August 2005.

2 CHECK. Write answers to the questions. Write complete sentences.

1. When do hurricane hunters collect information?

   Hurricane hunters collect information when they fly through the
   calm eye of the storm.

2. What are three things that a dropsonde checks?

   _____

3. What two important things about a hurricane do the pilots want to find out?

   _____

4. What do weather forecasters do with the hurricane hunters' information?

   _____

3 DISCOVER. Complete the exercises to learn about the grammar in this lesson.

A Read the sentences from the article in excercise **1**. Underline the passive in each sentence.

1. <u>Being caught</u> in the middle of a storm was no problem for Gibson.

2. The weather forecasters issue warnings about areas that they expect to be affected.

3. That way, they can avoid getting caught in dangerous situations.

4. They don't mind being asked to track dangerous storms.

B Look at the sentences in exercise **A** again. Then read the statements. Choose **T** for *true* or **F** for *false*.

1. You need to use a form of *be* in all passives.   **T**   **F**

2. Passives can be formed with both gerunds and infinitives.   **T**   **F**

3. The final verb form in passive phrases is always a past participle. **T**   **F**

LEARN

9.5 Passive Gerunds and Passive Infinitives

Passive Gerunds
(Not) Being + Past Participle
I dislike **being given** extra work.
I don't mind **not being invited** to the picnic.
I was angry about **being fired** from my job.

Passive Infinitives
(Not) To Be + Past Participle
I want **to be invited** to the party.
I tried **not to be caught** in the storm.
I was happy **to be given** some extra work.

1. The passive form of a gerund is *being* + the past participle.	She dislikes **being asked** a lot of questions. He was upset about **not being told** the news.
2. Like gerunds, passive gerunds can: a. be the subject of a sentence b. follow verbs such as *avoid, dislike, mind, risk, understand*[1] c. follow a preposition	a. **Being questioned** about my work made me nervous. b. I **don't mind being interviewed**. c. Are you interested **in being called** if a job opens up?
3. The passive form of an infinitive is *(not) to be* + the past participle.	She is determined **to be elected** president. The information is **not to be discussed** with anyone.
4. Passive infinitives can follow verbs and adjectives normally followed by an infinitive. a. Verbs: *ask, expect, hope, prefer, wait*[2] b. Adjectives: *afraid, determined, lucky, ready*[3]	a. We **waited to be picked up** at the station. b. I was **lucky to be given** the award.

[1] See page **A4** for a full list of verbs and phrases followed by gerunds.
[2] See page **A5** for a full list of verbs followed by infinitives.
[3] See page **A5** for a full list of adjectives followed by infinitives.

4 Circle the correct form of the verb to complete each sentence.

1. When hurricanes develop, hurricane hunters get ready **being sent / to be sent** into the storm.

2. Hurricane hunters risk **being injured / to be injured** on the job.

3. Hurricane hunters never complain about **being expected / to be expected** to help weather forecasters.

4. Buildings are often in danger of **being damaged / to be damaged** during a hurricane.

5. When a bad storm is coming, people shouldn't wait **being evacuated / to be evacuated**.

6. Sometimes homeowners need **being told / to be told** that they can't return to their homes.

7. Everyone looks forward to **being allowed / to be allowed** back into their homes.

8. After a storm, people hope **being given / to be given** assistance by the government.

9.6 *Get* Passives

1. You can use a form of *get* + the past participle to create a passive meaning. *Get* passives are commonly used:
   a. to describe something unwanted or unexpected
   b. to talk about something that will have a negative effect
   c. with certain verbs such as *accept, deliver, fire, hire, invite, offer, pay, promote, show*

   a. His dog **got hit** by a car. He's very upset.
   b. Kim i**s going to get punished** for staying out too late.
   c. I'm so happy. I **got accepted** to the University of Iowa.

2. The gerund form of a passive with *get* is *getting* + the past participle.

   I'm worried about **getting fired**.

   The infinitive form of a passive with *get* is *to get* + the past participle.

   I don't expect **to get fired**.

5 Complete the conversations with a correct form of *get* and the verbs in parentheses. In some cases, more than one form of the verb is possible.

Conversation A

Eve: Are tornadoes frequent where you live?

Al: Yes, they're pretty common. In fact, we (1) _____got hit_____ (hit) by one last month.

Eve: Were there any injuries?

Al: No, we were very lucky. Some windows (2) _____ (break) but no one (3) _____ (hurt).

Conversation B

Deb: Did you have any damage from the hurricane?

Vic: Our basement (4) _____ (flood), but the rest of the house was OK. Downtown (5) _____ (hit) much worse. Main Street was affected badly.

Deb: Why? Did the stores (6) _____ (damage)?

Vic: Yeah, especially the grocery store; a lot of food (7) _____ (ruin). I think it's going to take weeks before that store dries out.

Deb: Oh, no. So can you still buy food there?

Vic: Yeah, you can. There isn't much to buy there now, but I heard that more food (8) _____ (deliver) tomorrow.

► A bull tries to escape a running wildfire in Gradford, Texas.

PRACTICE

6 Read about the effects that weather has on wildlife. Complete the paragraph with the correct form of *get* or *be* and the verbs in parentheses. More than one answer is sometimes correct.

Many animals are in danger of (1) _____ (harm) during storms, especially during hurricanes. Violent storms can affect a variety of species. Even fish are not safe. During a hurricane, for example, fish habitats often (2) _____ (damage) when tree limbs and branches break off and fall to the ground. The wetlands (3) _____ (fill) with the tree parts. This reduces the amount of oxygen in the water and fish die as a result. Birds are at risk, too. During a hurricane, many birds (4) _____ (blow) out to sea. (5) _____ (remove) from their natural habitats can be very dangerous for birds, and many of them (6) _____ (kill) when this happens. The Puerto Rico parrot population, for example, (7) _____ (reduce) greatly after Hurricane Andrew. Normally, large sea animals such as manatees (8) _____ (not affect) by hurricanes, and they do not need (9) _____ (rescue). However, there are exceptions. For instance, after Hurricane Andrew, one manatee (10) _____ (find) far away from its home in coastal waters.

7 Complete the exercises.

A Complete the questions with the passive. Use the correct form of *get* and a verb from the box.

| bite | burn | ~~catch~~ | injure | rescue | sting |

1. Have you ever _gotten caught_ in a bad storm?

2. What should you do to avoid _____ in a wildfire?

3. Have you ever _____ from a dangerous situation?

4. Have you ever _____ in a car accident?

5. What do some people do when they _____ by a bee?

6. Have you ever _____ by an animal?

B **SPEAK.** Work with a partner. Ask and answer the questions in exercise **A**. Add details about your experiences.

8 **LISTEN** to the conversation about a camping trip. Then read the statements. Circle **T** for *true* or **F** for *false*.

1. Campers' garbage could bother some animals at the campground.   **T**   **(F)**

2. Julie woke up her friends when she heard a noise.   **T**   **F**

3. Julie and her friends hadn't thrown all the garbage away.   **T**   **F**

4. Skunks spray to defend themselves in the wild.   **T**   **F**

5. Julie was able to stop the skunk from spraying.   **T**   **F**

6. The campers felt lucky that their adventure only involved a skunk.   **T**   **F**

9 **EDIT.** Read the paragraph. Find and correct eight more errors with passives.

When I was a child, I remember being show [shown] a bird nest in a tree in our yard. It was a robin's nest, and it was amazing. There were four blue eggs in the nest. The bird didn't seem to mind be watched, and I was careful not to get too close. I was very young, maybe four, but I never needed telling not to touch the nest. Somehow I knew that without being remind. One day, I looked and saw baby robins in the nest. I don't think they liked be left alone by their mother, but sometimes she had to fly away to get food. When she came back, the babies made a lot of noise while they were waiting to being fed!

Since that time I have always loved birds, and I love to go on birdwatching trips. In recent years, I have traveled all over the world to observe birds. I sometimes get invite to speak at birdwatching conferences. Be asked to share my knowledge of birds with others gives me a lot of pleasure. Fortunately, birdwatching is a very safe hobby. I've never get injured while doing my favorite thing.

A Look at the photo. Then write sentences about it. Use your imagination. Use passive gerunds, passive infinitives, and *get* passives in your sentences.

1. This city _____ got hit by a snowstorm _____.

2. The taxi _____.

3. The woman doesn't want _____.

4. The dog doesn't mind _____.

5. _____ can be scary.

6. _____.

B Work in a group. Share your sentences from exercise **A**. Ask each other questions about your sentences. Try to use passive gerunds, passive infinitives, and *get* passives.

A: *This city got hit by a bad snowstorm.*

B: *Did anyone get hurt in the snowstorm?*

A: *No, no one got hurt, if I remember correctly.*

Charts
9.1–9.6

1 Circle the correct words to complete the conversation.

Elsa: I remember when I first started working at the animal preserve 40 years ago, one of my favorite animals was a young elephant named Lucy. But one day, (1) she **disappeared** / **was disappeared**, and she (2) **never saw / was never seen** again.

Paul: I remember Lucy. Then shortly after that, we (3) **noticed / were noticed** that every day another animal was missing. We realized that some thieves (4) **must have taken / must have been taken** them. Eventually, the thieves (5) **caught / were caught** by the police. If I remember correctly, they (6) **sent / got sent** to jail for three years.

Elsa: That's right. That was a harsh punishment at that time. I don't think those thieves expected (7) **to punish / to get punished** at all.

Paul: No, I don't think they did. But it was a good thing, because more and more animals (8) **are saving / are being saved** now. Since our departure, some of the animals (9) **have released / have been released** back into the wild.

Elsa: That's great news. It shows how much people (10) **have learned / have been learned** since we started our work.

Charts
9.1–9.4

2 Rewrite the sentences in the passive where possible. Begin each sentence with the underlined word(s). Use the correct form of the verb. Use *by* + the agent when necessary.

1. We find <u>bats</u> throughout most of the world.

   Bats are found throughout most of the world.

2. We can see <u>bats</u> all over the world.

   _____

3. In some parts of the world, <u>bats</u> live in caves.

   _____

4. Someone should stop <u>the destruction</u> of bat habitats.

   _____

5. A deadly disease has killed <u>more than 5.7 million bats</u>.

   _____

6. Organizations are investigating <u>the spread of the disease</u>.

   _____

7. The disease could threaten <u>the survival of bats</u>.

   _____

8. The government should have protected <u>these endangered animals</u> from this disease.

   _____

Charts
9.5–9.6

3 Complete the sentences with passive gerunds, passive infinitives, *get* passives and the correct form of the verbs in parentheses.

1. The old couple isn't worried about __being caught OR getting caught__ (catch) in the hurricane. They aren't ready _____ (evacuate). They hope _____ (leave) alone in their home until the hurricane is over.

2. The baby monkey _____ (hurt) when it fell out of a tree. Now it wants _____ (pick up) by its mother. It's asking _____ (feed) some fruit.

3. _____ (trap) in a fire can be very dangerous. If you play with fire in your home, you risk _____ (burn) very badly. A fire _____ (start) in a house last week by five children who were playing with matches. Luckily, the children _____ (rescue) by a firefighter. The firefighter _____ (promote) after she saved the children.

Charts
9.1–9.6

4 EDIT. Read the text. Find and correct seven more errors with passives.

Good News for Gray Seals, or Is It?

                                                    been
Good news for the gray seal population has ⌄announced. Seal populations are being grown off the north Atlantic coast of the United States. For many years, seals killed for their skins, oil, and meat. However, since 1972, they have be protected by U.S. law, and they cannot be killed. Many people worry, however, that the seal population is getting out of control, and that nothing will been done to manage it. Fishermen are complaining because large amounts of fish are eating by the seals. In addition, there is the shark problem. Sharks like to eat seals, so when seals move into an area, sharks usually follow. In fact, many more sharks can be seen in the areas where seal populations have increased. Naturally, swimmers are concerned about to be attacked by sharks. Swimmer Jon Turner says, "It's great that the gray seal population has come back, but now I have to be careful not to get bite by a shark!"

5 LISTEN & SPEAK.

Charts
9.1,
9.3–9.5

CD3-11

A Take the quiz. Circle the letters of the correct answers. Then listen and check your answers.

1. Which of the following is a major problem facing the world's oceans?

    a. Overfishing   c. Pollution

    b. Building in coastal areas   d. All of these things

2. Which of the following has been linked to climate change on Earth?

    a. Droughts (periods with little or no rainfall)   c. Melting ice caps

    b. Flooding   d. All of these things

3. On average, what are your chances of being struck by lightning in any given year?

    a. 1 in 7,000,000   c. 1 in 70,000

    b. 1 in 700,000   d. 1 in 7000

4. How many pounds of wild fish and shellfish are removed from the ocean every year?

    a. About 700,000 pounds   c. More than 170 billion pounds

    b. Less than 170 million pounds   d. About 100 million pounds

5. How big was the biggest wave that has ever been recorded?

    a. 12 feet (4 meters)   c. 75 feet (23 meters)

    b. 30 feet (9 meters)   d. 90 feet (27 meters)

CD3-11

B Listen again. Then write the answers to the questions in your notebook.

1. What is happening to Earth's oceans and the species that live in them?

2. What is happening to rainfall patterns and melting polar ice?

3. What role do activities such as golf and mountain climbing play during a thunderstorm?

4. Why are there fewer fish and shellfish in the ocean every year?

5. What caused the biggest wave?

C Work with a partner. Discuss your answers from exercise **B**.

A: *The ocean and its species are being harmed by pollution.*

B: *That's one problem. Another is overfishing.*

1 READ & NOTICE THE GRAMMAR.

A Look at the photo below. What do you know about this animal? Discuss with a partner. Then read the essay.

AFRICAN MANATEES

African manatees can be found in the rivers and coastal areas of western Africa. Unfortunately, the future of African manatees is uncertain. There are now fewer than 10,000 of these animals left. The destruction of their natural habitat and hunting are major threats.

A large part of the manatees' habitat is being destroyed by the building of dams. In Senegal, for example, manatees get stuck in the shallow water created by dams on the Senegal River. Pollution from boats on the river also damages their habitat, as does the clearing of wetlands.

Hunting is another problem. Hunting manatees is illegal, but their meat is still being sold in markets, and their bones are used to make parts of walking sticks. Because the laws are not strongly enforced, people who hunt manatees illegally do not get punished.

Although all manatees are endangered, the African manatees are especially at risk because of the serious problems they face. Many environmental groups are working to save African manatees. They hope that education and better law enforcement will help protect these animals.

GRAMMAR FOCUS

In this essay, the writer uses the passive with and without the agent.

• The agent is mentioned when it adds new information.
  *A large part of the manatees' habitat **is being destroyed by the building of dams**.*

• The agent *isn't* mentioned when it is already clear or obvious.
  *African manatees **can be found** in the rivers and coastal areas of western Africa.*

B Read the essay in exercise **A** again. Find two more examples of the passive. Indicate whether or not the agent is mentioned.

1. _____ can be found _____   _____ no agent _____

2. _____   _____

3. _____   _____

C Complete the chart with information from the essay in exercise **A**.

Endangered Species: ___African Manatee___	
Threat	**Specific Examples**
Habitat is being destroyed	1. 2. 3. Clearing of wetlands
	1. Meat is sold in markets 2. 3.

2 BEFORE YOU WRITE.

A In your notebook, make a list of all the endangered animals that you have heard of. Then choose the animal from your list that you know the most about.

B Make a chart in your notebook like the one in exercise **1C**. Think about the animal you chose in exercise **A**. What are the two biggest threats to its survival? Write notes in your chart. Use the chart from exercise **1C** as a model.

3 WRITE an essay about the endangered animal you chose. Use the information from your chart in **2B** and the essay in exercise **1A** to help you.

> **WRITING FOCUS**   Using *Especially*
>
> Notice how the writer uses *especially* in the essay in exercise **1A**. *Especially* indicates that the writer is adding an important or particular example of detail to a sentence.
>
> *Although all manatees are endangered, African manatees are **especially** at risk because of the serious problems they face.*

4 SELF ASSESS. Read your essay again. Underline the passive. Then use the checklist to assess your work.

- [ ] I used the passive correctly. [9.1–9.5]
- [ ] I used *by* + the agent only when it was important. [9.4]
- [ ] I used *especially* to give additional information. [WRITING FOCUS]

Causative Verb Patterns and Phrasal Verbs

◀ A female io moth, Little
Orleans, Maryland, USA

EXPLORE

CD3-12

1 **READ** the article about a popular annual event in Abu Dhabi. In what way does it celebrate the past?

Who's the loveliest of them all?

The contest participants come from near and far. They wear gold and silver and flutter[1] their long eyelashes. However, this is no ordinary beauty contest. The competition takes place in a remote part of Abu Dhabi, one of the United Arab Emirates. There are about 25,000 contestants and they all have large heads, floppy lips, and long legs. They come from all over the Arabian Peninsula for *Al Dhafra*, the annual beauty contest for camels. Yes, camels.

To prepare for the contest, experienced trainers **help owners to make their camels** look their best. The camels are fed special food to make them healthy and strong. They are also washed from top to bottom, which **makes their hair shine**. Sometimes the trainers **get the camels to loosen up** by massaging them. Then, the camels are decorated.

The beauty contest lasts ten days. Each day, the trainers **have the camels walk** in front of the judges. The judges evaluate the size of the camel's head, the length of the neck, and the size and shape of the hump.[2] The owners of top-scoring camels win millions of dollars. The most exciting day is the last one, when the judges choose the most beautiful camel of all.

A winning camel brings a lot of prestige[3] to an owner; however, the contest is about much more. Historically, the camel provided people of the desert with food, clothing, and transportation. *Al Dhafra* **lets this community celebrate** their traditional relationship with camels, the much loved "ships of the desert."

[1] **flutter:** to quickly move up and down
[2] **hump:** the large lump on a camel's back
[3] **prestige:** being admired or respected

▼ These long-legged, floppy-lipped, big-eyed camels are getting ready for a big day.

▼ The Rub al Khali or Empty Quarter is the largest sand desert in the world. It includes parts of Oman, Saudi Arabia, the UAE, and Yemen.

2 CHECK. Correct the error in each sentence according to the information in the article.

                                                      all over the Arabian Peninsula

1.   The beauty contest is for camels from ~~Abu Dhabi~~.

2.   Camel owners get help from family members before the contest.

3.   A camel's hair shines after it is massaged.

4.   The trainers evaluate the camels at the contest.

5.   On the last day, the judges choose the most skillful camel.

3 DISCOVER. Complete the exercises to learn about the grammar in this lesson.

A Find these sentences in the article from exercise **1**. Write the missing words.

1.   . . . experienced trainers _____ their camels look their best.

2.   They are also washed from top to bottom, which _____.

3.   Sometimes the trainers _____ by massaging them.

4.   Each day, the trainers _____ in front of the judges.

5.   *Al Dhafra* _____ their traditional relationship with camels . . .

B Look at the verb patterns in the phrases you wrote in exercise **A**. Then check (✓) the pattern that is used with each verb.

Verb	Object + Base Form of Verb	Object + Infinitive (*to* + verb)
1. help		
2. make		
3. get		
4. have		
5. let		

LEARN

10.1 *Have, Let,* and *Make*

Have/Let/Make + Object + Base Form
The teacher **has her students do** a lot of homework.
Amy **lets her children play** outside every day.
Jon's mother **makes him clean** his room once a week.

1. *Have/let/make* + object + the base form of a verb indicates that the subject causes or influences a person or thing to act.	The director **had the actor say** his lines again. He **made the actors wear** silly costumes. He **didn't let the actors choose** the costumes.
2. *Have someone do something* means to require or ask someone to do something.	The teacher **had the students** retake the test. Did you **have anyone read** your essay?
3. *Let someone do something* means to allow or permit someone to do something.	Jack's mother **lets him stay up** late.
4. *Make someone do something* means to force or cause someone to do something.	She **made the child drink** milk, but he hated it. That book **made me decide** to study history.

4 Circle the correct answers to complete the paragraph about a camel market in Abu Dhabi.

Today, the huge number of cars on the streets of Abu Dhabi might (1) **have / (make)** you think that camels are a thing of the past. However, a trip to the camel market in Al Ain is likely to change your mind. You can (2) **have / make** someone give you a tour of the market, or you can look around by yourself. Camels of all colors and sizes are kept in wire pens. That (3) **lets / makes** you see them up close. There is lively competition among the traders. Each man tries to (4) **let / make** people believe that his camels are the very best. Some owners (5) **have / let** tourists enter the camel pens, but the visitors often have to pay to do this. The cutest camels are the wide-eyed babies. They (6) **have / make** everybody smile. Some traders won't (7) **have / let** you take pictures. They will (8) **let / make** you put your camera away, so be sure to ask permission first. Take your time and look around. Perhaps a visit to the market will (9) **have / make** you want a camel of your own. You probably won't be able to (10) **let / make** it behave like a prize-winner, but you will still love it.

▲ Mother and baby camel, Abu Dhabi, UAE

10.2 *Get* and *Help*

> **Get + Object + Infinitive**
> I **get my friend to exercise** with me after work.

> **Help + Object + Base Form/Infinitive**
> I **help my son to do** his homework.
> I **help my son do** his homework.

1. *Get* + object + infinitive means to persuade or cause someone to do something.	He **got his brother to lend** him some money. The classes **get me to think** differently about history.
2. *Help* + object + the base form of the verb or infinitive means to assist or guide.	The teacher **will help you do** the report. The teacher **will help you to do** the report.

5 Complete the interview with a beauty contest participant. Use the correct forms of *get* or *help* and the words in parentheses. More than one answer is sometimes possible.

A: You entered your first beauty contest at age 16. Did your parents think you were too young?

B: Yes, at first, but I finally (1) ___got them to agree___ (them / agree). They knew how much I wanted to participate. But they (2) _____ (me / promise) to finish my college applications before I started preparing for the contest.

A: Was the contest all about appearance?

B: Absolutely not. We had to show we had talents and skills. Luckily, the trainers (3) _____ (us / prepare) for the contest. For example, my talent was tap dancing, so my trainer (4) _____ (me / practice) six times a week.

A: What about your relationship with the other contestants? How was that?

B: It was great! I made lifelong friends with some of the other people. We always (5) _____ (each other / do) our best.

A: What's the secret to winning a contest?

B: Well, for one thing, you have to (6) _____ (the judges / respect) you. They have to realize that there is more to you than your appearance.

A: You've won several contests, haven't you?

B: Yes, and the scholarship money (7) _____ (me / pay) for college.

A: That's great. A college degree will (8) _____ (you / get) a good job. Do you know what you're going to study?

B: I want to study psychology, so I can (9) _____ (people / solve) their problems.

A: That's a good goal. Well, good luck!

PRACTICE

6 Complete the exercises.

A Put the words in the correct order to complete the questions about personal appearance.

1. gotten / change / your / appearance / to / you

   Has anyone ever _gotten you to change your appearance_ ?

2. get / your / cut / hair / to

   Who do you _____ ?

3. people / about / make / their appearance / worry

   Do you think that advertisements _____ ?

4. you / wear / make / certain clothes

   Did your parents _____ when you were young ?

5. your clothes / anyone / borrow / let

   Have you ever _____ ?

6. for new clothes / you / shop / help

   Does anyone _____ ?

B **SPEAK.** Work with a partner. Ask and answer the questions from exercise **A**. Explain your answers.

A: *Has anyone ever gotten you to change your appearance?*

B: *Yes. Once my sister got me to curl my hair.* OR *No. My friends and I aren't really interested in appearance.*

7 Circle the correct words to complete the paragraph.

Flower Power

Flowers are beautiful, but how do they (1) **get** / **help** / (**make**) people feel? Research has shown that flowers can (2) **get** / **help** / **let** people to improve their mood and (3) **get** / **have** / **make** them smile. According to one study of older adults, receiving flowers (4) **got** / **had** / **made** 81 percent of the participants feel happier. Other studies showed that the smell of flowers can (5) **get** / **let** / **make** people feel more positive and might even (6) **help** / **make** / **get** them to sleep better. There is also evidence that flowers (7) **get** / **let** / **have** people to act friendlier toward one another.

So if you are feeling sad, take a walk in a garden. The owners probably won't (8) **get** / **let** / **make** you pick the flowers, but you can still smell them. Better yet, you can (9) **get** / **make** / **let** someone to send you some.

8 Read each conversation. Then complete the sentence about the conversation with the correct form of the verb in parentheses.

1. **Pam:** Alicia, can I borrow your sweater for the party tonight?

   Alicia: OK. But please be careful with it.

   Alicia is going to _let Pam borrow_ (let) her sweater.

2. **Polly:** Jake, the kitchen needs a paint job.

   Jake: Yes, I'm going to call the painters today.

   Jake is going to _____ (have) come to paint the kitchen.

3. **Jen:** I haven't had time to decorate the house for Cathy's birthday party yet.

   Andy: Don't worry. I can do it for you.

   Andy is going to _____ (help) the house for the party.

4. **Chen:** Kyle got mud all over himself at the soccer game!

   Miki: I know, but he's clean now. I told him to take a shower.

   Miki _____ (make) a shower.

5. **Lily:** You looked great at the party last night! Where did you get that dress?

   Amy: At Magnim's. I asked a salesperson to choose a dress for me!

   Amy _____ (get) a dress for her.

6. **Nora:** Do you think children should participate in beauty contests?

   Rex: No. Their parents shouldn't allow them to do that.

   Rex thinks that parents shouldn't _____ (let) in beauty contests.

7. **Ana:** The lawn really needs mowing.

   Hector: I'll talk to Jorge about mowing it tonight.

   Hector is going to _____
   _____ (get) the lawn.

8. **Maria:** I think orchids are really beautiful flowers. Don't you?

   Rachel: Yes, I do. I feel happy when I look at them.

   Orchids _____

   (make) happy.

▶ The orchid *Ophrys apifera* looks like a female bee.

273

9 LISTEN.

A Listen to the conversation about a man who loves beautiful plants. Then read the statements. Circle **T** for *true* or **F** for *false*.

1. Visiting Bahia made Alex Popovkin want to live there.   **T**   **F**

2. Alex had a dream, and he made it happen.   **T**   **F**

3. Alex has scientists help him identify plant species.   **T**   **F**

4. Alex's photos let people see animals they would never see otherwise.   **T**   **F**

5. Alex does not let people download his photos of plants on the Internet.   **T**   **F**

B Listen again and check your answers.

10 APPLY.

A Use the prompts to write questions about yourself, someone else you know, or people in general.

1. why / flowers / make / _____people_____ / feel happy

   Why do flowers make people feel happy?

2. how / team sports / make / _____ / act

   _____

3. how / travel / help / _____ / see things differently

   _____

4. what kind of music / get / _____ / relax

   _____

5. what / teachers / let / _____ / do in the classroom

   _____

6. what things / help / _____ / fall asleep

   _____

B Work with a partner. Ask and answer your questions in exercise **A**.

A: *Why do flowers make people feel happy?*

B: *Looking at flowers helps people forget their troubles.*

EXPLORE

CD3-14

1 **READ** this excerpt from a book about ancient Egyptians. Which of their techniques for improving personal appearance do people still use today?

Looking Good in Ancient Egypt

Thanks to the work of archaeologists, today we know a great deal about ancient Egyptian life. Consider, for example, four small jars on exhibit at the Louvre Museum in Paris. Experts first thought that the jars had contained the internal organs[1] of a pharaoh.[2] It was common for Egyptians to store the organs of the dead this way. However, when officials at the museum **had the jars examined** by chemists, they discovered that the jars had actually contained cosmetics.[3] In fact, a great many combs, brushes, mirrors, cosmetic containers, and different types of makeup have been found in tombs and temples. Ancient Egyptians clearly cared a lot about appearance.

Queen Cleopatra is one ancient Egyptian who is known for her beauty. Cleopatra had her own beauticians, as many wealthy Egyptians did. Research shows that she **had her hair dyed** and **styled** into complex hairdos. She also **had her nails polished**. Her hands were decorated with henna, a reddish-brown dye. Another famous beauty was Queen Nefertiti. Her husband **had large images** of her **painted** on the walls of tombs and temples. This let him share his wife's beauty with the people and communicate her power at the same time.

▲ Statue of Nefertiti, 1345 B.C.

Concern with appearance was not limited to women. Both men and women wore eye makeup to beautify themselves and prevent eye disease. (It seems that the chemicals in the makeup could fight infection.) Men also **had their hair cut**, and boys **got their heads shaved**. Evidently, the ancient Egyptians' focus on appearance was not very different from our own.

[1] **organ:** a part of the body that has a particular function such as the heart or lungs
[2] **pharaoh:** a ruler of ancient Egypt
[3] **cosmetics:** substances such as lipstick, powder, and skin cream that people put on their faces to look more attractive

2 **CHECK.** Read the statements. Circle **T** for *true* or **F** for *false*.

1. Scientists discovered that the jars at the Louvre contained ancient jewels.   **T**   **F**

2. The ancient Egyptians were buried with things that they used every day.   **T**   **F**

3. Wearing eye makeup benefited people's health as well as their appearance.   **T**   **F**

4. Women wore makeup, but men didn't.   **T**   **F**

5. Modern beauty techniques have little in common with those of
   the ancient Egyptians.   **T**   **F**

3 **DISCOVER.** Complete the exercises to learn about the grammar in this lesson.

A Find these sentences in the excerpt from exercise **1** on page 275. Write the missing words.
Do the subjects perform the actions? Discuss your answers with a partner.

1. Research shows that she _____
   into complex hairdos.

2. She also _____ .

3. Her husband _____
   on the walls of tombs and temples.

4. Men _____ cut, and boys _____ .

B What is the pattern of the verb phrases you wrote in exercise **A**? Circle the answer.

1. *have / get* + past participle

2. *have / get* + past participle + object

3. *have / get* + object + past participle

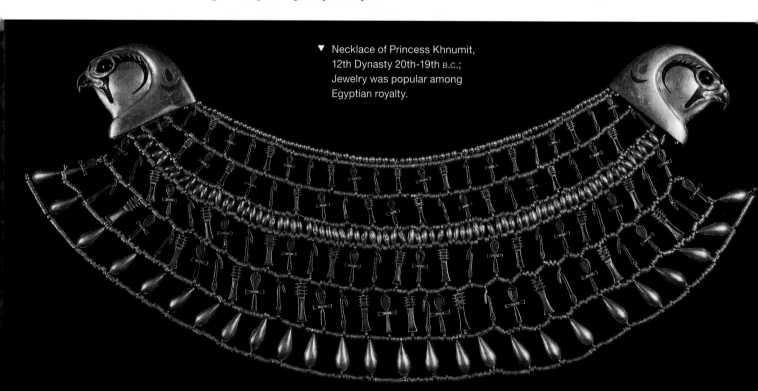

▼ Necklace of Princess Khnumit,
12th Dynasty 20th-19th B.C.;
Jewelry was popular among
Egyptian royalty.

LEARN

10.3 Passive Causative: *Have Something Done*

Have + Object + Past Participle

I **had my watch repaired** last week.

Did you **have the battery changed**?

1. Use passive causatives with *have* to talk about services that we have someone else do for us.	We **had the roof fixed** last year. (Someone else fixed the roof.)
2. The subject of a sentence with a passive causative did not perform the action. The action was done by someone else.	I **had the kitchen painted** by HMS Painters. (HMS Painters painted the kitchen.)
3. **Be careful!** The form of the verb *have* changes with different tenses and modal verbs.	I'm **having** the kitchen **painted** this week. I **have** the kitchen **painted** every two years. I **haven't had** the kitchen **painted** recently. I'm **going to have** the kitchen **painted** soon. **Should** we **have** the kitchen **painted**?
4. **Be careful!** The passive causative (*have something done*) looks similar to the present perfect (*have done something*), but the meanings are very different.	I never **have the house cleaned**. I **have never cleaned** the house.

4 Complete the paragraph about ancient Egypt. Use the correct form of *have* and the words in parentheses.

The pharaohs were very powerful rulers, and they (1) _____ had many things done _____

(many things / do) in their kingdoms to demonstrate their power. For example, they

(2) _____ (their portraits / paint). They also

(3) _____ (their images / put) on coins. In addition, the

pharaohs (4) _____ (large tombs / build) for themselves.

Women of high status (5) _____ (heads / shave). They

wore wigs instead of their own hair, and they (6) _____

(the wigs / dye) different colors: black, blond, gold, blue, or green.

The Egyptians believed in life after death, so they (7) _____

(their bodies / preserve) for the next life in a process called mummification. Because

they believed that they would need many of their possessions in the afterlife, they

(8) _____ (their belongings / place) near

them in their tombs. These belongings included weapons, jewelry, food and drink,

and cosmetics. They also (9) _____ (special

words / write) on their coffins to protect them from harm after death. Some pharoahs even

(10) _____ (their pets / bury) with them.

10.4 Passive Causative: *Get Something Done*

Get + Object + Past Participle
She **got** her hair **done**.
Did he **get** the car **washed**?
Why **have** you **gotten** the locks **changed**?

1. Use passive causatives with *get* to talk about services that people arrange for someone to do. *Have* and *get* usually have the same meaning in passive causatives.	I **got my teeth cleaned**. (The dentist cleaned my teeth.)
2. The form of the verb *get* changes with different tenses and modal verbs.	She's **getting** her hair dyed right now. She **gets** her hair dyed every two months. She **hasn't gotten** her hair dyed recently. She's **going to get** her hair dyed soon. She **shouldn't get** her hair dyed.

5 Complete the conversations. Use the correct form of *get* and the objects and verbs in parentheses.

REAL ENGLISH

Use *by* + the agent when it is necessary to say who did the action.

Did you get the pictures taken by your neighbor?

No, we had them taken by a professional photographer.

1. **A:** Your hair looks great.

   B: Thanks. I _____got it cut_____ (it / cut) last week at the new hair salon on First Street.

2. **A:** How's your eyesight?

   B: Excellent. I _____ (my eyes / check) last month.

3. **A:** These pants are too long. I need to _____ (them / shorten).

   B: You can take them to the tailor after work. He's open until seven o'clock.

4. **A:** Can you drive me to the mall?

   B: Sorry, my car is at the repair shop. I _____ (it / service) today.

5. **A:** I'll order a pizza. What time should we pick it up?

   B: Why don't we _____ (it / deliver)?

6. **A:** Do you have a credit card?

   B: No, but I'm going to get one. First, I have to _____ (the application / sign) by my parents.

7. **A:** Your car looks really clean. Did you wash it yourself?

   B: No, I _____ (it / wash) at the local car wash.

8. **A:** I like the pharmacist at Green Street Pharmacy. He fills prescriptions quickly.

   B: Yes, I always go there to _____ (prescriptions / fill).

PRACTICE

6 Look at the calendar for an Egyptian art exhibit. Today is April 10th. Complete the sentences. Use the correct form of *have* + object + past participle. More than one verb form may be used in some items.

APRIL Staff Assignments for Egyptian Art Exhibit (✓ = done)					Jim Morton, Director, City Center Museum	
Sunday	Monday	Tuesday	Wednesday	Thursday	Friday	Saturday
	1 ✓ print exhibit catalog	2	3	4 ✓ record audio tour	5	6
7	8	9 ✓ paint gallery	10 TODAY	11 install lighting	12 unpack artworks	13
14	15	16	17 arrange art	18	19	20
21	22 write labels for artworks	23	24	25 take photographs of exhibit	26	27
28	29	30 design and print tickets				

1. On April 1st, the director, _had the catalog printed_ .

2. By the end of last week, he _____ .

3. On April 9th, Mr. Morton _____ .

4. Tomorrow, he _____ .

5. The day after the lighting is installed, _____ .

6. The week of the 14th, he _____ .

7. After the art is arranged and labeled, he _____ .

8. At the end of the month, he _____ .

7 LISTEN & WRITE.

A Listen to the conversation about the exhibit. Decide who actually did each task. Check (✓) the correct column. Then compare your answers with a partner.

Task	The director did this.	Somebody else did this.
1. Painting the gallery		
2. Installing the lights		
3. Unpacking the artworks		
4. Arranging the artworks		
5. Preparing the labels		
6. Labeling the artworks		
7. Photographing the exhibit		
8. Designing and printing the tickets		

B Write three affirmative and three negative sentences about the museum director in exercise **A**. Use the correct form of *have* or *get*.

The director didn't paint the gallery. He had it painted by his assistants.

8 EDIT. Read the text. Find and correct six more errors with passive causatives.

The Maya Idea of Beauty

Thousand of years ago, the Maya often had things do̲ᵈᵒⁿᵉ to themselves to improve their looks. This is shown in the Maya art that archaeologists have found. We can see from the art that Maya kings and nobles got holes to make in their teeth. Then they had pretty stones put in the holes. Ordinary Maya probably couldn't afford to have pretty stones in their teeth. Pictures show them with sharp, pointed teeth. They probably had their teeth make sharp to decorate themselves. Upper-class people had fancy tattoos on their bodies. Researchers believe that they didn't create the tattoos themselves. They must have had decorated their bodies with these designs. Today, some people do similar things to their bodies. For example, it is common for people to have their ears pierce. Other people get dyed their hair or their nails painted. They do these things to look good. Will people still be getting these things done hundreds of years from now, or will they think that people in the twenty-first century had some very strange habits?

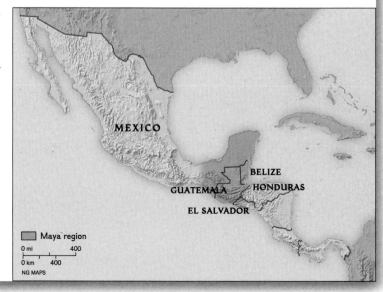

Maya region
0 mi 400
0 km 400
NG MAPS

MEXICO
BELIZE
GUATEMALA
HONDURAS
EL SALVADOR

◀ This Maya sculpture may show Pacal, who ruled from 615 A.D. for 68 years.

9 APPLY.

A Circle the things that someone else usually does for you.

Clean:	home	car	teeth		
Cut:	hair	beard	nails	grass	
Do:	laundry	homework	dry-cleaning	nails	
Fix:	laptop	phone/tablet	TV	car	bike
Paint:	home				
Pay:	tuition	rent	medical bills		
Take Care of:	children	pets			
Wash:	hair	car	dishes		

B Work in a group. Ask and answer questions about the things your classmates have circled on the list.

A: *Who do you get to cut your hair?*

B: *I go to a hairdresser on Center Street.*

C Write four or five sentences about your group's responses. Use *have* and *get*.

Felipe gets his sister to cut his hair.

Last week Charles had to get his laptop fixed. He had it fixed at the Tech Center.

EXPLORE

CD3-16

1 **READ** the article about an animal researcher who is interested in more than good looks. What is Lucy Cooke's message for the world?

Funny looking or beautiful?

It is often said that beauty is in the eyes of the beholder.[1] That is certainly true for zoologist[2] Lucy Cooke. While most people prefer cute pandas and kittens to odd-looking frogs and sloths, Cooke does not. Instead of being **turned off** by less attractive creatures, she is fascinated by them. She looks beyond their appearance and tries to **find out** as much as possible about how they behave and adapt to their environments.

Consider the sloth. This slow-moving animal lives in the tropical forests of South and Central America. It often hangs upside-down in trees, **holding on** with its long claws. Most people think that the sleepy sloth is lazy, dirty, and stupid. However, Cooke is quick to **point out** that sloths have been greatly misunderstood. In fact, their behavior **helps** them **out** in the wild. Their slow metabolism[3] helps protect them from poisons in the leaves they eat, and moving slowly keeps them hidden from predators.[4]

Cooke is concerned that attractive animals get all the attention. It troubles her that there is much less research on "uncute" animals such as sloths and frogs, yet many of these animals are in danger of **dying out**. Cooke wants to show the world how some of the strangest-looking creatures deserve attention and protection. To **get** her message **across**, she takes advantage of the Internet. People can watch humorous videos online about her adventures with the unloved species of the world. Just watch Cooke's video about sloths—you will probably **end up** loving them as much as she does.

Fun Sloth Facts

- Sloths are great at hiding.
- Sloths spend up to 70% of their time resting.
- Sloths can take up to a month to digest a meal.

[1] **beauty is in the eye of the beholder:** people have different ideas about what is beautiful
[2] **zoologist:** a scientist who studies animals
[3] **metabolism:** the processes in the body that cause food to be used for energy and growth
[4] **predator:** an animal that lives by killing and eating others

▼ Sleeping sloth

▶ Lucy Cooke's goal is to save ugly and unloved creatures that are dying out.

2 CHECK. Answer the questions. Write complete sentences.

1. What kind of animals are most interesting to Lucy Cooke?

   _____

2. What quality of the sloth helps it survive in its environment?

   _____

3. According to Cooke, what is the problem with attractive animals?

   _____

4. How does Cooke communicate her message to the world?

   _____

3 DISCOVER. Complete the exercises to learn about the grammar in this lesson.

A Find these bold words in the article in exercise **1**. Write the missing words to complete the phrase.

1. **turned** ____off____   4. **dying** _____

2. **point** _____   5. **get** her message _____

3. **helps** them _____   6. **end** _____

B Look back at the article and find the verbs in exercise **A**. Then read the statement. Circle **T** for *true* or **F** for *false*.

When you add a particle (*off, out,...*) to a verb, it can change the meaning of the verb.   **T**   **F**

LEARN

10.5 Phrasal Verbs: Transitive and Intransitive

Phrasal Verbs	
Transitive	He **looked over** <u>the contract</u> carefully. Direct Object
Intransitive	We **grew up** quickly.

1. Phrasal verbs usually mean something different from the two or three words that are used to form them.	Phrasal Verb: **Look out**! (*look out* = be careful) Regular Verb: **Look** out the window. Do you see the bird?
2. **Remember:** A transitive phrasal verb is followed by an object.	Could you **turn off** <u>the light</u>? Object
3. An intransitive phrasal verb cannot be followed by an object.	He **came over**.
4. Three-word phrasal verbs (*come up with, put up with, look forward to*) are always transitive.	Have you **come up with** an idea for the project? I can't **put up with** his behavior. It's very bad. I'm **looking forward to** the party this weekend.
5. Phrasal verbs are more common in spoken English and informal writing. They are often used in place of one or more words that express the same meaning.	Informal: *put off* The party was **put off** until next week. Formal: *postpone* I have to **postpone** the meeting until next week.

See page **A6** for a list of transitive and intransitive phrasal verbs.

4 Complete the exercises.

A Circle the correct phrasal verb to complete each sentence.

1. Can you **make out /** (**point out**) a website with information about sloths?

2. My friend and I once visited a sloth sanctuary in Costa Rica. We had planned to spend an hour there, but we **looked up / ended up** staying all day.

3. The people who **look after / look for** the sloths in the sanctuary are kind.

4. The sanctuary does important work by preventing sloths from **dying out / helping out**.

5. Would you like to **help out / turn out** the sloth rescue group in your free time?

6. Lucy Cooke has **come after / come up with** many great ways to communicate her message.

7. I recently **found out / got out** how to join the Sloth Appreciation Society, which tries to help sloths.

8. I'm going to **keep out of / keep up with** the society's activities through its website.

B **ANALYZE THE GRAMMAR.** There are six sentences with transitive phrasal verbs in exercise **A**. In your notebook, write the number of each sentence and the transitive phrasal verb + object.

1. *point out a website*

10.6 Transitive Phrasal Verbs: Separable and Inseparable

Separable
He **looked over** the report.
Direct Object
He **looked** the report **over**.
Direct Object

Inseparable
We can't **get over** the changes.
Direct Object

1. Most transitive phrasal verbs are separable. The object may come after the phrasal verb or between the two parts of the phrasal verb.	Who **picked out** the birthday card? Who **picked** the birthday card **out**?
2. When the object is a pronoun (*me, you, him,* . . .), it comes between the two words.	✓ She didn't **pick** it **out**. I did. ✗ She didn't <u>pick out it</u>.
3. In an inseparable phrasal verb, the object or object pronoun comes after the two parts of the phrasal verb.	✓ I **came across** an interesting article. ✓ I **came across** it while doing research. ✗ I <u>came it across</u> yesterday.
4. Three-word phrasal verbs are always inseparable.	✓ Gary **looked up to** his older brother. ✗ Gary <u>looked up his older brother to</u>.

See pages **A7–A10** for a list of separable and inseparable phrasal verbs and their meanings.

5 Complete the conversations with the correct form of the phrasal verb in parentheses and *her, him, it,* or *me.* You can check the meanings of the verbs on pages **A7–A10**.

1. **A:** Do you know the expression "Beauty is in the eye of the beholder"?

   B: Yeah. I ___looked it up___ (look up) on the Internet.

2. **A:** I saw an ad for a cool motorcycle. It's on sale. You should _____ (check out).

   B: No, thanks. Motorcycles _____ (turn off).

3. **A:** Remember Jim from our high school? I _____ (run into) yesterday.

   B: Yes, I _____ (get together with) sometimes. We play golf.

4. **A:** The first time my grandfather saw my grandmother, he _____ (fall for). At

   first she didn't like him, and she refused to _____ (go out with). He was really

   disappointed, and it took him a while to _____ (get over). But when they met

   again a few years later, she liked him a lot better . . . and eventually they got married!

   B: That's so romantic!

5. **A:** Vera, would you come with me to look for a wedding dress? I need someone to help me

   _____ (pick out).

   B: Sure, I'd love to.

6. **A:** Colin, I see something strange on this X ray. I've never _____ (come across)
   before in any other X ray.

   B: Let's ask Dr. Voltman to take a look.

PRACTICE

6 Circle the correct phrasal verbs to complete the paragraphs. You can check the meanings of the words on pages **A7–A10**.

What is beauty?

I read an interesting article about beauty the other day. I (1) **came across / came up with** it when I was (2) **looking after / looking up** something online. The article (3) **pointed out / picked out** that people around the world have different ideas about what beauty is. So many different things can be considered beautiful—human beings, works of art, music, and nature. Even if people (4) **go along with / go over** the idea that art, for example, is beautiful, they may not like the same kind of art. One person might love modern art, but it might (5) **turn off / turn up** another person.

One thing we do know is that beauty in all its different forms is something people just can't (6) **give in / give up**. People need beauty just like they need oxygen or water. It (7) **cheers them up / shows them up** when they are feeling sad, and it calms them down when they are feeling anxious.

Nobody can say for sure what beauty is, but some people have tried to (8) **figure it out / think it up**. One artist wanted to discover something that everyone in the world agreed was beautiful. He (9) **came up with / came over** an interesting idea, and he did experiments to test it. His research (10) **ended up / made up** showing that people around the world share at least one idea: a springtime scene with lakes, rivers, and forests is beautiful.

▲ Caryatids of Athens, Greece, show the classical Greek idea of beauty.

7 Match each bold phrasal verb with its correct meaning.

<u>c</u> 1. They **put** their paintbrushes **away** after art class.

_____ 2. Don't **give up**. You'll solve this problem if you keep trying.

_____ 3. My winter coat was getting old, so I **gave** it **away**.

_____ 4. He **put** his favorite shirt **on** to look his best.

_____ 5. I asked the movie star for her autograph, but she **turned** my request **down**.

_____ 6. In one fairy tale, a magician **turns** a frog **into** a handsome prince.

_____ 7. **Turn on** the lights. I can't see anything.

_____ 8. Lynn borrowed my laptop, but she **gave** it **back** last night.

_____ 9. She doesn't like horror movies. They **turn** her **off**.

_____ 10. I can't hear the TV. Can you **turn up** the volume?

a. give without charging money

b. place clothing, jewelry, or makeup on one's body

c̸. put something in its usual place

d. increase

e. make someone feel disgust

f. make equipment or lights start working

g. refuse

h. change to something different

i. return

j. quit

8 WRITE & SPEAK.

A Look at the meanings of the phrasal verbs in exercise **7**. Then complete the chart with an object for each phrasal verb. If the phrasal verb is separable, write the phrasal verb + object two ways.

give away	*give away money*	*give money away*
give back		
give up		
put away		
put on		
turn down		
turn into		
turn on		
turn up		

B Complete the sentences with your own ideas.

1. When I go to a special event, I put on _____.

2. I turn down invitations to parties when _____.

3. When I'm at a party, I turn into a _____ person.

4. I once put aside money for _____.

5. When _____ something difficult, I don't give up.

6. I sometimes give away _____.

7. When you _____, you should always give them back.

8. People should turn on their phones when _____.

C Work with a partner. Compare the sentences you wrote in exercise **B**.

9 EDIT. Read the conversation. Find and correct six more errors with phrasal verbs.

A: The other day I came ~~over~~ ^{across} an interesting article. It was about a beautiful bird called the Gouldian finch.

B: What was so interesting about it?

A: Well, when a male finch chooses a mate, he uses his right eye to pick out her. For some reason, his right eye helps him choose a better mate.

B: That's strange. How did they figure that up?

A: They covered the finch's right eye. They noticed that with its left eye, the finch chose any bird as a mate.

B: Wow. It's amazing how animals and plants choose mates in different ways.

A: Well, choosing a mate is really important. If animals and plants choose the wrong mates, their species could die over.

B: What does that say about the way that people choose mates?

A: The article points that human beings also choose mates to keep their species alive.

B: So when people go over with each other for a while and then break up, are they really trying to stay alive?

A: You could look at it that way.

B: Or maybe they just can't put up each other with anymore!

A: That's possible, too.

10 APPLY.

A Write responses to the questions. Replace the <u>underlined</u> words with the correct form of the phrasal verbs from the box.

fall for	figure out	~~get across~~	look up to	run into	stand out

1. What idea about beauty do you want to <u>make others understand</u>?

     I want to get across the idea that beauty involves more than appearance.

2. Can beauty alone make a person <u>fall in love with</u> someone else?

    _____

3. What problem have you <u>understood after thinking about it</u> recently?

    _____

4. Have you ever <u>unexpectedly met</u> a friend in another country?

    _____

5. Do most young people <u>admire</u> famous people?

    _____

6. What kind of people <u>do you notice</u> in a crowd?

    _____

B Work in a group. Discuss your answers to the questions in exercise **A**.

A: *I want to get across the idea that beauty involves more than appearance.*

B: *I agree.*

Charts
10.1, 10.2,
10.5, 10.6

1 Complete the paragraph with six of the eight words from the box.

| across | let | make | have | out | point | them | to |

Many animals are able to (1) _____ themselves look like their surroundings. This ability is called camouflage. Camouflage lets animals find food, and it also helps (2) _____ hide from predators. Scientists often (3) _____ out that stick insects are masters of camouflage.

◀ A stick insect

Because of their stick-like shape and color, these tiny bugs of the forest look just like the leaves and twigs of trees and plants. They don't stand (4) _____ from the background, and this helps (5) _____ protect them. Sometimes the insects look harmless, but they are not. If you come (6) _____ an American stick insect, be careful. They're poisonous.

Charts
10.1–10.4

2 Complete each sentence with the correct form of the verb in parentheses.

1. Hundreds of years ago in Venice, rich people had fancy masks _____ (make) for big parties.

2. They got others _____ (make) their masks. They didn't make them themselves.

3. Some had mask makers _____ (design) the masks to look like famous characters.

4. Some got masks _____ (design) to show emotions such as jealousy and anger.

5. Nowadays some people have masks _____ (decorate) with feathers.

6. Others get artists _____ (decorate) their masks with jewels.

7. Sometimes people like to have costumes _____ (create) to go with the masks.

8. When they have experts _____ (create) the designs, the results can be incredible.

3 **LISTEN** to the conversation between two people in a costume store. Then circle the correct verb according to what you hear.

1. The customer (**lets**) / **helps** the salesperson see the invitation to the party.

2. The salesperson **makes** / **has** the customer walk over to the display of masks.

3. The Venetian mask **helps** / **lets** the wearer eat, drink, and talk.

4. The mask with the feathers always **makes** / **has** people feel beautiful and exciting.

5. The tiger mask will probably **help** / **have** the customer feel good.

6. The salesperson **had** / **made** the assistant wrap up the mask.

4 **EDIT.** Read the text. Find and correct six more errors with causative verb patterns and phrasal verbs.

The Mystery of Masks

Wearing masks lets people ~~to~~ hide their identity from others. This can help to create a feeling of mystery at a masquerade ball, a dance where people wear costumes. In a normal situation, you might be able to come up with some ideas about people's qualities because you can see their faces and expressions. You think about whether they are good looking and how often they smile. Their appearance gets you form certain opinions about them. It may help you to decide if you want to talk to them.

Some masks stand up from all the rest because they are so fancy. People may pay a lot of money to have made these masks. Do such amazing masks make you to want to meet the people who are wearing them? Once a friend of mine fell her husband for at a costume party before she ever saw his face. She loved his voice and personality, and she didn't think about his appearance at all. Sometimes a masquerade ball can turn it out to be a very special day.

5 **SPEAK.** Work in groups. Discuss the answers to these questions.

1. Why do some people enjoy putting on costumes? Why do others dislike it?

2. When was the last time you wore a costume? Describe it. How did it make you feel?

3. What kinds of costumes stand out at a party?

4. Give examples of animals or insects that use camouflage. How does it help them?

1 READ & NOTICE THE GRAMMAR.

A What do people in your culture do to make themselves more attractive? How do they prepare themselves for special events? Tell a partner. Then read the blog.

Here comes the bride!

Hello, everyone. The last time I wrote, everyone in my family was looking forward to my sister's wedding. Well, the big day finally arrived, and it was my job to help her get ready. It is traditional for an Indian bride to wear elaborate[1] makeup and clothes.

My sister got her hair done at a salon, but she let me do her makeup. I used mascara and eyeliner to make her eyes stand out. Indian brides also have beautiful patterns painted on their hands with a reddish-brown dye called *henna*. I am not skilled enough to do this, so she had a professional henna artist paint her hands.

I helped her put a traditional *bindi* on her forehead, and then my mother and I helped her get dressed. My mother let my sister borrow some fancy gold jewelry.

My sister was stunning on her wedding day, and her husband looked attractive, too. He had gotten his hair cut, and his face was clean-shaven to show off his jawline and cheekbones. He was dressed in a modern suit. He also had on a cool expensive watch. He made his brother lend it to him for the wedding.

I'll write more about the wedding in my next post!

[1] **elaborate:** very fancy

GRAMMAR FOCUS

In the blog in exercise **A**, the writer uses the following types of causative verbs:

Have, let, and make	• show when one person causes someone to do something or gives permission to do something (*. . . she **let me do** her makeup.*)
Help	• shows when someone assists someone else (*It was my job to **help her get** ready . . .*)
Passive causatives	• talk about services that others do for someone (*My sister **got her hair done** at a salon . . .*)

B Read the blog in exercise **A** again. Underline the examples of causative verbs.

C Complete the diagram with information from the blog in exercise **A**. What did the bride get or have done to look attractive for the wedding? Discuss your answers with a partner.

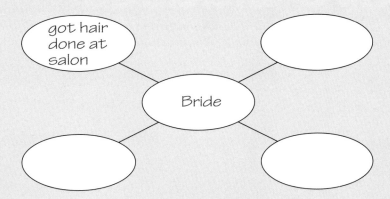

2 BEFORE YOU WRITE.

A Work with a partner. Brainstorm ways that men and women change their appearance to go to parties and weddings or to job interviews. Use exercise **1A** for ideas.

B Make a diagram like the one in exercise **1C**. Write ways that people from your culture make themselves look more attractive.

> **WRITING FOCUS   Gender and Adjective Choice**
>
> In English, some adjectives that describe appearance are more commonly used only for men or women. Some adjectives are used for either.
>
> *beautiful, pretty, stunning* (for women)
> *handsome* (for men)
> *attractive, striking, good looking* (women or men)

3 WRITE a blog entry describing a time when you helped someone prepare for a special event. Write two or three paragraphs. How did you make this person look different? Use your diagram from exercise **2B** and the blog in exercise **1A** to help you.

4 SELF ASSESS. Read your blog entry. Underline the verb forms. Then use the checklist to assess your work.

☐ I used causative verbs with objects correctly. [10.1, 10.2]

☐ I used the passive causative correctly. [10.3, 10.4]

☐ I used phrasal verbs correctly. [10.5, 10.6]

☐ I used appropriate adjectives for men and women. [WRITING FOCUS]

Relative Clauses

▲ A time-exposure image shows star trails over Geghard Monastery, Armenia.

EXPLORE

CD3-18

1 **READ** the web page and comments on a photography site. Then write your own comment below.

Myphotospace

share | like | post

Photo by Dipanjan Mitra

This photo was taken in the Sundarbans in West Bengal, India. The Sundarbans is an area **that is famous for its mangrove forest and royal Bengal tigers**. In this photo, the farmers **that live in the area** had recently experienced a devastating storm **that flooded the fields and destroyed crops**. You can see the water from the flood. However, the scene is not sad. Maybe that's because the boy, **whose feet dangle over the water**, seems untouched by the flood. We feel his calm.

Comments:

Greta M. Beautiful picture. I like the way it captures the child, **who seems to be living in the moment**.

Raul O. This photo, **which shows the highs and lows of life in the Sundarbans**, sends a powerful message. It shows how people, especially children, can survive even in the most difficult circumstances.

Post a comment _____

2 CHECK. Answer the questions about the web page in exercise **1**. Write complete sentences.

1. Where was the photo taken?

   _____

2. What is this area known for?

   _____

3. What weather recently affected this region?

   _____

4. How did it affect the region?

   _____

3 DISCOVER. Complete the exercises to learn about the grammar in this lesson.

A Write the missing words in each sentence from the Web page. Then draw an arrow to the word they describe.

1. In this photo, the farmers _that live in the area_ had recently experienced a devastating storm that flooded the fields and destroyed crops.

2. Maybe that's because the boy, _____ , seems untouched by the flood.

3. I like the way it captures the child, _____ .

4. This photo, _____ , sends a powerful message.

B Look back at the words *which, who, whose,* and *that* in the clauses you wrote in exercise **A**. Complete each statement with the correct word/s.

1. _____Who_____ and _____ are in clauses that describe people.

2. _____ and _____ are in clauses that describe things.

3. _____ is in clauses that describe possession.

LEARN

11.1 Subject Relative Clauses

After the Main Clause
This is the website. <u>The website</u> sells photos by Russian photographers.
This is the website **that sells photos by Russian photographers**.
Subject Relative Clause

Inside the Main Clause
The tourists were from Hawaii. <u>The tourists</u> took photos of the ski slopes.
The tourists **who took photos of the ski slopes** were from Hawaii.
Subject Relative Clause

1. A relative clause describes a noun or indefinite pronoun (*someone, anyone, something*) in a sentence. The relative clause* comes after the noun or pronoun it describes.	The people **that took the photos** are my friends. Someone **who was at the party** took this photo.
2. A subject relative clause starts with a relative pronoun (*that, which,* or *who*). The relative pronoun is the subject of the relative clause.	The people left. <u>The people</u> were here an hour ago. The people **that were here an hour ago** left.
3. In a subject relative clause, use: a. *that* or *who* as a subject for people b. *that* or *which* as a subject for places, things, animals, or ideas	a. That's the student **who got the scholarship**. b. Phones **that have computing ability** are called smartphones.
4. The verb in a subject relative clause agrees with the noun it describes.	There is **an app** that **shows** the weather forecast. There are **apps** that **show** the weather forecast.
5. **Remember:** The subject and verb in the main clause must agree.	**The photographer** who photographs animals **is going** to the Serengeti.

*Relative clauses are also called *adjective clauses*.

4 Underline five more relative clauses in the paragraph. Then draw an arrow from the relative pronoun to the noun or pronoun it describes.

Today anyone <u>who has a digital camera</u> can produce a clear photo. However, that is not enough to make it a great photo. Photographers who want to take powerful shots have to make sure that the photo has good composition. In photography, composition is the way that things or people in a picture are placed, or positioned. Look at some photos of your friends or family, and you'll see what I mean. Where are the people in the photo? Are they standing in the center with a lot of empty space in the background? If so, the picture probably isn't very interesting. Photographs are more striking when they show someone or something that is on the right or left, or off-center. In addition, a picture that does not have too many details will not have a clear focus. So think carefully about how you take your photos. Photos that have good composition will be the most successful.

5 Complete the exercises.

A Complete the advice for photographers. Write *who* or *which* and the correct form of the verb in parentheses.

1. When you're just starting out, don't buy equipment ___which costs___ (cost) a lot.

2. People _____ (keep) their camera with them at all times will get better photos.

3. Places _____ (not seem) unusual at first might still make great photos.

4. Look at photography magazines and websites _____ (can offer) you a range of information on technique.

5. Look closely at a photo _____ (demonstrate) strong composition and lighting.

6. Take a workshop from a photographer _____ (do) interesting work.

7. Copy the style of someone _____ (take) pictures that you admire.

8. Avoid subjects _____ (might be) extremely difficult to photograph.

B **SPEAK.** Work with a partner. Read the sentences in exercise **A** aloud, but change the relative pronouns to *that*.

> **REAL ENGLISH**
>
> The relative pronoun *that* is more common than *which* in subject relative clauses.

6 Read the sentences about photos from this book. Circle the correct words.

1. The leopard seal that **(was playing)** / **were playing** with Paul Nicklen **(was)** / **were** gentle. (pages 32–33)

2. The photo which **shows / show** mountains of Kauai **are / is** especially beautiful. (page 39)

3. The woman who **are sitting / is sitting** at the floor of the ice cave **has been taking / have been taking** pictures of ice formations with a special camera. (pages 90–91)

4. The old woman and girl who **appear / appears** in this picture **is from / are from** the Navajo tribe. (pages 114–115)

5. The girls that **are facing / is facing** away from us **lives / live** in Kabul, Afghanistan. (pages 142–143)

6. The sea turtle that **are drifting / is drifting** by the scuba diver **has never injured / have never injured** anyone. (page 179)

7. The volunteers who **work / works** for WWOOF **have been collecting / has been collecting** heather from a flower garden. (page 192)

8. The flowers that **has bloomed / have bloomed** on the cereus cactus **comes out / come out** only at night. (pages 246–247)

11.2 Non-Identifying Subject Relative Clauses

1. A non-identifying relative clause* gives extra information about a noun in the sentence. You don't need this information to understand who or what the noun refers to.	Cy went to Peru, **which is a beautiful place to visit.**
2. The relative pronoun *that* cannot be used in a non-identifying subject relative clause. Use *who* or *which*.	✓ Dave's father, **who lived in Peru**, always liked meeting people. ✗ Dave's father, <u>that</u> lived in Peru, always liked meeting people.
3. Use a comma before and after a non-identifying relative clause that is within a main clause.	✓ Facebook, **which started in 2004**, has over a billion users. ✗ Facebook <u>which started in 2004</u> has over a billion users.
4. Identifying and non-identifying clauses can change the meaning of a sentence.	My uncle who lives in New York owns a restaurant. (I also have an uncle in Los Angeles.) My uncle, who lives in New York, owns a restaurant. (I have only one uncle.)

*Non-identifying relative clauses are also called *non-restrictive relative clauses*.

7 Write the correct relative pronoun and add one or two commas to each relative clause.

1. Photo sharing, _____which_____ is now extremely popular, has changed over time.

2. Websites like Flickr _____ became available in 2010 offered lots of space.

3. Facebook _____ started in 2004 allows people to share messages and photos.

4. College students _____ were the first users of Facebook were later followed by users of all ages.

5. I just bought the latest smartphone _____ has a powerful built-in camera.

6. Kevin Systrom and Mike Kreiger _____ wanted a way to edit photos started Instagram in 2010.

7. Instagram _____ was originally an application for iPhones is now available for Android devices.

8. Have you ever met Dr. Jones _____ teaches Photography 101?

9. Amsterdam _____ is the capital of the Netherlands is a wonderful city to photograph.

10. The photography exhibition was created by my friend Laura _____ is a professional artist.

8 Complete the exercises.

A Combine the sentences. Make the second sentence of each pair a relative clause with *which* or *who*. Use correct punctuation.

1. Photography is a highly competitive profession. Photography can be very creative.

   Photography, which can be very creative, is a highly competitive profession.

2. My friend Erin is a great photographer. Erin has just started his own business.

   _____

   _____

3. Online photography classes can be a great way to learn the basics. Online photography classes are often free.

   _____

   _____

4. Disposable cameras are popular with tourists. Disposable cameras are usually good for one use only.

   _____

   _____

5. Digital storytelling is popular with Professor Wong. Professor Wong has experience telling stories with photos.

   _____

   _____

6. Displays on cameras give you valuable information. Displays on cameras can be difficult to use.

   _____

   _____

7. Camera reviews can help you choose a good camera. Camera reviews are easy to find online.

   _____

   _____

8. Digital photographs are extremely popular. Digital photographs are inexpensive.

   _____

   _____

B Work with a partner. Compare your answers from exercise **A**.

11.3 Relative Clauses with *Whose*

The photographer has a great website. His photos feature wildlife in Africa.

The photographer **whose photos feature wildlife in Africa** has a great website.
Relative Clause

1. Use *whose* + a noun in a relative clause to show possession. *Whose* replaces a possessive adjective or noun (*his, her, its, their, Jim's, . . .*).	I know the woman. Her son has won the award. I know the woman **whose** son has won the award.
2. *Whose* is used for people. It is also used for places, things, animals, and ideas.	New Zealand is a country **whose** official languages include English and Maori.
3. Relative clauses with *whose* can be identifying or non-identifying. Non-identifying clauses must have a comma before and after them.	People **whose seats are up front** can go in first. Mr. and Mrs. An, **whose seats are up front**, can go in first.
4. **Be careful!** Do not repeat the possessive pronoun in a relative clause with *whose*.	✓ Will the person **whose cell phone is ringing** please turn it off? ✗ Will the person whose his cell phone is ringing please turn it off?

9 Underline the relative clause in each sentence. Then draw an arrow from *whose* to the noun it modifies.

1. The statues, whose faces are difficult to see, show a king and gods. (pages 206–207)

2. Does the frog, whose face peeks out from the mushroom, feel the rain? (pages 234–235)

3. Jimbo Bazoobi is an Australian citizen whose goat Gary has become famous. (page 248)

4. An insect whose wings display beautiful colors is a hawk moth. (pages 266–267)

5. The sloth, whose eyes are closed, sleeps peacefully. (page 282)

6. The starry night picture was taken in Armenia, whose sky shows a meteor. (pages 294–295)

7. The photographer, whose image captures star trails, used time exposure. (pages 294–295)

10 Complete the exercises.

A Combine the sentences. Make the second sentence in each pair a relative clause with *whose*. Add punctuation if necessary.

1. The woman in the photo is from the Maori tribe. Her name is unknown.

   The woman in the photo, whose name is unknown, is from the Maori tribe.

2. The Maori woman in the photo has a mysterious expression. Her eyes are deep brown.

   _____

   _____

3. New Zealand is 14.6 percent Maori. New Zealand's population is mostly European.

_____

_____.

4. The Maori still live there today. Their ancestors came to New Zealand around 1250–1300 CE.

_____

_____.

5. The Maori mainly speak English. Their native language is close to Polynesian.

_____

_____.

6. New Zealand is a beautiful country. Its terrain is mountainous.

_____

_____.

7. The Maori have lost some of their traditions. Their culture has changed.

_____

_____.

8. We should try to respect people. Their cultures are different from ours.

_____

_____.

B Work with a partner. Compare your answers from exercise **A**.

◀ a Maori woman

PRACTICE

11 Complete the exercises.

A Complete the paragraph with relative clauses. Use *that, who, which*, or *whose* and the words in parentheses. Use the simple present.

Photography helps us to understand human psychology. The photographer is important because it is his or her (1) _viewpoint that comes_ (viewpoint / come) through in the photo. (2) _____ (the people / appear) in the photo are also relevant. People (3) _____ (expressions / show) more than one emotion are the most interesting. The way people interact can also say a lot. (4) _____ (people / influence) others or (5) _____ (people / be) powerful often stand in the center or in front. (6) _____ (groups of people / stand) together sometimes show a close relationship. (7) _____ (individuals / be) not comfortable with the group may stand off to the side or look away. A person (8) _____ (eyes / meet) the camera shows a connection with the photographer. Colors are also important. (9) _____ (red and orange / be) warm colors, attract our eyes first. (10) _____ (green and blue / be) cool colors, seem to move away from us. The photographer's choices are important in creating the mood of the picture.

B Write the numbers of the two non-identifying relative clauses in exercise **A**.

_____ , _____

12 Combine the sentences with relative clauses. Use *that, which, who*, or *whose*. Sometimes more than one relative pronoun is possible.

1. Photography can capture moments. The moments will be remembered forever.

    Photography can capture moments that will be remembered forever.

2. Photography is an activity. The activity will always hold your interest.

    _____

    _____

3. A photograph can communicate ideas. The ideas are hard to express in words.

    _____

    _____

4. Photos of loved ones become important possessions. The loved ones are far away.

    _____

    _____

5. With photography, we speak to people. Their language is different from ours.

_____

_____

6. Sharing photos allows you to connect to people. People are important to you.

_____

_____

7. Photography is an art. Its origins go back to the mid-1820s

_____

_____

8. The first surviving photograph shows a landscape. The photograph was taken in 1825 or 1826.

_____

_____

13 PRONUNCIATION. Read the chart and listen to the examples. Then complete the exercises.

CD3-19

> **PRONUNCIATION**   **Pauses with Non-Identifying Relative Clauses**
>
> Speakers pause before and after non-identifying relative clauses. The pauses make the information easier to understand. In writing, commas are used to indicate the pauses.
>
> **Examples:**
>
> *Colors, which affect our feelings, are important in photography.*
> *Black and white, which are not colors but tones, are important for contrast.*

CD3-20

A Listen to the sentences about a photo contest on the Internet. Insert commas where you hear pauses. Not all of the sentences contain non-identifying relative clauses.

1. The contest which is held once a year has a $5000 cash prize.

2. Many people who have won the prize have gone on to be successful photographers.

3. The judges who are professional photographers consider the creativity of each photo.

4. The judges who do not always agree have a difficult task.

5. The contestant whose photo gets the highest score is the winner.

6. The photo which won last year's prize was taken by a 15-year-old.

B Work with a partner. Take turns reading the sentences from exercise **A**.

14 LISTEN.

CD3-21

A Look at the two images from a photography contest and listen to the judges discuss them. Which photo is the winner, photo 1 or photo 2?

Photo 1

Photo 2

B Listen to the conversation again. Circle the correct answers.

1. Where was the photo with the buildings and the sea taken?

   a. In Malé, in the Republic of Maldives.   b. In a Mexican town.

2. What is bothering the judge about Photo 1?

   a. It's not realistic.   b. The composition.

3. What part of Photo 1 does the judge want to look at?

   a. The buildings in the back.   b. He is not sure what to look at.

4. What should Photo 1 have shown more of to provide a better perspective?

   a. The buildings.   b. The sea.

5. What makes Photo 1 powerful?

   a. Its warmth and liveliness.   b. The way the photographer uses space.

6. Why is the photographer of the Mexican buildings the winner?

   a. The color in his photo is intense.   b. His technical abilities and composition are excellent.

C Listen to the sentences and complete the relative clause in each. Add commas where necessary. Then listen again and check your answers. Listen for pauses where you put commas.

1. The photo _that shows the buildings and the sea_ was taken in Malé.

2. Malé _____ of the Republic of Maldives is located in the Indian Ocean.

3. Let's talk about the photo _____ in a small Mexican town.

4. We see a hand _____ .

5. The photographer has excellent technical abilities and a composition _____ the viewer's attention.

15 APPLY. Work in a group. Look through this book and choose three or four photos to discuss. Use relative clauses where appropriate. Then write the sentences in your notebook.

I really like the photo (on pages 294-295) that shows the star trails. In this picture, which was taken in Armenia, the photographer used time exposure to show the meteor moving in the sky.

EXPLORE

CD3-23

1 READ the article about photojournalist Michael "Nick" Nichols, whose work takes him deep into the wilderness. What is his goal?

A LOOK INSIDE

Shooting the Real Story

Michael "Nick" Nichols started taking pictures in his Photography 101 class over thirty years ago, and he hasn't stopped since. His passion has always been to photograph the things **that he cares about**. Today, Nichols is an award-winning photojournalist whose powerful images in *National Geographic Magazine* tell real stories about endangered lands and wildlife.

For Nichols, telling the real story is key. He takes pictures of animals and places whose future is threatened. He wants the photos to motivate people and governments to protect these endangered animals and lands. Thanks to Nichols's extraordinary skill and determination, he has been successful. His work with conservationist Michael Fay in Central Africa is a good example. Fay walked 2000 miles (3219 kilometers) from Congo's deepest rainforest to the Atlantic Coast of Gabon. Nichols and Fay studied Africa's wilderness and listed 13 areas that were critical habitats. As a result, the president of Congo made the 13 endangered areas **that Fay and Nichols had identified** into national parks. Over the years, Nichols's pictures have told the stories of several species that are rapidly disappearing in the wild. His images of lions, tigers, elephants, and gorillas in their natural habitats are unforgettable.

Nichols knows his photos need to be realistic. If they aren't, people won't believe the stories **that the images tell**. "I can't stand a photograph **that I've made**, no matter how cool it is, if I set it up,"[2] he says. The wild and unpredictable nature of the animals is a great challenge. However, Nichols has a special ability to work in rough environments **which others find too difficult**. Time and time again, he shows the way life truly is in some of the most remote parts of the world.

[1] **set up:** arrange or create something

2 CHECK. Correct the error in each sentence to make it true according to the article.

1. Michael "Nick" Nichols is concerned about the future of zoo animals.

2. Fay walked a total of 500 miles through Africa's wilderness.

3. Nichols thinks it is most important for his photos to look cool.

4. The subjects of Nichols's photographs are usually easy to manage.

5. Nichols works in some of the most populated parts of the world.

3 DISCOVER. Complete the exercises to learn about the grammar in this lesson.

A Look at the bold relative clauses in the sentences from the article. Write the missing relative pronoun.

1. His passion has always been to photograph the things _____ **he cares about**.

2. The president of Congo made the 13 endangered areas _____ **Fay and Nichols had identified** into national parks.

3. People won't believe the stories _____ **the images tell**.

4. "I can't stand a photograph _____ **I've made**, no matter how cool it is, if I set it up," he says.

5. Nichols has a special ability to work in rough environments _____ **others find too difficult**.

B Work with a partner. Look at the relative pronouns you wrote in exercise **A**. Are they the subjects of the relative clauses?

◀ A pride of African lions walks through tall savanna grass. Masai Mara National Reserve, Kenya.

LEARN

11.4 Object Relative Clauses

After the Main Clause
We liked many works in the photo contest. Zeyna won <u>the contest</u>. Object
We liked many works in the photo contest **that Zeyna won**. Object Relative Clause

Inside the Main Clause
The photo tells a story. Ricardo posted <u>the photo</u> on the Internet. Object
The photo **that Ricardo posted on the Internet** tells a story. Object Relative Clause

1. In an object relative clause, the relative pronoun is the object. The relative pronoun may be *that, who, whom,* or *which.*	The wallet belongs to her. You found **the wallet**. Object The wallet **that you found** belongs to her. Object Relative Clause
2. The verb in an object relative clause agrees with the subject of the relative clause.	The trip **that Joe is taking** will be fun. The trip **that Joe and Ann are taking** will be fun.

3. Object relative clauses can be identifying or non-identifying.
  a. In identifying object relative clauses, the relative pronoun can be omitted.
 	
  b. In non-identifying object relative clauses, use commas, but do not omit the relative pronoun.
	a. The man **that she was interviewing** is famous.
	   The man **she was interviewing** is famous.
	b. Vietnam, **which my family left over 30 years ago**, has changed a lot.
	✗ Vietnam <u>my family left over 30 years ago</u> has changed a lot.

4. Do not use *that* as the object relative pronoun in a non-identifying relative clause.	✓ Dr. Tam, **who(m) we have met**, is a surgeon. ✗ Dr. Tam, <u>that</u> we have met, is a surgeon.
5. Do not repeat the object at the end of an identifying object relative clause. The relative pronoun is the object.	✓ Where's the man **you were helping**? ✗ Where's the man you were helping <u>him</u>?

REAL ENGLISH
In formal English, *whom* is sometimes used instead of *who* in object relative clauses. *The employees **whom the director dismissed** had all worked at the bank for over 15 years.*

4 Complete the exercises.

A Complete each sentence with *that, who, whom,* or *which*. Sometimes more than one answer is possible.

1. Michael "Nick" Nichols has photographed 27 stories for *National Geographic Magazine*. This is work _____that_____ he has enjoyed.

2. He photographed orphan elephants _____ he saw in an elephant nursery in Nairobi.

3. The elephant nursery has created a home for the elephants _____ it has saved.

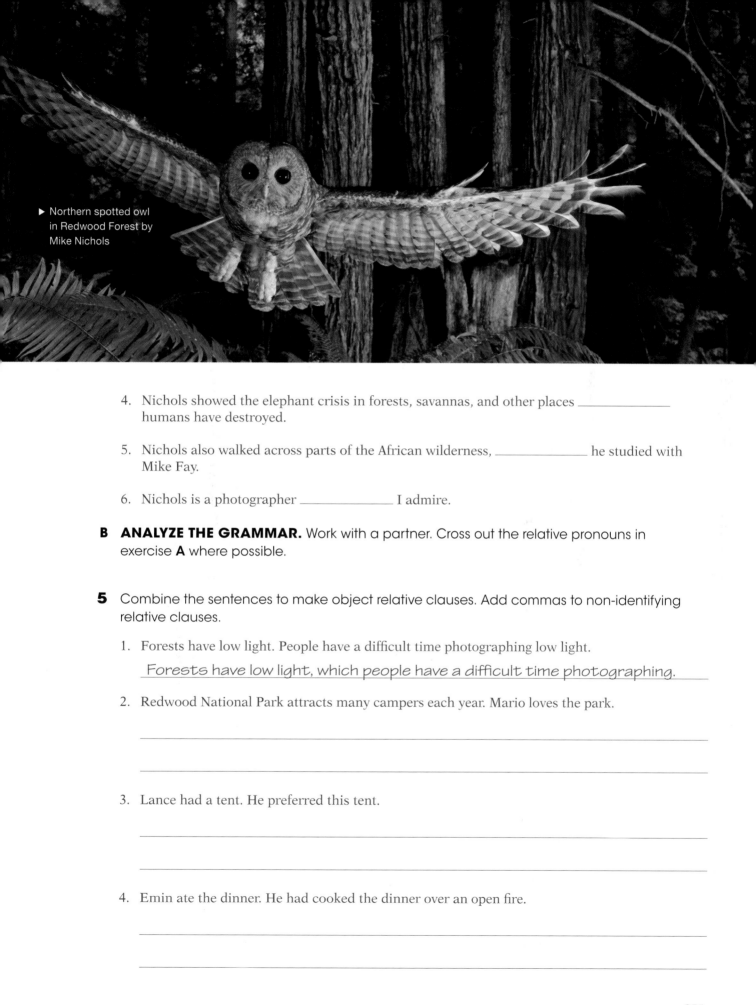

Northern spotted owl in Redwood Forest by Mike Nichols

4. Nichols showed the elephant crisis in forests, savannas, and other places _____ humans have destroyed.

5. Nichols also walked across parts of the African wilderness, _____ he studied with Mike Fay.

6. Nichols is a photographer _____ I admire.

B ANALYZE THE GRAMMAR. Work with a partner. Cross out the relative pronouns in exercise **A** where possible.

5 Combine the sentences to make object relative clauses. Add commas to non-identifying relative clauses.

1. Forests have low light. People have a difficult time photographing low light.

   Forests have low light, which people have a difficult time photographing.

2. Redwood National Park attracts many campers each year. Mario loves the park.

   _____

   _____

3. Lance had a tent. He preferred this tent.

   _____

   _____

4. Emin ate the dinner. He had cooked the dinner over an open fire.

   _____

   _____

5. Joe was very knowledgable. Nancy asked him for directions.

_____

_____

6. The redwood trees were beautiful. The campers saw them.

_____

_____

11.5 Object Relative Clauses with Prepositions

After the Main Clause
I like the professor. I spoke to <u>him</u>.
I like the professor **who I spoke to**. Relative Clause

Inside the Main Clause
The student left the program. I met with <u>him</u>.
The student **that I met with** left the program. Relative Clause

1. A relative pronoun (*that, which, who,* or *whom*) can be the object of a preposition. The preposition usually comes after the verb in an object relative clause.	The movie **that we were talking about** won an award. The photos **that we were looking at** were amazing.
2. **Remember:** We often omit object relative pronouns from identifying relative clauses in conversation and informal writing.	The meeting **that I forgot about** was important. The meeting **I forgot about** was important.
3. In formal English, the preposition can come at the beginning of the object relative clause, before *whom* (for people) or *which* (for things).	My father, **after whom I was named**, died before I was born. The article **to which you are referring** is no longer available.
4. **Be careful!** Do not use a preposition + *who* or *that*.	✗ The person <u>to who</u> I sent the message isn't here. ✗ The club <u>of that</u> she is a member is private.

6 Complete the sentences. Use *that, which, who,* or *whom* or a preposition (*about, for, in, with*).

1. The profession _____ I'm going to tell you about is quite challenging.

2. Portrait photography, which most people don't know much _____, is my job.

3. The people for _____ I work are called clients.

4. Clients describe the kind of portraits they're looking _____ when I meet them.

5. I enjoy the children whom I work _____.

6. The contract on _____ we agree gets finalized.

7. I go to the home _____ which the photo shoot will take place early in the day.

8. I have to get the people _____ I take pictures of to relax.

9. My clients review the photographs _____ I take.

10. I always thank the people _____ I take pictures of.

7 Combine the sentences to make object relative clauses with prepositions. Use *that, which*, or *who(m)*. More than one answer is possible.

1. Take photos of areas. Endangered animals are found in the areas.

   Take photos of areas that endangered animals are found in.

2. Look up information on the animals. You take pictures of the animals.

   _____

3. Volunteer for a citizen science project. You care about the project.

   _____

4. Take photos for environmental groups. You want to contribute to the groups.

   _____

5. Take photos of environmental projects. You have volunteered for these projects.

   _____

6. Write information about the scientists. You work with the scientists.

   _____

7. Be respectful of natural areas. You work in the areas.

   _____

8. Collect stories of the subjects. You have taken pictures of the subjects.

   _____

9. Know the issues. People often argue about these issues.

   _____

10. Start a blog about current topics. People will be interested in these topics.

    _____

PRACTICE

8 Complete the sentences. Circle all the correct answers.

1. Photographers _____ include Annie Griffiths.

   (a.) who National Geographic works with   (c.) that National Geographic works with

   b. that Griffiths which National Geographic works with

   (d.) National Geographic works with

2. Griffiths was one of the first women _____.

   a. to whom National Geographic gave an assignment

   c. National Geographic gave an assignment to

   b. National Geographic gave an assignment to her

   d. that National Geographic gave an assignment to

3. Some of the countries _____ include Australia, New Zealand, and Jordan.

   a. that Griffiths has worked in

   c. in which Griffiths has worked

   b. Griffiths has worked in

   d. which Griffiths has worked

4. Many of the strangers _____ have been friendly.

   a. Griffiths has met with

   c. who Griffiths has met with

   b. that Griffiths has met with

   d. to which Griffiths has met with

5. The people in Pakistan _____ were always warm and hospitable.

   a. which she stayed with

   c. she stayed with

   b. that she stayed with

   d. whom she stayed with

◀ A child peers between her sisters' robes in southern Pakistan.

6. The Zambian natives _____ allowed her to take the pictures.

    a. with whom she went swimming   c. who she went swimming with

    b. which she went swimming with   d. she went swimming with

7. Griffiths wants people to understand the women _____.

    a. she has taken photos of   c. of whom she has taken photos

    b. whom she has taken photos of them   d. of which she has taken photos

8. Griffiths and an organization _____ help women and girls in developing countries.

    a. that she started   c. which she started

    b. whom she started   d. she started

9 Complete the nature photographers' website with object relative clauses. More than one answer is possible.

Frequently Asked Questions

1. **What parts of your job do you like the most?**

   The parts of my job _____ *that I like the most* _____ are meeting new people and doing something artistic every day.

2. **What do you eat when you are on assignment?**

   The food _____ isn't very good. In fact, sometimes it's absolutely awful.

3. **Do you usually take your family with you?**

   No, my trips are not fun for them. The only people _____ are assistants to help with the lighting on complex assignments.

4. **Do you work with local guides and translators, or do you use assistants for that kind of work?**

   The guides and translators _____ are always local people.

5. **Have you ever been frightened by a wild animal?**

   One time there was a gorilla _____. It came very close and looked at me. I didn't know what it was going to do.

6. **What do you most enjoy taking pictures of?**

   The subjects _____ are endangered species.

7. **Has the average person heard of the animals you photograph?**

   Probably not. I like to photograph unusual creatures, the ones _____ _____. Photographs of uncommon animals can increase people's awareness of them.

8. **Do you ever observe other photographers?**

   Yes. I learn something from every photographer _____, from wildlife photographers to celebrity photographers.

10 LISTEN.

A Complete the paragraph about Joel Sartore, a longtime photographer for *National Geographic Magazine* and other publications. Use the information in the box to write relative clauses. Add commas where necessary.

> They may never see certain animals.
> He has great passion for his projects.
> ~~He has photographed many subjects.~~
> He is deeply committed to the Photo Ark project.
> He has traveled all over the world for his magazine assignments.

Joel Sartore is known for his ability to tell compelling stories about a wide range of topics. The subjects (1) <u>he has photographed</u> range from beekeepers to soccer fans. He is also deeply concerned about animals that are in danger of extinction. Therefore, in addition to his magazine assignments (2) _____,
he has initiated a few projects of his own. One is called the Photo Ark. The goal of the Photo Ark project (3) _____ is to bring people eye to eye with certain animals (4) _____ and to make them care about these creatures. Take a look at some of Sartore's photos online. You will begin to appreciate the great passion (5) _____.

B Listen to the professor and the students discuss Joel Sartore. Check your answers.

CD3-24

▶ Sartore photographed this female Diana monkey as part of his Photo Ark project.

11 **EDIT.** Read the text. Find and correct five more errors with relative clauses. There is more than one way to correct some errors.

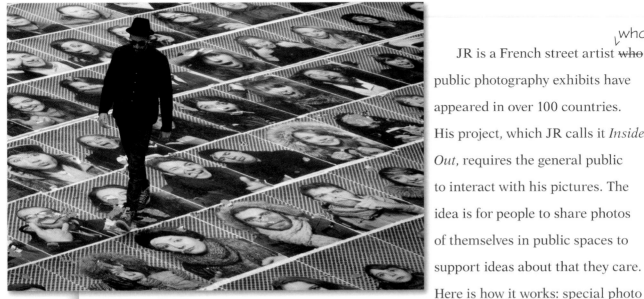

▲ Artist JR with exhibit

JR is a French street artist ~~who~~ ^whose^ public photography exhibits have appeared in over 100 countries. His project, which JR calls it *Inside Out*, requires the general public to interact with his pictures. The idea is for people to share photos of themselves in public spaces to support ideas about that they care. Here is how it works: special photo booths in which people can take their own pictures there are set up. The self-portraits are then printed and made into huge posters are displayed on the street. These photos attract attention to the causes, such as human rights.

JR, for who *Inside Out* is a way to make the world a better place, believes in the power of ordinary people. He is convinced that they can create positive change in the world. In JR's words, "Together, we'll turn the world inside out."

12 **APPLY.**

A Match the photojournalists with the issues that are most important to them.

_____ 1. Annie Griffiths   a. endangered species

_____ 2. Michael Nichols   b. life in the wild

_____ 3. Joel Sartore   c. women and children

B Write sentences in your notebook to describe the work of each photojournalist in exercise **A**. Include information that you learned in this lesson. Use relative clauses.

Annie Griffiths, who tries to help women and children in developing countries, has met many people in her travels.

C Imagine that you are a photojournalist who is concerned about a global issue, such as world hunger. What do you want to photograph and why? Write sentences using relative clauses in your notebook.

I want to take pictures of natural disasters, which can change people's lives in a single minute.

EXPLORE

CD3-25

1   **READ** the website about films in India. How are Bollywood films powerful for Indians living outside of their country?

Bollyblog
news

like share post

The Changing Face of Bollywood

The Indian film industry has been an important part of Indian cultural life for many years. The center of the industry, **nicknamed Bollywood**, is located in Mumbai (formerly Bombay). Bollywood, **where mostly Hindi language films are made**, makes over 1000 films a year. These days, the films are enjoyed by people around the world.

In the past, the movies were set in India and included singing and dancing, acting, romance, and always a happy ending. This type of film, **mixing all of these elements together**, was called *masala*. In Hindi this means a mixture of spices.

Modern times brought changes. Large numbers of Indians were living in other places: Asia, Africa, the Caribbean, Australia, Europe, and North America. In the late 1990s, **when new technology was developing**, Bollywood filmmakers realized they could make films for this diaspora[1] with satellite television, DVDs, and the Internet. The films were made with modern life in mind. The main characters were often Indians **living outside their country**. The films were shot where these Indians lived and in India. The new films were a bit different from *masala*s, but still about Indian values and traditions.

Bollywood films have had a powerful effect on the Indian diaspora. Even for Indians living far away, the films connect them to their homeland. Thanks to Bollywood, there is now a stronger sense of identity and community among Indians all over the world.

[1] **diaspora:** people who come from a particular nation, but who now live in many different parts of the world

2 CHECK. Read each statement about the article. Write **T** for *true* or **F** for *false*.

_____ 1. Bollywood has made a total of 1000 films.

_____ 2. The capital, Delhi, is the center of the Indian movie industry.

_____ 3. *Masala* films usually end sadly.

_____ 4. It is not unusual to see scenes outside of India in today's Bollywood films.

_____ 5. Indian films help connect Indians living in other countries to India.

3 DISCOVER. Complete the exercises to learn about the grammar in this lesson.

A Complete the sentences to match the sentences from the website. Change the underlined words.

1. The center of the industry, <u>which is nicknamed Bollywood</u>, is located in Mumbai.

   The center of the industry, _nicknamed Bollywood_ , is located in Mumbai.

2. This type of film, <u>which mixed all of these elements together</u>, was called *masala*.

   This type of film, _____ all of these elements together, was called *masala*.

3. The main characters were often Indians <u>who live</u> outside their country.

   The main characters were often Indians _____ outside their country.

B Underline the relative clauses that begin with *when* or *where* in the article. Circle the nouns that *when* and *where* refer to.

LEARN

11.6 Reduced Relative Clauses

> The woman <u>who stars in the movie</u> has a beautiful voice.
>
> The woman **starring in the movie** has a beautiful voice.

1. A subject relative clause can be reduced or shortened to a relative phrase.	The girl <u>who was riding the bike</u> fell off. The girl **riding the bike** fell off.
2. In a relative phrase, the relative pronoun (*who, that, which*) and any form of *be* is omitted.	People <u>who are driving hybrid cars</u> like them. People **driving hybrid cars** like them. The film <u>that was shown last night</u> was exciting. The film **shown last night** was exciting. He is the person <u>who is most interested in the job</u>. He is the person **most interested in the job**.
3. With some verbs other than *be*, you can omit the relative pronoun and add *-ing* after the base form of the verb.	Anyone <u>who wants to learn about film history</u> should read this book. Anyone **wanting to learn about film history** should read this book.
4. Use commas when a non-identifying relative clause is reduced.	The film festival, <u>which was held in Brazil</u>, attracted people from all over the world. The film festival, **held in Brazil**, attracted people from all over the world.

4 Complete the exercises.

A Complete each sentence with a reduced relative clause.

1. Nollywood, which was named after Bollywood, is the Nigerian film industry.

   Nollywood, ___named after Bollywood___ , is the Nigerian film industry.

2. Nollywood films, which are mostly made in English, are shown around Africa and overseas.

   Nollywood films, _____ , are shown around Africa and overseas.

3. Some Somali films are made in Eastleigh, which is a neighborhood in Nairobi, Kenya.

   Some Somali films are made in Eastleigh, _____.

4. Last night we saw a film that was set in Nairobi.

   Last night we saw a film _____.

5. A Somali production company that is known as Eastleighwood is popular in many parts of the world.

   A Somali production company _____ is popular in many parts of the world.

6. Anyone who is interested in world politics would enjoy the movie.

   Anyone _____ would enjoy the movie.

B Complete each sentence with a reduced relative clause.

1. My favorite Indian movies are films that have a lot of singing and dancing.

   My favorite Indian movies are films <u>having a lot of singing and dancing</u>.

2. The African film festival has movies that feature beautiful scenery.

   The African film festival has movies _____.

3. That Nigerian director only produces films that promote social awareness.

   That Nigerian director only produces films _____.

4. I enjoy movies that star my favorite actors.

   I enjoy movies _____.

5. We want to see the thriller that is showing at midnight.

   We want to see the thriller _____.

6. The critic loved the new film that shows life in Mumbai.

   The critic loved the new film _____.

5 Complete the exercises.

A Underline the relative clause in each sentence. Then check (✓) the sentences that contain relative clauses that can be reduced.

___✓___ 1. Bollywood, <u>which was named after Hollywood</u>, makes different kinds of films.

_____ 2. Bollywood, which is also referred to as Hindi cinema, is one of the largest film producers in India.

_____ 3. Bollywood films, which many people enjoy, do not pretend to show reality.

_____ 4. Bollywood, which inspired many cinema movements, was followed by Nollywood.

_____ 5. Bollywood's production studio, which the government built, is called Film City.

_____ 6. The actors who appear in Bollywood movies come from all over India.

B In your notebook, write reduced relative clauses for the sentences you checked in exercise **A**.

▼ The Nairobi skyline. Some Somali films are made in Nairobi, Kenya.

11.7 Relative Clauses with *Where* and *When*

> We visited the region **where the film was made.**
> I remember the day **when I first saw a lion in the wild.**

1. Use *where* in a relative clause to describe a place (for example, *home, neighborhood, city, country, place*).	Istanbul is a city. Europe and Asia meet there. Istanbul is a city **where Europe and Asia meet.**
2. Use *when* in a clause to describe a time (for example, *day, weekend, year, time*).	I'll never forget the summer. Our team won the championship then. I'll never forget the summer **when our team won the championship.**
3. *Where* and *when* can be used in identifying and non-identifying relative clauses. They can be omitted only in identifying relative clauses.	Do you remember the time **when we met**? Do you remember the time **we met**? The movie is in Paris, **where we first met.**
4. **Be careful!** Do not use a preposition in a relative clause with *where* or *when*.	✓ The late 1920s was the time **when talking films replaced silent films.** ✗ The late 1920s was the time <u>during when</u> talking films replaced silent films.
5. Instead of *where*, you can use a preposition: a. before *which* b. following the verb in the relative clause	a. The apartment building **in which I was born** no longer exists. b. The apartment building **which/that I was born in** no longer exists.
6. Instead of *when*, you can use *in which* in identifying relative clauses.	Last year was the year **when they got married.** Last year was the year **in which they got married.**

6 Combine the sentences about silent movies. Use *when, where*, or a preposition with *which*. Add commas where necessary.

1. The history of film starts in the late nineteenth century. Movies had no sound then.

   <u>The history of film starts in the late nineteenth century when movies</u>

   <u>had no sound.</u>

2. People wanted to go to a relaxing place. They could escape from their troubles there.

   _____

   _____

3. Moviegoers saw silent movies in theaters. There were usually pianos or organs in the theaters.

   _____

   _____

4. The age of silent movies ended in the late 1920s. Talking movies became popular then.

   _____

   _____

5. The movie *The Artist* (2011) takes place during the last years of silent films. People were losing interest then.

   _____

   _____

6. Today, there are a few silent film festivals. People show modern silent movies there.

   _____

   _____

PRACTICE

7 Complete the blog with the words in the box. Some words can be used more than once.

meaning	showing	when	which	where

Tips for Independent Filmmakers

Are you a new independent filmmaker starting out? Here are some tips to help you set up your movie and find a good location (1) _____*where*_____ you can make your film.

First, think about what scenes you need to film. You should probably make a storyboard, (2) _____ a series of drawings in (3) _____ you visualize your scenes. You can draw sketches of scenes or use computer software to make it. The storyboard will help you plan your film. Now you are ready to decide on your location and schedule.

To save money, think about places (4) _____ you might be able to film for free. For example, perhaps you can use a warehouse, a field, a back alley, or a quiet restaurant. Don't forget that you can't film in a location without permission. Be sure to contact the owner first. You will need to be flexible about the hours (5) _____ you will be at the location. A restaurant might let you film for free in the middle of the night, but not at 6:00 p.m.

For more information (6) _____ you how to make a basic film, visit www.grexfilms.com.

8 Look at the information and the notes in the filming schedule. Then complete the conversation between two production assistants. Use *when* or *where* and the correct form of the words in parentheses.

Preliminary Filming Schedule for *The Talented Mr. Ripley*					
Day	Scene	Description	Location	Characters	Requirements
SHOOT DAY 1 (October 8)					
9:00–10:00	10	Tom Ripley gets off bus	Ischia Ponte, Italy	Tom, crowd	bus
10:30–2:30	10	Tom introduces himself to Richard and Marge	Bagno Antonio (Antonio Beach)	Tom, Richard, Marge, crowd	bathing suits, towels, shoes
BREAK FOR LUNCH					
3:00–4:15	13	Tom, Marge, and Richard have coffee	Marge's house	Tom, Richard, Marge	coffee cups
4:15–6:00	30	Tom gives Marge a letter	Marge's house	Tom, Marge	letter, perfume
6:00–7:15	31	Marge reads letter	Marge's house	Marge	letter

1. A: Do you know the first day _____ when filming begins _____ (filming / begin)?

   B: Yes, it starts on October 8.

2. A: Is Ischia Ponte the place _____ (the bus scene / happen)?

   B: Yes, on the Ischia Ponte bridge.

3. A: Can you tell me the location _____ (Tom, Richard, and Marge / meet)?

   B: Bagno Antonio.

4. A: Do you remember the scene _____ bathing suits? (we / need)

   B: Scene 10.

5. A: Do you know the time of day _____ (we / stop) for lunch?

   B: Yes, we'll have lunch at 2:30.

6. A: Did the director tell you the area _____ (Marge's house / be) located?

   B: No. I'll ask.

7. A: Can you remind me of the crowd scenes _____ (the director / want) extras?

   B: Yes, we need extra people for the scenes at Ischia Ponte and Bagno Ischia.

8. A: Do you know the hours _____ (Tom / be) on camera today?

   B: Most of the day. He's in scenes 10, 13, and 30.

9. A: The moment _____ (Tom / give) Marge the letter is always such a bad scene.

   B: I know! It's a really serious part of the movie.

10. A: Are the actors staying on the island _____ (the film / take) place?

    B: The actors are, but it's so expensive there that the film crew is staying somewhere else.

9 Complete the sentences about movie extras. Use the information in the box to write reduced relative clauses.

> Particular clothes are required for scenes.
> Information about your age is requested.
> Photographers' fees are posted on websites.
> Extras should not talk while filming.
> ~~Some people want to be an extra in a movie.~~
> Jobs are listed on movie studio websites.
> Being an extra requires long hours.

1. Anyone _wanting to be an extra in a movie_ should get a professional photo made.

2. Call photographers to find out how much they charge. Don't rely on the fees _____.

3. You can find jobs _____.

4. Be honest when you send the information _____.

5. Extras usually use their own clothing. Make sure you have the particular clothes _____.

6. Being an extra is a job _____. You might be on set for up to 14 hours.

7. Don't talk during filming. Extras _____ will have to leave and won't get paid.

10 **EDIT.** Read the memory about a scary movie. Find and correct five more errors with relative clauses.

A Memorable Movie

                                     when
    I will never forget how I felt the night ~~where~~ I saw the movie "The Birds." I was watching it on TV with my family in the house where grew up. The movie, was directed by Alfred Hitchcock, was made many years ago, but to this day just thinking about it scares me to death. I'll never forget the moment in when the woman was locked in a room with all the birds attacking her. My oldest brother, who wanting to be funny, started making loud bird noises and moving his arms like wings. The shadows created by his moving arms frightened me even more. Since then I have never been able to look at a lot of birds are sitting on a telephone wire or on tree branches without getting scared. I will never forgive Alfred Hitchcock, or my brother, for that.

11 APPLY.

A Read the description of the movie. Underline the reduced relative clauses and the relative clauses with *when* and *where*.

What movie is it?

This is a horror movie <u>directed by Alfred Hitchcock</u>. The film, released in 1963, is based on a short story written by British author Daphne du Maurier. It takes place in a northern California town where birds start attacking people for no obvious reason. The main characters are Melanie and Mitch. Melanie Daniels, played by actress Tippi Hedren, is a rich young woman who follows a San Francisco lawyer named Mitch Brenner to the coastal town of Bodega Bay, where his mother and sister live. Strangely, on the day when Melanie arrives to town, birds start attacking people. At the end of the movie, Melanie hears noises coming from the attic of the Brenner home. Hundreds of birds rush at her as she opens the attic door. It's a terrifying movie!

The Birds
introducing Tippi Hedren

B Think about a movie you remember well. Write a description of the movie. Use the model in exercise **A** and the questions in the box to help you. Include at least three reduced relative clauses and three relative clauses starting with *where* or *when*.

Who are the main characters?	Where does the story take place?
Who starred in the movie?	Who directed the movie?
When was the movie released?	What is the most memorable scene in the movie?
Is the movie based on a book?	How does the movie end?
Is the movie a true story?	What happens to the main character(s)?

C Work in a group. Listen to your classmates read their movie descriptions. Try to guess the movie. Ask questions if you aren't sure.

A: *Is the movie* The Birds?   B: *Yes, it is.*

1 Read the paragraph. Then complete the statements with *that, who, whom, when, where, which,* or *whose.*

> Shirin Neshat is a visual artist from Iran. She came from a wealthy family. She left Iran in 1974 at age 17 to study art in Los Angeles. Neshat now lives in New York and makes visual art, photographs, and films. Her works look at the role of women in the Islamic world. In 2010 she was named the Artist of the Decade by the *Huffington Post*. Her work explores religion, human rights, and women's identity. Her works have been shown in many museums across the world, including New York, Greece, and Istanbul. Neshat says that artists are there to bring hope and become the voice of the people.

1. Shirin Neshat, _____ is from a wealthy family, is a visual artist from Iran.

2. In 1974 Neshat traveled to Los Angeles, _____ she planned to study art.

3. Neshat, _____ work explores women in Islamic society, has become famous.

4. Neshat makes different kinds of art, _____ include photographs and films.

5. Places _____ Neshat's works have appeared include museums in the west and east.

6. Neshat, _____ many people find a source of hope, wants to speak for people _____ can't speak for themselves.

Charts
11.1–11.5,
11.7

2 Add *that, which, who, whom, whose, when,* or *where* to complete the relative clause in each sentence.

1. In classrooms ʌ *where* presentations are done well, images can be a powerful teaching tool.

2. In the past, professors used fewer images, students had to rely on listening skills.

3. Most people remember things they see better than things they listen to.

4. The images hold an audience's attention are the most successful.

5. During presentations, are done in all kinds of classes, presenters use images in different ways.

6. There are many presentations use still or moving images to illustrate a difficult concept.

7. Other presentations use images encourage discussion and debate.

8. Sometimes a presenter's goal is to surprise students with an image gets them to look at an issue in a new way.

Charts
11.1–11.7

3   **EDIT.** Read an excerpt from a class lecture about the role of images in advertising. Find and correct seven more errors with relative clauses. There is more than one way to correct some errors.

How do images influence our actions?

                                                           that

    Images communicate meanings ∨can't always be expressed as quickly in words. That's why images are so important in advertising. We see ads everywhere, and they affect us in ways in we don't realize. For example, we might see an ad for a candy bar before a movie is shown at the local theater. Maybe a few days later, we're in the supermarket and we buy the same candy bar, that we didn't plan to buy. When we put it into the shopping cart, we probably aren't thinking about the candy we saw it in the movie.

    Some people think they're not influenced by advertising because they don't buy products from ads whom they see. They don't realize that ads don't usually lead us to act immediately. This is the way ads work, though—they give us ideas that we act on them later.

    Consider this photo of someone selling flowers and other products in Thailand, floating markets are common. What kinds of thoughts do you associate with the image? Do you think this is a better advertising image for a travel company or for a company that sells products made in Thailand?

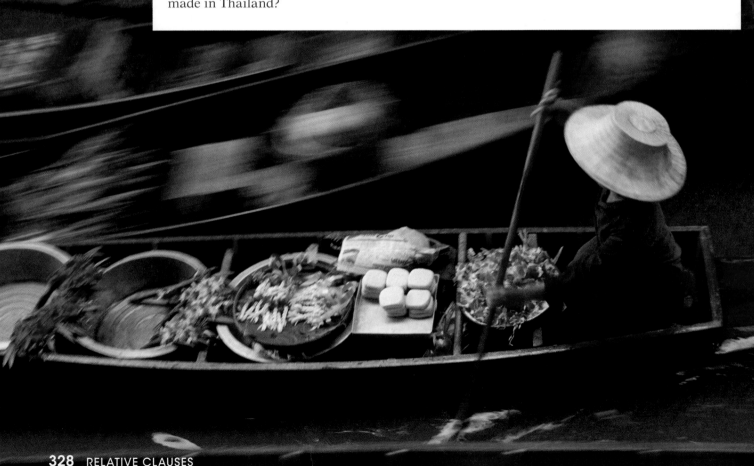

4 LISTEN.

A Listen to the radio ad. What product is it advertising?

B Listen again. Complete each sentence with a relative clause that answers the question in parentheses.

1. The coconut is a fruit _____ .
   (What can coconuts provide you with?)

2. This tropical fruit, _____
   (How long have humans been using coconuts?)
   _____ , is a great source of iron and other minerals.

3. It's the perfect drink for people _____ on a hot summer day.
   (Who is coconut milk the perfect drink for?)

4. Just take one sip and you'll be transported to a beautiful tropical island _____
   _____ .
   (What will you see on the tropical island?)

5. The Hoolehua post office, _____ of these postcards each
   (How many coconut postcards does the post office
   year, is in Hawaii.   ship each year?)

6. Send some coconuts to your friends, _____ with such
   (How will your friends feel about the gift of coconuts?)
   a tasty and unusual gift.

5 WRITE & SPEAK.

A Work in a group. Choose a product and write an ad for it in your notebook. Include at least three relative clauses.

| a car | perfume | hiking boots | a smartphone | your idea: _____ |

Try on a pair of our XXG6 boots, and you'll love them. These boots, which are lightweight and waterproof, will be comfortable from the moment you put them on . . .

B Discuss one or two images that might be effective in your ad. Use a relative clause in your answer.

We'd like to illustrate our ad with a photo showing a hiker who is on a trail that goes through a beautiful forest. The focus should be on the hiker's boots . . .

Connect the Grammar to Writing

1 READ & NOTICE THE GRAMMAR.

A Have you recently seen a movie that had a big impact on you? Exchange ideas with a partner. Then read the review.

MOVIE REVIEW: *The Deep*

The Deep is a 2012 Icelandic film directed by Baltasar Kormákur. It is based on the true story of a fisherman whose boat sank at sea in 1984.

Gulli, played by Ólafur Darri Ólafsson, is stranded in freezing cold waters after he survives an accident that sinks his fishing boat. In an instant, he changes from an ordinary person to a man who must make a heroic effort to survive. The movie is a beautiful and moving reflection on human endurance.

The whole movie does not take place only in the icy waters where Gulli floats and tries to swim (although these are certainly the most dramatic parts). We also see many scenes of the town where he lives, both before and after the accident. The gray colors and tough, weather-beaten look of everything really give viewers a taste of a different world; it is one in which people must work hard and take great risks living. Scenes from the real life event, shown at the end of the film, add to the emotional impact.

The Deep reminds us of the simple and at times dangerous lives that many people must live and the incredible choices that they sometimes have to face. It will leave you with a deep respect for Icelandic fishermen. Unsurprisingly, Kormákur dedicated the film to them.

GRAMMAR FOCUS

In this movie review, the writer uses the following types of relative clauses to describe or give extra information about a noun.

Subject relative clause . . . *an accident **that sinks his fishing boat***.

Object relative clauses . . . *the incredible choices **that they sometimes have to face***.

B Read the movie review in exercise **A** again. Find and underline three more relative clauses (including one reduced relative clause) and label what type each one is. Then circle the noun that the relative clause describes or gives extra information about.

C Complete the chart with information from the review in exercise **A**. Then discuss your answers with a partner.

> Title of movie: _The Deep_   Year movie was released: _____
>
> Director: _____
>
> Main character: _____   Actor: _____
>
> Plot/Story: An Icelandic fisherman must try to survive after his fishing boat sinks.
>
> Setting (place) or visual effects: _____
>
> This is a powerful/interesting movie because _____
>
> _____

2 BEFORE YOU WRITE.

A Work with a partner. Create a list of the three best movies that you have seen in the past year. Help each other remember the actors in each one.

B Choose one movie from your list and prepare to write a review of it. In your notebook, make a chart like the one in exercise **1C** and fill in as much information as you can.

3 WRITE two or three paragraphs about the movie that you chose. Tell the basic plot and the setting. What made the movie powerful or interesting? Use your chart from exercise **2B** and the review in exercise **1A** to guide you. Use at least three relative clauses in your review.

> **WRITING FOCUS**   Discussing Plot in the Simple Present
>
> When we discuss the plot (the basic storyline) of a movie or a novel, we usually use a present form of the verb. Even though we saw the movie or read the book in the past, the events in the story continue to exist. Every time we watch the movie or read the novel, the same events will occur. Notice the simple present in the first sentence of the plot summary:
>
> *Gulli, played by Ólafur Darri Ólafsson,* **is stranded** *in freezing cold waters after he* **survives** *an accident that* **sinks** *his fishing boat.*

4 SELF ASSESS. Underline the relative clauses in your review. Then use the checklist to assess your work.

- [ ] I used identifying and non-identifying subject relative clauses correctly. [11.1, 11.2]
- [ ] I used relative clauses with *whose, when,* and *where* correctly. [11.3, 11.7]
- [ ] I used object relative clauses correctly. [11.4, 11.5]
- [ ] I used the simple present when describing the plot of the movie. [WRITING FOCUS]

Adverb Clauses

Skyscrapers in New York
City's Financial District,
New York, USA

EXPLORE

CD3-27

1 READ the book review. According to Edward Glaeser, why do many people want to live in cities?

Triumph of the City by Edward Glaeser

We are becoming an urban species. More than half of the world's people live in cities today, and cities are still growing. For economist Edward Glaeser, this is good news. In his fascinating book, *Triumph of the City*, Glaeser explains why cities continue to attract people.

Glaeser sees great advantages to urban life. **Whenever people live close together**, they can exchange ideas, from business to technology to the arts. This exchange makes cities exciting and productive centers of opportunity.

He also believes that cities are good for the planet because they reduce pollution. **Since urban residents don't drive much**, cities have fewer carbon emissions.[1] For example, fewer than one third of New York City residents drive to work as compared with 86 percent of people living elsewhere in the United States.

> "Cities are our species' greatest invention."
> —Edward Glaeser

Glaeser thinks that cities are good for everyone—for people of all incomes. He does not believe that cities make people poor. He writes that we should build more skyscrapers **so that large numbers of people can live in relatively small areas**. Then housing will be affordable. However, **even though Glaeser has some interesting suggestions**, he underestimates the high cost of city living. Millions of urban residents can't afford food, clothing, and housing **because they are too expensive**. It is a serious problem.

Triumph of the City is a thoughtful book. **Although you may not agree with all of Glaeser's ideas**, you will probably enjoy his lively discussion.

[1] **carbon emissions:** the release of carbon dioxide into the air

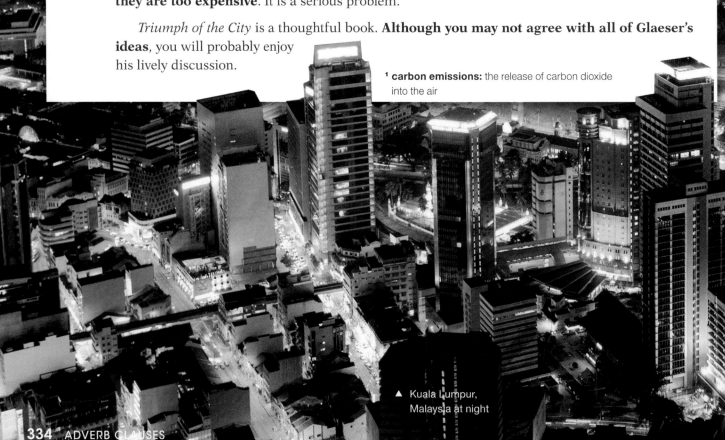
▲ Kuala Lumpur, Malaysia at night

2 CHECK. Correct the error in each sentence to make it true according to the book review.

1. About one third of the world's population lives in cities.

2. Cities today are decreasing in size.

3. According to Glaeser, cities cause pollution.

4. Eighty-six percent of New York City residents drive to work.

5. The reviewer agrees with all of Glaeser's ideas.

3 DISCOVER. Complete the exercises to learn about the grammar in this lesson.

A Find these sentences in the book review from exercise **1**. Write the missing words.

1. _____Whenever_____ people live close together, they can exchange ideas.

2. _____ urban residents don't drive much, cities have fewer carbon emissions.

3. He writes that we should build more skyscrapers _____ large numbers of people can live in relatively small areas.

4. Millions of urban residents can't afford food, clothing, and housing _____ they are too expensive.

5. _____ you may not agree with all of Glaeser's ideas, you will probably enjoy his lively discussion.

B Look at the words you wrote in exercise **A**. Write the words that show:

1. a contrasting idea: _____   3. reasons: _____ , _____

2. a purpose: _____   4. a time relationship: _____

LEARN

12.1 Adverb Clauses of Time

<u>Whenever I hear that song</u>, <u>I get sad.</u>
    Adverb Clause   Main Clause

<u>It started to snow</u> **just as we were leaving the theater**.
    Main Clause   Adverb Clause

1. Adverb clauses of time begin with a time word or phrase (*when, whenever, as, as long as, as soon as*). They tell when the action or event in the main clause happens.	**As I was leaving my dormitory**, I ran into an old friend.
2. *As* means when or while something is or was happening.	**As I was walking home**, it started to thunder.
Just as means that an action or event happened at exactly the same moment as another action or event.	My roommate called **just as I was leaving**.
3. *As long as* means from beginning to end.	I'll never forget that day **as long as I live**.
4. *Whenever* means any time or every time.	**Whenever she tells a story**, I laugh a lot.
5. Time clauses can come before or after the main clause. The meaning is the same.	We went on vacation **as soon as we finished classes**.
Remember: Use a comma after the time clause when it comes first in the sentence.	**As soon as we finished classes**, we went on vacation.

4 Underline five more adverb clauses of time in the paragraph. Add commas where necessary.

Singapore

<u>As you fly over Singapore</u> you'll see enormous skyscrapers. Five million people live in just 270 square miles (700 sq. km) there, so most people live in tall buildings. Whenever people think of skyscrapers they usually think of crowded spaces. However, this is not true of the Pinnacle@Duxton in Singapore. The Pinnacle is a huge skyscraper with 1800 apartments. You'll be amazed as you walk around it. As soon as you reach the 20th floor you'll see a 2625-foot (800 m) jogging track. You'll feel like you're running in the clouds whenever you go there to exercise. The skyscrapers in Singapore look like something from a science fiction movie. They're truly amazing works of architecture. You'll remember them as long as you live!

◄ The Singapore skyline

5 Circle the correct word(s) to complete each sentence.

1. Some people use elevators **as long as / whenever** they leave the building.

2. **As soon as / As** the new skyscraper was completed, people started complaining about it.

3. The power went out **as long as / just as** the elevator reached the twelfth floor.

4. **Whenever / As** people live close to each other, there is less privacy.

5. **Just as / Whenever** our neighbors have a party, they invite us.

6. **As / As soon as** I was driving home, I saw that new apartment building.

7. I'll remember my trip to Singapore **whenever / as long as** I live.

8. Oleg got to the station **just as / as long as** the train was leaving.

9. Please call me **as along as / as soon as** you get to Hong Kong.

10. **Whenever / As** we go to New York City, we always visit the Empire State Building.

12.2 Adverb Clauses of Contrast

<u>**Although I've studied a lot**</u>, <u>I'm still nervous about the exam</u>.
    Adverb Clause   Main Clause

<u>I'm still nervous about the exam</u> <u>**even though I've studied a lot**</u>.
      Main Clause   Adverb Clause

1. Adverb clauses beginning with *although*, *even though*, and *though* introduce a contrast. The information may be unexpected or surprising.	**Although Joe studied a lot**, he's still nervous about the exam. **Even though she loves him**, she is not going to marry him. **Though I slept well last night**, I'm very tired today.
2. *Even though* shows more contrast than *though*.	He bought a new car **even though he has trouble paying his rent every month**.
3. *Though* is more common in informal English.	Informal: **Though** I have the qualifications, they're not going to give me the job. Formal: **Although** you have the right qualifications, I'm afraid we can't offer you the position.
4. **Be careful!** Do not use *but* in sentences with *although*, *even though*, and *though*.	✓ **Though it was raining**, I went for a walk. ✗ Though it was raining, <u>but</u> I went for a walk.
5. **Remember:** Use a comma after the adverb clause when it comes first in the sentence.	**Although we enjoy the countryside**, we prefer city life.

6 Choose the best ending for each sentence. Then add commas where necessary.

1. Singapore has a population of five million although _____.

   a. it is only 270 square miles (700 sq. km) wide

   b. it has a lot of interesting architecture

2. Even though Chicago is a large city, _____.

   a. it has a lot of tall buildings

   b. it has a lot of parks and gardens

3. Some of the world's oldest cities are in Egypt although _____.

   a. Greek cities are not as old

   b. there are many ancient cities and towns in China, too

4. Toronto is the largest city in Canada although _____.

   a. it is not the country's capital

   b. it has a population of about 5.6 million

5. Although Yamoussoukro is the capital city of the Ivory Coast _____.

   a. it is the political capital

   b. it began as a very small village

6. Even though many ancient cities had walls around them _____.

   a. the walls did not always stop invaders

   b. the walls protected the city from invaders

▼ The walled city of Dubrovnik, Croatia

7. Shanghai, China has the largest population of any city in the world though _____.

   a. almost as many people live in Beijing

   b. far fewer people live in Jaipur, India

8. Though some large cities such as Tokyo and London have skyscrapers _____.

   a. their streets are inhabited by millions of people

   b. tiny streets in some sections show their ancient beginnings

12.3 Adverb Clauses of Reason and Purpose

Since I don't know how to get there, I'm going to use my GPS.
_____Adverb Clause_____   _____Main Clause_____

Now that I have a GPS, I never get lost.
___Adverb Clause___   ___Main Clause___

We're going to leave early **so that we can avoid traffic**.
___Main Clause___   ___Adverb Clause___

1. *Because* and *since* show reasons.	**Because I didn't do well on the exam**, I'm going to take it again. **Since we're late**, let's take a taxi.
2. **Be careful!** *Since* can also refer to time.	**Since I got here**, I've done very little work.
3. *Now that* shows a reason. It means *because . . . now*.	**Now that I know English**, I can get a good job. **Now that Ed's retired**, he's going to have more free time.
4. *So that* shows a purpose. It means *in order to*. Modal verbs (*can, could, would*, etc.) are often used with *so that*.	I'm putting on my glasses **so that I can read the menu**. We studied hard **so that we would do well on the exam**. Max moved to the front of the classroom **so that he could see better**.

REAL ENGLISH

In conversation, *that* is often omitted after *so*.

*I texted Bill **so he could get the information fast**.*

7 Circle the correct word(s) to complete each sentence.

1. **Because** / So that people live close together in cities, they can interact more.

2. **Since / So that** our city has excellent public transportation, we don't need a car.

3. More people want to live in big cities **now that / so that** they are safer and cleaner.

4. Cities need police **so that / since** they will be safe places to live.

5. Cities are important **now that / because** they are economic, political, and cultural centers.

6. **Now that / So that** I have a bike, I don't have to take the bus to work.

7. **So that / Since** the world population is growing, cities are becoming larger.

8. Some people move to big cities **so that / now that** they can live more exciting lives.

8 Complete the conversation with *because, since, now that,* or *so that*. More than one answer is sometimes correct.

Ali: How was your trip to Malaysia? Did you get to see much of Kuala Lumpur?

Bill: Yes, I did. The weather was nice. It was really warm (1) _____ Kuala Lumpur has a tropical rainforest climate. There's a lot to see there, especially religious sites. A lot of people go there (2) _____ they can visit the mosques and the Batu Caves outside the city.

Ali: What are the Batu Caves?

Bill: They're an important religious site. The Batu Caves are a group of cave temples cut into the side of a hill. Some people climb all 272 steps (3) _____ they can see all of the caves, but I didn't get to see many of the caves (4) _____ I didn't have that much time.

Ali: It sounds interesting. I've never heard of them.

Bill: A lot of people have never heard of them. But (5) _____ they have become famous, they attract a lot of tourists.

Ali: Really? So, what else did you do there?

Bill: Well, we visited Putrajaya (6) _____ it is so close to Kuala Lumpur. That was nice, too. It's a new city. The government built it not long ago.

PRACTICE

9 Circle the correct words to complete the sentences about Putrajaya, Malaysia.

1. Putrajaya was created **because / so that / though** Kuala Lumpur would be less crowded.

2. **Because / Just as / Although** there are a lot of government offices in Putrajaya, many government workers live there.

3. **Even though / Just as / Now that** many government workers live in Putrajaya, there is less traffic there than in Kuala Lumpur.

4. Government workers enjoy living in Putrajaya **even though / since / whenever** it has good public services.

5. You can see attractive buildings, parks, and bridges **as / even though / since** you walk down the streets of Putrajaya.

6. **As long as / So that / Although** Putrajaya does not have historical buildings, it does have interesting places, such as Wasana Park.

7. **Even though / So that / Since** Putrajaya is a big city, it also has a lot of green space, such as parks and botanical gardens.

8. **Although / Since / Whenever** people visit Putrajaya, they are surprised by its natural beauty.

▶ Tanguá Park,
Curitiba, Brazil

10 Read the sentences about Curitiba, Brazil. Then combine each pair of sentences into one sentence with an adverb clause. Use the word in parentheses. Add a comma where necessary. Sometimes there is more than one way to combine the sentences.

1. Curitiba is an attractive city. It has historic buildings and beautiful woods around it. (because)

   Because Curitiba has historic buildings and beautiful woods around it, it

   is an attractive city. OR _Curitiba is an attractive city because it has_

   historic buildings and beautiful woods around it.

2. Curitiba has a diverse population. Immigrants from Europe and Japan have made it their home. (since)

   _____

   _____

3. The population began to grow rapidly. Curitiba's mayor tried to reduce crowding. (as)

   _____

   _____

4. There are no cars on "The Street of Flowers." It's a nice place to walk and shop. (because)

   _____

   _____

5. Many people own cars in Curitiba. Two million people take public transportation every day. (although)

   _____

   _____

6. Curitiba developed a good recycling program. It can keep the city clean. (so that)

_____

_____

7. Children bring cans and bottles to recycling centers. They receive small gifts. (whenever)

_____

_____

8. Not all of the city's garbage is recycled in Curitiba. Seventy percent of it is. (though)

_____

_____

11 WRITE & SPEAK.

A Complete the blog entry with *since, because, although, even though, though, whenever,* or *so that*. Sometimes more than one answer is correct.

World Traveler

April 12

Rome and Dubai are two of my favorite cities (1) _____ they are very different. (2) _____ there are a lot of huge skyscrapers in Dubai, it has a very modern look and feel. The architecture is amazing. In fact, many people go there (3) _____ they can visit the Burj Khalifa—the tallest building in the world. (4) _____ Dubai is well known for its impressive buildings, there are also many beautiful parks and gardens there. My favorite park is Dubai Miracle Garden, which has over 45 million flowers! Dubai is also a great city for shopping. (5) _____ I visit Dubai, I always go to the famous Wafi shopping mall.

Rome is my other favorite city. Like many other people, I go there (6) _____ I can visit the historical sites and see the famous art. (7) _____ Rome is one of the most ancient cities in Europe, there is a lot to see, such as Renaissance palaces, the Pantheon, the Colosseum, and the Spanish Steps. Also, (8) _____ many of the sites in Rome are close together, it's a very walkable city. And the food in Rome is fantastic! (9) _____ I go to Rome, I gain weight!

Rome and Dubai are two wonderful cities with very different atmospheres. I highly recommend visiting them both!

B Complete the sentences to make them true about yourself and your city.

1. Although my city _is very crowded and noisy_ , _it's a great place to live_ .

2. _____ is the best time of year to visit my city since _____ .

▼ Rome, Italy

3. _____ is my favorite city because _____ .

4. Even though _____ is a _____ city,
   it's _____ .

5. Many people visit my city so that _____ .

6. Whenever I travel, I always _____ .

7. I want to visit _____ someday so that I _____ .

8. Whenever I visit my family, _____ .

C Work with a partner. Share your sentences from exercise **B**. Ask follow-up questions.

A: *Although my city is very crowded and noisy, it's a great place to live.*

B: *Really? What do you like about it?*

12 LISTEN & SPEAK.

CD3-28

A Listen to the conversation. Then answer the questions.

1. What is the Eurosky Tower? _____

2. Where is it? _____

3. Is Sergio's opinion of the Eurosky Tower positive or negative? _____

CD3-28

B Listen again. Choose the correct answer to complete each sentence.

1. In the past, Rome had _____ .

   a. no skyscrapers   b. only a few skyscrapers

2. The Eurosky Tower _____ .

   a. does not use sustainable energy   b. uses solar energy

3. Sergio believes that skyscrapers in Rome _____.

    a. destroy its beauty   b. add to its beauty

4. The Eurosky tower is a new tower _____ of Rome.

    a. in the residential and business district   b. in the old city

5. Sergio does not think that _____ will live in the Eurosky Tower.

    a. only rich residents   b. regular residents of Rome

6. Sergio's feeling about skyscrapers is that they _____.

    a. are bad for most cities   b. need to be a proper fit with cities

13   **EDIT.** Read the paragraph about urban sprawl. Find and correct five more errors with adverb clauses and commas. There is more than one way to correct some errors.

Urban Sprawl

Even [^though] a lot of people who work in cities would prefer to live closer to their jobs, not all can afford to do so. Although the cost of housing in cities is usually very high, a lot of people have to live outside of the city in the suburbs and commute to work. The spread of cities into outside areas is called urban sprawl. Unfortunately, urban sprawl can have serious consequences. For example, in Mexico City, developers built new buildings as fast as possible so that could make money. They also built new housing, but it was far away from the city center. It can take two to five hours to get to work every day, so a number of people have moved in with family members who live in the city. Since they are now more crowded, they are closer to their jobs. Even though many people have moved back to Mexico City, there are now a great number of empty homes in the suburbs. It will take time and careful planning to solve this problem. People will have to be patient just as urban planners try to find a solution.

14   **APPLY.**

A   Work in a group. Imagine that you are going to build an ideal city together. Choose one of the topics from the box. Discuss your decisions and preferences. Use adverb clauses.

> **Geography:** mountains, hills, beaches, oceans, lakes, islands
> **Buildings:** skyscrapers, low buildings, historical, modern, futuristic buildings
> **Transportation:** car, bus, subway, bicycles, futuristic vehicles
> **Industries:** tourism, finance, technology, arts, restaurants

Our city is only going to have public transportation. There won't be any roads for cars. Even though cars are convenient, they use too much energy . . .

B   Present your group's ideas to the class.

EXPLORE

CD3-29

1 READ the article about Amsterdam. What makes this city so safe for cycling?

Amsterdam: A Cyclist's Dream

On a Monday morning in Amsterdam, the workday began as usual for Rokus Albers. **While finishing his coffee**, Albers checked messages on his phone. Then, he grabbed his backpack and headed for the nearest railway station. He wasn't there to take the train, though. Instead, Albers chose one of the public bicycles lined up outside the station. **After unlocking the bike with a smart card,**[1] he set out for his job on the other side of the city. He joined dozens of other cyclists in the bike lanes, safely apart from car traffic.

Amsterdam wasn't always bicycle friendly. In fact, cycling used to be dangerous, especially during the second half of the twentieth century. This was a time of rapid economic growth in the Netherlands. As people's incomes rose, they were able to afford expensive goods such as cars for the first time, and driving became popular. Highways were built to accommodate all of the cars. This meant there was less space for cyclists. **Having had a long tradition of cycling**, this was a big change for the country. Unfortunately, as car traffic increased, so did the number of fatal biking accidents. Many of the cyclists were children.

The Dutch were outraged.[2] They organized huge protests in the city streets. Government officials and urban planners listened. **Hoping to solve the problem quickly**, they started to think of ways to make the city safe for cyclists again. Soon there were separate bike lanes, and some areas were permanently closed to cars. The changes were so effective that today Amsterdam is a model of biking safety for other cities around the world.

[1] **smart card:** a small plastic card that can store and process computer data
[2] **outraged:** extremely angry and shocked

► Herengracht Canal, Amsterdam, Netherlands

2 CHECK. Read the statements. Circle **T** for *true* or **F** for *false*.

1. Rokus Albers rode his own bicycle to work. **T** **F**

2. Bike riding in Amsterdam was safe throughout the twentieth century. **T** **F**

3. Driving became popular when the Dutch economy improved. **T** **F**

4. Highways helped cyclists get around the city. **T** **F**

5. The Dutch people helped make biking safe again in their country. **T** **F**

3 DISCOVER. Complete the exercises to learn about the grammar in this lesson.

A Find these sentences in the article from exercise **1** on page 345. Write the missing words.

1. _____, Albers checked messages on his phone.

2. _____,
   he set out for his job on the other side of the city.

3. _____, this was a big
   change for the country.

4. _____, they started to think of
   ways to make the city safe for cyclists again.

B Look at the reduced adverb clauses you wrote in exercise **A**. Then answer the questions.

1. Which clauses give information about time? Write the numbers of the sentences. _____ , _____

2. Which clauses express a reason? Write the numbers of the sentences. _____ , _____

3. Which words show that two of the clauses are about time? _____ , _____

4. Do the clauses about reason include a reason word? _____

◄ A woman rides
a bicycle in
Amsterdam.

LEARN

12.4 Reduced Adverb Clauses of Time

I saw the accident <u>while I was walking down the street</u>.
Adverb Clause

I saw the accident **while walking down the street**.
Reduced Adverb Clause

1. An adverb clause of time can be shortened or reduced when the subject of the adverb clause and the main clause are the same. To reduce an adverb clause of time, omit the subject and use the *-ing* form of the verb.	I always have coffee <u>before I leave home.</u> I always have coffee **before leaving home**. Lois has been very busy <u>since she started college</u>. Lois has been very busy **since starting college**.
2. When an adverb clause of time is in the progressive, omit the subject and *be* and use the *-ing* form of the verb.	I got tired <u>while I was riding my bike</u>. I got tired **while riding my bike**.
3. Adverb clauses of time that begin with *after, before, since*, and *while* can be reduced.	**After seeing me do the trick**, Mike did it, too.
4. **Be careful!** It is not possible to reduce an adverb clause if the subject of the main clause and the subject of the adverb clause are different.	✓ **After the dog barked**, I opened the door. ✗ <u>After barking</u>, I opened the door.
5. **Remember:** Use a comma when the reduced adverb clause comes first in the sentence.	**Before leaving for work**, I watered the plants.

4 Rewrite each sentence. Change the adverb clause to a reduced adverb clause. Add commas where necessary.

1. Since Amsterdam started a bike-share program, the city has improved conditions for cyclists.

   <u>Since starting a bike-share program,</u> Amsterdam has improved conditions for cyclists.

2. After the city closed the downtown area to cars, it opened the area to bikes.

   _____ the city opened the area to bikes.

3. Dutch people spend years learning bike safety rules before they get their driver's licenses.

   Dutch people spend years learning bike safety rules _____.

4. After they get a bike diploma, Dutch children can ride their bikes alone.

   _____ Dutch children can ride their bikes alone.

5. While they are taking a road test, drivers show how they watch out for cyclists.

   _____ drivers show how they watch out for cyclists.

6. Drivers must turn and open the door with their right hands before they exit the car.

   Drivers must turn and open the door with their right hands

   _____ .

7. While drivers are turning to open their doors, they look for any cyclists on the road.

_____, drivers look for any cyclists on the road.

8. After Amsterdam improved its road safety, it has become one of the world's best places to bike.

_____, Amsterdam has become one of the world's best places to bike.

12.5 Reduced Adverb Clauses of Reason

Because he felt tired, he went to bed early.
Adverb Clause

Feeling tired, he went to bed early.
Reduced Adverb Clause

1. In many cases an adverb clause of reason can be reduced. Omit the subject and *because* or *since*. Then change the verb to the *-ing* form. Put *not* before the *-ing* form of the verb to make a negative.	Because she is an only child, she is often lonely. **Being an only child**, she is often lonely. Because she was an only child, she was often lonely. **Being an only child**, she was often lonely. Since I don't know Chinese, I can't understand him. **Not knowing Chinese**, I can't understand him.
2. To reduce an adverb clause of reason in the present perfect or past perfect, change *have* or *had* to *having*.	Since she has spent all her money, she needs more. **Having spent all her money**, she needs more. Since she had spent her money, she needed more. **Having spent her money**, she needed more.
3. **Remember:** In order to reduce an adverb clause, the subject of the adverb clause and the main clause must be the same.	✓ **Because Jake won the race**, his sister was happy for him. ✗ Having won the race, his sister was happy for him.

5 Complete the sentences about the subway system in Seoul, Korea. Change the adverb clauses in parentheses to reduced adverb clauses.

1. _____ Having 316 miles of track _____, Seoul's subway system is one of the longest. (because it has 316 miles of track)

2. _____, the trains make travel around Seoul easy. (because they run every two minutes during rush hour)

3. _____, the stations are a great source of information. (since they provide digital maps and schedules)

4. _____, the mayor of Seoul lowered the price of subway fares. (because he had heard complaints about high subway fares)

5. _____, the subway cars are excellent for winter travel. (since they have heated seats)

6. _____, the subway is very convenient. (since it has opened a lot of new stations)

7. _____, the Seoul subway provides passengers with easy Internet access. (because it offers free wi-fi in stations and on subway cars)

8. _____, I want to ride the subway when I go to Seoul. (because I have read about it)

PRACTICE

6 WRITE & SPEAK.

A Read the statements. Check (✓) the statement if the adverb clause can be reduced.

_✓_ 1. After they arrived in London, Pam and Emily took a bus to their hotel.

_____ 2. After he had spent a year in Mexico, Matt spoke Spanish fluently.

_____ 3. Before Linda left for Australia, we had a party for her.

_____ 4. After he saw the pyramids outside Cairo, Ed wanted to learn more about them.

_____ 5. Jackie learned some Turkish before she moved to Istanbul.

_____ 6. Since Claudia loves to dance, her trip to Brazil during Carnival was wonderful.

_____ 7. While Cara was driving to the airport, her car broke down.

_____ 8. Because she's an art history major, Tanya really enjoyed her trip to Florence.

_____ 9. After he left Lisbon, Scott went to Madrid.

_____ 10. Since she had never been to Iceland, Anita was excited to spend a day there on her way to Moscow.

B In your notebook, rewrite the sentences you checked in exercise **A** with reduced adverb clauses.

After arriving in London, Pam and Emily took a bus to their hotel.

C In your notebook, write two more sentences with reduced adverb clauses about other cities, but don't include the names of the cities. Read your sentences to the class. Your classmates will try to guess the cities.

A: *After arriving in this city, I visited Shinjuku.*

B: *The city is Tokyo!*

7 In your notebook, combine each pair of sentences into one sentence with a reduced adverb clause. Use the words in parentheses when they are provided. Add commas where necessary.

1. She had driven everywhere for years. Ella wanted to move to a more walkable neighborhood.

   Having driven everywhere for years, Ella wanted to move to a more walkable neighborhood.

2. Ella made a decision. Ella looked for a website about walkability. (before)

3. Ella was doing some research online. She found a "walkability" website. (while)

4. The website considers factors such as walking distance to stores and public transportation. It gives a walkability score. (after)

5. Some communities had gotten bad walkability scores. These communities made changes to improve their scores.

6. They have everything they need nearby. That's why Ella's family is happy in their new home.

7. Ella's children walk home from school. Her children can stop at a park and play. (while)

8. Ella had been dependent on a car for years. Ella is happy that she doesn't need one now.

8 **EDIT.** Read the paragraph. Find and correct six more errors with reduced adverb clauses and commas. There is more than one way to correct some errors.

City Life

After ~~grow~~ ^growing up in the suburbs, many young people in the United States are choosing to live in cities. Have attended college in lively cities, a lot of young people don't want to give up their urban lifestyles after they graduate. Cities offer a variety of interesting things to do plus the convenience of having everything nearby. After experience city life, many young people find living in the suburbs boring. Transportation is another factor that makes cities attractive to them. Having spent their early years riding around in the family car a lot of young people prefer to get around on public transportation, by bike, or on foot. These forms of transportation give them more independence. Being more independent, their parents are proud of them. There are other benefits, too. For example, walking can be a social activity. While friends are walking together, they can have a conversation or stop and have coffee. Since there are sidewalks, bike lanes, and public transportation, there's no need to have a car in many cities. Not own cars, young people don't have to spend money on parking and gas. Whenever they want to leave the city they can rent a car or take a bus or train. Cities offer everything that many young people want these days.

9 APPLY.

A Look at the walkability map of San Francisco, California. In your notebook, write answers to the questions below. Use reduced adverb clauses and the words in parentheses in your answers. More than one answer may be possible.

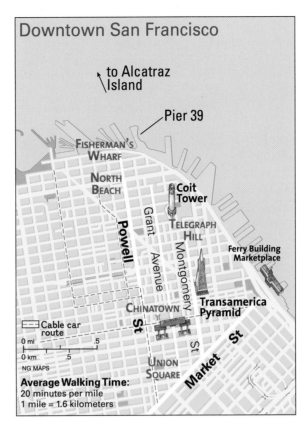

1. I'm leaving the Transamerica Pyramid now. How long will I need to walk to Coit Tower? (after)

   After leaving the Transamerica Pyramid, you will need about 15-20 minutes to walk to Coit Tower.

2. I want to go to Fisherman's Wharf after I leave Union Square. How can I get there quickly? (after)

3. What will I see while I am traveling from Union Square to Fisherman's Wharf? (while)

4. I'm going to walk from Powell Street to Telegraph Hill. Which streets or avenues will I cross on my way there? (while)

5. I'm planning to walk from Ferry Building Marketplace to Chinatown. What will I see before I arrive there? (before)

6. I'm having dinner with a friend tomorrow night at Pier 39. I hear there are a lot of nice shops there. Should we plan to spend some time shopping there before we have dinner? (yes)

B In your notebook, draw a map of part of your city or hometown. Label some of the main streets and important places.

C Work with a partner. Ask and answer questions about your maps from exercise **B**. Use reduced adverb clauses and the questions in exercise **A** to help you.

A: *What will I see while I'm walking along the river?*
B: *Some boats and a lot of cyclists.*

Charts
12.1–12.3,
12.5

1 Read the sentences about the city of Pontevedra in Spain. Underline the adverb clauses and circle the reduced adverb clauses. Add commas where necessary.

1. Although Pontevedra has only around 85,000 people traffic congestion used to be a problem.

2. Being the major city in the region it has attracted a lot of commuters.

3. Since it now has a free bike-lending service the city has set a new lower speed limit for cars.

4. The city council designed a special map with walking times so that the city would become more walkable.

5. People can leave their cars at one of the free parking lots whenever they visit the city.

6. Though people disliked the new policies at first they now support them.

7. Being a small city Pontevedra was never very well known outside of the region.

8. Now that it is such a walkable city it has become popular with urban planners.

Charts
12.1–12.4

2 Read the sentences about London, England. Circle the correct word(s) to complete each sentence.

1. London started making drivers pay to enter the city **so that / just as** there would be less traffic.

2. **Whenever / Although** you plan to drive into London, try to pay the charge before you go. It's cheaper.

3. **As long as / Just as** people had gotten used to the charge, the price increased.

4. **So that / Though** drivers have to pay on weekdays, they don't pay on weekends.

5. Most drivers pay the charge **so that / whenever** they avoid a large fine.

6. **While spending / Having spent** hours in traffic in the past, taxi drivers like the charge.

7. **Even though / Since** there was less traffic in London after the charge, it seemed like it was working well.

8. **Although / Since** there were fewer cars in London at first, the amount of traffic has been increasing lately.

Charts
12.1–12.3

3 LISTEN & SPEAK.

CD3-30

A Listen to the podcast. Check (✓) the names of smart cities you hear.

☐ Amsterdam   ☐ Detroit   ☐ St. Petersburg   ☐ Beijing

☐ Cairo   ☐ Dubai   ☐ Stockholm   ☐ Yokohama

B Listen again. Choose the correct answer to complete each statement.

1. Smart cities have certain things in common _____.
   a. since people agree on everything
   b. although people don't agree on everything

2. Whenever a city invests in its people and new communication technology, _____.
   a. it becomes more expensive
   b. it creates more jobs and improves the quality of life

3. Smart cities want to offer a good quality of living _____.
   a. so that more skilled professionals move to them
   b. even though they pay workers less money

4. Being a smart city, _____.
   a. Stockholm pays its workers a little less than most cities
   b. Stockholm offers its residents a good quality of life

5. Smart cities try to use natural resources carefully _____.
   a. so that they will last a long time
   b. although they show few signs of running out

C Work with a partner. Compare your answers from exercise **B**.

Charts 12.1, 12.2, 12.4, 12.5

4 EDIT. Read the paragraph about Melbourne, Australia. Find and correct seven more errors with adverb clauses, reduced adverb clauses, and commas. There is more than one way to correct some errors.

Melbourne, Australia

though
Even ^Sydney is more famous, Melbourne, Australia is one of the most livable cities in the world. What makes a city livable? Excellent education, quality health care, good roads, and public transportation are essential. People need to feel safe that they can walk around day or night without feeling afraid. Even though it has a great tram system, people can get around Melbourne easily. Having so many restaurants, unique shops, and music festivals Melbourne offers a wide variety of leisure activities. Although it's located on the beautiful Yarra River, it's perfect for water sports. Melbourne has great weather, too. Whenever they are in the mood residents can go to the beach. Though Melbourne has so much to offer, it has visitors from all over the world. After come to the city, people don't want to leave.

Charts 12.1–12.5

5 SPEAK & WRITE.

A Work in a group. Discuss the city or town that you are in now. As a group, write as many sentences as you can about the city. Use adverb clauses and reduced adverb clauses.

Although Washington, DC, is a big, crowded city, it feels very livable to me.

B Share your sentences with the class. Ask and answer follow-up questions.

1 READ & NOTICE THE GRAMMAR.

A Think about a city you know well. What is your favorite place in that city? What is your least favorite part of it? Tell a partner about it. Then read the text.

A Vital Restoration

Like any city, Seoul can be a stressful place to live. City residents living with crowds and pollution need outdoor spaces to experience nature. This is why the Cheonggyecheon project, a new park built around an ancient stream, has a great design.

Before the park was built, the stream was covered by a big, noisy highway. Having lived near the highway at that time, I remember it. It was not a nice place to walk around because there was so much traffic. In 2003, the city began removing the highway and building a park next to the stream.

Whenever I go for a walk in that area now, I feel refreshed. Seeing the greenery and flowing stream, I can leave behind the stress of city life. It's a great place to hang out with friends or to sit and relax. Now that Cheonggyecheon is such a nice park, people visit it more often and take more walks.

Even though the project cost a lot of money, I think it was worth it. Having brought beautiful scenery to Seoul, Cheonggyecheon was good for the city. Other cities should build similar parks so that their residents can have a beautiful place to go and relax.

GRAMMAR FOCUS

In the text, the writer uses the following types of adverb clauses:

Clauses of time to tell when the action or event in the main clause happens.
Before the park was built, the stream was covered by a big, noisy highway.

Clauses of contrast to express an idea that is the opposite of the idea in the main clause.
Even though the project cost a lot of money, I think it was worth it.

Clauses of reason to explain the idea in the main clause.
It was not a nice place to walk around **because there was so much traffic.**

Clauses of purpose to express a reason or purpose for something.
Other cities should build similar parks **so that their residents can have a beautiful place to go and relax.**

B Read the text in exercise **A** again. Notice the adverb clauses. Find and write two more reduced adverb clauses in the first column of the chart. Then write each as a full adverb clause in the second column. Then work with a partner and compare your answers.

Reduced Adverb Clauses	Changed into Full Adverb Clauses
Having lived near the highway . . .	Since I lived near the highway . . .

C Read the text in exercise **A** again. What are the positive and negative aspects of the project? Write them in the chart. Then discuss your ideas with a partner.

Positive Aspects	Negative Aspects
adds beauty to the city	was very expensive

2 BEFORE YOU WRITE.

Choose a city project, for example, a park, a bridge, a plaza, or a building. What are the positive and negative aspects about it? In your notebook, make a chart like the one in exercise **1C**. Complete the chart with your ideas.

3 WRITE about the city project you chose. Write three or four paragraphs. Do you think it has improved the city? Explain why or why not. Use your chart from exercise **2** and the text in exercise **1A** to help you.

> **WRITING FOCUS** Using *Like* to Make a Comparison
>
> Use *like* + a noun phrase to tell your reader that the subject in the main clause and the noun after *like* are similar. Remember to put a comma after the phrase with *like*.
>
> ***Like any city,*** *Seoul can be a stressful place to live.*

4 SELF ASSESS. Read your text. Underline the adverb clauses. Then use the checklist to assess your work.

☐ I used adverb clauses of time and contrast correctly. [12.1, 12.2]

☐ I used adverb clauses of reason and purpose correctly. [12.3]

☐ I used reduced adverb clauses of time and reason correctly. [12.4, 12.5]

☐ I used *like* in a prepositional phrase to show similarity. [WRITING FOCUS]

13 Choices

Conditionals

▶ People trying to decide which way to go in the middle of multiple waterfalls (Plitvice Lakes National Park, Croatia)

EXPLORE

CD4-02

1 **READ** the article about why people do not always make logical decisions. What often influences the decisions we make?

Making Decisions: Are you in control?

It's vacation time. You are planning a trip to visit your family, so you compare airlines. You learn that 87 percent of Flyright flights arrive on time and that Skyway flights are late 13 percent of the time. Which airline will you choose the next time you fly?

If you are like most people, you will probably choose Flyright. It seems more efficient than Skyway. However, **if you stop and think, you will find no difference between the two flight records**. Then, why did Flyright seem better at first? Psychologists explain that we are greatly influenced by the way we see information. For example, **if an option[1] is presented in a positive way, people usually prefer it**. That's why an 87 percent success rate seems better than a 13 percent failure rate. **Unless we think carefully, we don't realize the facts** are the same. Instead, we make a decision based on our first reaction.

The way we perceive[2] information greatly affects our decisions whether we are buying toothpaste or a car. It also has a powerful effect in politics and on the way people vote. Studies show that in the United States, people prefer candidates who talk about political issues in positive, encouraging ways. A politician's physical appearance matters, too. Voters like people who appear to be good leaders.

Even if we think our decisions are completely rational,[3] they are not. We make a lot of choices because information is presented in a certain way. However, **if we know this, we will be able to do something about it in the future**. We can try to think more seriously about our choices and consider them from different points of view. In that way, we can better control our decisions, both large and small.

[1] **option:** a choice

[2] **perceive:** become aware of something through the senses; understand something

[3] **rational:** showing clear, logical thought

2 CHECK. Read the statements. Circle **T** for *true* or **F** for *false*.

1. Flyright has a better flight record than Skyway.   **T**   **F**

2. We often make decisions because the options are presented to us in certain ways.   **T**   **F**

3. A politician's appearance is not important to voters.   **T**   **F**

4. We think our decisions are rational, but they aren't always.   **T**   **F**

5. There is nothing that we can do to control our decision making.   **T**   **F**

3 DISCOVER. Complete the exercises to learn about the grammar in this lesson.

A Find these sentences in the article from exercise **1**. Write the missing words.

1. _____ like most people, you will probably choose Flyright.

2. However, _____ , you will find no difference between the two flight records.

3. . . . _____ in a positive way, people usually prefer it.

4. _____ our decisions are completely rational, they are not.

5. However, _____ ,we will be able to do something about it in the future.

B Look at the sentences in the box. Then answer the questions.

> a. Unless we think carefully, we don't realize the facts are the same.
> b. However, if we know this, we will be able to do something about it in the future.

1. Which sentence talks about a future result?   Sentence a.   Sentence b.

2. Which sentence talks about a fact that is generally true?   Sentence a.   Sentence b.

3. Which verb form is used after *if* and *unless*?

     a. *will* + the base form of the verb   b. the simple present

▲ **Sunrise in Times Square, New York City**

LEARN

13.1 Present Real Conditionals

1. A conditional sentence describes a condition and a result. The *if* clause gives the condition. The main clause tells the result.	If I eat late at night, I don't sleep well. *If Clause (Condition)* *Main Clause (Result)*
Present real conditionals describe facts, general truths, habits, or routines.	If it's very cold, my car doesn't start. If I take the train, I always bring a book. If the weather is nice, I walk to work.
2. A present tense verb is used in both clauses.	If you **talk** to friends, you **make** better decisions. **Do** you **make** better decisions if you **get** advice? If Tom **is** on the phone, he**'s talking** to Joe.
3. The *if* clause can come before or after the main clause with no change in meaning. Use a comma when it comes first.	I listen to the news in the morning **if I have time.** **If I have time in the morning,** I listen to the news.
4. A conditional clause can also begin with *unless*. *Unless* has the same meaning as *If . . . not*.	If I don't sleep ten hours, I feel tired. **Unless I sleep ten hours,** I feel tired.
5. A conditional clause can also begin with *even if*. *Even if* is used when the information in the main clause is unexpected or surprising.	**Even if Ari sleeps only five hours,** he has a lot of energy. I feel tired **even if I sleep for eight hours.**
6. In real conditionals, *when* can be used instead of *if*. The meaning is similar.	**If he has time**, he practices the piano. **When he has time**, he practices the piano.

4 Complete the exercises.

A Read each statement. Then choose the statement that is closest in meaning.

1. If my friends are wearing a certain brand of jeans, I buy the same brand.

    a. My friends wear a certain brand of jeans, so I wear the same brand.

    b. I buy a certain brand of jeans, so my friends wear them, too.

2. I don't go in a store if it is empty.

    a. When a store is empty, I don't go in.

    b. When I don't go into a store, nobody else does, either.

3. If I make a bad decision once, I don't make the same decision a second time.

    a. When I make a bad decision, I don't do it a second time.

    b. Once I made a bad decision, but I didn't make the same mistake again.

4. When I need advice, I ask a friend.

    a. My friends know I need advice when I ask.

    b. If I have a problem, I ask my friends for advice.

B Complete each sentence with the correct form of the verbs in parentheses.

1. If my friends _____drive_____ (drive) nice cars, I _____want_____ (want) one, too.

2. If a store _____ (have) an attractive window display, I _____ (go) in.

3. If I _____ (see) designer labels, I _____ (not be) impressed.

4. When my dad _____ (make) a mistake, he _____ (try) to correct it.

5. If my sister _____ (need) to make an important decision, she always _____ (think) carefully first.

6. If I _____ (buy) something that doesn't fit, I _____ (return) it.

7. When I _____ (have) a question about a product, I _____ (ask) a salesperson.

8. If I _____ (shop) when I'm tired, I _____ (not make) good decisions.

C **SPEAK.** Work with a partner. Look at the statements in exercises **B**. Are these statements true for you? Why, or why not?

Statement 1 is not true for me. If my friends have nice cars, I don't care. I want a car that's safe and doesn't use a lot of gas.

5 Complete the exercises.

A Circle the correct word(s) to complete each sentence.

1. (**If**)/ **Unless** you think you make rational decisions, you are mistaken.

2. Some people go shopping every weekend **if / even if** they don't need anything.

3. We often make decisions based on our emotions **when / unless** we don't have a lot of information.

4. We often buy brands that we know **even if / if** others are less expensive.

5. People often do something **if / even if** they see other people doing it.

6. **If / Unless** the salespeople in a store are rude to me, I leave.

7. **If / Unless** we understand the influences on our decisions, they continue to influence us.

8. I have friends who always wear stylish shoes **even if / if** they hurt their feet.

B **SPEAK.** Work with a partner. Complete the sentences with information about yourself.

1. When I need to make an important decision, I . . .

2. If someone gives me a gift I don't like, I . . .

3. Unless . . ., I don't buy it.

4. Even if I'm very tired, I . . .

When I need to make an important decision, I ask my friends and family for advice.

13.2 Future Real Conditionals

1. Future real conditionals describe possible conditions in the future and real results.	If he passes the exam, he will be very happy.
	    Condition Future Result
	He won't graduate unless he passes.
	    Future Result Condition

2. Use the simple present in the *if* clause. Use *will* or a form of *be going to* in the main clause.	If you **go** to Caracas next year, you **will like** it. If I **finish** by 8:00, **I'm going to meet** my friends.
3. Other modals (*can, have to, could, may, might, must, should*) can be used in the *if* clause or main clause.	If I don't have to work late, I **may go** to a movie. If I **can't do** the work, I'll tell you.
4. Imperatives can also be used in the main clause.	If you go to the store, **buy some coffee.**
5. **Remember:** *Unless* means *If . . .not.*	**Unless** we leave soon, we'll be late.

6 Complete the exercises.

A Complete each sentence with the correct form of the verbs in parentheses. Use *will*.

1. Unless you _____ make _____ (make) a decision, someone else
   _____ will choose _____ (choose) for you.

2. If you _____ (make) the wrong decision, it _____ (hurt)
   your future.

3. If a person _____ (worry) too much about always making the right
   decision, it _____ (not be) good for his or her health.

4. If someone _____ (think) too much about making the best decision, he or
   she _____ (have) a hard time making any decision at all.

5. If you _____ (not sleep) enough, it _____ (be) harder
   for you to make important decisions.

6. Unless you _____ (ask) someone who knows you for advice, you
   _____ (not get) advice that is right for you.

7. If you _____ (be) afraid of change, you _____ (not try)
   anything new.

8. If a person _____ (keep) an open mind, he or she _____
   (learn) new things.

B **SPEAK.** Work with a partner. Compare your answers from exercise **A**. Then discuss where
other modals can be used in the sentences.

*I think "might" can be used in number 1. Unless you make a decision, someone else might
choose for you.*

7 Paulo is trying to decide whether or not to do an internship. Use the words to write future real conditionals. Add commas where necessary.

1. Condition: Paulo / take the internship   Result: he / get some useful job experience

   If _Paulo takes the internship, he will get some useful job experience_ .

2. Condition: his coworkers / teach him new skills   Result: he / be interested

   _____ if _____ .

3. Condition: he / do the internship   Result: it / be good for his résumé

   If _____ .

4. Condition: he / accept the position   Result: he / meet new people

   If _____ .

5. Condition: the work / be physically demanding   Result: he / not get in shape

   _____ unless _____ .

6. Condition: he / have a paying job   Result: he / not be able to pay his bills

   _____ unless _____ .

7. Condition: his work hours / be 7:00 a.m. to 7:00 p.m.   Result: he / not accept the offer

   _____ if _____ .

8. Condition: he / enjoy the internship   Result: he / apply for the job

   If _____ .

PRACTICE

8 Put the words in the correct order to make sentences. Put the conditional clause first in 2–4. Put the conditional clause second in 5–8. Add commas where necessary.

1. a career that matches your talents / you / your job / will be more enjoyable / choose / if

   If you choose a career that matches your talents, your job will be more
   enjoyable. OR Your job will be more enjoyable if you choose a career that
   matches your talents.

2. have / don't realize it / we each / we / a personal work style / even if

   _____

   _____

3. a set schedule / you / will be happier / in a job that has flexible hours / if / don't like / you

   _____

   _____

4. you / a job that requires travel / don't take / to be away from home / don't like / if

_____

_____

5. helps you to succeed / if / a stressful job / a lot of pressure / good for you / might be

_____

_____

6. if / don't choose / important to you / making a lot of money / is / a low-paying career

_____

_____

7. you / excited about the job / the interviewer / won't be / seem / interested in you / unless

_____

_____

8. it / you / is / know all of your career possibilities / hard to make a decision / unless

_____

_____

9 WRITE & SPEAK.

A In your notebook, write three sentences about the careers in the box. Then write one sentence about another career that you know about. Use conditionals.

| accounting | business | computer science | education | engineering | medicine |

If you are good with numbers, you might like to work in accounting.

B Work with a partner. Share your sentences from exercise **A**. Do you agree with your partner's ideas? Why, or why not?

10 EDIT. Read the paragraph. Find and correct six more errors with conditionals.

      If
~~Even if~~ you don't want to work in an office every day, you should consider starting your own business. That's right, you can be your own boss! If you have a hobby that you are very good at, you might be able to earn a living doing it. For example, if you will have a talent for web design, you could sell your services to small companies. To get started, choose a company that you know about and show them some examples of web pages you've designed. Unless they like your work, offer to design a web page for them for a small fee. If you will do a good job the first time, they will probably hire you again. They may also recommend you to other businesses. Soon you'll have a lot of customers contacting you, and you'll be running your own business. If you don't make a lot of money, you'll feel satisfied and successful. You will also be doing something you love. Running your own business can be a lot of work, but it's worth it. If people will enjoy their jobs, they are usually happier. You won't know for sure unless you are going to try.

11 WRITE & SPEAK.

A Look at the information in the chart about the advantages and disadvantages of having your own business. In your notebook, write 6–8 sentences. Use present and future real conditionals and the information from the chart.

Having Your Own Business	
Advantages	Disadvantages
be your own boss	work 60–80 hours a week
have a lot of freedom	not have much free time
do something you love	take risks
make a lot of money	not have any paid vacation time

If you have your own business, you can be your own boss.

B Work in a group. Discuss this question: Would you prefer to have your own business or work for someone else? Give reasons. Use present and future real conditionals.

12 LISTEN.

CD4-03

A Listen to the talk about making decisions. Check (✓) the things that the speaker says may influence the decision-making process.

☐ the place ☐ eating ☐ too many choices ☐ color

☐ the time of day ☐ advice from friends ☐ exercise ☐ language

CD4-03

B Listen again. Then read the statements. Circle **T** for *true* or **F** for *false*.

1. It's often not helpful to spend a long time making a decision. **T   F**

2. The best time to make decisions is early afternoon. **T   F**

3. People should take a relaxing break before they make a decision. **T   F**

4. Eating before making a decision will make you tired. **T   F**

5. It's better to make emotional decisions in your native language. **T   F**

13 APPLY.

A Read each situation. Then in your notebook, write 2–3 sentences about each situation. Use conditionals.

1. Harry is thinking of getting a motorcycle. It's less expensive than a car, but a car is safer.

   He'll save money if he gets a motorcycle.

2. Sophia is about to graduate from college. She would like to do volunteer work abroad for a year. However, her friends are going to graduate school or are getting jobs.

3. Veronica is taking a semester off from college to travel around Brazil for five months. She doesn't speak Portuguese. She is trying to decide if she should travel alone, with a friend, or with a tour group.

B Work in a group. Discuss the consequences for each situation in exercise **A** and the best decision for each person.

EXPLORE

CD4-04

1 READ the article about the debate over animals from the past. What is the main question in this debate?

Back to Life

Woolly mammoths, saber-toothed cats. These animals went extinct[1] thousands of years ago. Today, more animals continue to go extinct, and every year the number increases. **Scientists wish they could change the situation.** Some of them would like to bring extinct animals back to life. Experiments with a few species of birds and frogs suggest that this might be possible someday. Is it a good idea to revive[2] extinct animals? Some people say yes, but others don't agree.

The Argument for Revival

Reviving some species could help the environment. Consider, for example, the woolly mammoths. They lived on grass-covered land in Siberia, Russia, 12,000 years ago. However, after mammoths disappeared, the land turned into tundra.[3] Not many plants can grow there now. **If large numbers of mammoths were brought back, they could improve the land.** Scientists would also benefit. **If researchers could study a large variety of revived animals, they would learn a lot**; and much of the information could be used to help living species.

The Argument against Revival

Natural habitats change over time. **Would animals survive if they were revived? Would they die without their old habitats? Would they be a danger to creatures living in those regions now?** Perhaps they would be harmed by hunting or pollution and die out again. In addition, **if scientists focused on extinct species, they might not have time to spend on living species.**

There are still many questions about extinct species revival. **Even if scientists had more answers, people would continue to debate the issues.**

[1] **extinct:** no longer living
[2] **revive:** bring back to life
[3] **tundra:** treeless flat land found mostly in the Arctic Circle

A museum worker checks the hair on this woolly mammoth replica. (Victoria, British Columbia, Canada)

2 CHECK. Answer the questions. Write complete sentences.

1. What do woolly mammoths and saber-toothed cats have in common?

   _____

2. What is happening to more animals every year?

   _____

3. How has the ancient woolly mammoth's habitat changed?

   _____

4. What are some dangers that revived species might experience today?

   _____

3 DISCOVER. Complete the exercises to learn about the grammar in this lesson.

A Read each sentence from the article in exercise **1**. Then read the statements below. Write **T** for *true* or **F** for *false*.

1. Scientists wish they could change the situation.

   _____ Scientists are not sure that they can change the situation.

2. If large numbers of mammoths were brought back, they could improve the land.

   _____ It is certain that large numbers of mammoths will be brought back.

3. If researchers could study a large variety of revived animals, they would learn a lot.

   _____ Researchers can't study a large variety of revived animals now.

4. Even if scientists had more answers, people would continue to debate the issues.

   _____ Scientists don't have all of the answers now.

B Look at sentences 2–4 in exercise **A** again. Circle **T** for *true* or **F** for *false*.

1. In sentences 2 and 4, the simple past is used in the *if* clause.   T   F

2. In sentences 2–4, the simple past is used in the main clause.   T   F

3. In sentence 2, the verb form in the *if* clause describes an action in the past.   T   F

4. In sentences 2–4, the sentences are about real situations.   T   F

LEARN

13.3 Present and Future Unreal Conditionals

1. Present and future unreal conditionals describe situations that are untrue, impossible, or imaginary.	**If I lived in Rio de Janeiro,** I would go to the beach every day. (I don't live in Rio de Janiero.)
2. The *if* clause gives the condition, and the main clause gives the result.	If I lived downtown, I would walk to work.
	If Clause (Condition) Main Clause (Result)
Use the simple past in the *if* clause. Use *would* + the base form of the verb in the main clause. (*Could* and *might* can also be used in the main clause. *Could* is sometimes used in the *if* clause.)	**Would** we **save** money if we **bought** a smaller car? What **would** you **do** if you **won** the lottery? If you **didn't have** to work, you **could go** with us. If I **could travel** anywhere, I'**d go** to Peru.
3. **Be careful!** The verb after *if* is simple past, but the situation or event refers to the present or future.	If I **had a dog**, I would name it Rufus. If you **came here tomorrow**, we would have fun.
4. Use *were* for all subjects in the *if* clause. In informal conversation, *was* is often used for *I*, *he*, *she*, and *it*.	If **I were** rich, I would live somewhere different.
5. **Be careful!** The contracted *'d* has two meanings: *would* and *had*.	**He'd come** with us if he had the time. **He'd already left** when we arrived.
6. **Remember:** Use a comma when the *if* clause comes first in a sentence.	She'd take art classes **if she had more free time.** **If she had more free time,** she'd take art classes.

4 Complete the sentences with the correct form of the verbs in parentheses. Use *would*.

1. If extinct animals _____ *were* _____ (be) brought back to life, there _____ *would be* _____ (be) consequences.

2. Most people _____ (not believe) it if they _____ (see) a dinosaur.

3. Animals that have gone extinct _____ (cause) problems if they _____ (be) revived.

4. What _____ (happen) if woolly mammoths _____ (live) in Siberia now?

5. _____ it _____ (improve) the land if woolly mammoths _____ (be) alive today?

6. If my government _____ (spend) money on reviving extinct species, I _____ (be) unhappy.

7. If I _____ (be) a scientist, I _____ (be) interested in researching extinct species.

8. I _____ (major) in biology if I _____ (get) into a good program.

9. _____ fewer species _____ (go) extinct if people

_____ (take) better care of the environment?

10. It _____ (be) better for the environment if scientists _____
(spend) their energy on living species, not extinct species.

13.4 *Wish* + Simple Past/*Would*

1. Use the simple past or past progressive after *wish* to talk about present or future situations that you would like to be different.	We wish we **lived** in a nicer place. I wish I **didn't have to work** tomorrow. I wish I **were sitting** on a beach right now.
2. Use *were* for all subjects after *wish*. *Was* is often used in informal conversation.	**I wish** it **were** warmer. Then, I could go swimming. I can't pay my bills. **I wish I were** rich.
3. *Could* (not *can*) can be used after *wish*.	I wish I **could go** to the party next week.
4. Use *would* + the base form of the verb when you are dissatisfied or unhappy with something or someone.	**I wish** it **would stop** raining. **I wish** you **wouldn't leave** your dishes in the sink.
5. **Be careful!** Do not confuse *wish* with *hope*. *Wish* expresses a regret for something that will not happen. *Hope* expresses a desire for something that might happen. The simple past is used with *wish*, while the simple present is used with *hope*.	**I wish** I **did** better on tests, but I never do. **I hope** I **do** better on this test. I've studied a lot.

5 Complete the exercises.

A Circle the correct word(s) to complete each statement.

1. I wish I **am /(were)** a scientist.

2. I hope I **am helping / were helping** the environment.

3. I wish I **do / did** more interesting work every day.

4. I hope I **can find / could find** a better job.

5. I wish I **can work / could work** on a team.

6. I wish I **am sitting / were sitting** outside right now.

7. I wish I **live / lived** someplace else.

8. I wish my parents **called / calls** me more often.

9. I wish I **have / had** a fancy car.

10. I wish our teacher wouldn't **gave / give** us a lot of tests.

B **SPEAK.** Work with a partner. Say which of the statements in exercise **A** are true for you. Change the other statements to make them true for you.

Number 1 isn't true for me. I wish I were a musician, not a scientist.

PRACTICE

6 Complete the text about keeping wild animals as pets. Use present and future unreal conditionals and *wish* + the simple past or *would*. More than one answer is sometimes correct.

Wild Pets

Sometimes people find animals in the wild that are injured or orphaned and want to bring them home and keep them as pets. However, if they (1) _____understood_____ (understand) some of the issues involved with keeping wild animals as pets, they (2) _____ (change) their minds. One issue is cost. Keeping certain kinds of animals can be very expensive. For example, some people want pet tigers, but if these people (3) _____ (realize) that tigers need about 5000 pounds (2 metric tons) of meat a year, they (4) _____ (think) again. Safety is another issue. Even if such people (5) _____ (know) a lot about wild animals, they (6) _____ (not be) able to keep the animals safe and healthy. They and other people might also be in danger, since attacks by wild animals are common. This can be a problem for both the pet and the owner.

Different countries have different laws about keeping wild animals as pets. For example, in England people are sometimes permitted to keep owls as pets. However, some people wish this (7) _____ (change). Animal rights groups wish the laws (8) _____ (be) stricter. Many people argue that if people (9) _____ (stop) buying and selling wild animals, it (10) _____ (help) more endangered species survive.

▼ A trainer with Ada the owl in Aragon, Spain. In some countries such as England, some people are permitted to keep owls as pets.

7 Read the sentences. What does each person wish for? Write a sentence about each person. Use *wish* + the simple past or *wish* + *would*.

1. Kate really wants a pet owl and is sad because she doesn't have one.

   Kate wishes she had a pet owl.

2. Len sees an injured deer in the road and doesn't know how to help it.

   _____

3. Josh's car broke down, and he doesn't have his cell phone with him.

   _____

4. Cars drive fast down Molly's street. She thinks it's very dangerous.

   _____

5. Jen wants to go to Australia, but her parents won't let her.

   _____

6. Meg can't sleep because her neighbors play loud music every night.

   _____

7. Anna's sister borrows her clothes without asking first. This bothers Anna very much.

   _____

8. It bothers Roland that his roommate never cleans their apartment.

   _____

8 WRITE & SPEAK.

A Complete the sentences to make them true about yourself.

1. I wish I _____.

2. I wish people _____.

3. I wish my family _____.

4. I wish my neighbors _____.

5. My family wishes I _____.

6. My family hopes I _____.

B Work with a partner. Share your sentences from exercise **A**. Ask your partner follow-up questions.

A: *I wish I could play the guitar really well.*

B: *Really? Do you want to be in a band?*

9 WRITE & SPEAK.

A Read the situations. Then give advice for each.
Use *If I were you . . . .*

1. I don't feel well, but I have two final exams tomorrow.

   If I were you, I'd try to take the exams on another day.

2. I really want to get a cat, but my roommate is allergic to them.

   _____

3. My parents want me to go to college next year, but I want to get a job so that I can make money.

   _____

4. My neighbor keeps parking his car in my parking space. I've already spoken to him once about it.

   _____

5. I'm very tired, but I haven't finished my assignment for tomorrow yet.

   _____

6. I have a friend who is always late. Sometimes I have to spend a long time waiting for her. It's very annoying!

   _____

7. I'm supposed to turn in an important assignment tomorrow for one of my classes, but I don't think I can finish it on time.

   _____

8. One of my coworkers is always interrupting me to tell me about his problems. I want to help him, but I can't get any work done!

   _____

B Think of three problems that you have. Write sentences about them.

   My roommate stays up late every night watching movies. This is a

   problem for me because I have to get up early every morning.

   _____

   _____

   _____

C Work with a partner. Share your problems from exercise **B**. Take turns giving each other advice. Use *If I were you . . . .*

   A: *My roommate stays up late every night listening to music. This is a problem for me because I have to get up early every morning.*

   B: *If I were you, I would talk to him first. If he doesn't stop, I would move out.*

10 **PRONUNCIATION.** Read the chart and listen to the examples. Then complete the exercises.

> CD4-05

| PRONUNCIATION | Contractions of *Would* and *Would Not* |

Would and *would not* are often contracted after pronouns in conversation.

Examples: **Full Pronunciation**

I **would** get a dog if I could.
You **would** like him if you knew him.
I **would not** open the door if I were you.
I **would not** read it even if I had the time.

Contraction

I**'d** get a dog if I could.
You**'d** like him if you knew him.
I **wouldn't** open the door if I were you.
I **wouldn't** read it even if I had the time.

The pronunciation of *it'd* sounds like /itəd/.

It would be nice if you came.

It'd be nice if you came.

> CD4-06

A Listen to the the statements. Write the full form of the missing words you hear.

1. If scientists could revive extinct animals, _____it would_____ be interesting to see them.

2. _____ help the environment if all species were preserved.

3. If extinct animals were brought back to life, _____ be happy.

4. _____ want to put more creatures on the planet if it were possible.

5. _____ be selfish if I wanted to see all the extinct animals revived.

6. If someone asked me to support a de-extinction project, _____ do it.

7. _____ help the environment more if we used fewer natural resources.

8. _____ be good for society if people shared more.

B Work with a partner. Take turns reading the sentences from exercise **A** aloud. Use the contracted forms of *would* and *would not*.

11 **WRITE & SPEAK.**

A Complete each sentence according to your own opinion and ideas. Use *would* or *would not* and an appropriate verb.

1. If scientists could revive extinct species, it __would be / wouldn't be__ useful.

2. If we released captive animals from zoos, they _____ in the wild.

3. If someone gave me a fur coat, I _____ it.

4. If I knew that a company harmed animals, I _____ their products.

5. If people were vegetarians, they _____ healthier lives.

6. If I found an injured bird, I _____ it as a pet.

7. There _____ less pollution if we used fewer natural resources.

8. If people shared more resources, it _____ the environment.

B Work with a partner. Compare your sentences from exercise **A**. Explain your ideas and opinions. Practice using the contracted forms of *would* and *would not*.

If scientists could revive extinct species, it'd be useful. They might learn things that could help endangered species.

12 WRITE & SPEAK.

A Read the sentences. Then rewrite each sentence with a present or future unreal conditional. Add commas where necessary. Sometimes there is more than one correct way to rewrite the sentence.

1. People want to keep wild animals as pets because they don't understand the consequences.

   If people understood the consequences, they would not want to keep wild animals as pets. OR People wouldn't want to keep wild animals as pets if they understood the consequences.

2. My sister is allergic to dogs, so we can't get one.

   _____

3. I can't go to the movies tonight because I have to work late.

   _____

4. Nick wants to take guitar lessons, but he doesn't have the time.

   _____

5. I'd like to walk to work every day, but I don't live near my office.

   _____

6. Lila isn't going to run in the race because she isn't in shape.

   _____

7. Tom and Sarah don't need a new car, so they aren't going to buy one.

   _____

8. I don't feel well, so I'm not going to go to the gym this afternoon.

   _____

B In your notebook, write three sentences about yourself. Use present or future unreal conditionals.

If my sister lived closer, I could see her more often.

C Work with a partner. Share your sentences from exercise **B**. Ask follow-up questions.

A: *If my sister lived closer, I could see her more often.*

B: *Where does she live?*

A: *In San Diego. I wish she didn't live so far away. I really miss her.*

13 **EDIT.** Read the conversation. Find and correct five more errors with conditionals and *wish*.

A: If someone on the street offered you money, ~~you would~~ *would you* take it?

B: No, I don't.

A: Why not? I often wish a stranger would give me money.

B: I guess I don't trust strangers. If a stranger tries to give me money, I'd think it was a trick. Nobody just gives money away without a reason.

A: What would you do if money would fall out of a window?

B: That would never happen either.

A: I guess you're right. I wish things like that happen, but they never do.

B: I know. I wish making money is that easy, but it's not.

14 **READ & LISTEN.**

A Read the text about sharing money. If a friend had to share $100 with you, how much do you think you would probably get?

What would *you* do?

What would you do if a stranger on the street offered you some money to share with a friend? Would you accept it? Would you give your friend half the money even if you wanted to keep more? Do you think your friend would accept less than half?

According to some economists, if people were being completely rational, they would offer as little money as possible. Researchers wanted to test that idea, so they did an experiment. Surprisingly, they found that when most people were given money to share, they offered their partners between 40 and 50 percent of it. Other studies showed that when people offered their partners less than 30 percent, their partners refused to take it. The results of the experiment clearly show that fairness plays an important role in people's decisions about sharing.

 B Listen to the conversation. Do Mike and Jack get to keep the money?

 C Listen again. Write the missing words that you hear.

Jack: Only five? Why not ten, Mike? That's what I (1) _____ you if I (2) _____ the money with you.

Mike: That's crazy. The woman gave me the money, not you. If I (3) _____ in your shoes, I (4) _____ happy with five dollars.

Jack: No, you (5) _____. You (6) _____ upset if I (7) _____ it in half.

Mike: I wish you (8) _____ arguing with me.

15 WRITE & SPEAK.

A Use the words to write questions with conditional clauses. Add commas where necessary. Sometimes there is more than one correct way to write the question.

1. you / talk / to a stranger / if / he or she / stop / you on the street

   Would you talk to a stranger if he or she stopped you on the street?

2. if / a stranger / offer / you / money / take / it

   _____

3. if / you / get / some money / from a stranger / you / share / it

   _____

4. it / be / fair / if / you / keep / all the money / for yourself

   _____

5. if / your friend / not share / the money / you / get / angry

   _____

6. you / be / annoyed / if / the stranger / take / the money back

   _____

B Work in a group. Ask and answer the questions from exercise **A**.

A: *Would you talk to a stranger if he or she stopped you on the street?*

B: *Probably. But if the person seemed unfriendly, I don't think I would. I'd be afraid.*

16 APPLY.

A Work in groups. Discuss the answers to these situations.

1. Sometimes people buy wild animals to keep as pets. What would you do if one of your friends wanted to buy a baby tiger to keep as a pet?

2. Many people try to smuggle[1] exotic animals into or out of countries through airports. One man had a python[2] tied to him. Others have had snakes and spiders in their luggage and socks. One man even had a crocodile in his bag! What would you do if you saw this kind of activity?

   [1] **smuggle:** to bring things into or out of another country or area illegally
   [2] **python:** a large snake that wraps itself around its victims

B Choose one of the situations from exercise **A** and role-play it for the class.

EXPLORE

CD4-08

1 **READ** the article about Paul Salopek and his seven-year walk around the world. How does he stay in touch with the world?

21,000 miles, 3 miles per hour

Paul Salopek wants to slow down. He wants to learn more about our planet at a human pace . . . three miles per hour. That's why he's walking. Salopek is on a seven-year, 21,000-mile (33,796-kilometer) walk to follow the path of human migration[1] out of Africa, which occurred about 60,000 years ago. **If he had continued his work as a newspaper journalist, he would never have begun this incredible journey.**

Salopek's travels began in Ethiopia, across the Afar Triangle, one of the hottest deserts in the world. Water there is very scarce,[2] and the heat is overpowering.[3] Without his guides, Salopek knew he couldn't survive in such a harsh environment. In addition, **if the guides hadn't been so knowledgeable, Salopek could never have learned as much as he did about the land and its people.**

Thanks to modern technology, Salopek has been able to share the things he has learned so far through regular Internet postings. **This wouldn't have been possible if he hadn't taken along a laptop, satellite phone, camera, and digital recorder.**

Even with these devices that connect him with people thousands of miles away, Salopek knows that there will be times of loneliness. There might even be days when he **wishes he had never left home.** However, he also knows that there will be moments of great excitement and discovery, which will strengthen his deep commitment[4] to this journey of a lifetime.

[1] **migration:** movement from one place to another
[2] **scarce:** If something is scarce, there is not enough of it.
[3] **overpowering:** too strong
[4] **commitment:** a strong belief in an idea

▶ Journalist Paul Salopek leads a pair of camels across Ethiopia's Afar desert (Afar, Ethiopia).

2 CHECK. Correct the error in each statement to make it true according to the article.

1. Salopek is walking to follow the path of animal migration out of Africa.

2. Salopek walked across Ethiopia alone.

3. People can follow Salopek's journey by reading his newspaper articles.

4. Salopek sometimes feels lonely during his journey, and this may stop his future travels.

3 DISCOVER. Complete the exercises to learn about the grammar in this lesson.

A Read each sentence. Then choose the sentence that is closest in meaning.

1. If Salopek had kept his newspaper job, he would never have begun this incredible journey.

   a. He was able to begin the journey because he didn't keep his newspaper job.

   b. He didn't begin the journey because he had to continue working for the newspaper.

2. If the guides hadn't been so knowledgeable, he could never have learned as much as he did.

   a. Because the guides weren't very knowledgeable, he had to learn everything on his own.

   b. Because the guides were very knowledgeable, he could learn a lot from them.

3. Posting messages wouldn't have been possible without modern technology.

   a. Posting messages wasn't possible because Salopek didn't take along electronic devices.

   b. Electronic devices made it possible for Salopek to post messages.

4. There might be days when Salopek wishes he had never left home.

   a. There might be days when Salopek regrets that he left home.

   b. There might be days when Salopek feels he couldn't have left home.

B Look at sentences 1–4 in exercise **A** again. Then choose the correct answer for each question.

1. What time period do the sentences 1–3 refer to?

   a. the past   b. the present   c. the future

2. What verb form is used in the *if* clause in sentences 1 and 2?

   a. the simple past   b. the simple present   c. the past perfect

3. What verb form is used in the main clause in sentences 1 and 2?

   a. *would/could* + verb   b. *would/could have* + past participle   c. the past perfect

4. What verb form is used after *wish* in sentence 4?

   a. the simple past   b. the simple present   c. the past perfect

LEARN

13.5 Past Unreal Conditionals

1. Past unreal conditionals describe past conditions and results that did not happen. The conditions and results are impossible, not true, or imaginary.	**If he had gone to class, he would have seen her.** (He didn't go. He didn't see her.) **I wouldn't have gotten lost if I had used the GPS.** (I got lost. I didn't use the GPS.)
2. The *if* clause gives the condition, and the main clause gives the result. Use *if* + the past perfect in the *if* clause. Use *would have* + the past participle in the main clause.	<u>If you had seen the movie,</u> <u>you would have liked it.</u> *If Clause (Condition)* *Main Clause (Result)* She **would have come** if you **had invited** her. Would he **have taken** the job if they **had offered** it to him? If the weather **had been** nice, **would** you **have gone** to the beach?
3. Other modals such as *could* and *might* can also be used in the main clause.	If I had read the book, we **could have discussed** it. If he had stayed, he **might have enjoyed** himself.
4. **Remember:** Do not use the simple past after *if* to refer to the past. Use the past perfect.	✓ If he **had come** last week, I would have known. ✗ If he <u>came</u> last week, I would have known.
5. **Remember:** Use a comma when the *if* clause comes first in a sentence.	I would have graduated **if I had passed the test.** **If I had passed the test,** I would have graduated.

4 Complete the exercises.

A Circle the correct form of the verb to complete each sentence.

1. Would you have joined Salopek if he **invited /** ⟨**had invited**⟩ you on his journey?

2. If Salopek **had asked / asked** me to go on his journey, I might have said yes.

3. My family **hadn't been / wouldn't have been** happy if I had gone on such a trip.

4. If I had crossed the Afar Triangle, I **would have kept / had kept** a journal.

5. If I had stayed in the desert for a long time, I **had gotten / might have gotten** sick.

6. If I **had gone / went** to Ethiopia with Salopek, I would have brought a good camera with me.

7. If I **was / had been** in Ethiopia with Salopek, I would have wanted to try some Ethiopian coffee.

8. If you had traveled across the desert with Salopek, what would you **had worn / have worn**?

B **SPEAK.** Work with a partner. Take turns asking and answering questions 1 and 8 from exercise **A**.

A: *Would you have joined Salopek if he had invited you on his journey?*

B: *Yes, I would have.* OR *No, I wouldn't have.*

> **REAL ENGLISH**
>
> We do not repeat the verb in short answers with *would have*.
>
> A: *Would you have come?*
>
> B: *No, I **wouldn't have**.*

5 Complete the sentences about a walk in Kenya. Use the correct form of the verbs in parentheses and *would*.

1. If people _____hadn't chosen_____ (not choose) to participate in the walk, the Makindu Children's Program _____wouldn't have raised_____ (not raise) so much money.

2. The trek through Kenya's Rift Valley _____ (be) easier if it _____ (not rain) so much.

3. The participants _____ (not be able) to walk for 10 days if they _____ (not be) in good shape.

4. If they _____ (not have) so much energy, the trekkers _____ (have) a lot of difficulty covering all 150 miles.

5. They _____ (get) sick if they _____ (not drink) a lot of water every day.

6. If they _____ (not use) camels to carry supplies, the trip _____ (not be) a success.

13.6 *Wish* + Past Perfect

1. Use the past perfect after *wish* to express regrets about events or situations that happened (or did not happen) in the past.	I wish I **had studied** harder for last week's test. I'm sorry now. I wish I **hadn't eaten** so much cake. Now I feel sick.
2. **Be careful!** Even though you are referring to a past time, do not use the simple past after *wish* to express regrets.	✓ I wish I **had gone** home yesterday. ✗ I wish I <u>went</u> home yesterday.
3. In short answers, do not include the past participle of the verb after *had*. The past participle can also be omitted in follow-up statements.	A: Do you wish you **had grown up** in California? B: Yes, I wish I **had**. A: Did you grow up in California? B: No, I didn't, but I wish I **had**.

6 WRITE & SPEAK.

A Complete the sentences. Use the correct form of the verb in parentheses.

1. I wish I _____had walked_____ (walk) to class today.

2. I wish I _____ (do) something different last weekend.

3. I wish I _____ (go) to bed earlier last night.

4. I wish I _____ (bring) a cup of coffee to class.

5. I wish our teacher _____ (not give) us any homework last night.

6. I wish I _____ (spend) more time on the last homework assignment.

7. I wish I _____ (not move) to this city.

8. I wish I _____ (wear) a different pair of shoes today.

B SPEAK. Work with a partner. Change the statements in exercise **A** to questions, and take turns asking and answering them. Add follow-up statements to your answers.

A: *Do you wish you had walked to class today?*

B: *Yes, I wish I had. I could have gotten my exercise!*

PRACTICE

7 READ & WRITE.

A Read the story from the movie *All Is Lost*.

> A man is on a sailboat in the Indian Ocean. When he wakes up one morning, he sees water in the bottom of the boat. He realizes that his boat has hit a large container that fell off a ship, and the crash has resulted in a hole in his boat. The man is very skillful, so he is able to repair the hole. Soon after, there is a bad storm, and his boat gets badly damaged. Before it sinks, the man takes some supplies and gets into a life raft. When two ships pass near his raft, he tries to signal them. Neither of the ships notices him. He is running out of food and water, so he is very worried. On the eighth night he sees a light in the distance and thinks it might be another boat. He lights a fire in the life raft, but the fire gets out of control, and the raft catches fire. The man falls off the raft into the ocean.

B Rewrite each sentence about the movie as a past unreal conditional. Add commas where necessary. Sometimes there is more than one correct way to rewrite the sentence.

1. There was water in his boat because it hit a large container.

   If his boat hadn't hit the large container, water wouldn't have gotten into the boat. OR Water wouldn't have been in his boat if it had not hit the large container.

2. The man was able to fix the hole because he was skillful.

   _____

   _____

3. He survived because he got into the life raft.

   _____

   _____

4. The people on the other ships didn't see him, so they didn't rescue him.

   _____

   _____

5. The man fell into the ocean because his life raft caught on fire.

_____

_____

6. The man had this terrible experience because he went out on his boat.

_____

_____

C Read the sentences. Then write sentences about what the man probably wishes. Begin each sentence with *He wishes* . . . .

1. The shipping container hit his boat.

   He wishes the shipping container hadn't hit his boat.

2. The weather wasn't good.

   _____

3. The people on the other ships did not notice him.

   _____

4. He didn't take a lot of food and water from his boat.

   _____

5. He couldn't put out the fire on the life raft.

   _____

6. He didn't stay home.

   _____

▶ A rough sea

8 PRONUNCIATION. Read the chart and listen to the examples. Then complete the exercises.

CD4-09

PRONUNCIATION	Reduced Forms of *Would Have*

Would have and *would not have* are often reduced in conversation. *Have* is often pronounced like the word *of*.

Examples: Full Pronunciation	Reduced Pronunciation
If Meg had known, she **would have** called.	If Meg had known, she ***would of*** called.
If I had seen her, I **would have** told you.	If I'd seen her, I ***would of*** told you.
If you had stayed, Ray **would not have** left.	If you'd stayed, Ray ***wouldn't of*** left.
If it had been cold, we **would not have** gone.	If it'd been cold, we ***wouldn't of*** gone.

In informal conversation, *woulda* is common.

If you had asked me, I **would have** *helped.* | *If you'd asked me, I* **woulda** *helped.*

CD4-10

A Listen to the sentences. Write the full forms of the missing words you hear.

1. If the weather hadn't gotten so bad, the ship _____ stuck in ice.

2. The ship _____ its destination if it hadn't gotten stuck.

3. If a helicopter hadn't rescued the people, they _____ in danger.

4. The people _____ if the ship hadn't had plenty of food.

5. If there hadn't been an Internet connection, the people _____ able to communicate with the outside world.

6. If they had stayed much longer, many people _____ to worry.

B Work with a partner. Take turns saying the sentences from exercise **A**. Practice the reduced pronunciation of *would have* and *would not have*.

9 WRITE & SPEAK.

A Complete the sentences to make them true about yourself.

1. I wish my parents <u>had encouraged me to take risks</u> when I was a child.

2. If I hadn't heard about _____.

3. I wouldn't have met _____.

4. I wouldn't have tried _____.

5. I wish I _____ last weekend.

6. I would have gone _____.

7. I wish I _____ when I was in school.

8. I wish I _____ before class.

9. If I had known _____.

10. My _____ wishes _____.

B Work with a partner. Share your sentences from exercise **A**. Ask each other questions for more information.

A: *I wish my parents had encouraged me to take risks when I was growing up.*

B: *What kind of risks?*

A: *Well, I wanted to start my own business, but they thought it would be too expensive to start.*

10 APPLY.

A Think about a decision you made that has affected your life. In your notebook, write a short paragraph about this decision that answers the following questions. Use past unreal conditionals and *wish* + the past perfect.

What do you wish you had done differently?

What might have made you change your mind about your decision?

How would the consequences have been different if you had made a different decision?

How did the decision affect your life?

I once had the chance to take a long trip by myself, but I decided not to. Now I wish I had. I might have gone if my parents had encouraged me, but they were nervous about the idea. If I had traveled alone for six months, I would have learned to make decisions on my own.

B Work in a group. Take turns reading your paragraphs from exercise **A**. Ask each other questions for more information.

Charts
13.1, 13.2,
13.3, 13.5

1 Match the beginning of each sentence in Column A with the correct ending in Column B.

Column A

1. If I had more time, __f__ .

2. If I drink coffee in the afternoon, _____ .

3. If I hadn't wasted time on the weekend, _____ .

4. Unless it rains on Saturday _____ .

5. Will you be able to finish our project _____ ?

6. You would save time _____ .

7. Even if I had studied more, _____ .

8. I wouldn't have finished the report _____ .

Column B

a. I can't fall asleep at night.

b. if I leave early today

c. if you took the subway instead of driving

d. if you hadn't helped me with it

e. I wouldn't have passed the test

f. I'd go to the movies more often

g. I'm going to go hiking

h. I would've finished all my work

Charts
13.2, 13.3

2 WRITE.

A Read each sentence about the future. Is the situation likely or unlikely for you? Write **L** (*likely*) or **N** (*not likely*) next to each sentence.

_____ 1. I will get a very well-paying job.

_____ 2. I will have my own business.

_____ 3. I will go to graduate school.

_____ 4. I will live to be 100.

_____ 5. I will become famous.

_____ 6. I will buy a house next year.

_____ 7. I will work abroad in 10 years.

_____ 8. I will move this year.

B In your notebook, write real and unreal conditionals according to your answers in exercise **A**.

__L__   If I get a very well-paying job, I'll retire at the age of 50.

__N__   If I got a very well-paying job, I'd retire at the age of 50.

Charts
13.4, 13.6

3 Complete each conversation with the correct form of the verb in parentheses.

1. **Jesse:** Are you happy to be living in the twenty-first century?

   Carla: Well, sometimes I wish things _____ moved _____ (move) more slowly.

2. **Elena:** Why didn't you mention the new book about time travel in your report?

   Eric: I wish someone _____ (tell) me about it. I didn't realize it had been published.

3. **Dan:** I decided to change my topic. I couldn't find information about time machines.

   Kate: I wish I _____ (know). I could've helped you do research.

4. **Deema:** I miss working with you and your team on physics projects.

   Antonio: We miss you, too. We wish you _____ (be) here.

5. **Matt:** I wish Craig _____ (arrive) on time for our meetings.

   Lily: I know. He's always late.

6. **Bill:** We missed you in the lab today. We made a lot of progress.

   Rosa: I wish I _____ (be able) to come, but I had to go to a meeting.

7. **Kitty:** What's the matter? Didn't you like the movie?

   Paul: I wish I _____ (not see) it. It was terrible!

8. **Chris:** Are you reading *The Time Machine* by H. G. Wells?

   Zahra: Yes. We have to read it for class. Some of my classmates wish we _____ (not have to) read it. I love science fiction, though, so I'm enjoying it.

4 EDIT & SPEAK.

Charts 13.1–13.6

A Read the text. Find and correct eight more errors with conditionals and *wish*.

Would you travel in time?

            were
Some people wish it ~~is~~ possible to travel back into the past. If it were possible, they can go back to any time they wanted. At least, that's what they think. Actually, this isn't true, but it's easy to get the wrong idea. When you will see movies about time travel, you don't always get the full story. In fact, you can only go back to the time when your time machine was created. For example, if your time machine was created on January 1st, and you traveled in it six months later, then you can't travel back in time any earlier than January 1st.

    Why is time travel such an attractive idea? We all have done things in the past that we wish we hadn't done. We wish things happened differently. For example, if I didn't go to the store the day of my car accident, the accident wouldn't have happened. I wouldn't have gotten hurt if it didn't happen. If time travel allowed us to go back in time, it will be possible to prevent bad experiences. Wouldn't we all want to do that if we could? It's too bad we can't.

    Future time travel, however, is possible. If scientists figure out how to do it, people will be able to see their lives 20 or 30 years into the future. If you could travel 20 or 30 years into the future, will you want to do it?

B Work in a group. Discuss these questions.

If you could go back in time, what year or time period would you want to visit?

Why would you want to go back to that year or time period?

What do you think you would see?

What would you want to change about that year or time period?

Chart
13.1, 13.3,
13.5

🎧
CD4-11

5 LISTEN & SPEAK.

A Read the questions in the chart. Then listen to the podcast about a physicist and take notes on the answers.

1. Why did young Mallett want to go back in time?	*His father died.*
2. What did he read that made him think about making a time machine?	
3. What could Mallett do if he had a time machine?	
4. Why did Mallett keep his work a secret?	
5. What does Mallet believe will happen if he keeps making progress?	
6. How could time machines be helpful?	

B In your notebook, write sentences using the information from the chart in exercise **A**. Use conditionals.

If his father hadn't died, Mallett wouldn't have wanted to go back in time.

Charts
13.1–13.6

6 WRITE & SPEAK.

A Work with a partner. Your teacher will assign you one of the opinions below. In your notebook, write a list of reasons to support this opinion.

1. Governments should fund research on time machines.

2. Governments should not fund research on time machines.

B Get together with another pair of students who discussed the opposite opinion. Have a debate about this question: Do you think governments should fund research on time machines? Use conditionals when giving your reasons.

Governments should fund work on time machines. If researchers were able to do more work in this area, they might make other important discoveries about our world.

C Decide which team had the better argument. Then discuss your real opinion about this topic.

Connect the Grammar to Writing

1 READ & NOTICE THE GRAMMAR.

A When you think about choosing a career, what is most important to you? The salary? The hours? Helping others? Tell a partner your ideas. Then read the essay.

Choosing the Right Career

Parents always ask what we want to be when we grow up. Very often, they wish that we would choose a career that makes a lot of money. They might think this is in our best interest. After all, if you have money, you have fewer financial worries. However, this doesn't mean that a high-paying career will make you happy. For me, having a meaningful, family-oriented job is more important.

I would make this choice for a couple of reasons. First, people who choose a high-paying career just for the money might find they really don't like it. For example, I knew a woman who was a successful attorney, but she was very unhappy. She didn't find any meaning in the work at all. She spent all day doing legal paperwork and preparing tax documents for corporations. You spend most of your life at work, so it is terrible to dislike your job. I think that people who dislike their jobs are not truly happy even if they are wealthy. Unless I made enough money to retire early, I would not choose a job that I disliked. I want to enjoy my work even if it means I will make less money.

In addition, spending time with my family and friends is very important to me. High-paying careers, such as those in finance, law, or medicine, require very long hours. I know a man in finance who is gone about 12 hours a day. He comes home at 7 or 8 p.m. Sometimes he also works at night from home. His wife raises the kids. He really only spends time with them on the weekends. If I had no time for my kids, I would be very unhappy. I know several retired people who wish that they had spent more time with their families. They can't change that now. I don't want to have the same regrets.

Some people value wealth and their careers more than anything else. They may not care if the work they do is interesting, as long as it pays very well. Some people never have children, and their job is their life. But for me, I want a job that I enjoy—one that will give me enough time to spend with family and friends.

GRAMMAR FOCUS

In the essay in exercise **A**, the writer uses the following conditionals to describe conditions and results.

Present real conditionals	• are used to describe facts, general truths, habits, or routines. *. . . **if you have money, you have fewer financial worries**.*
Present unreal conditionals	• are used to describe situations that are untrue, impossible, or imaginary. *If I **had no time with my kids, I would be very unhappy**.*

B Read the essay in exercise **A** again. Underline the conditionals. Decide if each conditional is real or unreal. Write **R** (*real*) or **U** (*unreal*) above each conditional. Then work with a partner and compare your answers.

C Complete the chart with information from the essay in exercise **A**. Then work with a partner and compare your answers.

> Introduction (Background Information):
> _I don't want a job that I don't like even if it pays well._

> Main Idea: _I want a meaningful job that lets me spend time with my family._

> Reason #1: _____

> Reason #2: _____

2 BEFORE YOU WRITE.

A Work with a partner. Discuss these questions: What careers would you enjoy or not enjoy? Do these careers pay well? How important is money to you when choosing a career?

B In your notebook, make a chart like the one in exercise **1C** and complete it in response to this question: What is the most important factor for you when choosing a job or career? Write notes about your ideas and reasons in your chart.

3 WRITE about your response to the question in exercise **2B**. Write three or four paragraphs. Use your chart from exercise **2B** and the text in exercise **1A** to help you.

> **WRITING FOCUS**   Avoiding Sentence Fragments
>
> An *if* clause must be attached to a main clause to be a complete sentence.
> An *if* clause by itself is a sentence fragment. To correct a fragment, connect the
> *if* clause to the main clause.
>
> ✗ *I want to enjoy my work. Even if it means I will make less money.*
> ✓ *I want to enjoy my work even if it means I will make less money.*

4 SELF ASSESS. Underline the verb forms in your essay. Then use the checklist to assess your work.

- ☐ I used a comma in conditional sentences when the *if* clause came first. [13.1]
- ☐ I used real conditionals correctly. [13.2]
- ☐ I used unreal conditionals and *wish* correctly. [13.3, 13.4]
- ☐ I avoided sentence fragments. [WRITING FOCUS]

Noun Clauses and Reported Speech

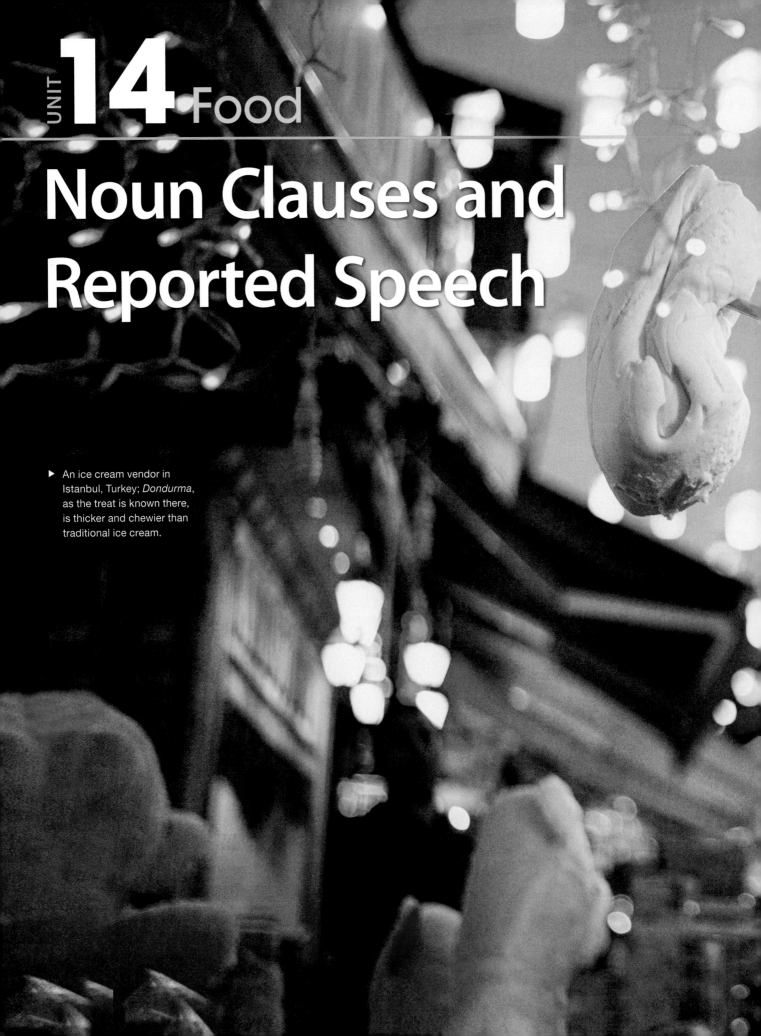

▶ An ice cream vendor in Istanbul, Turkey; *Dondurma*, as the treat is known there, is thicker and chewier than traditional ice cream.

1 **READ** the article about the relationship between food and the brain. According to some scientists, what made the brain of early humans grow fast?

The Power of a Hot Meal

The human brain is considerably larger than the brain of most animals. In fact, our brains have about three times as many neurons[1] as those of gorillas and chimpanzees. Scientists believe **that the human brain grew faster than the brains of other animals**. Research shows **that our brains grew most rapidly about 1.8 million years ago**. Researchers are trying to explain **why this happened**.

Biological anthropologist[2] Dr. Richard Wrangham thinks **that the brain began to grow rapidly when humans first learned to cook**. Cooking made it easier and faster for humans to digest food and gain energy for the brain and the body. By contrast, gorillas, chimps, and other apes continued to eat raw food, which took longer to eat and was harder to process. It also provided less energy.

Neuroscientist[3] Suzana Herculano-Houzel supports the cooking theory. One of her studies looked at the effect of raw food on the body. Her findings showed **that a raw-food diet doesn't provide enough energy for significant brain growth**.

Other scientists wonder **if the cooking theory is right**. Some of them aren't sure **whether or not people were cooking over one million years ago**. That's because there is no evidence of fire being used for food preparation until much later. Scientists also point out the importance of the greater variety of foods that early humans began to eat, which included more protein and fat.

Perhaps we will never know exactly **what caused the rapid growth of the brain**. However, continuing scientific research brings us closer to the truth all the time.

[1] **neuron:** a cell that sends messages to and from the brain
[2] **biological anthropologist:** a scientist who studies the physical and social development of humans and animals
[3] **neuroscientist:** a scientist who studies the brain

2 CHECK. Work with a partner. Discuss answers to the questions according to the information in the article. Then discuss your answers as a class.

1. What is one advantage of cooking food?
2. Why doesn't a raw-food diet support brain growth?
3. Why do some scientists doubt the cooking theory?

3 DISCOVER. Complete the exercises to learn about the grammar in this lesson.

A Find these sentences in the article from exercise **1**. Write the missing words.

1. Research shows _____*that*_____ our brains grew most rapidly about 1.8 millions years ago.

2. Researchers are trying to explain _____ this happened.

3. Other scientists wonder _____ the cooking theory is right.

4. Some of them aren't sure _____ people were cooking over one million years ago.

B What follows each word or phrase that you wrote in exercise **A**?

a. an adjective + verb   b. a verb + object   c. a subject + verb

◀ Replica of a Stone Age house. People have been cooking with fire since prehistoric times. (Senales, Bolzano, Italy)

LEARN

14.1 Noun Clauses with *That*

Noun/Noun Phrase	Noun Clause
Gina discovered **the problem**. The problem is **her food**.	Gina discovered **that her refrigerator is broken**. The problem is **that her food will go bad**.

1. A noun clause can replace a noun or a noun phrase in a sentence. *That* can introduce a noun clause. **Remember:** A clause always has a subject + a verb.	Gina knows **that her food will go bad**. Subject Verb
2. Certain verbs that involve thinking or mental activity are often followed by noun clauses.* agree feel hope realize believe find out know show discover forget notice think	I **thought** that you knew the answer. Do you **feel** that you're working too hard?
3. A noun clause can follow *be* + certain adjectives. afraid glad sorry true certain interesting sure upset concerned lucky surprised worried	He **was surprised** that the door isn't locked. It **is interesting** that the door is open.
4. A noun clause can be used after the verb *be*.	The problem is **that I don't have my keys**.
5. In speaking and informal writing, *that* is often omitted.	I realized **that I needed some help**. I realized **I needed some help**.

*See page **A11** for a list of verbs followed by noun clauses.

4 Read the paragraph about raw-food diets. Underline eight more noun clauses.

Is a raw-food diet better for us?

Some people feel <u>that we should eat the way our ancestors did</u>. In other words, they believe that raw food is healthier for human beings. People that think like this eat only raw food, including some meats. Often they believe that a raw-food diet is better for the environment. Some hope they will lose weight by eating only raw food. But not everyone agrees.

"If you're healthy, this is a terrible idea," said neuroscientist Suzana Herculano-Houzel. The problem is that humans have to eat lots of raw food to get all the necessary nutrients. That takes a lot of time. Also, people forget that our bodies have changed over time. Thus, we may not be able to eat exactly as our ancestors did. However, it is true that many diets of the past were healthier. We probably should try to eat more simply as our ancestors did. For example, we can avoid food that is processed. Most people agree that we should eat more vegetables. Some people are also certain that a diet of different-colored foods (red radishes, green spinach, blueberries) is especially beneficial.

5 WRITE & SPEAK.

A Write sentences in your notebook. Combine words from the first column with a noun clause in the second. Express your own opinions.

I (don't) agree	our ancestors had a better diet
I (don't) believe	eating raw food is healthier
I (don't) feel	cooked food tastes better than raw food
I'm (not) surprised	a raw-food diet is a good way to lose weight

I agree that cooked food tastes better than raw food.

B Work with a partner. Discuss your sentences. Give reasons for your opinions.

I don't agree that cooked food always tastes better than raw food. For example, cooked carrots are OK, but I prefer raw ones.

14.2 Noun Clauses with *If* and *Whether*

Yes/No Question	Noun Clause with *If/Whether*
Is dinner ready?	I'm not sure. I'll ask **if dinner is ready**.
Does he eat meat?	I don't know **whether he eats meat**.
Have you had food poisoning?	I'm not sure **if I've had food poisoning**.

1. Use *if* or *whether* to express a *Yes/No* question as a noun clause. A noun clause with *if* or *whether* can be part of a statement or a question.	*Yes/No* Question: Does he have my number? I'm not sure **if he has my number**. Do you know **whether he has my number**?
2. Use statement word order after *if* or *whether*. Do not use question word order.	✓ Do you know whether **he is** coming? ✗ Do you know whether <u>is he</u> coming?
3. Use *whether*, not *if*, after a verb + preposition.	✓ She **talked about whether** she should move. ✗ She talked about <u>if</u> she should move.
4. When *if* or *whether* begins a noun clause, *or not* is sometimes added to the end of the clause. It is possible to add *or not* directly after *whether*, but not after *if*.	I didn't notice **if** the car was locked **or not**. I didn't notice **whether** the car was locked **or not**. ✓ I don't know **whether or not** I passed the test. ✗ I don't know <u>if or not</u> I passed the test.

6 Complete the exercises.

A Complete the sentences. Change each *Yes/No* question to a noun clause. Add a period (.) or question mark (?) to each sentence.

1. Is it a good idea to eat different colored foods?

   Can you tell me whether _it's a good idea to eat different colored foods?_

2. Should people drink more water?

   I'm not sure if _____

3. Does a salt-free diet benefit everyone?

   Do you know if _____

4. Do most people eat a lot of carbs?

   I'm not sure whether _____

5. Is coffee good for your health?

   Is there research about whether _____

6. Do most people follow a specific diet?

   I'm not sure whether or not _____

7. Have you had an allergic reaction to a food?

   I can't remember if _____

8. Are artificial colors in foods harmful?

   Do you know whether _____

B SPEAK. Work with a partner. Compare your answers to exercise **A**. Then read and respond to each sentence you completed using your own knowledge.

A: *Can you tell me whether it's a good idea to eat different colored foods?*

B: *I think it is a good idea. My mother always said, "A colorful plate is a healthy plate!"*

14.3 Noun Clauses with *Wh-* Words

Wh- Question
Why did you miss the deadline?
When did the teacher arrive?
What time do you want to leave?

Noun Clause with *Wh-* Words
Please explain **why you missed the deadline**.
I wonder **when the teacher arrived**.
Can you tell me **what time you want to leave**?

1. A noun clause can begin with a *wh-* word such as *when, where, why, who, what, how, whose, how many, how much,* and *how old*.	I wonder **when the cooking class is starting**. Do you remember **how the oven works**? Did you write down **what the instructor said**? Can you tell me **how much the ring costs**?
2. A noun clause with a *wh-* word can be part of a statement or a question. Use statement word order (subject + verb) in noun clauses with *wh-* words.	✓ I'm not sure **where the park is**. ✗ I'm not sure where <u>is the park</u>. ✓ Can you tell me **how far the park is**? ✗ Can you tell me how far <u>is the park</u>?
3. Do not use *do, does, did* in noun clauses with *wh-* words.	*Wh-* Question: Where do the Smiths live? ✓ I have no idea **where the Smiths live**. ✓ Do you know **where the Smiths live**? ✗ I have no idea where <u>do the Smiths live</u>.

7 Circle the correct answers.

1. I don't understand this recipe. I'm not sure what
   should I do / (I should do) next.

2. Can you tell me how **is this lasagna made / this lasagna is made**?

3. I can't remember when **I've ever eaten / have I ever eaten** such good lasagna.

4. Could you tell me what spices **you have added / have you added** to the lasagna?

5. Do you remember when **were you given / you were given** this recipe?

6. I'm not sure what **foods do I prefer / foods I prefer** the most. I like everything!

7. I don't understand why **some people don't like / don't some people like** cooking?

8. My mother doesn't understand why **cooking is / is cooking** my favorite hobby. She hates being in the kitchen.

> **REAL ENGLISH**
>
> Use words such as *Could you tell me. . .* , or *Can I ask. . .* before a noun clause with a *wh-* word to make a question sound more polite.
>
> **Could you tell me** what time it is?
> **Can I ask** where the restroom is?

8 Complete the sentences. Change each question in parentheses to a noun clause. Add a period (.) or question mark (?) to each sentence.

1. We've been waiting a long time for a table. Can I ask <u>how much longer we have to wait?</u>
   (How much longer do we have to wait?)

2. Nobody has taken our order yet. Could you tell me _____
   (Who is our server?)

3. Can you tell me _____ I'd like to make it at home.
   (How is this salad made?)

4. I've never seen the word *stew* before. Could you explain _____
   (What does *stew* mean?)

5. I'm allergic to peppers. I'd like to know _____
   (What vegetables are in the soup?)

6. I need to get some cash. Do you have any idea _____
   (Where is there an ATM?)

7. I'm not that hungry. Could you tell me _____
   (How much does a half order cost?)

8. I reserved a table. I wonder _____
   (Why isn't my table ready?)

PRACTICE

9 Complete the sentences with *if, that,* or *whether.* Write all possible answers.

1. Did you know _____ that _____ we are quickly losing many different varieties of food?

2. Experts believe _____ we used to have more than 7000 types of apples. Now we have fewer than 100.

3. The problem is _____ we may lose even more food varieties in the future.

4. Some people wonder _____ the food varieties we depend on might become extinct.

5. Do you know _____ or not anything can be done to prevent the loss of more foods?

6. Many people hope _____ we will be able to protect our future food supply by saving seeds today.

7. Are scientists worried _____ our food sources will be threatened by climate change?

8. I wonder _____ governments around the world are doing anything to help.

10 Complete the exercises.

A Put the words in the correct order to complete the conversations. Add the correct end punctuation. Each sentence has a noun clause.

Conversation 1

Jen: _Do you know where potatoes were first grown?_
     (1) where / were / know / potatoes / you / first grown / do

Dan: _____
     (2) originally came / think / I / from Ireland / that / potatoes

Jen: _____ They came from Peru.
     (3) that / you're / I'm / wrong / afraid

Dan: _____
     (4) potatoes / I / never realized / South America / came from / that

_____
     (5) I / how many / are grown there / wonder / varieties of potatoes

Jen: Thousands. They are really important to the people of Peru, too.

Dan: Really?

Jen: Yes. _____
     (6) I / heard / hold a special ceremony / they / after the potato harvest / that

Conversation 2

Leo: I missed class yesterday. _____
(7) you tell me / can / we covered / what

Ann: Yes. We talked about the Great Potato Famine in Ireland in the 1860s. There wasn't enough to eat, and about a million people died.

Leo: Wow. That's terrible. _____
(8) caused the famine / did / learn / you / what

Ann: _____
(9) that / a harmful fungus / believe / I / destroyed the potatoes

Leo: Can you explain? _____
(10) what / is / I'm not / a fungus / sure

Ann: It's the stuff that can grow on plants and animals. It can kill them. It destroyed all of the potatoes in Ireland.

Leo: What happened then? A lot of people must have left because of the famine.

Ann: Yes, they did.

Leo: _____
(11) you / know / do / where / went / they

Ann: _____
(12) that / over one million people / I / think / emigrated to the United States

▼ The ruins of the village of Slievemore on Achill Island, Ireland.
The people left the village during the Great Potato Famine.

B SPEAK. Work with a partner. What other places have experienced a famine? Why? Discuss your answers.

A: *I read about a famine in Ethiopia in the early 1980s.*   B: *Do you know what caused it?*
A: *I'm not sure why it happened.*

11 Complete the exercises.

A Complete the sentences. Change each question in parentheses to a noun clause. Add a period (.) or question mark (?) to each sentence.

1. Is it true _____ *that people cooked over open fires in prehistoric times?* _____
   (Did people cook over open fires in prehistoric times?)

2. Do you know _____
   (Were the first cast-iron stoves built by the French?)

3. Do you know _____
   (How did people cook in China before cast-iron stoves were invented?)

4. I'm not sure _____
   (Where was the first wood-burning stove invented?)

5. I have no idea _____
   (When were gas stoves invented?)

6. Can you tell me _____
   (What country was the gas stove invented in?)

7. I'm not certain _____
   (Did people in America use ovens shaped like beehives?)

8. I wonder _____
   (Did people cook first with gas or electricity?)

9. Do you have any idea _____
   (When did people start using microwaves in their homes?)

10. Do you know _____
    (Where did people start using solar ovens?)

B **SPEAK.** Work with a partner. Look at the timeline. Take turns asking and responding to the questions or statements in exercise **A**.

A: *Is it true that people cooked over open fires in prehistoric times?*

B: *Yes, the timeline shows that people cooked over open fires in Egypt then.*

Open-fire cooking	Cast-iron stoves	Wood-burning stove	Gas stove	Beehive-shaped ovens	Electric stove	Microwave ovens in homes	Solar ovens in homes
Egypt (prehistoric)	China (220 AD)	France (1490)	England (1826)	Early America (1800s)	Canada (1882)	US (1960s)	California, US (1980s)

◄ Beehive-shaped ovens (Utah, USA)

12 LISTEN & SPEAK.

CD4-13

A Listen to the beginning of a radio show about solar cooking. Check the benefits you hear.

- ☐ convenient
- ☐ easy
- ☐ fast
- ☐ fun
- ☐ healthy
- ☐ inexpensive
- ☐ modern
- ☐ safe

▲ A solar oven made by Stephen Heckeroth. Mendocino, California

CD4-14

B Listen to the rest of the radio show. Complete the noun clauses with information you hear. More than one correct answer may be possible.

1. The host, Jack, wants to know what _Molly is making_____.

2. Molly is not sure whether _____ better with solar cooking or not.

3. Molly knows that _____ a terrific way to save energy.

4. Jack has always wondered if _____ only on a warm day.

5. Jack asks Molly to explain how _____.

6. Jack can't understand why _____ with solar energy.

7. Molly thinks that _____ more popular.

8. Molly believes that _____ a very healthy way to cook.

C Work with a group. Take turns answering the questions. Begin your answers with phrases such as, *I (don't) think . . ., I (don't) believe . . ., I'm (not)sure . . ., I (don't) know . . .*

1. According to the audio, how does solar cooking work?

2. Are there any possible problems with solar cooking?

3. Would you like to try solar cooking? Why or why not?

A: *I'm sure the sun cooks the food, but I'm not sure how, exactly.*

B: *I think the woman said something about the color of the pan, but I'm not sure, either.*

13 EDIT. Read the text about prehistoric people's use of spices. Find and correct five more errors with noun clauses.

Ancient Foodies?

Researchers have found ~~if~~ *that* ancient Europeans were cooking with garlic mustard seeds over 5000 years ago. The findings come from archaeological sites in Denmark and Germany, where the seeds were found inside pieces of pottery. Archaeologists think people used the seeds in their cooking. Because the seeds have no nutritional value, archaeologists are convinced that were used to add flavor to other foods.

The researchers have explained why are their findings important. Although other examples of ancient spices have been found, these seeds are the first to be linked to cooking. In earlier studies, scientists weren't sure if or not these spices had been used in cooking. Experts believed that prehistoric people simply ate food for energy without caring about its taste. Until the garlic mustard seed discovery, they had no idea how much did early humans think about their food preparation. Now scientists realize that flavor was important to people long ago. In the future, researchers would like to find out what other spices did early humans use, but it won't be an easy task.

14 APPLY.

A Write in your notebooks. Use noun clauses with the phrases in the box to answer the questions. Use your own ideas.

I think (that) . . .	I'm (not) concerned (that) . . .	I don't know if / whether . . .
I believe (that) . . .	I'm (not) sure (that) . . .	I wonder if/whether . . .

1. Is solar cooking a good idea?

   I *believe solar cooking is a good idea because it saves energy.*

2. Why do you believe that some people choose to become vegetarians?

3. Are you worried about our food varieties disappearing?

4. Are you concerned about eating food that has chemicals in it?

5. A lot of food is wasted. Do you think this is a big problem? Why, or why not?

B Work with a partner. Share your answers to exercise **A**.

A: *I believe solar cooking is a good idea because it saves energy.*

B: *I agree. I think it's healthier, too.*

EXPLORE

CD4-15

1 **READ** the web page about Charles Spence's research on food and the senses. According to Spence, what senses besides taste and smell play a role in our eating experiences?

Flavor and the Senses: Can we taste with our ears and eyes?

Not all scientific research takes place in labs. Just consider the work of Oxford University psychologist, Charles Spence. Spence does some of his work in restaurants because he studies people's perceptions[1] of flavor.

In one of Spence's experiments, guests were served a chocolate-covered sweet and given some printed instructions to follow. The instructions said **the guests should press number 1 or number 2 on their cell phones**. The people who pressed 1 heard the high notes of fast, upbeat music. These people thought the dessert was sweet. Those who pressed 2 heard low, slow, serious music. For this group, the dessert seemed bitter.[2] Spence said **the results show the role of the brain**. It uses information from one sense, such as hearing, to inform another sense—taste.

Comment   Posted 2 hours ago by Chef Charles

I'm sure that music can affect taste. Last night, one of our regular guests at the café asked **who had chosen the music**. He told his server **that the songs made everything taste better**.

Comment   Posted 50 minutes ago by Haley

In an interview I read, Spence said, "We cannot ever eat or drink without being influenced by the environment." He explained how the brain processes all the information around us—sound, color, and even the weight of the dishes.

Comment   Posted 10 minutes ago by Noah

Spence has said, "In many ways, we really do taste with our eyes." He showed that a dessert on a white plate will taste sweeter than one on a black plate. I tried that at home. It's true!

[1] **perception:** the way you notice or understand something using one or more of the five senses
[2] **bitter:** not sweet and slightly unpleasant

2 CHECK. Answer the questions. Write complete sentences.

1. Where does Charles Spence do some of his research?

   Charles Spence does some of his research in restaurants.

2. Which two senses (seeing, hearing, smelling, tasting, touching) play a big part in the chocolate-covered sweet experiment?

   _____

3. What does the brain do when we eat?

   _____

4. How does Spence think a chef could make a dessert taste sweeter?

   _____

3 DISCOVER. Complete the exercises to learn about the grammar in this lesson.

A Complete the sentences with words from the web page. Add commas where necessary.

1. Spence _____ the results show the role of the brain.

2. He _____ that the songs made everything taste better.

3. Spence _____ "We cannot ever eat or drink without being influenced by the environment."

4. Spence _____ "In many ways, we really do taste with our eyes."

B Look at the sentences in exercise **A**. Check the two true statements.

1. _____ *That* is used before quotation marks.

2. _____ *That* is used when there are no words in quotation marks.

3. _____ A comma is used before words in quotation marks.

4. _____ A comma is used when there are no words in quotation marks.

LEARN

14.4 Reported Speech: Statements

Quote	Reported Speech
Troy: "I'm not cooking."	Troy **told me (that) he wasn't cooking**. Noun Clause
Carla: "It's going to rain."	Carla **said (that) it was going to rain**. Noun Clause

1. In reported speech,* you report what someone said using a reporting verb** + a noun clause. No quotation marks (" ") or commas are used. *That* can be omitted.	Anna: "I have to leave the party." Anna **said that she had to leave the party**. Anna **said she had to leave the party**.
2. In reported speech, pronouns must be changed to keep the speaker's original meaning.	Jim: "I need to rest because **my** back hurts." Jim said **he** needed to rest because **his** back hurt.
3. If the reporting verb is in the past (*said, told*), the verb form in the noun clause usually changes.*** a. Simple present changes to simple past. b. Present progressive changes to past progressive. c. Present perfect and simple past both change to past perfect.	 a. Sam: "I **don't want** to go." Sam **said** that he **didn't want** to go. b. Mary: "I**'m taking** cooking lessons." Mary **said** she **was taking** cooking lessons. c. Tod: "I**'ve made** a cake." / "I **made** a cake." Tod **said he had** made a cake.
4. It is not necessary to change the verb form in the noun clause from present to past when it is about: a. a general truth b. something still true	 a. I told him that I **love** to cook. b. Mary said Jack **is** in the kitchen.

*Reported speech is sometimes called indirect speech.
See page **A11 for a list of reporting verbs in addition to *say* and *tell*.
***See page **A11** for a list of verb tense changes in reported speech.

4 Read each quote. Then circle the correct answer to complete each sentence in reported speech.

1. Jake: "I'm applying to a culinary art school in New York.

   Jake said he **was applying / has applied** to a culinary art school in New York.

2. Fay: "I want to take a class in restaurant management."

   Fay said she **wanted / had wanted** to take a class in restaurant management.

3. Ray: "We were studying with one of the finest baking instructors."

   Ray: He said that they **are studying / had been studying** with one of the finest baking instructors.

4. Igor: "We gained hands-on experience in the cooking labs."

   Igor said that **he gains / they had gained** hands-on experience in the cooking labs.

5. Nida: "A famous French chef teaches at our school."

   Nida said that a famous French chef **taught / had taught** at their school."

6. Marcel: "I am taking a nutrition class."

   Marcel said he **had taken / was taking** a nutrition class.

7. Antonia: "The college has offered me financial assistance."

   Antonia said the college **was offering / had offered** her financial assistance.

8. Miguel: "Some of the students are having trouble with the nutrition class because it has a lot of information about the science of cooking."

   Miguel said some of the students **had been having / were having** trouble with the nutrition class because it **had / had had** a lot of information about the science of cooking.

5 Jane and Peter graduated from a cooking school and are at a party. Read the conversation. Then complete the sentences with reported speech.

Jane:	I need to leave the party. I feel sick.
Peter:	I'm sorry you're feeling bad. This is such a good party. I want to stay, if that's all right with you.
Jane:	I don't mind. I have my car. I don't need a ride.
Peter:	All right. I hope you feel better. Be safe. I want you to call me when you get home.

1. Jane said that _____ to leave the party.

2. She told Peter that _____ sick.

3. Peter said _____ sorry that _____ bad.

4. He told Jane _____ to stay.

5. Jane told him that _____. She said that _____ car so _____ a ride home.

6. Peter wanted to make sure she was safe. He told her that _____ to call him when _____ home.

14.5 Reported Speech: Modals

Quote	Reported Speech
Students: "We'll be late for class." Lisa: "We can't leave early."	They **mentioned** (that) they would be late for class. She **said** (that) they couldn't leave early.

1. These modals often change as follows in reported speech.
 	
  a. *will* → *would*
 	
  b. *can* → *could*
 	
  c. *must* → *had to*
 	
  d. *may* → *might*
	a. Joe: "I'll see you later."
	  Joe said he **would see** us later.
	b. Lucy: "I can't see."
	  Lucy said she **couldn't see**.
	c. Jen: "You must leave by noon."
	  Jen said that we **had to leave** by noon.
	d. Tim: "I may come later."
	  Tim said that he **might come** later.

2. The modals *should, ought to, could,* and *might* do not change in reported speech.	Oscar: "You **should be** a chef." Oscar told Jane that she **should be** a chef.

6 Complete the conversations. Use an appropriate modal in each sentence. Sometimes more than one answer is possible.

1. **A:** We should go to the party on Saturday after dinner.

   B: I thought you said we _____ *should go* _____ early. You said they would have dinner.

2. **A:** I may bake a loaf of bread for the party.

   B: You didn't tell me you _____ a loaf of bread! I love your bread.

3. **A:** I'll bring some beverages, too.

   B: OK, but yesterday you said you _____ a dessert.

4. **A:** We can't drive there. The highways will be busy.

   B: Really? Yesterday you said that we _____ there easily, with no traffic.

5. **A:** We may need to leave early to get to the party on time.

   B: Did you say that we _____ to leave early? I'm not sure I can leave before 4:00.

6. **A:** The party will be fun.

   B: I thought you said the party _____ boring and that you didn't want to go.

7. **A:** We can go swimming at the party.

   B: Swimming? You never told me we _____ swimming. Is there a pool?

8. **A:** Alex may bring his drums.

   B: I don't think so. Last night Alex mentioned that he _____ his guitar.

14.6 Reported Speech: Questions

Quote	Reported Speech
Ben: "Is the cake going to be ready?"	Ben **asked if the cake was going to be ready.**
Olive: "Did the café open?"	Olive **wanted to know whether the café had opened.**
Celia: "Who has been taking notes?"	Celia **wanted to know who had been taking notes.**

1. Use statement word order when reporting *Yes/No* questions and *wh-* questions. Do not use question word order.	Omar: "How long has she been talking?" ✓ Omar asked **how long she had been talking.** ✗ Omar asked how long <u>had she been</u> talking.
2. Use *if* or *whether* to report *Yes/No* questions.	Carol: "Did the reporter take photos?" Carol asked **if the reporter had taken photos.** Carol asked **whether the reporter had taken photos.**
3. If the reporting verb is in the past (*asked, wanted to know*), the verb form in the noun clause usually changes.	Ed: "**Will** Li **be able to attend** the concert?" Ed **asked if Li would be able to attend** the concert.
4. **Remember:** Pronouns are often changed to keep the speaker's original meaning.	Ms. Lee: Do **you** smell the pie in the oven? Ms. Lee asked if **we** smelled the pie in the oven.

7 Read the chef's interview questions in parentheses. Complete the sentences with reported speech.

1. The interviewer asked me _____ *if there was a food I hated* _____ .
   (Is there a food that you hate?)

2. He asked me _____ .
   (Can anyone learn to be a great chef?)

3. He wanted to know _____ .
   (Will you be opening your restaurant soon?)

4. The interviewer asked _____ .
   (How do you think people's eating habits have changed?)

5. The interviewer wanted to know _____ .
   (How big is your garden?)

6. He asked _____ .
   (Is there anything people should eat for their health?)

7. He asked _____ .
   (Do you cook for your family, too?)

8. He asked _____ .
   (Could you share one of your favorite recipes?)

9. I asked _____ .
   (Are you going to post our interview on your blog?)

10. I asked _____ .
    (What time is the photo shoot?)

PRACTICE

8 Read the conversation. Then complete the paragraphs below. Change the speakers' exact words to reported speech.

Dim Sum, Anyone?

Vendor:	The dumplings are delicious!
Man:	I don't know. They've made me sick before.
Vendor:	They won't make you feel bad. Everyone loves the dumplings.
Woman:	Can I try the shrimp dumplings?
Vendor:	Absolutely. You're going to love them. Do you want spicy sauce?
Woman:	I don't think so.
Vendor:	What do you think?
Woman:	I think they're great!

▼ Har Gow, or shrimp dumplings, one of the most popular dishes in Chinese dim sum

The street vendor said that the dumplings (1) __were__ delicious. The man said

(2) _____ because they'd made him sick before. The street vendor

told the man the dumplings (3) _____ feel bad. He also said

(4) _____ them.

The man's wife asked (5) _____ the shrimp dumplings.

The vendor said (6) _____ them. Next he asked her

(7) _____ spicy sauce. She said (8) _____ so.

Then he asked her (9) _____ and she said (10) _____ great.

9   Complete the exercises.

A   Match the questions with the answers about street food in Nepal.

_e_ 1. **Kate:** Are you going to have the dumplings?   a. **Jenny:** All of them are.

___ 2. **Rudy:** How's the rice?   b. **Dena:** I had some on Sunday.

___ 3. **Luke:** Have you tried the spicy sauce yet?   c. **Yuri:** They grow wild in the Himalayas.

___ 4. **Rosa:** Where do the spices come from?   d. **Elsie:** It tastes delicious.

___ 5. **Dave:** How many of the dishes are Nepalese?   e̶. **Tony:** I might try one or two.

B   **WRITE.** Report what the speakers said in exercise **A**. Write in your notebook.

1. Kate asked Tony if he was going to have the dumplings.
   Tony told her he might try one or two.

10   **EDIT.** Read the story about a foreign student in France. Find and correct seven more errors with reported speech.

                                                   she was

Last week, I called Catherine and asked her what ~~was she~~ doing. She said that she and some friends are going out. I asked her whether I can go with them. She said that I was welcome to come along. We met at a bakery. Catherine ordered a cake I had never seen before. She asked me if had I ever tried that kind of cake. I hadn't, so she ordered me a piece. I took a bite and bit something hard. She laughed and said that there is a toy inside. She told me that I am eating a special cake for French holidays. I told her that you should have told me before. I thought maybe I had broken my tooth. She apologized and asked me that I forgave her. I said that I did.

11   **READ, WRITE & SPEAK.**

A   Work with a partner. Look at the pie chart showing the results of a survey. What does it show?

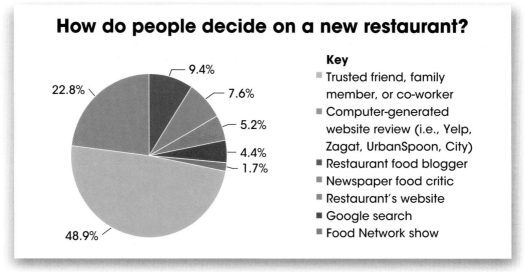

Source: Angelsmith digital marketing agency.

B Look at the results in the chart in exercise **A**. Use the phrases in the box to report what the survey respondents said. Write in your notebook.

> check out a restaurant's website   look at recommendations in food blogs
> do a Google search   read reviews in newspapers
> watch TV shows   pay attention to consumer reviews online

Nearly 49 percent said they followed the recommendations of relatives, friends, and coworkers.

C Work in groups. Discuss how you choose a new restaurant. Then work with a student from another group. Report the results of students from your group. Use reported speech.

12 APPLY.

A Read the restaurant reviews. Write what the food critic said when talking about the restaurants. Write four sentences using reported speech.

FOOD NEWS: ★★★★ Restaurants

Molly's Place: Great bread, tasty soups and salads, popular and busy but worth the wait
Sally Smith, *Food News*

Oishi Ramen: Best noodles in town; cheap, friendly staff. Don't miss the Won Ton soup!
Juanita Gomez, *About Town*

The Casbah: Delicious Middle Eastern food, romantic atmosphere, piano bar
Ravi Gupta, *Dining Out*

Dee's Desserts: Homemade ice cream and cupcakes; great place to eat after the movies!
Hector Vega, *Where To Eat*

The food critic of Food News said that the food was tasty at Molly's Place and that it was worth the wait.

B Work with another student. Compare the sentences you wrote in exercise **A**. Then tell each other your opinion of a restaurant that you have tried. Take notes in your notebook about what your partner says.

I loved the Mongolian Hot Pot. Cooking at the table was a lot of fun. I've never been to a place like it before, but I'm sure I'll go back there again.

C Use your notes to report to the class what your partner told you.

Sally said she loved the Mongolian Hot Pot. She said she'd never been to a place like it before, but she was sure she'd go back there again.

EXPLORE

CD4-16

1 **READ** the blog post about a cooking class. What did the writer learn how to do?

Baking in Ravello

October 15, Ravello, Italy

As we came to the door, Francesco smiled and offered us fresh tomatoes and cheese. We were there for our first cooking class in Ravello, Italy. Francesco was going to teach us how to make pizza.

First, he **told us to knead the dough**.[1] He explained that this makes it easier to work with the dough. He **told us not to stop until it was smooth and slightly sticky**. After that, we left the dough for a while. It needed time to rise, so we toured Francesco's fabulous vegetable garden. He also introduced us to Mamma Lena, a local cheese maker. We **asked her to explain why she was adding lemon juice to the hot milk**. She said it turns hot milk into ricotta, a soft cheese. Apparently, it is easy to make ricotta at home, so I'm looking forward to trying to make it.

Back in Francesco's kitchen, we rolled out the balls of dough into flat round shapes and chose the toppings—sauce, cheese, tomatoes, herbs. Then we used wooden paddles[2] to slide the pizzas into the huge brick oven. Francesco **told us not to get too close to the fire**. He said people cook at high temperatures in order to get the toppings and the crust[3] to cook at the same rate.

When the pizzas were done, we took them out of the oven and waited for them to cool. They made a terrific snack after a very satisfying day.

[1] **knead the dough:** to press a mixture of flour, liquid, and other ingredients with the hands to prepare it for baking
[2] **paddle:** a tool with a handle attached to a broad, flat surface
[3] **crust:** the hard, bread-like layer of a pizza or pie

2 **CHECK.** Read each statement about the article. Circle **T** for *true* or **F** for *false*.

1. First, the class worked on the sauce for the pizza.   **T**   **F**

2. Francesco explained how to work with the dough.   **T**   **F**

3. The students met Mamma Lena, a baker.   **T**   **F**

4. The writer of the blog wants to make ricotta in her own kitchen.   **T**   **F**

5. According to Francesco, you should bake pizza at a low temperature.   **T**   **F**

3 **DISCOVER.** Complete the exercises to learn about the grammar in this lesson.

A Find these sentences in the blog post from exercise **1**. Write the missing words.

1. First he told us _____ the dough.

2. He told us _____ until it was smooth and slightly sticky.

3. We asked her _____ why she was adding lemon juice to the hot milk.

4. Francesco told us _____ too close to the fire.

B Look at the sentences in exercise **A**. What form follows the reporting verb + object in each sentence? Choose the correct answer.

a. a noun clause with *that*   b. an infinitive (+ object)

◄ The beautiful hillsides of the town of Ravello on the Amalfi Coast, Italy

LEARN

14.7 Reported Speech: Commands, Advice, and Requests

Quote	Reported Speech
Chef: "Stir the soup." Friend: "You shouldn't add sugar." Manager: "Can you help me?"	The chef **told me to stir the soup**. Her friend **advised her not to add sugar**. The manager **asked me to help her**.

1. Use an infinitive phrase* to report commands.	Teacher: "Turn off your phones." The teacher told us **to turn off our phones**.
2. Often an infinitive phrase is used to report advice or requests with modals.	Jim: You should bake a chocolate cake. Jim told me **to bake a chocolate cake**. Ann: "Could you turn off the oven?' Ann asked me **to turn off the oven**.
3. For negative commands, advice, or requests, *not* comes before the infinitive phrase.	Joe: "Don't cut the cake yet." Joe told me **not to cut** the cake yet.
4. Do not include *please* when reporting a command or request.	Receptionist: "Please wait in the hallway." The receptionist **told us to wait in the hallway**.

*infinitive phrase: *to* + the base form of a verb (+ an object)

4 Complete each sentence with the correct statement from the box. Use reported speech.

"Move it to a cooler spot."	"Don't continue until you wash your hands."
"Weigh the sugar on the scale first."	~~"Stand away from the oven."~~
~~"Could you show me how to do it?"~~	"You should stop mixing the dough."
"Would you explain step 3, please?"	"Can you please tell me how to prepare it?"

1. Chef McClellan said I wasn't stirring properly. I asked <u>her to show me how to do it</u>.

2. I didn't want Jack to burn himself, so I told <u>him to stand away from the oven</u>.

3. Lisa set the dough on the hot stovetop, so I told _____.

4. Jay often mixed the dough too long. I advised _____.

5. I didn't understand one step in the recipe, so I spoke to Chef McClellan. I asked _____.

6. Jack didn't put the right amount of sugar in the bowl, so I told _____.

7. His hands were covered with flour, so I told _____

   _____.

8. Chef (Jane) Grubart hadn't taught us how to make a white sauce, so I asked _____

   _____.

14.8 Reported Speech: Time and Place Changes

1. Words that describe the time and place often change in reported speech. This is done to preserve the speaker's original meaning.	Bob: "I'll be out of the office <u>this afternoon</u>." When I talked to Bob last week, he said he'd be out of the office **that afternoon**.
2. Time words change as follows when reporting speech at a later date (e.g., the next week, year, etc.). now → then this afternoon → that afternoon tomorrow → the next day yesterday → the day before next week → the following week last year → the year before	Jim: "I tried sushi <u>yesterday</u>." I saw Jim last month. He said he'd tried sushi **the day before**.
3. Sometimes *here* changes to *there* when our location is farther from the reference point.	The chef: "Put the plates **here**." The chef said to put the plates **there**.
4. Sometimes *this* changes to *that* and *these* to *those*.	Valerie: "**This recipe** is easy to follow." Valerie said **that recipe** was easy to follow.

5 Circle the correct answers.

1. Ana said, "I took a baking class last week."

   When I saw Ana, she said that she had taken a baking class **last week /** **the week before**.

2. Karim said, "I'm going to be on TV next week."

   I just saw Karim. He said he was going to be on TV **next week / the following week**.

3. Nick asked, "Can I sign up for courses here?"

   When Nick was at the school, he asked if he could sign up for courses **here / there**.

4. Dahlia opened the oven and said, "These cupcakes are perfect!"

   Dahlia said **these / those** cupcakes were perfect.

5. We were at a party. Samantha said, "I think this is the best party I've ever been to."

   The next day, Samantha said she thought **that / this** was the best party she'd ever been to.

6. Alex said, "I start my new job tomorrow."

   Alex was excited when I saw him. He said he was starting his new job **tomorrow / the next day**.

7. Yuri said, "I'm planning to open a business next year."

   When I saw Yuri two years ago, he said he was planning to open a business **next year /
   the following year**.

8. At noon I asked Rob, "Are you leaving now?"

   At noon yesterday I asked Rob if he was leaving **then / now**.

PRACTICE

6 Read what a health inspector and restaurant owner said to each other during a health
inspection last month. Rewrite the quotations in reported speech.

1. "Get the freezer fixed."

   The health inspector told the owner _to get the freezer fixed_.

2. "Could I have ten days to get the freezer fixed?"

   The owner asked _____.

3. "Give all employees a food safety training tomorrow."

   The inspector told the owner _____

   _____.

4. "Put labels on the food before closing time this evening."

   The inspector told the owner _____

   _____.

5. "Don't leave any boxes on the floor anymore."

   The inspector told the owner _____

   _____.

6. "Could you come back later this afternoon?"

   The owner asked the inspector _____

   _____.

7. "You should get the door fixed by next week."

   The inspector told the owner _____

   _____.

8. "Can you show me the inspection report tomorrow?"

   The owner asked the inspector _____

   _____.

7 LISTEN.

A Listen to a conversation between a hotel restaurant manager and a new employee. Check (✓) the things the manager talks about.

_____✓____ a. coffee

_____ b. continental breakfast

_____ c. delivery

_____ d. garbage

_____ e. hotel check-in

_____ f. orange juice

_____ g. purchase order

_____ h. room keys

CD4-17

B Listen again. Then complete the sentences with the manager's requests and instructions.

1. The manager asked Jimmy ___to come over___ so she could explain his tasks.

2. First, she told him _____ to every floor of the hotel.

3. She also told him _____ any garbage or newspapers.

4. After she talked about the continental breakfast, she told him _____ to the side entrance at 5:00 a.m. to pick up the donuts and rolls.

5. She advised him _____ the donuts and _____ there was a variety.

6. Finally, she advised him _____ the night auditor at the hotel front desk if he had any questions.

8 READ, WRITE & SPEAK.

A Read an airline attendant's description of a stressful day at the airport. Underline the commands, advice, or requests.

It was another stressful day at LaGuardia Airport. Everyone was in a hurry. The lines were extremely slow because there weren't enough security guards on duty that day. Passengers were furious that the lines were slow. They yelled, "<u>Hurry!</u> We're going to miss our flight." One airline attendant was saying to passengers, "Calm down! Don't panic!" Another attendant ran to the gate. He yelled, "Wait!" at the crew. An announcer said, "Everyone flying to Brazil should get in the express line." The passengers lined up. We began taking their food orders. Some customers were worried that the food wouldn't come. We said, "Don't worry about the food."

B Complete the sentences using information from exercise **A**.

1. The passengers told airport security employees ___to hurry___.

2. The airline attendant told passengers _____.

3. An attendant told the crew _____.

4. An announcer told passengers flying to Brazil _____.

5. The airline attendant told the passengers _____.

C Write three more commands or instructions from an airline attendant to a passenger or a passenger to an attendant. Then report them to your partner.

The attendant told the passenger to turn off his phone.

9 APPLY.

A Complete the chart. Write statements or things people have told or advised you to do at some time in your life.

Person	Quote
my mother	"Don't be an art major. Study engineering."

B Work with a partner. Take turns reporting what each person in exercise **A** said. When your partner reports to you, write the exact words (quote) in the chart.

My mother told me not to be an art major. She told me to study engineering.

Person	Quote
my mother	"Don't be an art major. Study engineering."

C Look at the chart in exercise **B** in your partner's book. Do your partner's sentences match the sentences you wrote in exercise **A**?

Charts
14.1–14.8

1 Circle the correct answers.

1. Sally asked the server who **the chef is / was the chef**.

2. Do you know **whether / if** or not the café is open on Sundays?

3. Do you know what time it **is. / is?**

4. When a friend needed money to pay for cooking school, I advised her
   don't borrow / not to borrow it from the bank.

5. I met an old friend for coffee last week. She said she **saw / had seen** our high school teacher
   the day before / yesterday.

6. I told you **don't / not to** overcook the beans.

7. I wonder what **she was / was she** doing in the kitchen.

8. After Jen dropped the cake dough on the floor, Joe told her that **she / you** shouldn't worry.

9. When I was young, my grandfather told me that I **can / could** one day have his secret recipes.

10. Do you know who **did make / made** the dessert last night?

11. The customer asked the server when the meal **will / would** be ready**. / ?**

12. After cutting my finger last month, my boss said that I **must / had to** take a few days off.

Charts
14.1–14.8

2 **LISTEN & WRITE.**

CD4-18

A Read each statement. Then listen. Circle **T** for *true* of **F** for *false*.

1. The woman said the fireworks had smelled like different kinds of fruit.	T	F
2. The woman said she never wanted to experience anything like that again.	T	F
3. The woman said the inventors of the firework display were experienced chefs in a famous restaurant.	T	F
4. The man mentioned that he had read an article about an exhibit which featured a chocolate waterfall.	T	F
5. The woman said she had visited the chocolate waterfall exhibit and had thought it was a cool idea.	T	F
6. The woman said she didn't know what the inventors' next project would be.	T	F

B Listen again. Write the missing words.

CD4-18

1. **Dennis:** How ___was your trip___ to London?

2. **Dennis:** Tell me _____ like.

3. **Nedra:** I've never _____ like it.

4. **Dennis:** I'd like to know _____ this crazy idea.

5. **Dennis:** Do you have any idea _____ their next project _____?

6. **Nedra:** No, but whatever it is, I'm sure _____ pretty outrageous.

C Now report what the speakers in exercise **A** said. Write in your notebooks.

He asked her how her trip to London was.

▼ At midnight on January 1, 2013, fruit-flavored
fireworks went off over London, England.

3 EDIT. Read the story about a child's first cooking experience. Find and correct eight more errors with noun clauses and reported speech.

My First Kitchen Blunder

                        whether

I can't remember ~~if~~ or not I've had any extraordinary experiences with food, but I'm certain that have had some unusual cooking experiences. The funniest was when I was about 12 years old. Before then, I had asked my mother many times when would I be allowed to cook dinner. Finally, one Thursday night, she told me I could make roast chicken tomorrow. She told me to wash the chicken first. I asked if I was supposed to wash only the skin of the chicken. She said that I should wash the inside, too. She also told me don't forget to put salt and pepper on the chicken before putting it in the oven. I wrote down exactly what my mother did tell me to do. The next day, I took the chicken out of the fridge and went over to the sink. I turned on the water and put soap all over the inside and the outside of the chicken. When my brother came in, he asked what was I doing. I told him that Mom had said I could make chicken for dinner. He asked where the chicken is. He said all he saw was soap. I said that Mom had told me to wash the chicken. He told me he would never eat it. Then, he called my mother to tell her I had done. I was so embarrassed. It was years before I ever cooked chicken again.

4 SPEAK & WRITE.

A Walk around the class. Take turns asking your classmates whether they have had the experiences in the chart. If they say *yes*, write their names and ask for details.

Who has . . . ?	Name
made a big mistake when cooking	
cooked a gourmet meal	
eaten food at a street fair	
eaten something strange	
used food to create art	
seen a celebrity in a restaurant	

A: *Have you ever made a big mistake when cooking?*

B: *Oh, lots of times. The worst was when I put hot peppers in Hungarian goulash. I wasn't sure whether or not the peppers I had were hot peppers . . . I thought they were just regular ones . . .*

B Write the most interesting story you heard. Then report to the class what the person said.

Connect the Grammar to Writing

1   READ & NOTICE THE GRAMMAR.

A   What are some of the best places to eat in town? Tell a partner your ideas. Then read the text.

Finding Food to *Die* For

Everyone knows how useful online restaurant reviews are, but you can also get great suggestions from your friends. You trust them, and they know what you like and dislike. I surveyed three of my classmates—Nayma, Esra, and Oscar—because I wanted to know where I could go to get some really delicious food.

They each had different opinions. First of all, Nayma is crazy about desserts, so she told me to go to a place called the Chocolate Room. She said that a dessert called "Death by Chocolate" would change my life. Unlike Nayma, Esra is very health conscious. She asked me if I liked salads. When I said that I pretty much liked everything, she told me to try a place called Omer's Garden. According to her, no one else in the world makes such delicious salad. Finally, Oscar likes to eat meat. He asked me if I had ever eaten Brazilian barbecue. When I told him that I had not, he said that I absolutely had to try the Brasilia Grill. I asked him why it was so great. He described how the waiters walk around with freshly grilled meats and slice them directly onto your plate.

All my friends' suggestions sounded terrific. Which place will I try first? Like Nayma, I really love desserts, so I think I will try the Chocolate Room first. I hope that I get a chance to try the other places soon, too. I can't wait to tell my classmates what I think of their recommendations!

GRAMMAR FOCUS

In this essay, the writer used:

Noun Clauses	• to act as the object in a sentence. . . . *they know* **what you like and dislike**.
Reported Speech	• to report statements and questions. *She* **said that a dessert called** *"Death by Chocolate"* **would change my life**.

B   Read the text in exercise **A** again. Underline all examples of noun clauses and reported speech. Then work with a partner and identify whether the reported speech examples are statements, questions, or commands.

The first one—"told me to go to a place called the Chocolate Room"—is a reported command.

C Complete the chart with information from the text in exercise **A**. Discuss your answers with a partner.

Restaurant	Recommended Food & Why
Omer's Garden	
	grilled meat; very fresh

2 **BEFORE YOU WRITE.** Survey three classmates about restaurants that they like. What are their favorite places to eat? Are there any dishes in particular that they recommend? Why? Complete the chart with their answers.

Restaurant	Recommended Food & Why

3 **WRITE** two or three paragraphs discussing the results of your survey. Use your chart from exercise **2** and the text in exercise **1A** to guide you.

WRITING FOCUS Using *According To* to Report an Opinion

To state someone's opinion, you can use *according to* followed by the person's name or *him/her*.

According to her, *no one else in the world makes such delicious salad.*

Put a comma after *according to* + (name/pronoun).

---

4 **SELF ASSESS.** Underline the noun clauses and the reported speech in your survey results. Then use the checklist to assess your work.

☐ I used noun clauses with statements and questions correctly. [14.1–14.3]

☐ I used reported speech for statements correctly. [14.4]

☐ I used reported speech for questions correctly. [14.5]

☐ I used reported speech with commands, advice, and requests correctly. [14.6]

☐ I used *according to* correctly to report an opinion. [WRITING FOCUS]

15 Learning

Combining Ideas

▲ The third-class cabin of the ship
Titanic is re-created in a traveling
exhibit (Denver, Colorado).

EXPLORE

CD4-19

1 READ the article about how Brendan Mullan motivates people to learn about astronomy. What are some of the ways that Mullan communicates information?

Where are the aliens?

"Hey Aliens, Earth for Sale." With this advertisement written on a large sign, Brendan Mullan began his science presentation. Mullan, an astrobiologist,[1] asks difficult questions about the universe. The biggest question is why aliens have never visited our planet. As Mullan explains, conditions on Earth are perfect to support life. **As a result,** it should be an excellent place for aliens to live. Not only could they live here, Mullan explains, but they could travel here easily. After all, we have sent astronauts into space for years. **Nevertheless,** no aliens have ever appeared. For Mullan, **however,** this does not mean that there is no life on other planets. In fact, he is convinced that in other parts of the universe, there must be life.

Mullan's presentations captivate[2] audiences. They are just one way he shares his passion for astrobiology. **In addition,** he uses social media, with podcasts about the universe for scientists, students, and ordinary people. Mullan directs the planetarium[3] and observatory at the Carnegie Science Center. The center allows people to see stars and planets in the dome[4] or through telescopes. Mullan is an expert scientist and talented teacher with a unique sense of humor. **As a result,** he makes astronomy fascinating to learn about.

[1] **astrobiologist:** a scientist who studies life on Earth and in space
[2] **captivate:** hold the attention of
[3] **planetarium:** a building where lights on the ceiling show the planets, moons, and stars
[4] **dome:** a rounded roof (in this case, of an observatory)

2 CHECK. Read the statements. Circle **T** for *true* or **F** for *false*.

1. Brendan Mullan is an astronaut.   **T**   **F**

2. Mullan believes that Earth is the only planet with living things.   **T**   **F**

3. The Internet plays an important part in Mullan's teaching strategy. **T**   **F**

4. At the Carnegie Science Center, people study clouds.   **T**   **F**

5. Mullan makes studying the universe exciting.   **T**   **F**

3 DISCOVER. Complete the exercises to learn about the grammar in this lesson.

A Find these sentences in the article from exercise **1**. Write the missing words and punctuation.

1. _____ no aliens have ever appeared.

2. For Mullan _____ this does not mean that there is no life on other planets.

3. _____ he uses social media, with podcasts about the universe for scientists, students, and ordinary people.

4. _____ he makes astronomy fascinating to learn about.

B Look at the article in exercise **1** again. Find the sentence that comes just before each sentence in exercise **A**. Then complete the statements below with the words you wrote in exercise **A**.

1. __Nevertheless__ and _____ are similar in meaning to *but*.

2. _____ is similar in meaning to *so*.

3. _____ is similar in meaning to *and*.

▲ Stargazers view the nighttime
sky from Mount Wu Fen, Taipei.

LEARN

15.1 Contrast: *However, Nevertheless, On the Other Hand*

1. Transition words connect ideas between or within sentences. They are commonly used in formal writing and speaking. Transition words of contrast are similar in meaning to *but*.	The professor knew his subject well, but his lectures were hard to understand. The professor knew his subject well. **However**, his lectures were hard to understand.
2. Transition words often come at the beginning of a sentence. Some can also occur within or at the end of a sentence. a. When a transition occurs at the beginning, put a comma after it. b. When it occurs within the sentence, put a comma before and after it. c. When it occurs at the end, put a comma before it and a period after it.	a. It can be cold in April in New York. **However,** it doesn't snow very often. b. It can be cold in April in New York. It does not**, however,** snow very often. c. It can be cold in April in New York. It doesn't snow very often**, however.**
3. Use *however* and *nevertheless* to introduce information that is surprising or that contrasts with what has just been said.	The exam was difficult. **However**, everyone in the class got a good grade. Jan got very good grades. **Nevertheless**, she didn't get into graduate school.
4. Use *on the other hand* to introduce the second of two ways of looking at something.	The job is not interesting. **On the other hand**, it pays well.

4 Read each statement. Then choose the statement that logically follows it.

1. In my city, it's hard to see the stars because there are too many lights.

    (a.) On the other hand, the lights from the buildings and bridges are beautiful.

    b. On the other hand, it's hard to see the stars from my apartment.

2. I never liked studying science in high school.

    a. However, in college I developed an interest in astronomy.

    b. However, I studied history in college.

3. At first, I thought astronomy would be boring.

    a. Nevertheless, I decided to sign up for a course in it.

    b. Nevertheless, I didn't sign up for a course in it.

4. When I began to study astronomy, finding individual stars was hard.

    a. On the other hand, I couldn't find one.

    b. On the other hand, finding them was very rewarding.

5. The class lectures were not always interesting.

    a. The video presentations, however, were boring.

    b. The video presentations, however, were fascinating.

6. By my sophomore year, I loved to study the planets and stars.

    a. Nevertheless, I didn't choose astronomy as my major.

    b. Nevertheless, I decided to major in astronomy.

7. I took several more courses in astronomy.

    a. However, none of them were as captivating as the first course I took.

    b. However, they were all as captivating as the first course I took.

8. I'm still fascinated by the nighttime sky.

    a. However, I regret not having majored in astronomy.

    b. However, I don't regret my decision not to major in astronomy.

5 Read each statement below and notice the word in parentheses. Find the sentence in the box that logically follows it. Rewrite the sentence from the box using the word in parentheses. Add commas where necessary.

They must work alone during the exam.	They shouldn't ask questions that are too personal.
Many students still prefer traditional classes.	Reading is better for visual learners.
They must not hurt anyone's feelings.	~~They need to make their expectations clear.~~

1. It is fine for teachers to have high expectations for their students. (however)

    However, they need to make their expectations clear.

2. Students should feel free to ask about their classmates' interests. (on the other hand)

    _____

3. It it is fine for students to study together for exams. (however)

    _____

4. It can be helpful for students to comment on their classmates' writing. (however)

    _____

5. Listening to lectures is the best way for some students to learn new information. (on the other hand)

    _____

6. Online classes are becoming more popular. (nevertheless)

    _____

15.2 Result: *As a Result, Therefore, Thus*

1. Transition words of result are similar in meaning to *so*. Notice the difference in punctuation.	The exam was long, so it was tiring.
	The exam was long. **Therefore,** it was tiring.
2. *Therefore* can come at the beginning or within a sentence. It is similar in meaning to "for that reason."	Pat missed the lecture. **Therefore,** he's going to ask Rina for her notes.
	Pat missed the lecture. He is, **therefore,** going to ask Rina for her notes.
3. *Thus* can come at the beginning or within a sentence. It is similar in meaning to *therefore*.	Mars has a rocky surface. **Thus,** it is the same type of planet as Mercury, Venus, and Earth.
4. *As a result* is usually used at the beginning of a sentence.	She has a good telescope. **As a result,** she was able to see the rings around Saturn.

See chart 15.1 on page **428** for rules on comma usage with transition words.

6 Rewrite each sentence as one or two sentences. Replace *so* with the words in parentheses. Add commas where necessary.

1. Digital learning is becoming more popular, so teachers' roles are changing. (as a result)

    Digital learning is increasing. As a result, teachers' roles are changing.

2. Digital learning gives students more control, so they become more active learners. (thus)

    _____

    _____

3. Digital learning gives students more responsibility, so they become more independent. (as a result)

    _____

    _____

4. We can often both see and hear content online, so it is more interactive. (therefore)

    _____

    _____

5. That course is very popular, so it fills up quickly. (therefore)

    _____

    _____

6. Our university has an excellent biology department, so many students major in biology. (thus)

    _____

    _____

7. The final exam was very difficult, so many students didn't pass. (as a result)

_____

_____

8. Professor Chen is well known in her field, so a lot of students want to take her classes. (therefore)

_____

_____

15.3 Addition: *In Addition, Moreover*

1. Transition words of addition are similar in meaning to *and*. Notice the difference in punctuation.	Lisa recommended me for the job, and she introduced me to the head of the company.
	Lisa recommended me for the job. **In addition,** she introduced me to the head of the company.
2. *In addition* and *moreover* usually come at the beginning of a sentence.	An essay should be clear and well organized. **In addition,** it should be interesting.
	He had enough money to build a new lab. **Moreover,** he received funding to do more research.

7 Read the sentences about learning with video chat applications (apps). Then rewrite the sentences using the words in parentheses. Add commas where necessary.

1. With video chat apps, you can talk online for free. They're easy to use. (in addition)

    With video chat apps, you can talk online for free. In addition, they're

    easy to use.

2. Video chat apps allow you to make phone calls. They let you have group chats. (in addition)

    _____

    _____

3. These apps make it easy for you to talk to your classmates. They connect you to other students. (moreover)

    _____

    _____

4. Teachers can give feedback with these apps. Students can comment on each other's work. (in addition)

    _____

    _____

5. During video chats, students can watch artists at work. They can learn about the artists' techniques. (moreover)

_____

_____

6. You can learn about foreign countries through video chats. You can find a language partner. (moreover)

_____

_____

7. With video chatting, students can listen to authors read their work. They can talk to the authors. (in addition)

_____

_____

8. Students can use these apps to go on virtual field trips. They can give presentations. (in addition)

_____

_____

PRACTICE

8 Circle the correct words to complete the article.

Social Media: Good or Bad?

Social media is changing the way we learn and communicate with each other, and there are both advantages and disadvantages to using it. Social media allows us to connect with people from all parts of the world and learn from them. (1) **In addition, / Nevertheless,** we can communicate with those who share our interests. Age, gender, and nationality become less important online. (2) **However, / As a result,** we can make friends that we would not otherwise make. Thanks to social media, we are able to discuss important political, social, and environmental issues with a wide variety of people. (3) **Moreover, / However,** it helps us connect with other professionals in our field.

(4) **On the other hand, / Moreover,** social media has some drawbacks.[1] For example, more online communication means less face-to-face communication. (5) **However, / As a result,** people can start to forget how to communicate in person. (6) **In addition, / Nevertheless,** online communication can make us less sensitive to other people's feelings. We can't see people's facial expressions on social media. (7) **Therefore, / Nevertheless,** it's more difficult to know how someone feels about a comment we've made. We may be less polite when communicating online, or we might post comments that are hurtful without realizing it. Social media has made learning and communication easier in many ways. (8) **However, / Thus,** we need to think carefully about how we use it.

[1] **drawback:** a disadvantage

9 Complete the sentences with the words in the boxes. Add commas where necessary.

> however   in addition   therefore

1. Social media sites are a great way to communicate with friends. _____However,_____ spending too much time on them can be unhealthy.

2. You can meet new people through social media sites. _____ you can contact old friends.

3. People's posts aren't always honest. _____ you shouldn't believe everything you read.

> as a result   moreover   nevertheless

4. Frank joined a social networking site. _____ he has been able to connect with other doctors.

5. It's sometimes necessary to provide personal information online. _____ you should make sure the site is secure.

6. Social media is a great way to keep in touch with family and friends. _____ it allows us to share and broaden our interests.

10 Circle the correct transition words to complete the sentences about Internet research.

1. The Internet is an amazing source of information. **In addition, / Nevertheless,** much of the information is free and easy to use. **Therefore, / However,** it is important to remember that not all websites are accurate and up to date.

2. Anyone can post content on the Internet, both experts and non-experts alike. **Therefore, / Moreover,** student researchers may find it difficult to tell whether or not the information on a particular site is reliable.

3. Online encyclopedias are popular and often excellent sources of information. **Nevertheless, / Thus,** the information in them is not always up to date. Students, **therefore, / however,** need to be careful and cross-check the information they find with other sources.

4. Even articles on the websites of major newspapers can contain errors. **As a result, / However,** these errors are often corrected within minutes. **Moreover, / Therefore,** many professors encourage students to use newspaper websites for their research.

5. Online professional journals are also good sources of information. **In addition, / Thus,** student researchers may find reliable information on the websites of university libraries.

11 **SPEAK & WRITE.** Work with a partner. Write a sentence that logically follows each sentence below. Use the transition words in the box and your own ideas. Add commas where necessary.

| however | nevertheless | on the other hand | therefore |
| ~~as a result~~ | in addition | moreover | thus |

1. Some students have been using video chatting to practice their English.

   As a result, their English is getting better and better.

2. The Internet helps students find and check information quickly.

   _____

3. Tablets are easy to carry from place to place.

   _____

4. The Internet has a lot of useful information.

   _____

5. Many educational apps are free.

   _____

6. Some students like to use apps to study for exams.

   _____

7. Other students prefer to use textbooks.

   _____

8. Others form study groups.

_____

12 LISTEN & WRITE.

A Listen to the conversation about MOOCs. Circle **T** for *true* or **F** for *false*.

1. Sarah explains what the letters M-O-O-C stand for.   **T**   **F**

2. Sarah tells her friend the subject of the course she is taking.   **T**   **F**

3. Sarah says there are a lot of requirements for the course.   **T**   **F**

4. Sarah will never sign up for another MOOC.   **T**   **F**

B Listen again. Match each sentence in Column A with the correct sentence in Column B according to the conversation.

Column A

1. Students comment on each other's essays. __*b*__

2. Sarah didn't get college credit. _____

3. There were lectures, readings, and discussion questions. _____

4. The subject of the course was interesting. _____

5. Sarah enjoyed the course. _____

6. Students do not have to take a test before signing up. _____

Column B

a. Anyone can register for a MOOC.

b. They get a lot of feedback on their writing.

c. She plans to sign up for another MOOC.

d. She got a certificate of completion.

e. The lectures were great.

f. There were no final exams.

C In your notebook, write six sentences to connect the information in exercise **B**. Use *as a result, however, in addition, moreover, nevertheless,* and *therefore*.

13 APPLY.

A Check (✓) the things you have used as learning tools.

_____ Apps _____ MOOCs _____ Tablets _____ Digital textbooks _____ Social media _____ Other

B Work in a group. Discuss these questions about the learning tools in exercise **A**.

What is the most effective learning tool you have ever used?
How did it help you? How could it have worked better?
What new learning tool would you like to try?
How would you use it?
How do you think it could help you?

C In your notebook, write five sentences about two or more of the questions you discussed in exercise **B**. Connect your ideas with transition words where appropriate.

The most effective learning tool I've ever used is YouTube. There are a lot of free lectures on it. As a result, I've learned about some very interesting topics . . .

EXPLORE

CD4-21

1 **READ** the article about a learning experiment. What did the students learn how to do?

Let Learning Happen

Professor Sugata Mitra wanted to do an experiment. He went to a part of New Delhi, India, where children rarely attended school and had never seen a computer. Mitra set a computer into one of the walls on the street and connected it to the Internet. Then he turned on the computer and left.

Surprisingly, the children learned to use the computer in a few hours. **Despite** their lack of formal education, they figured out how to browse and download information, and they helped each other learn. When Mitra repeated the experiment in India and other countries, the same thing happened. **As a result of** these findings, Mitra became convinced that students will learn what they want to learn.

Mitra did more experiments to see what else groups of students could learn. He found that some figured out how to play music and send e-mails; others learned complex subjects such as biotechnology.[1] All of the students improved their English. They were **so** successful **that** Mitra wanted to provide them with even more opportunities to teach themselves.

The benefit of group learning was an important discovery for Mitra. He realized that students learn more in groups **due to** their constant communication with each other. They do **such** a good job in groups **that** Mitra decided to build SOLEs (self-organized learning environments). These allow groups of students to do Internet research on a wide range of subjects. There is no teacher in the traditional sense. SOLEs reflect Mitra's strongly held view: "It's not about making learning happen. It's about *letting* learning happen."

[1] **biotechnology:** the use of living things, such as cells or bacteria, for industrial purposes

▲ Boys exploring the Internet at one of Sugata Mitra's experiment sites

2 **CHECK.** Read each statement about the article. Circle **T** for *true* or **F** for *false*.

1. Sugata Mitra began his learning experiments with wealthy children.   **T**   **F**

2. It took the children a few days to learn to use the computer.   **T**   **F**

3. Mitra's research shows that students learn best in groups.   **T**   **F**

4. Mitra discovered that children learned complex subjects when they wanted to.   **T**   **F**

3 **DISCOVER.** Complete the exercises to learn about the grammar in this lesson.

A Find these sentences in the article from exercise **1**. Write the missing words.

1. _____ their lack of formal education, they figured out how to browse . . .

2. _____ these findings, Mitra became convinced that students will learn what they want to learn.

3. They were _____ successful _____ Mitra wanted to provide them with even more opportunities to teach themselves.

4. He realized that students learn more in groups _____ their constant communication with each other.

5. They do _____ a good job in groups _____ Mitra decided to build SOLEs.

B Choose the correct answers based on the sentences you completed in exercise **A**.

1. *Despite* introduces _____.   a. a result   b. a contrast

2. *Due to* and *as a result of* introduce _____.   a. a cause   b. a contrast

3. *Despite, due to,* and *as a result of* are followed by _____.   a. a noun phrase   b. a noun clause

◄ Kolkata, India (formerly Calcutta)

437

LEARN

15.4 Cause and Effect: *As a Result of, Because of, Due to*

Effect	Cause
	Prepositional Phrase
She will get good grades We didn't take the field trip The class was canceled	**as a result of** her hard work. **because of** the weather. **due to** a lack of interest.

1. *As a result of, because of,* and *due to* are multi-word prepositions. They begin a prepositional phrase that gives the cause of or reason for the event in the rest of the sentence.	The tree fell **as a result of the storm**. Driving was difficult **because of the snow**. Class was cancelled **due to the bad weather**.
2. **Remember:** A prepositional phrase is a preposition + a noun or noun phrase. When a prepositional phrase is first in a sentence, put a comma after it.	**Because of the traffic**, we were late. We were late **because of the traffic**.
3. **Be careful!** *Because of* and *because* are similar in meaning, but they are used with different structures: 　a. *because of* + noun/noun phrase 　b. *because* + subject + verb	 　a. We stayed home **because of** the rain. 　b. We stayed home **because** it was raining.
4. In formal writing, *due to the fact that* + subject + verb is sometimes used instead of *due to* + noun phrase.	They left town **due to** the hurricane. They left town **due to the fact that** a hurricane was approaching.
5. **Be careful!** *As a result of* is used to introduce the cause of an event. *As a result* introduces the effect or result of the cause mentioned in the previous sentence.	**As a result of** poor sales, the company closed. 　　　Cause　　　　　　　Effect Sales were poor. **As a result**, the company closed. 　Cause　　　　　　　Effect

4 Circle all correct words. Sometimes more than one answer may be correct.

1. Children learned to use Mitra's computer **because / because of** their curiosity and intelligence.

2. **Because / Due to the fact that** children organized their own learning, Mitra thinks they can learn without a teacher.

3. Mitra wants learning to change **because / because of** he thinks schools are not effective.

4. **As a result, / Due to** recent research, the teachers have changed their methods.

5. Children learn differently **because / because of** different learning styles.

6. **As a result of / Because** computers, students do not practice writing as much as before.

7. Computers are common in schools today. **As a result, / As a result of** students do not practice writing as much as before.

8. The test scores went up this year, perhaps **due to / because** the tutoring program.

9. Some students are good at group work **due to / due to the fact that** they enjoy interacting with others.

10. Teachers pay attention to different learning styles **due to / due to the fact that** their influence on learning.

5 Complete each sentence with the correct prepositional phrase from the box. Add a comma where necessary.

because of the noise	~~because of the teachers' strike~~
as a result of their low test scores	as a result of the fire
due to the class website	due to the spread of the flu

1. _____Because of the teachers' strike,_____ classes were cancelled.

2. The students had to sign up for tutoring _____.

3. Some students dislike working in groups _____.

4. _____ more shy students were participating in discussions.

5. _____ the school nurse was working long hours.

6. The school received insurance money _____.

▶ Educators around the world now use a variety of methods to teach their students. Here, a Chinese astronaut speaks to students from space.

15.5 Cause and Effect: *So/Such . . . That, So Many/Much . . . That*

Cause	Effect
So . . . / Such . . .	*That* Clause
Jonathan was **so** funny	**that** people were crying.
He ran **so many** miles	**that** he needed new shoes.
There was **so little** time	**that** we had to run.
It was **such** a nice day	**that** we ate outside.

1. Use *so* + an adjective/adverb to give a cause or reason; the effect or result follows in a *that* clause.	The exam was **so easy that** we finished it early. He drove **so quickly that** he crashed the car.
2. *Many, much, few,* or *little* + a noun can also go between *so* and a *that* clause.	He had **so much homework that** he didn't go out. She had **so few friends that** she often felt lonely.
3. You can also use *such* + an adjective + a noun to give a cause or reason for an effect or result in a *that* clause.	It was **such an easy exam that** I finished it early.
4. **Remember:** *That* is often omitted in conversation.	It was such an easy exam **that I finished early.** It was such an easy exam **I finished early.**

6 Circle the correct answers to complete the text.

Learn Anything in Just 20 Hours!

Has this happened to you? You try to learn a new skill, but you are (1) **so / such** bad at it that you give up. Practicing the skill becomes (2) **so / such** boring that you stop after an hour or two. Or you might think it will take (3) **so many / so much** hours to learn, you will never learn it. But Josh Kaufman, writer and entrepreneur, says you can learn any skill. First, realize you don't have to become an expert. Second, don't spend (4) **so many / so much** time worrying about failing that you never try to learn anything new. Third, give yourself 20 hours to learn the skill. The first few hours can be (5) **so much / such** a frustrating time that you will want to give up. However, Kaufman says, you will soon get better at it. When you do, you will feel (6) **so / so much** good that you will keep practicing. Kaufman taught himself (7) **so many / so much** new skills in one year that he wrote a book about it. It is (8) **so much / such a** good book that you'll want to read it twice!

7 Complete the sentences with the correct missing words. Use *so, so much, so many, so little,* or *such.*

1. There are _____so many_____ ways to teach yourself that you can learn just about anything.

2. The Internet offers _____ a wide range of information that you can learn about anything.

3. There is _____ art on museum websites that you can see famous paintings without leaving home.

4. Speakers on podcasts are _____ interesting that it's easy to listen and learn.

5. YouTube has _____ how-to videos that it makes learning by watching easy.

6. E-books are _____ easy to download that you can read them in minutes.

7. It takes _____ time to look up new words on smartphones that learning words is easier.

8. I have _____ a good time learning new things that I spend hours online.

15.6 Contrast: *Despite, In Spite of*

	Despite/In Spite of + Noun/Noun Phrase
Some people did well on the test Others didn't do very well	**despite** the pressure. **in spite of** their hard work.

1. *Despite* and *in spite of* introduce information that is surprising or unexpected or that contrasts with information in the rest of the sentence.	She got the job **despite her lack of experience.** She got the job **in spite of her lack of experience.**
2. *Despite* and *in spite of* are followed by a noun or noun phrase.	We went on a picnic **despite the storm.** We went on the picnic **in spite of the storm.**
3. *Despite of* and *in spite of* can come at the beginning or end of a sentence. Use a comma when they come at the beginning of the sentence.	**Despite the cold water,** I went swimming. I went swimming **despite the cold water.**
4. In formal writing, *the fact that* + subject + verb is sometimes added to *despite* and *in spite of*.	We went on a picnic **in spite of the fact that there might be a storm.**

8 Use the choices in the box to complete the sentences. Add a comma where necessary.

my inexperience singing on stage	I didn't know anything about music
I don't play the guitar well now	~~I took lessons as a child~~
my dreams of being a musician	my fear of failure
my parents' threats of punishment	my lack of singing talent

1. Despite the fact that _____ I took lessons as a child, _____ I never learned to play the piano well.

2. In spite of the fact that _____
   I taught myself the guitar.

3. I didn't practice the piano often despite _____.

4. I won a piano competition in spite of _____.

5. Despite the fact that _____
   I played it a lot when I was young.

6. Despite _____
   I will probably have to work a regular job.

7. In spite of _____
   I got to sing in the school play.

8. Despite _____ I was very relaxed on stage.

PRACTICE

9 Complete the text. Circle the correct words.

A Self-Taught Painter: Paul Gauguin

He was a famous artist from the nineteenth century. (1) **Despite** / **As a result of** his fame and talent, Paul Gauguin was never formerly trained as a painter. (2) **Despite** / **Despite the fact that** he was never trained in art, he excelled at it. Gauguin first saw art when he was a child. His family went to Peru, where his father was from. (3) **As a result,** / **Despite** Gaugin experienced the art of Indian cultures. Gauguin always wanted to be an artist (4) **despite the fact that** / **in spite of** he worked in business.

Finally, (5) **despite** / **as a result of** his success as a businessman, Gauguin made enough money to quit his job and start painting. He spent his free time in the cafés of Paris. (6) **As a result of** / **In spite of** this, he made friends with other artists. Gauguin painted and traveled. He especially liked islands. He liked them (7) **so much** / **such** that he left Europe for Tahiti and never came back. Tahiti was a spiritual place for Gauguin. It inspired him (8) **such** / **so much** that he painted his best works there. (9) **Because of** / **In spite of** Gauguin's interest in other cultures, he used painting styles from Africa and Japan. Gauguin died at age 54. He had completed over 228 paintings. (10) **Despite** / **Due to** his early death, Gauguin was an important influence on modern art.

▲ Oil painting (1892) by Paul Gauguin

10 Use the words in parentheses to combine the sentences. Add a comma where necessary.

1. Kate had a fear of heights. She learned to ski. (in spite of)

   <u>In spite of Kate's fear of heights, she learned to ski.</u>

   <u>OR Kate learned to ski in spite of her fear of heights.</u>

2. Margaret is an excellent dancer. She was not chosen by the dance company. (despite the fact)

   _____

   _____

3. Josh has a passion for winter sports. He learned to snowboard. (due to)

   _____

   _____

4. Maya worked on a farm. She never learned how to grow vegetables. (in spite of the fact)

   _____

   _____

5. Mark has natural musical talent. He learned to play the violin by himself. (as a result of)

   _____

   _____

6. Ben is a very impatient person. He stopped taking art lessons after just one month. (so)

   _____

   _____

7. Henry has good computer skills. He was able to build his own website without any help. (because of)

   _____

   _____

8. Tomas is a wonderful pianist. His friends love to hear him play. (such)

   _____

   _____

11 WRITE & SPEAK.

A Use the words in parentheses to write sentences about your own experiences. Use the present or past.

1. (so difficult) <u>Learning English was so difficult at first that I thought I would</u> <u>never speak.</u>

2. (so easy) _____

_____

3. (so fascinating) _____

_____

4. (such an interesting place) _____

_____

5. (so much fun) _____

_____

6. (so many mistakes) _____

_____

B Work with a partner. Share your sentences.

A: *Learning English was so difficult at first that I thought I would never speak.*

B: *Really? It wasn't hard for me to speak, but writing is still hard.*

12 EDIT. Read the text about learning how to dance. Find and correct six more errors with phrases of cause and effect, contrast, and result. There is more than one way to correct some errors.

Shall we dance?

    Watching a friend compete in a dance contest was ~~so~~ ^such a great experience that I decided to learn how to dance. Despite my lack of rhythm, I wanted to learn. I watched such many YouTube videos that I started to dream about dancing. However, I got very frustrated. It was so hard for me to learn from the videos that I almost gave up. Then, my friend told me about a dance class. I signed up, but the first time I went I was shy that I couldn't move. In spite of my fear, I kept going. I had so few free time that I couldn't practice a lot. But a half hour before dinner every night, I put on music and practiced the steps I had learned in class. Because the teacher's patience, I eventually learned to dance. I'm such good dancer now that I'm going to be my friend's partner in a dance contest. As a result my experience, I am convinced that a person can learn just about anything. All you need is the desire and an effective way to learn.

13 APPLY.

A Work with a partner. Look at the picture and imagine that you are one of the dancers. Write three or four sentences about learning to dance. Use the phrases in the box. Then read your sentences to the class.

| as a result of | because of | due to | despite | in spite of | so . . . that | such . . . that |

My legs hurt so much at the end of every class that I had to sit down!

B Work in groups. Think of something you have learned to do or would like to learn to do. Speak for one minute about the experience or what you think it would be like. Use some of the phrases in the box in exercise **A**.

Last summer I took a folk dance class in my country. My dancing was so bad at first that I stepped on my partner's feet. But soon I was having so much fun that I didn't want to stop.

▼ Chinese national dancers perform a traditional dance in Chengdu, China.

Charts
15.1,
15.4–15.6
1 Circle the correct words to complete the article.

Science for Non-Scientists

We can learn about many things, even the stars, with social media. In the past, to learn about the stars, we used books and maps. (1) **However, / Moreover,** today, we use different sources such as astronomy websites. (2) **As a result of / On the other hand**, sites like Twitter, we can post new scientific information. (3) **Due to / Despite** all of these sources, there are now more opportunities for everyday people to get involved with science. (4) **Despite the fact that / Due to the fact that** we need scientists to lead experiments, non-scientists can also play a part in scientific research. (5) **Because of / In spite of** the need for a lot of data, non-scientists can help. They can collect data for scientists. When a lot of people collect data, scientists are able to get information more quickly. Today, more scientists are encouraging non-scientists to get involved. (6) **In spite of / Due to** social media sites, it is now possible for scientists and non-scientists to work together on many projects. For many non-scientists, these projects are (7) **so / such** interesting that they want to help out as volunteers.

2 WRITE. Read the sentences. Then rewrite them using the words in parentheses. Add commas where necessary.

1. Zooniverse is a web portal. It is a citizen science project. (In addition)

   _____

   _____

2. Non-scientists are welcome in many science projects. They can't always be included. (Despite the fact that)

   _____

   _____

3. Some sciences require specific advanced knowledge. Other sciences are more accessible. (However)

   _____

   _____

4. Most scientists of the past were professionally trained. Isaac Newton was a citizen scientist. (On the other hand)

   _____

   _____

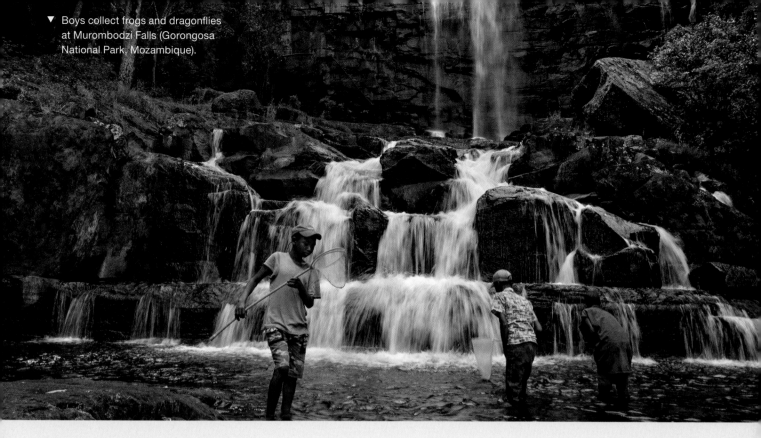

▼ Boys collect frogs and dragonflies at Murombodzi Falls (Gorongosa National Park, Mozambique).

Charts
15.1–15.6

3 READ & WRITE. Read the information about a kind of nature project called a bioblitz. Then complete the sentences using information from the text. Add commas where necessary.

Bioblitz

We often don't notice the biodiversity—the variety of plants and animals—right in our own backyards. Participating in a bioblitz can change that. A bioblitz lasts 24 hours. During that time, both scientists and non-scientists look around in one area carefully. They try to locate and identify as many different species of living things as possible. Hundreds of people look for species of plants, mammals, fish, birds, and insects. Large groups can cover a lot of ground. Although they usually find known species, sometimes new ones are discovered. Everyone gets very tired and dirty, but the work can be fun, and it's a great learning experience. In fact, most people want to do it again.

If you'd like to participate in a bioblitz, here are some important reminders:

- You have to register by a certain date in order to participate, so check the schedule.

- No experience is necessary.

- Weather conditions may change during the day, so wear layers of clothing.

- You will need sunglasses, sunscreen, and a hat.

- The event will take place rain or shine.

1. We don't often consider the biodiversity around us. However _____

_____.

2. In a bioblitz, people look for different species of plants. In addition _____

_____.

3. Despite the fact that _____ sometimes new species are discovered.

4. People who participate in bioblitzes usually get very dirty. Nevertheless, _____

_____.

5. It's such _____ most people want to do it again.

6. The weather may change. Therefore _____.

7. If it's hot and sunny, you need to protect yourself. Thus _____.

8. Bioblitzes are hardly ever canceled because of _____.

Charts
15.1–15.6

4 LISTEN.

CD4-22

A Listen to the report about a bioblitz in New York City's Central Park. Check (✓) the names of the creatures mentioned.

| _____ ants | _____ bears | _____ catfish | _____ spiders |
| _____ bats | _____ birds | _____ frogs | _____ turtles |

CD4-22

B Listen again. Write the missing words you hear. Add commas where necessary.

1. _____ the people had only 24 hours to work, they were able to find a great variety of wildlife.

2. _____ insect experts were pleased to find 44 beetle species and 31 types of spiders.

3. _____ during a bioblitz, nighttime is especially important. Participants were able to identify many different species of animals in the dark, such as owls and bats.

4. There is _____ a variety of species in Central Park _____ scientists are trying to find out why.

5. Many believe that it is _____ the conservation work that has been going on for years.

6. _____ the improvements in the land and water, a large number of living things are now living happily there.

7. _____ their bioblitz work, they now realize that there's a lot of natural beauty as well.

8. In fact, they saw _____ new things _____ they will never think of New York City in quite the same way again.

5 EDIT. Read the blog post about an expedition in Mongolia. Find and correct eight more errors with transition words and phrases of cause and effect, result, and contrast. There is more than one way to correct some errors.

Trekking Tina

OCTOBER 6

On our first day in Mongolia, we saw ~~such~~ so many amazing mountains that I didn't know what to photograph first. We came for the Eagle Festival. Later, our guide gave a talk about eagles and life in Mongolia. We learned that because Western influences, many young people in Mongolia move to the cities. Despite this, traditional life in Mongolia is threatened.

We saw Kazakhs training their eagles. They do so a good job that the eagles will hunt for them. We spent time on horseback with the Kazakhs. In fact, we spent such time on the horses that I was in a lot of pain later. After the Eagle Festival, we visited with a Kazakh family. Despite of the fact that I was very tired, I was very interested in learning about their lives. However, I stayed up very late talking to them.

We have been such busy that I have hardly had time to think about home, though I do miss my family. Therefore, I'm having a wonderful time.

6 WRITE & SPEAK.

A Read the statements. Write the number that best describes your opinion:

1 = strongly agree	3 = neither agree nor disagree	5 = strongly disagree
2 = agree somewhat	4 = disagree somewhat	

_____ 1. Some things can never be learned in a classroom.

_____ 2. We learn more useful things from experience than from classroom learning.

_____ 3. Learning is only possible when we're interested in what we're trying to learn.

_____ 4. We learn better if we have someone to guide us.

_____ 5. We learn from our mistakes.

B In your notebook, write sentences that explain your opinions from exercise **A**. Use words and phrases that show cause and effect, result, and contrast.

We can learn a lot from our mistakes. Therefore, we should try to keep a positive attitude when we make one.

C Work in a group. Share your sentences from exercise **B** and discuss your opinions.

Connect the Grammar to Writing

1 READ & NOTICE THE GRAMMAR.

A Have you ever taken an online class? Do you know anyone who has? How was the experience? Share your thoughts with a partner. Then read the essay.

Online Learning: Here to Stay

One of the most exciting new developments in higher education in the past few years has been the growth of online learning, especially MOOCs, massive open online courses. Despite some of the disadvantages, I believe that online classes are better than traditional college classes for a number of reasons.

To begin with, they are free. College tuition rates have been increasing for many years. As a result of these high rates, many people can't afford a traditional college education. Moreover, people all around the world can access MOOCs as long as they have a computer and an Internet connection. Thus, the student body is much more diverse than in a traditional classroom.

It is true that MOOCs provide fewer opportunities for direct contact with the professor. On the other hand, you learn from experts from all over the world. It is also true that you don't meet with your classmates face to face; however, you can interact with them online.

Due to the exciting opportunities that MOOCs offer, I think that the traditional college classroom will have a difficult time competing. Who wants to pay for a traditional class when you can be taught by the best in the world for free?

GRAMMAR FOCUS

In this essay, the writer uses transition words and prepositional phrases to indicate contrast, cause, effect or result, and addition.

Transition word	• *Moreover, people all around the world can access . . .*
Prepositional phrase	• *Despite some of the disadvantages, I believe that online classes . . .*

B Read the essay in exercise **A** again. Find examples of sentences that use transition words and prepositional phrases. Then work with a partner and indicate what each of your examples indicates: contrast, cause, effect or result, or addition.

Transition words

1. _____

2. _____

Prepositional Phrases

1. _____

2. _____

C Complete the charts below with information from the text in exercise **A**. Write in your notebook if you need more room. Then work with a partner and compare your answers.

Traditional College Classroom		Online Learning or MOOC	
Advantages	**Disadvantages**	**Advantages**	**Disadvantages**
direct contact with professor	expensive	diverse student body	

2 BEFORE YOU WRITE.

A Work with a partner. Brainstorm more advantages and disadvantages of both traditional college classes and online classes. List your ideas in your notebook.

B Make a chart like the ones in exercise **1C**. Decide which has more benefits: traditional classes or online classes.

3 WRITE to convince your reader that either traditional college classes or online classes are better. Write three or four paragraphs. Use your chart from exercise **2B** and the text in exercise **1A** to help you.

> **WRITING FOCUS**   Using Semicolons
>
> Writers use semicolons when they want to connect two sentences that have closely related ideas. They are commonly used when the second sentence begins with a transition word. See the examples below:
>
> *College tuition rates have been increasing for many years**; as a result, many people are not able to afford a traditional college education**.*
>
> *It is also true that you don't meet with your classmates face to face**; however, you can interact with them online**.*
>
> Remember to put a comma after a transition word.

4 SELF ASSESS. Read your essay. Underline the transition words and prepositional phrases that indicate contrast, cause, effect or result, or addition. Then use the checklist to assess your work.

- [ ] I used transition words indicating contrast, result, and addition correctly. [15.1–15.3]
- [ ] I used prepositional phrases indicating cause and contrast correctly. [15.4–15.6]
- [ ] I used semicolons correctly. [WRITING FOCUS]

1 Stative Verbs

Description	Feelings	Desires	Measurements	Mental States	Possession	Senses
appear* be consist of look look like resemble seem	appreciate care dislike forgive hate like love mind miss	hope need prefer want wish	cost measure weigh	agree believe concern disagree doubt forget guess know imagine mean recognize remember suppose surprise think understand	belong contain have own possess	feel hear hurt notice see smell sound taste

*Verbs in blue have both a stative and active meaning

2 Spelling Rules for the *-ed* Form of Verbs

1. Add *-ed* to the base form of most verbs that end in a consonant.	start-start**ed** talk-talk**ed**
2. Add *-d* if the base form of the verb ends in *-e*.	dance-danc**ed** live-liv**ed**
3. For one-syllable verbs that end in a consonant + a vowel + a consonant (CVC), double the final consonant and add *-ed*.	stop-stop**ped** rob-rob**bed**
Do not double the last consonant of verbs that end in *-w, -x,* or *-y*.	follow-follow**ed** fix-fix**ed** play-play**ed**
4. When the base form of the verb ends in a consonant + *-y*, change the *-y* to *-i* and add *–ed*.	cry-cr**ied** worry-worr**ied**
Do not change the *-y* to *-i* when the verb ends in a vowel + *-y*.	stay-stay**ed**
5. For two-syllable verbs that end in CVC and have stress on the first syllable, add *-ed*. Do not double the final consonant.	ORder-order**ed** HAPpen-HAPpen**ed**
For two-syllable verbs that end in CVC and have stress on the last syllable, double the final consonant and add *-ed*.	ocCUR-occur**red** preFER-prefer**red**

3   Spelling Rules for the *-ing* Form of Verbs

1. Add *-ing* to the base form of most verbs.	eat-eat**ing** do-do**ing** speak-speak**ing** carry-carry**ing**
2. For one-syllable verbs that end in a consonant + a vowel + a consonant (CVC), double the final consonant and add *-ing*. Do not double the final consonant for verbs that end in CVC when the final consonant is *-w, -x,* or *-y*.	stop-stop**ping** sit-sit**ting** show-show**ing** fix-fix**ing** stay-stay**ing**
3. When the verb ends in a consonant + *-e*, drop the *-e* and add *-ing*.	ride-rid**ing** write-writ**ing**
4. For two-syllable verbs that end in CVC and have stress on the first syllable, add *-ing*. Do not double the final consonant. For two-syllable verbs that end in CVC and have stress on the last syllable, double the final consonant and add *-ing*.	ENter-enter**ing** LISTen-listen**ing** beGIN-begin**ning** ocCUR-occur**ring**

4   Spelling Rules for Regular Plural Nouns

1. Add *-s* to most nouns.	student-student**s** teacher-teacher**s** pen-pen**s**
2. Add *-es* to nouns that end in *-ch, -s, -sh,* and *-x*.	watch-watch**es** class-class**es** dish-dish**es** box-box**es**
3. Add *-s* to nouns that end in a vowel + *-y*.	boy-boy**s** day-day**s**
4. Change the *-y* to *-i* and add *-es* to nouns that end in a consonant + *-y*.	city-cit**ies** country-countr**ies**
5. Add *-s* to nouns that end in a vowel + *-o*.	video-video**s** radio-radio**s**
6. Add *-es* to nouns that end in a consonant + *-o*. Exceptions: photo → photo**s** piano → piano**s**	potato-potato**es** tomato-tomato**es**

5 Common Irregular Verb Forms

Base Form	Simple Past	Past Participle
be	was, were	been
beat	beat	beaten
become	became	become
begin	began	begun
bend	bent	bent
bite	bit	bitten
blow	blew	blown
break	broke	broken
bring	brought	brought
build	built	built
buy	bought	bought
catch	caught	caught
choose	chose	chosen
come	came	come
cost	cost	cost
cut	cut	cut
dig	dug	dug
dive	dived/dove	dived
do	did	done
draw	drew	drawn
drink	drank	drunk
drive	drove	driven
eat	ate	eaten
fall	fell	fallen
feed	fed	fed
feel	felt	felt
fight	fought	fought
find	found	found
fit	fit	fit/fitted
fly	flew	flown
forget	forgot	forgotten
forgive	forgave	forgiven
freeze	froze	frozen
get	got	got/gotten
give	gave	given
go	went	gone
grow	grew	grown
hang	hung	hung
have	had	had
hear	heard	heard
hide	hid	hidden
hit	hit	hit
hold	held	held
hurt	hurt	hurt
keep	kept	kept
know	knew	known

Base Form	Simple Past	Past Participle
lay	laid	laid
lead	led	led
leave	left	left
lend	lent	lent
let	let	let
lie	lay	lain
light	lit/lighted	lit/lighted
lose	lost	lost
make	made	made
mean	meant	meant
meet	met	met
pay	paid	paid
prove	proved	proved/proven
put	put	put
quit	quit	quit
read	read	read
ride	rode	ridden
ring	rang	rung
rise	rose	risen
run	ran	run
say	said	said
sit	sat	sat
sleep	slept	slept
slide	slid	slid
speak	spoke	spoken
spend	spent	spent
spread	spread	spread
stand	stood	stood
steal	stole	stolen
stick	stuck	stuck
strike	struck	struck
swear	swore	sworn
sweep	swept	swept
swim	swam	swum
take	took	taken
teach	taught	taught
tear	tore	torn
tell	told	told
think	thought	thought
throw	threw	thrown
understand	understood	understood
upset	upset	upset
wake	woke	woken
wear	wore	worn
win	won	won
write	wrote	written

6   Patterns with Gerunds

Verb + Gerund

*They **enjoy dancing**.*
*She **delayed going** to the doctor.*

admit	detest	miss	resent
advise	discuss	permit	resist
anticipate	dislike	postpone	risk
appreciate	enjoy	practice	stop
avoid	finish	put off	suggest
can't help	forbid	quit	tolerate
complete	imagine	recall	understand
consider	keep	recommend	
delay	mention	regret	
deny	mind	remember	

Verb + Preposition + Gerund

*He **succeeded in winning** the prize.*
*Are you **thinking about taking** another course?*

apologize for	concentrate on	object to	thank (someone) for
argue about	dream about/of	plan on/for	think about
believe in	insist on	succeed in	warn (someone) about
complain about	keep on	talk about	worry about

Noun + Preposition + Gerund

*What's the **purpose of doing** this exercise?*
*I don't know his **reason for being** late.*

benefit of	interest in	purpose of
cause of	problem with	reason for

Adjective + Preposition + Gerund

*I'm **excited about studying** abroad.*
*Are you **interested in going**?*

accustomed to	excited about	nervous about	tired of
afraid of	famous for	responsible for	upset about/with
bad/good at	(in)capable of	sick of	used to
concerned about	interested in	sorry about/for	worried about

7 Patterns with Infinitives

Verb + Infinitive

They need to leave.
I am learning to speak English.

agree	claim	know how	seem
appear	consent	learn	swear
arrange	decide	manage	tend
ask	demand	need	threaten
attempt	deserve	offer	try
be able	expect	plan	volunteer
beg	fail	prepare	want
can afford	forget	pretend	wish
care	hope	promise	would like
choose	intend	refuse	

Verb + Object + Infinitive

I want you to leave.
He expects me to call him.

advise	convince	hire	require
allow	dare	instruct	select
appoint	enable	invite	teach
ask*	encourage	need*	tell
beg*	expect*	order	urge
cause	forbid	pay*	want*
challenge	force	permit	warn
choose*	get	persuade	would like*
command	help**	remind	

*These verbs can be either with or without an object. (*I want [you] to go.*)

**After *help*, *to* is often omitted. (*He helped me move.*)

8 Adjectives Followed by Infinitives

afraid	embarrassed	lucky	sad
ashamed	excited	necessary	shocked
careful	glad	pleased	sorry
certain	good	proud	stupid
challenging	happy	ready	surprised
determined	hard	relieved	upset
difficult	important	reluctant	useful
disappointed	impossible	rewarding	willing
easy	likely	right	wrong

9 Transitive Verbs

arrest	control	found	observe	refuse	steal
avoid	cost	generate	offer	regard	take
attract	create	get	order	release	threaten
bother	damage	give	owe	remove	throw
bring	destroy	harm	pass	repair	train
buy	discover	hurt	plant	report	trap
call	disturb	identify	pollute	rescue	use
catch	do	kill	post	save	want
chase	estimate	lend	prepare	say	wash
complete	expect	limit	produce	see	tell
conserve	feed	locate	propose	send	surround
consider	find	lock	protect	shape	
consume	follow	make	provide	show	
contact	force	name	put	solve	

Intransitive Verbs

appear	exist	occur	stay
arrive	fall	rain	survive
be	fly	rise	take place
come	go	run	talk
cough	happen	sit	wait
cry	laugh	sleep	walk
die	live	smile	
disappear	look	snow	
dry (up)	matter	stand	

Verbs That Are Transitive and Intransitive

answer	increase	promise	teach
bite	know	read	think
clean (up)	leave	sell	try
eat	lose	serve	visit
finish	move	sign	walk
flood	pay	sing	write
hunt	play	start	

10   Phrasal Verbs and Their Meanings

Transitive Phrasal Verbs (Separable)		

(s.o. = someone   s.t. = something)

Phrasal Verb	Meaning	Example Sentence
blow (s.t.)* up	cause something to explode	The workers **blew** the bridge **up**.
bring (s.t.) back	return	She **brought** the shirt **back** to the store.
bring (s.t.) up	1. raise from childhood 2. introduce a topic to discuss	1. My grandmother **brought** me **up**. 2. Don't **bring up** that subject.
call (s.o.)** back	return a telephone call	I **called** Rajil **back** but there was no answer.
call (s.t.) off	cancel	They **called** the wedding **off** after their fight.
call (s.t.) out	say something loudly	He stood up when someone **called** his name **out**.
check (s.t.) out	find out information	I **checked** several places **out** before making a decision.
cheer (s.o.) up	make someone feel happier	Her visit to the hospital **cheered** the patients **up**.
clear (s.o.) up	clarify, explain	She **cleared** the problem **up**.
cut (s.t.) down	cut through the trunk of a tree so that it falls down	The town **cut** many trees **down** to make room for new roads.
do (s.t.) over	do again	His teacher asked him to **do** the essay **over**.
figure (s.t.) out	solve, understand	The student **figured** the problem **out**.
fill (s.t.) in	complete information on a form	I **filled** the blanks **in** on a hob application.
fill (s.t.) out	complete an application or form	I had to **fill** many forms **out** at the doctor's office.
find (s.t.) out	learn, uncover	Did you **find** anything **out** about the new plans?
get (s.t.) across	succeed in making people understand an idea	Leo **gets** his ideas **across** with pictures.
give (s.t.) away	offer something freely	They are **giving** prizes **away** at the store.
give (s.t.) back	return	The boy **gave** the pen **back** to the teacher.
give (s.t.) up	stop doing	I **gave up** sugar last year. Will you **give** it **up**?
help (s.o.) out	aid, support someone	I often **help** my older neighbors **out**.
lay (s.o.) off	dismiss workers from their jobs	My company **laid** 200 workers **off** last year.
leave (s.t.) on	allow a machine to continue working	I **left** the lights **on** all night.
let (s.o./s.t.) in	allow someone or something to enter	She opened a window to **let** some fresh air **in**.
look (s.t.) over	examine	We **looked** the contract **over** before signing it.
look (s.t.) up	find information by looking in something like a reference book or list	I **looked** the word **up** in the dictionary.
make (s.o./s.t.) into	change someone or something to become someone or something else	They **made** the book **into** a movie.
make (s.t.) out of	produce something from a material or existing object	Lily **made** the costume **out of** old clothes.
make (s.t.) up	say something untrue or fictional (a story, a lie)	The child **made** the story **up**. It wasn't true at all.
pay (s.o./s.t.) back	return money, repay a loan	I **paid** my friend **back**. I owed him $10.
pick (s.o./s.t.) up	1. get someone or something 2. lift 3. acquire a skill over time without a lot of effort	1. He **picked up** his date at her house. 2. I **picked** the ball **up** and threw it. 3. Joe **picked** the language **up** just by talking to people
point (s.t.) out	tell someone about a fact or mistake	I **pointed** the problem **out** right away.
put (s.t.) aside	keep something to be dealt with or used at a later time	Let's **put** the list of names **aside** until we need them.
put (s.t) away	put something in the place where it is normally kept when it is not used	Please **put** your books **away** before we start the test.

Transitive Phrasal Verbs (Separable) *(Continued)*		
put (s.t.) off	delay, postpone	*Don't **put** your homework **off** until tomorrow.*
put (s.t.) on	place clothing or makeup on your body in order to wear it	*Emma **put** her coat **on** and left.*
put (s.t.) out	1. take outside 2. extinguish	1. *He **put** the trash **out**.* 2. *Firefighters **put out** the fire.*
set (s.t.) up	1. arrange 2. start something	1. *She **set** the tables **up** for the party.* 2. *They **set up** the project.*
show (s.t) off	make something obvious to a lot of people because you are proud of it	*Tom's mother **showed** his award **off** to everyone.*
shut (s.t.) off	1. stop something from working 2. stop the power	1. *Can you **shut** the water **off**?* 2. *I **shut** the oven **off**.*
slip (s.t.) off	remove clothing quickly	*They **slip** their shoes **off** when they enter a room.*
sort (s.t.) out	make sense of something	*We have to **sort** this problem **out**.*
straighten (s.t.) up	make neat and orderly	*I **straightened** the living room **up**. It was a mess.*
take (s.t.) back	own again	*He **took** his tools **back** that he loaned me.*
take (s.t.) out	remove	*I **take** the trash **out** on Mondays.*
talk (s.t.) over	discuss a topic until it is completely understood	*Let's **talk** this plan **over** before we do anything.*
think (s.t.) over	reflect, ponder	*She **thought** the job offer **over** carefully.*
throw (s.t.) away/ throw (s.t.) out	get rid of something, discard	*He **threw** the old newspapers **away**. I **threw out** the old milk in the fridge.*
try (s.t.) on	put on clothing to see if it fits	*He **tried** the shoes **on** but didn't buy them.*
turn (s.o./s.t.) down	refuse	*His manager **turned** his proposal **down**.*
turn (s.o.) off	disgust or offend	*People who brag **turn** me **off**.*
turn (s.t.) off	stop something from working	*Can you **turn** the TV **off**, please?*
turn (s.t.) on	switch on, operate	*I **turned** the lights **on** in the dark room.*
turn (s.t.) up	increase the volume	***Turn** the radio **up** so we can hear the news.*
wake (s.o.) up	stop sleeping	*The noise **woke** the baby **up**.*
write (s.t.) down	write on paper	*I **wrote** the information **down**.*

*s.t. = something   **s.o. = someone

Transitive Phrasal Verbs (Inseparable)		
*We'll **look into** the problem.*		
Phrasal Verb	**Meaning**	**Example Sentence**
account for (s.t.)	explain or give the necessary information about something	*What **accounts for** Ned's problems in school?*
come across (s.t.)	find something accidentally	*I **came across** a very old family photo.*
come from (somewhere)	be a native or resident of	*She **comes from** London.*
come up with (s.t.)	invent	*Let's **come up with** a new game.*
count on (s.o/s.t.)	depend on	*You can always **count on** good friends to help you.*
drop out of (s.t.)	quit	*Jin **dropped out of** the study group.*
fall for (s.o.)	be strongly attracted to someone and to start loving the person	*Chris **fell for** her the moment he saw her.*
follow through with (s.t.)	complete	*You must **follow through with** your promises.*
get off (s.t.)	leave (a bus/a train)	*I forgot to **get off** the bus at my stop.*
get on (s.t.)	board (a car/a train)	*I **got on** the plane last.*

Transitive Phrasal Verbs (Inseparable) (Continued)

get out of (s.t.)	1. leave (a car/a taxi) 2. avoid	1. *I got out of the car.* 2. *She got out of doing her chores.*
get together with (s.o.)	meet	*I got together with Ana on Saturday.*
get over (s.t.)	return to a normal state	*I just got over a bad cold. I feel much better now!*
go over (s.t.)	review	*Let's go over our notes before the exam.*
keep up with (s.o./s.t.)	move at the same speed or progress at the same rate	*Slow down. I can't keep up with you.*
look after (s.o./s.t.)	take care of	*He has to look after his sister. His parents are out.*
look for (s.o./s.t.)	try to find someone or something that you want or need	*I'm looking for someone who can help me.*
look into (s.t.)	investigate	*The police looked into the crime and solved it.*
pass by (s.o./s.t.)	go past a person, place, etc., on your way to another place	*If you pass by the house, call first.*
put up with (s.t.)	tolerate or accept something even though you find it unpleasant	*We have to put up with a lot of noise in this building.*
run into (s.o.)	meet accidentally	*She ran into Mai on campus.*
turn into (s.t.)	become something different	*The trip turned into a nightmare.*
turn to (s.o.)	ask someone for help or advice	*I turn to my parents when I need advice.*
take up (s.t.)	use an amount of time, space, or effort	*The table takes up too much space.*

Intransitive Phrasal Verbs (Inseparable)

My car broke down again!

Phrasal Verb	Meaning	Example Sentence
add up	make sense	*What he says does not add up.*
break down	stop working	*This machine breaks down all the time.*
break up	separate	*Their marriage broke up after a year.*
catch up	reach the same level as others in a group	*You can catch up with the others in the class, but you have to work hard.*
check out	pay the bill and leave a hotel	*We have to check out by noon.*
come back	return	*I'll come back soon.*
come on	(of a machine) start working	*It takes a few minutes for the copier to come on.*
come out	reach a result	*The meeting came out well. We were all satisfied.*
cry out	make a loud sound because you are frightened, unhappy, or in pain	*When the children saw the bear, they cried out.*
die out	become less and less common and eventually disappear completely	*Many languages have died out.*
dress up	put on more formal clothes	*He dressed up in his best suit to attend the wedding.*
drop in	visit without an appointment	*Drop in when you can.*
drop out	leave or stop	*She dropped out of school very young.*
eat out	eat in a restaurant	*She hates to cook so she eats out frequently.*
end up	come finally to a particular place or position	*We couldn't decide where to eat. We ended up at a pizza place.*
fall down	fall accidentally	*I wasn't looking and fell down.*
fool around	play with	*He fools around with old cars for fun.*
get ahead	succeed, improve oneself	*Now that she has a new job, she is getting ahead.*
get along	have a friendly relationship	*My coworkers and I get along well together.*

		Intransitive Phrasal Verbs (Inseparable) *(Continued)*	
get around	go from one place to another in a certain way	I **get around** by bike.
get up	awaken, arise	I **got up** late this morning.
give up	stop trying	I played the piano for seven years but then **gave up**.
go ahead	begin or continue to do	You can **go ahead**. We'll wait for Jane.
go away	leave, depart	The rabbits in the garden finally **went away**.
go down	decrease	Prices of cars have **gone down** recently.
go on	continue	How long do you think this speech will **go on**?
go out	1. leave one's home 2. have a romantic relationship with someone	1. Jon has **gone out**. He should return soon. 2. Lee and Sam have been **going out** for a year.
go up	rise, go higher	The price of gasoline has **gone up**.
grow up	become and adult	Our daughter has **grown up** now.
hang on	wait	**Hang on** while I change my shoes.
hang out	spend time with others informally	My friends and I like to **hang out** on Friday nights.
hold on	1. struggle against difficulty 2. keep your hand on or around something	1. **Hold on** just a little longer. It's almost over. 2. **Hold on** so that you don't fall.
look around	examine an area	We **looked around** before choosing a place to camp.
look out	be careful	**Look out**! You'll fall!
loosen up	become more relaxed	My boss used to be very tense, but she has **loosened up** over the years.
make up	agree to be friends again	They had a fight, but soon **made up**.
move in	start to live in	We **moved in** last week. We love the area!
move out	leave a place permanently	When is your roommate **moving out**?
pass away	die	My father **passed away** last year.
run out	use all of something	Is there more of paper for the printer? We **ran out**.
set out	start a journey	We're going to **set out** at 6 a.m.
show up	arrive (sometimes unexpectedly or late)	They **showed up** after the train left.
sign up	join, agree to do something	The course looked interesting, so I **signed up**.
sit down	seat oneself	I **sat down** on a bench in the park.
speak up	talk louder	Will you **speak up**? I can't hear you?
stand out	be very noticeable	Can you make his face **stand out** more so that everyone can see him?
stand up	get on one's feet	The teacher asked the students to **stand up**.
stay on	remain somewhere after other people have left or after when you were going to leave	We haven't seen everything, so we'll **stay on** another day.
stay up	keep awake	The student **stayed up** all night to study.
take off	1. leave the ground and start flying 2. increase quickly	1. After a long wait, the airplane finally **took off**. 2. Sales of the new product have **taken off**.
turn out	happen in a particular way or have a particular result	I hope everything **turns out** well.
watch out	be careful	**Watch out**! There's a lot of ice on this road.
work out	exercise	The football player **works out** three times a week.

11 Verbs Followed by Noun Clauses

Learning & Noticing Verbs	Predicting Verbs	Reporting Verbs	Showing Verbs	Suggesting Verbs	Thinking & Feeling Verbs
learn	anticipate	answer	demonstrate	advise	agree
discover	expect	add	indicate	propose	assume
find (out)	hope	claim	reveal	recommend	believe
hear	predict	explain	show	suggest	consider
notice		inform			dream
read		mention			fear
realize		notify			feel
		promise			forget
		remind			know
		reply			remember
		respond			think
		say			understand
		scream			worry
		shout			
		state			
		tell			
		warn			

12 Reported Speech Verb and Modal Changes

Tense Changes

Tense	Quote	Reported Speech		
Simple present	"I **eat** lunch."		ate	
Present progressive	"I'm **eating** lunch"		was eating	
Simple past	"I **ate** lunch."	Sue said she	ate *or* had eaten	lunch.
Present perfect	"I **have eaten** lunch."		had eaten	
Past perfect	"I **had eaten** lunch."		had eaten	
Be going to	"I'm **going to eat** lunch."		was going to eat	

Modal Changes

Modal	Quote	Reported Speech		
Can	"We **can** come."		could	
May	"We **may** come."	They said they	might	come.
Must	"We **must** come."		had to	
Will	"We **will** come."		would	

No Modal Changes

Modal	Quote	Reported Speech		
could	"I **could** help."		could	
might	"I **might** help."	Bill said he	might	help.
ought to	"I **ought to** help."		ought to	
should	"I **should** help."		should	

13 Guide to Pronunciation Symbols

Vowels		
Symbol	Key Word	Pronunciation
/a/	hot	/hat/
	far	/far/
/æ/	cat	/kæt/
/aɪ/	fine	/faɪn/
/aʊ/	house	/haʊs/
/ɛ/	bed	/bɛd/
/eɪ/	name	/neɪm/
/i/	need	/nid/
/ɪ/	sit	/sɪt/
/oʊ/	go	/goʊ/
/ʊ/	book	/bʊk/
/u/	boot	/but/
/ɔ/	dog	/dɔg/
	four	/fɔr/
/ɔɪ/	toy	/tɔɪ/
/ʌ/	cup	/kʌp/
/ɛr/	bird	/bɛrd/
/ə/	about	/əˈbaʊt/
	after	/ˈæftər/

Consonants		
Symbol	Key Word	Pronunciation
/b/	boy	/bɔɪ/
/d/	day	/deɪ/
/dʒ/	just	/dʒʌst/
/f/	face	/feɪs/
/g/	get	/gɛt/
/h/	hat	/hæt/
/k/	car	/kar/
/l/	light	/laɪt/
/m/	my	/maɪ/
/n/	nine	/naɪn/
/ŋ/	sing	/sɪŋ/
/p/	pen	/pɛn/
/r/	right	/raɪt/
/s/	see	/si/
/t/	tea	/ti/
/tʃ/	cheap	/tʃip/
/v/	vote	/voʊt/
/w/	west	/wɛst/
/y/	yes	/yɛs/
/z/	zoo	/zu/
/ð/	they	/ðeɪ/
/θ/	think	/θɪŋk/
/ʃ/	shoe	/ʃu/
/ʒ/	vision	/ˈvɪʒən/

Source: The *Newbury House Dictionary plus Grammar Reference, Fifth Edition*, National Geographic Learning/Cengage Learning, 2014

Unit 9, Lesson 1, Exercise 8B, Page 242

1. Researchers say that at least 60 million sharks are killed each year. Many estimate that the number is much higher, possibly well over 200 million sharks per year.
2. Fewer than 100 people are attacked by sharks each year.
3. The megamouth shark was discovered in 1976.
4. More than 100 shark species are threatened by human activity.
5. The fins are sold for food.
6. Shark-fin soup is most popular in Asia.
7. Shark-fin soup is often served at weddings.
8. Sharks can be protected if people stop hunting them.

action verb: a verb that shows an action.
> ➤ He **drives** every day.
> ➤ They **left** yesterday morning.

active voice: a sentence in which the subject performs the action of the verb**.** (See *passive.*)
> ➤ *Michael ate the hamburger.*

adjective: a word that describes or modifies a noun or pronoun.
> ➤ She is **friendly**.
> ➤ Brazil is a **huge** country.

adjective clause: (See *relative clause.*)

adverb: a word that describes or modifies a verb, an adjective, or another adverb.
> ➤ He eats **quickly**.
> ➤ She drives **carefully**.

adverb clause: a kind of dependent clause. Like single adverbs, they can show time, reason, purpose, and condition.
> ➤ **When the party was over**, everyone left.

adverb of frequency: (See *frequency adverb.*)

adverb of manner: an adverb that describes the action of the verb. Many adverbs of manner are formed by adding *-ly* to the adjective.
> ➤ You sing **beautifully**.
> ➤ He speaks **slow**ly.

affirmative statement: a statement that does not have a verb in the negative form.
> ➤ *My uncle lives in Portland.*

article: a word used before a noun; *a, an, the.*
> ➤ I looked up at **the** moon.
> ➤ Lucy had **a** sandwich and **an** apple for lunch.

auxiliary verb: (Also called *helping verb.*) A verb used with the main verb. *Be, do, have,* and *will* are common auxiliary verbs when they are followed by another verb. Modals are also auxiliary verbs.
> ➤ I **am** working.
> ➤ He **won't** be in class tomorrow.
> ➤ She **can** speak Korean.

base form: the form of the verb without *to* or any endings such as *-ing, -s,* or *-ed.*
> ➤ *eat, sleep, go, walk*

capital letter: an uppercase letter.
> ➤ *New York, Mr. Franklin, Japan*

clause: a group of words with a subject and a verb. (See *dependent clause* and *main clause.*)
> ➤ *We watched the game.* (one clause)
> ➤ *We watched the game after we ate dinner.* (two clauses)

comma: a punctuation mark that separates parts of a sentence.
> ➤ *After he left work**,** he went to the gym.*
> ➤ *I can't speak Russian**,** but my sister can.*

common noun: a noun that does not name a specific person, place, thing, or idea.
> ➤ *man, country, book, help*

comparative: the form of an adjective used to talk about the difference between two people, places, or things.
> ➤ I'm **taller** than my mother.
> ➤ That book is **more interesting** than this one.

conditional: a structure used to express an activity or event that depends on something else.
> ➤ **If the weather is nice on Sunday**, we'll go to the beach.

conjunction: a word used to connect information or ideas. *And, but, or,* and *because* are conjunctions.
> ➤ He put cheese **and** onions on his sandwich.
> ➤ I wanted to go, **but** I had too much homework.
> ➤ We were confused **because** we didn't listen.

consonant: a sound represented by the following letters and combinations of the letters:
> ➤ *b, c, d, f, g, h, j, k, l, m, n, p, q, r, s, t, v, w, x, y, z.*

contraction: two words combined into a shorter form.
> ➤ *did not* → **didn't**
> ➤ *I am* → **I'm**
> ➤ *she is* → **she's**
> ➤ *we will* → **we'll**

count noun: a noun that names something you can count. They are singular or plural.
> ➤ I ate an **egg** for breakfast.
> ➤ I have **six apples** in my bag.

definite article: the article *the.* It is used when you are referring to a specific, person, place, or thing.
> ➤ I found it on **the** Internet.
> ➤ **The** children are sleeping.

demonstrative pronoun: a pronoun that identifies a person or thing.
> ➤ **This** is my sister, Kate.
> ➤ **Those** are Jamal's books.

dependent clause: a clause that cannot stand alone as a sentence. It must be used with a main clause.

> I went for a walk **before I ate breakfast**.

direct object: a noun or pronoun that receives the action of the verb.

> Aldo asked a **question**.
> Karen helped **me**.

direct quote: a statement of a speaker's exact words using quotation marks.

> Our teacher said, **"Do exercises 5 and 6 for homework."**

exclamation point: a punctuation mark that shows emotion (anger, surprise, excitement, etc.) or emphasis

> We won the game**!**
> It's snowing**!**

formal: describes language used in academic writing or speaking, or in polite or official situations rather than in everyday speech or writing.

> Please do not take photographs inside the museum.
> May I leave early today?

frequency adverb: an adverb that tells how often something happens. Some common adverbs of frequency are *never, rarely, sometimes, often, usually,* and *always*.

> I **always** drink coffee in the morning.
> He **usually** leaves work at six.

frequency expression: an expression that tells how often something happens.

> We go to the grocery store **every Saturday**.
> He plays tennis **twice a week**.

future: a form of a verb that expresses an action or situation that has not happened yet. *Will, be going to,* present progressive, and simple present are used to express the future.

> I **will call** you later.
> We**'re going** to the movies tomorrow.
> I**'m taking** French next semester.
> The show **starts** after dinner.

future conditional: expresses something that we believe will happen in the future based on certain conditions; the *if* clause + simple present gives the condition, and *will* or *be going to* + the base form of the verb gives the result.

> If you don't go to practice, the coach will not let you play in the game.

future perfect: a verb form used to talk about an action or event that will happen before a certain time in the future.

> I**'ll have finished** the work by the time you return.

generic noun: a noun that refers to people, places, and things in general

> **Hospitals** are for sick **people**.
> I like **music**.

gerund: an *-ing* verb form that is used as a noun. It can be the subject of a sentence, or the object of a verb or preposition. (See page A4 for lists of common verbs followed by gerunds.)

> **Surfing** is a popular sport.
> We enjoy **swimming**.
> The boy is interested in **running**.

gerund phrase: an *-ing* verb form + an object or a prepositional phrase. It can be the subject of a sentence, or the object of a verb or preposition.

> **Swimming in the ocean** is fun.
> I love **eating chocolate**.
> We are thinking about **watching the new TV show**.

helping verb: (See *auxiliary verb*.)

***if* clause:** a clause that begins with *if* that expresses a condition.

> **If you drive too fast,** you will get a ticket.

imperative: a sentence that gives an instruction or command.

> **Turn** left at the light.
> **Don't use** the elevator.

indefinite article: *a* and *an,* articles used when you are not referring to a specific person, place, or thing. They are used before singular count nouns.

> We have **a** test today.
> She's **an** engineer.

indefinite pronoun: a pronoun used to refer to people or things that are not specific or not known. *Someone, something, everyone, everything, no one, nothing,* and *nowhere* are common indefinite pronouns.

> **Everyone** is here today.
> **No one** is absent.
> Would you like **something** to eat?

independent clause: a clause that can stand alone as a complete sentence. It has a subject and a verb.

> **I went for a walk** before breakfast.

infinitive: *to* + the base form of a verb.

> He wants **to see** the new movie.

infinitive of purpose: *to* + the base form of the verb used to express purpose or to answer the question *Why?* (also *in order to*)

> Scientists studied the water **in order to learn** about the disease.
> We went to the store **to buy** milk.

informal: language used in casual, everyday conversation and writing.
  - ➢ *Who are you talking to?*
  - ➢ *We'll be there at eight.*

information question: (See *Wh-* question.)

inseparable phrasal verb: a phrasal verb that cannot have an noun or pronoun between its two parts (verb + particle). The verb and the particle always stay together.
  - ➢ *I **ran into** a friend in the library.*
  - ➢ *Do you and your coworkers **get along**?*

intonation: the rise or fall of a person's voice. For example, rising intonation is often used to ask a question.

intransitive verb: a verb that cannot be followed by a direct object.
  - ➢ *We didn't **agree**.*
  - ➢ *The students **smiled** and **laughed**.*

irregular adjective: an adjective that does not change form in the usual way.
  - ➢ *good → better*
  - ➢ *bad → worse*

irregular adverb: an adverb that does not change form in the usual way.
  - ➢ *well → better*
  - ➢ *badly → worse*

irregular verb: a verb with forms that do not follow the rules for regular verbs.
  - ➢ *swim → swam*
  - ➢ *have → had*

main clause: a clause that can stand alone as a sentence. It has a subject and a verb. (See *independent clause*.)
  - ➢ *I **heard the news** when I was driving home.*

main verb: the verb that is the main clause.
  - ➢ *We **drove** home after we had dinner.*

measurement word: a word used to talk about a specific amount or quantity of a non-count noun.
  - ➢ *We need to buy a **box** of pasta and a **gallon** of milk.*

modal: an auxiliary verb that adds a degree of certainty, possibility, or time to a verb. *May, might, can, could, will, would,* and *should* are common modals.
  - ➢ *You **should** eat more vegetables.*
  - ➢ *Julie **can** speak three languages.*

negative statement: a statement that has a verb in the negative form.
  - ➢ *I **don't** have any sisters.*
  - ➢ *She **doesn't** drink coffee.*

non-count noun: a noun that names something that cannot be counted.
  - ➢ *Carlos drinks a lot of **coffee**.*
  - ➢ *I need some **salt** for the **recipe**.*

non-identifying relative clause: a relative clause that gives extra information about the noun it is describing. The information is not necessary to understand who or what the noun refers to.
  - ➢ *Nelson Mandela, **who was a great leader**, died in 2013.*

noun: a word that names a person, place, or thing.
  - ➢ *They're **students**.*
  - ➢ *He's a **teacher**.*

noun clause: a kind of dependent clause. A noun clause can be used in place of a noun, a noun phrase or a pronoun.
  - ➢ *Could you tell me **where the bank is**?*

object: a noun or pronoun that receives the action of the verb.
  - ➢ *Mechanics fix **cars**.*

object pronoun: takes the place of a noun as the object of the sentence; *me, you, him, her, it, us, them.*
  - ➢ *Rita is my neighbor. I see **her** every day.*
  - ➢ *Can you help **us**?*

passive: a verb form that expresses who or what receives the action of the verb, not who or what performs the action
  - ➢ *My wallet **has been stolen**.*

past perfect: a verb form used to talk about an action that happened before another action or time in the past.
  - ➢ *They **had met** in school, but then they didn't see each other again for many years.*

past perfect progressive: *a verb form used for an action or event that was happening until or just before another action, event, or time.*
  - ➢ *He'd **been driving** for twelve hours when they ran out of gas.*

past progressive: a verb form used to talk about an action that was in progress in the past.
  - ➢ *He **was watching** TV when the phone rang.*

period: a punctuation mark used at the end of a statement.
  - ➢ *She lives in Moscow.*

phrasal verb: a two-word or three-word verb. The phrasal verb means something different from the two or three words separately. (See pages A7–A9 for lists of common phrasal verbs.)
  - ➢ ***Turn off** the light when you leave.*
  - ➢ *She's **come up with** an interesting idea.*

phrase: a group of words that go together; not a complete sentence (i.e., does not have both a subject and a verb).

> ➢ He lives **near the train station**.

plural noun: the form of a noun that indicates more than one person, place, or thing.

> ➢ He put three **boxes** on the table.
> ➢ Argentina and Mexico are **countries**.

possessive adjective: an adjective that shows ownership or a relationship: *my, your, his, her, its, our, their*.

> ➢ **My** car is green.
> ➢ **Your** keys are on the table.

possessive noun: a noun that shows ownership or a relationship. To make most singular nouns possessive, use an apostrophe (') + *-s*. To make plural nouns possessive, add an apostrophe.

> ➢ **Leo's** apartment is large.
> ➢ The **girls'** books are on the table.

possessive pronoun: a pronoun that shows ownership or a relationship: *mine, yours, his, hers, ours, theirs*. Possessive pronouns are used in place of a possessive adjective + noun.

> ➢ My sister's eyes are blue. **Mine** are brown. What color are **yours**?

preposition: a word that describes the relationships between nouns; prepositions show space, time, direction, cause, and effect. Often they occur together with certain verbs or adjectives.

> ➢ I live **on** Center Street.
> ➢ We left **at** noon.
> ➢ I'm worried **about** the test.

present continuous: (See *present progressive*.)

present perfect: a verb form that connects the past to the present.

> ➢ Julia **has lived** in London for 10 years.
> ➢ Monika **has broken** the world record.
> ➢ Zack and Dan **have never been** to Germany.

present perfect progressive: a verb form used for ongoing actions that began in the past and continue up to the present.

> ➢ You**'ve been working** too hard.

present progressive: (also called *present continuous*) a verb form used to talk about an action or event that is in progress at the moment of speaking; the form can also refer to a planned event in the future.

> ➢ That car **is speeding**.
> ➢ I **am taking** three classes this semester.
> ➢ We **are eating** at that new restaurant Friday night.

pronoun: a word that takes the place of a noun or refers to a noun.

> ➢ The teacher is sick today. **He** has a cold.

proper noun: a noun that names a specific person, place, or thing.

> ➢ **Maggie** lives in a town near **Dallas**.

punctuation: a mark that makes ideas in writing clear. Common punctuation marks include the comma (,), period (.), exclamation point (!), and question mark (?).

> ➢ John plays soccer**,** but I don't.
> ➢ She's from Japan**.**
> ➢ That's amazing**!**
> ➢ Where are you from**?**

quantifier: a word used to describe the amount of a noun.

> ➢ We need **some** potatoes for the recipe.
> ➢ I usually put **a little** milk in my coffee.

question mark: a punctuation mark used at the end of a question.

> ➢ Are you a student**?**

regular: a noun, verb, adjective, or adverb that changes form according to standard rules.

> ➢ apple $\longrightarrow$ apple**s**
> ➢ talk $\longrightarrow$ talk**ed**/talk**ing**
> ➢ small $\longrightarrow$ small**er**
> ➢ slow $\longrightarrow$ slow**ly**

reported speech: part of a sentence (a noun clause or infinitive phrase) that reports what someone has said.

> ➢ They said **they would be late**.
> ➢ They told **us not to wait**.

sentence: a thought that is expressed in words, usually with a subject and verb. A sentence begins with a capital letter and ends with a period, exclamation point, or question mark.

> ➢ The bell rang loudly.
> ➢ Don't eat that!

separable phrasal verb: a phrasal verb that can have a noun or a pronoun (object) between its two parts (verb + particle).

> ➢ **Turn** the light **off**.
> ➢ **Turn off** the light.

short answer: a common spoken answer to a question that is not always a complete sentence.

> ➢ A: Did you do the homework?
> ➢ B: **Yes, I did./No, I didn't.**
> ➢ A: Where are you going?
> ➢ B: **To the store.**

simple past: a verb form used to talk about completed actions.

> ➢ Last night we **ate** dinner at home.
> ➢ I **visited** my parents last weekend.

simple present: a verb form used to talk about habits or routines, schedules, and facts.

> He *likes* apples and oranges.
> Toronto *gets* a lot of snow in the winter.

singular noun: a noun that names only one person, place, or thing.

> They have *a son* and *a daughter*.

statement: a sentence that gives information.

> *My house has five rooms.*
> *He doesn't have a car.*

stative verb: a verb that does not describe an action. Non-action verbs indicate states, sense, feelings, or ownership. They are not common in the progressive.

> I *love* my grandparents.
> I *see* Marta. She's across the street.
> They *have* a new car.

stress: to say a syllable or a word with more volume or emphasis.

subject: the noun or pronoun that is the topic of the sentence.

> *Patricia* is a doctor.
> *They* are from Iceland.

subject pronoun: a pronoun that is the subject of a sentence: *I, you, he, she, it,* and *they.*

> *I* have one brother.
> *He* lives in Miami.

superlative: the form of an adjective or adverb used to compare three or more people, places, or things.

> Mount Everest is *the highest* mountain in the world.
> Evgeny is *the youngest* student in our class.

syllable: a part of a word that contains a single vowel sound and is pronounced as a unit.

> The word *pen* has one syllable.
> The word *pencil* has two syllables (pen-cil).

tense: the form of the verb that shows the time of the action.

> They *sell* apples. (simple present)
> They *sold* cars. (simple past)

third-person singular: in the simple present, the third-person singular ends in *–s* or *–es.* Singular nouns and the pronouns *he, she, it,* take the third-person singular form.

> She *plays* the piano.
> Mr. Smith *teaches* her.

time clause: a clause that tells when an action or event happened or will happen. Time clauses are introduced by conjunctions, such as *when, after, before, while,* and *since.*

> I have lived here **since I was a child.**
> **While I was walking home,** it began to rain.
> I'm going to call my parents **after I eat dinner.**

time expression: a phrase that tells when something happened or will happen. Time expressions usually go at the end or the beginning of sentence.

> **Last week** I went hiking.
> She's moving **next month.**

transitive verb: a verb that is followed by a direct object.

> We **took** an umbrella.

transition word: a word or phrase that connects ideas between sentences.

> I'd like to go. **However,** I have too much work to do.

unreal: used to describe situations that are contrary-to-fact, impossible, or unlikely to happen.

> If I **weren't learning** English, I **would have** more free time.
> I wish I **had** a million dollars.

verb: a word that shows action, gives a state, or shows possession.

> Tori **skated** across the ice.
> She **is** an excellent athlete.
> She **has** many medals.

voiced: a sound that is spoken with the vibration of the vocal cords. The consonants *b, d, g, j, l, m, n, r, th* (as in *then*), *v, w, z,* and all vowels are typically voiced.

voiceless: a sound that is spoken without the vibration of the vocal cords. The consonants *k, p, s, t,* and *ch,* sh, *th* (as in *thing*) are voiceless.

vowel: a sound represented in English by the letters: *a, e, i, o, u,* and sometimes *y.*

Wh- question: a question that asks for specific information, not *"Yes"* or *"No."* (See *Wh- word.*)

> **Where do they live?**
> **What do you usually do on weeeknds?**

Wh- word: a word such as *who, what, when, where, why,* or *how* that is used to begin a *Wh-* question.

Yes/No question: a question that can be answered by *"Yes"* or *"No."*

> **Do you live in Dublin?** Yes, I do./No I don't.
> **Can you ski?** Yes, I can./No, I can't.

INDEX

Note: All page references in blue are in Split Edition B.

Outofedenwalk.nationalgeographic.com/2013/02/08/gona-first-kitchen; scienceblogs.com/purepedantry/2007/06/25/did-cooking-allow-for-the-incr. **394:** Exercise 4. Source: news.nationalgeographic.com/news/2012/10/121026-human-cooking-evolution-raw-food-health-science. **401:** Exercise 12. Source: http://video.nationalgeographic.com/video/solar-cooking. **402:** Exercise 13. Source: http://news.nationalgeographic.com/news/2013/08/130823-prehistoric-hunter-gatherers-garlic-mustard-spices. **403:** Exercise 1. Source: http://www.theglobeandmail.com/life/food-and-wine/food-trends/the-5-senses-of-flavour-how-colour-and-sound-can-make-your-dinner-taste-better/article9957597. **410:** Exercise 11: http://angelsmith.net/inbound-marketing/groundbreaking-survey-reveals-how-diners-choose-restaurants. **426:** Exercise 1. Source: www.nationalgeographic.com/explorers/bios/brendan-mullan; science.psu.edu/news-and-events/Brendan-mullan-selected-as-a-2013-national-geographic-emerging-explorer. **436:** Exercise 1. Sources: www.ted.com/prize/sole_toolkit#intro; newswatch.nationalgeographic/tag/sugata-mitra; huffingtonpost.com/sugata-mitra/2013-ted-prize_b_276598.html. **440:** Exercise 6. Source: http://www.forbes.com/sites/danschawbel/2013/05/30/josh-kaufman-it-takes-20-hours-not-10000-hours-to-learn-a-skill/ **447:** Exercise 1. Source: Nationalgeographic.com/explorers/projects/bioblitz. **449:** Exercise 5. Sources: http://www.nomadicexpeditions.com/trip-finder/golden-eagle-festival; http://www.geoex.com/trips/mongolia-golden-eagle-festival; http://discover-bayanolgii.com/golden-eagle-festival.

Definitions for glossed words: Sources: *The Newbury House Dictionary plus Grammar Reference,* Fifth Edition, National Geographic Learning/Cengage Learning, 2014; *Collins Cobuild Illuminated Basic Dictionary of American English,* Cengage Learning 2010, Collings Cobuild/Harper Collins Publishers, First Edition, 2010; *Collins Cobuild School Dictionary of American English,* Cengage Learning 2009, Collins Cobuild/Harper Collins Publishers, 2008; Collins Cobuild Advanced Learner's Dictionary, 5th Edition, Harper Collins Publishers, 2006.

Photo Credits:

Inside Front Cover, left column: ©Cristina Mittermeier/National Geographic Creative, Courtesy of The Thayer Collection, Reprinted with permission of Barton Seaver, photo by Katie Stoops, ©Calit2, Erik Jepsen, ©Vander Meulen, Rebecca J/National Geographic Creative; right column: ©Cengage/National Geographic Creative, ©Tyrone Turner/National Geographic Creative, ©Cengage/National Geographic Creative, ©Rebecca Hale/National Geographic Creative, ©Jay Ullal/Black Star/Newscom.

2-3: ©Design Pics Inc/National Geographic Creative; **4, 5:** ©Michael Nichols/National Geographic Creative; **9:** ©Makoto Fujio/Getty Images; **12:** ©Echo/Getty Images; **13:** ©Genevieve Naylor/Corbis; **17:** ©KeithSzafranski/iStockphoto; **18:** ©National Geographic Image Collection/Alamy; **19:** ©Jodi Cobb/National Geographic/SuperStock, **22:** ©alkir/iStockphoto; **24:** ©INTERFOTO/Alamy; **28:** ©Catchlight Visual Services/Alamy; **30-31:** ©Jimmy Chin and Lynsey Dyer/National Geographic Creative; **32, 33:** ©Paul Nicklen/National Geographic Creative; **38:** ©Joel Sartore/National Geographic Creative; **39 top:** ©Jeff Compasso/Alamy, **bottom:** ©Diane Cook and Len Jenshel/National Geographic Creative; **41 top:** Courtesy of the Thayer Collection, **bottom:** ©David Pluth/National Geographic Creative; **42:** ©David Pluth/National Geographic Creative; **46:** Reprinted with permission of Barton Seaver, photo by Katie Stoops; **48-49:** ©Jimmy Chin/National Geographic Creative, **55:** ©Hulton Archive/Getty Images; **56:** ©Bill Hatcher/National Geographic Creative; **57:** ©www.sand3r.com/Getty Images; **58:** ©Frans Lanting/National Geographic Creative; **59:** ©Lui Siu Wai/Xinhua/Photoshot/Newscom; **60:** ©Christopher Futcher/iStockphoto; **62-63:** ©southeast asia/Alamy; **64:** ©Koichi Kamoshida/Getty Images; **65:** ©Yoshikazu Tsuno/AFP/Getty Images; **71 top:** ©Gry Karin Stimo/SINTEF, **bottom:** © Danita Delimont/Getty Images; **72:** ©Yoshikazu Tsuno/AFP/Getty Images; **78, 79:** ©Rex Features via AP Images; **84, 88:** ©Bloomberg via Getty Images; **90-91:** ©Piriya Photography/Getty Images; **92-93:** ©Image Asset Management Ltd./Alamy; **94:** ©European Space Agency/NASA; **96-97:** ©JPL-Caltech/NASA; **99:** ©Blaine Harrington III/Alamy; **100 left to right:** ©Matthew Jacques/Shutterstock, ©Top Photo Corporation/Thinkstock, © CatchaSnap/Shutterstock; **101 background:** ©Julia Ivantsova/Shutterstock; **101 both, 102:** ©Borge Ousland/National Geographic Creative; **105:** ©David Liittschwager/National Geographic Creative; **106:** ©Raymond Gehman/National Geographic Creative; **107:** ©Bobby Model/National Geographic Creative; **109:** ©Calit2, Erik Jepsen; **110:** ©James Stanfield/National Geographic Creative; **112 background:** ©Miro Novak/Shutterstock; **114-115:** ©Alison Wright/National Geographic Creative; **116-117:** ©Jon Bower at Apexphotos/Getty Images; **116:** ©Edmund Lowe/Alamy; **122:** Photo by Draycat; **123:** ©katorisi; **124-125:** ©Michael Nichols/National Geographic Creative; **129:** ©epa european pressphoto agency b.v./Alamy; **131, 132:** ©David McLain/National Geographic Creative; **135 background:** ©Odua Images/Shutterstock; **136 background:** ©Feng Yu/Shutterstock; **138:** ©Aaron Juey/National Geographic Creative; **140:** ©Rachid Dahnoun/Getty Images; **142-143:** ©Shah Marai/AFP/Getty Images; **144-145:** ©Bill Hatcher/National Geographic Creative; **148:** ©Dan Kitwood/Getty Images; **149:** ©Silvia Reiche/Minden Pictures/Getty Images; **152:** ©Wade Davis/Getty Images; **153:** © blickwinkel/Alamy; **158:** ©wacpan/Shutterstock; **161, 162:** ©Feliciano dos Santos/National Geographic Creative; **166:** ©Cengage/National Geographic Creative; **168:** ©ZUMA Press, Inc./Alamy; **172:** ©Fitbit, Inc.; **174-175:** ©Frans Lanting/National Geographic Creative; **176-177:** ©Tim Laman/National Geographic Creative; **176:** ©Paul Sutherland/National Geographic Creative; **179:** ©LOOK-foto/SuperStock; **184-185:** ©Iakov Kalinin/Shutterstock; **184:** ©Gary Dublanko/Alamy; **185:** ©LOOK Die Bildagentur der Fotografen GmbH/Alamy; **187:** ©Hemis/Alamy;